LAW AND JUSTICE IN BUGANDA

By

E. S. HAYDON, B.A. (READING)

of Gray's Inn, Barrister-at-Law,
formerly Judicial Adviser, Buganda

WITH A FOREWORD BY

OWEKITIIBWA J. P. MUSOKE

Minister of Justice in the Government of
His Highness the Kabaka of Buganda

LONDON
BUTTERWORTHS
1960

ENGLAND: BUTTERWORTH & CO. (PUBLISHERS) LTD.
                LONDON: 88 Kingsway, W.C.2.

AFRICA: BUTTERWORTH & CO. (AFRICA) LTD.
                DURBAN: 33/35 Beach Grove

AUSTRALIA: BUTTERWORTH & CO. (AUSTRALIA) LTD.
                SYDNEY: 6–8 O'Connell Street
                MELBOURNE: 430 Bourke Street
                BRISBANE: 240 Queen Street

CANADA: BUTTERWORTH & CO. (CANADA) LTD.
                TORONTO: 1367 Danforth Avenue, 6

NEW ZEALAND: BUTTERWORTH & CO. (NEW ZEALAND) LTD.
                WELLINGTON: 49/51 Ballance Street
                AUCKLAND: 35 High Street

U.S.A.:   BUTTERWORTH INC.
                WASHINGTON, D.C.: 7235 Wisconsin Avenue, 14

PRINTED IN GREAT BRITAIN

BY

PAGE BROS. (NORWICH) LTD.

LAW AND JUSTICE
IN
BUGANDA

Butterworth's African Law Series

No. 1. Essays in African Law, by Antony Allott, M.A., Ph.D.

No. 2. Law and Justice in Buganda, by E. S. Haydon, B.A.

FOREWORD

I have been asked by Mr. E. S. Haydon, the author of this book and formerly Judicial Adviser, Buganda, if I would write a Foreword to his book; I welcome this request.

One of the greatest safeguards of Human Rights and the Rule of Law is the certainty of law itself. For the most part, Customary Law in Buganda is unwritten. Yet this part of the Law still greatly affects the rights and duties of our people. Written works, like this one, import into customary law that certainty and predictability necessary in any legal system.

The vitality of the Kiganda customary law will substantially depend on our people's consent to continue to be bound by it. Education begets inquiring minds which will only be satisfied by concrete facts. The validity of customary law, therefore, will be greatly affected by the people's knowledge that the application of that part of the law is not merely the " Conscience " of each individual judge but a body of rules of human conduct which have their roots in antiquity. Mr. Haydon stresses this point sufficiently; he also makes it abundantly clear that the advent of English Law towards the close of the last century did not come to fill a complete legal vacuum in Buganda.

For the last sixty years the Kiganda customary law and English law have worked closely side by side to produce progress and peace of mind among our people. This is a very good indication that the two systems are not repugnant but complementary to each other. The result of the interaction of the Kiganda custo-mary law and English law must be as clearly ascertained as possible. This book happily reveals that the issue of marriage between the two systems, which are compatible but yet unlike in various instances, has been, and is likely to continue to be, at least satisfactory.

Mr. Haydon's application and scholarship throw an exception-ally bright beam of light on " the development of Buganda Customary Law and the Buganda judicial institutions from the middle of the last century until the present day," to quote the author himself. I am glad to be able to say that this book will be very useful to the legal profession, the lay reader and research students.

J. P. MUSOKE
OMULAMUZI

DEDICATED
TO MY WIFE

PREFACE

In 1926 the late Kabaka of Buganda, His Highness Sir Daudi Chwa, wrote to this effect:

> " After consultation with my three Ministers, I perceive that there should be a Code of Buganda Native Law, which my Chiefs shall employ in their Councils as well as in the Great Lukiko of the Kingdom of Buganda for at the present time the major part of the laws is unwritten—as, for example, the Law of Stealing; and others in like manner."[1]

The particular project, which the late Kabaka therein had in mind, never in fact came to fruition[2] but the following year Sir Daudi Chwa wrote:

> " I am quite convinced that the proposed book, if and when done properly, will be most useful to the Native Community of Buganda especially the educated section of it, and will remove certain irregularities at present existing in the trial of cases by Native Courts which I very much fear will cause in a very short time bitter discontent among the more enlightened Baganda."[3]

During the thirty years that have since elapsed, those who have specialized in the study of native customary law have tended to reject the codification of that law by statute in favour of the piecemeal recording of it over a period of years by consultation with native court members and tribal authorities, by comparison with records of native court cases and by submission of the resultant draft for approval to chiefs and people in council. " At the end of that period a legal text book might be produced which would take knowledgeable account of the trends of change in the growth of customary law . . . ".[4]

---

[1] Translation of passage in a letter dated 24th August, 1926, addressed to the Provincial Commissioner, Buganda.

[2] *I.e.* Compilation of Native Agreements, Laws and of Instructions issued by the Omulamuzi, by Blasio Mwebe Kagwa, Native Courts Adviser to the High Court—see below p. x.

[3] Passage in a letter written in July, 1927, to the Provincial Commissioner, Buganda.

[4] R. E. Robinson—" Methods of Recording Native Customary Law "— *The Digest of African Local Administration No.* 2; March, 1948, reprinted in *Journal of African Administration*, Vol. I No. 3, July, 1949; and Chapter V of *Records of Judicial Advisers' Conferences 1953 and 1956* published as special supplements to Journal of African Administration, October, 1953, and April, 1957; A. N. Allott—" Methods of Legal Research into Customary Law " J.A.A. Vol. V p. 172 and Julius Lewin—*Studies in African Native Law*, 1947, p. 3.

The fundamental importance of maintaining a system of law " that is certain and yet flexible " has been stressed by the local press[1] and is now accepted by public opinion generally. My aim has therefore been to produce a legal text book which describes the development of Buganda customary law and of the Buganda judicial institutions from the middle of the last century until the present day. In pursuit of that aim I have purposely omitted any description of the constitution and jurisdiction of the Protectorate Courts which also have existed since the advent of the British administration in Buganda.

In reviewing Monsieur Edouard Bustin's recent book[2] on the constitutional development in British East Africa a critic refers to Monsieur Henri Rolin's first text book on the Laws of Uganda[3] and writes:

> " It is surely a judgment on English Scholarship that after nearly half a century it should fall to another Belgian writer at Liege to bring up to date the account of political and administrative organisation in East Africa."[4]

Rolin in fact was primarily concerned with " le droit britannique de l'Uganda " and not with " le droit indigène, formé presque entièrement de coutumes ", except to determine to what extent native customary law in Uganda was upheld by British legislation.[5] Bustin's work is a comprehensive and comparative handbook of modern political development in East African territories. Of legal text books devoted to the description of the customary law of any tribe in Uganda there have to date been none. And in making that assertion, I am not overlooking the valuable report on land tenure in the Buganda Kingdom produced in 1906 by Mr. Justice (late Sir William) Morris Carter and rightly described as " the foundation upon which the observations of the majority of subsequent students have erected ".[6]

That absence of strictly legal works should not be taken to imply that there is a dearth of written material on the subject of Buganda custom. On the contrary there is a wealth of such

---

[1] Editorial in *Uganda Argus* of 9th August, 1956.

[2] Edouard Bustin, *La Décentralisation Administrative et l'Évolution des Structures Politiques en Afrique Orientale Britannique*, Liège, 1958.

[3] Henri Rolin, *Le Droit de l'Uganda*, Bruxelles, 1910.

[4] J. S. Read, *Journal of African Law*, Spring 1959, Vol. 3 No. 1, p. 75.

[5] *Op. cit.*, p. 15.

[6] Thomas and Spencer, *A History of Uganda Land and Surveys and of the Uganda Land Survey Department*, 1938, p. 52.

accumulated learning to be found in the published works and despatches of the early explorers, missionaries and administrators of the last century. The first author, however, who calls for individual mention is that great man of affairs and savant, Sir Apolo Kagwa, a Prime Minister of Buganda for many years, whose book on the history of the Kings of Buganda, first published in 1901,[1] was followed in 1905 by his more important work on Buganda custom,[2] and posthumously in 1949 by his description of the Baganda clans.[3] Culling most of his information through Sir Apolo Kagwa, then came the Reverend John Roscoe of the Church Missionary Society, whose classic work on the native customs and beliefs of the Baganda[4] is still of the highest authority[5] on that early period of Buganda's development at the turn of the century.

During the years of the First World War and subsequently the Kabaka's Government published a series of booklets of Lukiko decisions and instructions, which contain a number of circulars issued by Ministers of Justice. It should be noted that such circulars have no binding legal force[6] and are accordingly mentioned rarely in the pages which follow. The most important material included was Sir Apolo Kagwa's collection of Buganda custom which ought to be followed.[7]

The next author of a work on Buganda custom who deserves especial mention is a White Father, Pierre Gorju, who published in 1920 the results of his observations of the Baganda during a quarter of a century.[8] Thereafter there is a gap in published works of authority on this subject until 1934 when two appeared— Miss Lucy Mair's anthropological study[9] and Ggomotoka's description of Baganda custom.[10] Both these works are of great value to our present purpose but must nevertheless be employed with reserve: Mair's because she admittedly collected most of

---

[1] *Ekitabo kya Basekabaka BeBuganda*, 1901.

[2] *Ekitabo kye Mpisa za Buganda*, 1905.

[3] *Ekitabo kye Bika bya Baganda*, 1949.

[4] *The Baganda*, 1911.

[5] See opinion of Francis, J., in H.C.C.R. 17 of 1935 *Njirwa* v. *Kagangama*, 5 U.L.R. 146, on Roscoe's lesser but sister work— " The Banyankole ".

[6] See decision of Sheridan, J., in H.C.Misc.A. 3 of 1957 D.N.G. *Jakana & Another* v. *Lukiko*. (1957) E.A. 587.

[7] *Akatabo ke Biragiro na Mateka ebyatesebwa Olukiko Olukulu olwe Buganda okuva* 1916 *okutusa* 1919, pp. 8 and 18.

[8] *Entre le Victoria, l'Albert et l'Edouard*, 1920.

[9] *An African People in the Twentieth Century*, 1934.

[10] *Magezi Ntakke*, 1934.

her information from one informant, a certain Yokana Wasswa Ssalango, who was moreover employed by a Mission; and Ggomotoka's, because, although he was Ssabalangira[1] and thereby entitled to the greatest respect, his work sets out to describe all types of custom including mere social conventions which have no validity in legal process.[2]

There was, however, one compiler of Buganda native law in the 1920's, to whose work reference was made above,[3] but which unfortunately was never published. Blasio Mwebe Kagwa was the elder son of the famous Katikkiro, Sir Apolo Kagwa. From 1924 until 1928 when the post lapsed into abeyance on his appointment as an Assistant Katikkiro, Blasio Kagwa was Native Courts Adviser to the High Court and spent his time inspecting the records of the subordinate Buganda courts. Sir Daudi Chwa's proposal, mentioned above,[4] that Blasio Kagwa should be seconded for two years to revise the judicial procedure employed by the Baganda chiefs, eventually for extraneous reasons was whittled down to a secondment of two months only in mid-1927. That short secondment sufficed only for Blasio Kagwa to consider the existing Agreements and Native Laws and their respective translations. Due to lack of co-operation from the then Omulamuzi, Blasio Kagwa was unable to carry out his third term of reference and examine thoroughly the Lukiko Instructions and Standing Orders, or his fourth term of reference and make overall recommendations for the improvement of the judicial work of the Native Courts in Buganda.[5] It is notable that his terms of reference did not include and Blasio Kagwa did not accordingly attempt the recording of unwritten customary law then or formerly obtaining in Buganda.

After Mair came other sociologists, who for the most part restricted their research to particular aspects of life in Buganda or to particular areas. Their works are occasionally relevant to our present purpose as are also certain articles to be found in the *Uganda Journal*, the periodical of the Uganda Society.

It behoves me to lay my credentials for this task before the reader. I confess that I start with the disadvantage of being an Englishman, but I have served in the Provincial Administration

---

[1] *I.e.* Head of the Princely Clan.
[2] See Lewin, *op. cit.*, p. 13.
[3] See p. vii, above. [4] *Loc. cit.*
[5] Report of Blasio M. L. Kagwa, Native Courts Adviser, dated 2nd September, 1927.

in Uganda for more than thirteen years and most of that service has been in the Kingdom of Buganda. For the last five and a half years I have held the post of Judicial Adviser, Buganda. Perhaps my best reference is the fact that the Baganda have given me the nickname of " omusai omuto ".[1]

My methods of study have been threefold:

Firstly I have examined all the important decisions of the Principal Court of His Highness the Kabaka of Buganda for the last twenty years. In fact the series of civil case files starts with the year 1939 and the criminal with the year 1944. Prior to those years the files of cases in each register are not kept in ordered sequence and are for the most part missing. The more important decisions of the Principal Court on Buganda customary law have been included in the series of Customary Law Reports published by the Kabaka's Government.[2] For study of cases decided in the thirty years 1911–1940 I have relied upon the unpublished records of the decisions of the Provincial Commissioner, Buganda, sitting as a revisional authority in respect of cases arising in the Buganda courts. In addition I have, of course, examined all published and the more important unpublished decisions of Her Majesty's High Court of Uganda on points of Buganda customary law whether arising in revisional or appellate proceedings or otherwise. Finally I have studied those few leading cases decided by Her Majesty's Court of Appeal for Eastern Africa wherein matters concerning Buganda customary law came up for decision.

Secondly, following in the footsteps of Henri Rolin and Blasio Kagwa, I have scrutinised Imperial and Protectorate legislation from the year 1889 onwards to discover those portions which affected Buganda native law or Buganda judicial institutions. Likewise I have carefully examined all Agreements made between His Britannic Majesty and His Highness the Kabaka, Chiefs and people of Buganda. The Buganda Native Laws have naturally been accorded studious consideration but for reasons explained above,[3] I have given circular instructions issued by Ministers of Justice only cursory attention.

Thirdly I have, with the kind permission of the Minister of Justice in His Highness' Government, discussed various categories and points of Buganda customary law with the judges

---

[1] *I.e.* " the young blood ".
[2] For list see bibliography.
[3] See above p. ix.

of the Principal Court of Mmengo, " the highest authority on Buganda Custom ",[1] and with Ssaza, Ggombolola, Muluka and Batongole chiefs, magistrates and members of the Buganda subordinate courts clan elders and notables throughout the main centres of population on the mainland of the Kingdom of Buganda. For to quote the words of the late Sir Charles Dundas, a former Governor of the Uganda Protectorate:

" . . . in the long run native courts cannot function otherwise than in accordance with accepted native opinion of what their own law and practice should be. Old ideas cannot altogether be eradicated while they still retain vitality, new ideas cannot be disregarded when they have come to be commonly accepted. But only the native can say whether he himself accepts one or the other, or how both can be brought into harmony."[2]

In conducting these discussions I made it plain that the objective was to collect unwritten *Buganda* custom, which had legal validity, and that that object excluded the customary law of the neighbouring tribes who had now been incorporated in the Kingdom of Buganda such as the Bakoki, the Basesse or the Bavuma, to give three examples. Furthermore I have only included in this book customary law which I have tested in several different areas of Buganda and have found to be generally agreed to be the custom of the Baganda.[3] In posing questions to these meetings I have found many suggestive lines of approach in Hans Cory's *Sukuma Law and Custom* and Schapera's *Handbook of Tswana Law and Custom*. Finally with the approval and assistance of the Katikkiro I interviewed certain high officials at Mmengo who are concerned with the administration of particular aspects of customary law, namely the Assistant Katikkiro in charge of Clan Matters, the Lukiko Land Officer who is concerned with immovables in succession, the Succession Secretary who is concerned with movables in succession, the Omuwanika Nkuluze and the Katikkiro we Byalo bya Ssabasajja Kabaka who control his Highness' official estates and last but by no means least the Omukulu ow'Olubiri, who is the major domo in His Highness' Palace.

---

[1] Pearson, J., in H.C.Cr.A. 127 of 1949, *Kagimu* v. *Lukiko*, *Notes* pp. 25–28.
[2] Undated minute on Native Courts.
[3] See decision of Manning, J., in H.C.Cr.A. 125 of 1942, *Kivu* v. *Lukiko* (unpublished), following *Esugbayi Eleko* v. *Government of Nigeria*, A.I.R. 1931 P.C. 253 and [1931] A.C. 662, and decision of Griffin, C. J., and Ainley, J., in H.C.Cr.A. 98 of 1953, *Musoke* v. *Lukiko*, *Notes* p. 53–58.

I am most grateful to Owekitiibwa Mikaeli Kintu, Katikkiro of Buganda, and to Owekitiibwa Joseph P. Musoke, Minister of Justice, for their support in the preparation of this work; to the Chief Judge, Buganda, the Judges and Registrar of the Principal Court and the Magistrates and Members of the Buganda subordinate courts for their ready assistance and advice in the compilation; to the Clan Authorities for their help in ascertaining the machinery for dealing with clan matters, and, in particular, succession affairs, which lie outside the jurisdiction of courts of law; and to the many other officials of high and low degree in the Kabaka's Government who lent their aid to make this work possible.

I further owe a perennial debt to the Honourable C. A. L. Richards, C.M.G., Resident, Buganda, for his never-failing encouragement in the work of recording and publishing Buganda customary law. Dr. A. N. Allott of the Department of Law in the London School of Oriental and African Studies I thank for his helpful advice in the arrangement of this book.

It is my hope that this book will be of use as a statement of Buganda customary law to all those who are concerned with its administration be they holders of office or private individuals, students of comparative law or members of legislative bodies.

E. S. HAYDON

ACKNOWLEDGMENTS

To provide a proper historical and sociological background for the consideration of Ganda customary law I have thought it better to cite the authorities in their own words rather than to paraphrase the information they provide. In this resolve I have been strengthened by the difficulty of consulting the original works when in the field in Africa.

I am grateful to the following publishers and authors for permission to quote from the works indicated: William Blackwood & Sons, Ltd., in respect of Speke's " Journal of the Discovery of the Source of the Nile ", although the book is now out of copyright; Sampson Low, Marston & Co., Ltd., in respect of Ashe's " Two Kings of Uganda " and " Life in Uganda "; Macmillan & Co., Ltd., in respect of Roscoe's " The Baganda "; Routledge & Kegan Paul, Ltd., and Miss L. P. Mair in respect of Miss Mair's " An African People in the Twentieth Century "; the Controller of Her Majesty's Stationery Office in respect of Lord Hailey's " Native Administration in British African Territories "; Heffers and Dr. Audrey I. Richards, C.B.E., in respect of Dr. Richard's " Economic Development and Tribal Change "; the Government of Uganda Protectorate and Messrs. H. B. Thomas, O.B.E., and A. E. Spencer, C.B.E., in respect of Thomas and Spencer's " A History of Uganda Land and Surveys "; and The East African Institute of Social Research and Professor A. W. Southall and Mr. P. Gutkind in respect of Southall and Gutkind's " Townsmen in the Making ".

E.S.H.

NOTE

This work has been compiled by the author
purely in his personal capacity.

TABLE OF CONTENTS

Page

FOREWORD v
PREFACE vii
ACKNOWLEDGMENTS xv
CITATION xxi
TABLE OF LEGISLATION CITED xxiii
TABLE OF CASES CITED xxvii
INTRODUCTION xxxvii
    Terminology and delimitation of subject xxxvii
    Description of land and people xxxviii

PART I.—CONSTITUTIONAL

Chapter
1. THE NINETEENTH CENTURY 3
    Ancient Political Organisation 3
    Early legislation 7
    Ancient judicial system 11
2. THE 1900 AGREEMENT 18
3. THE TWENTIETH CENTURY 23
    Modern political organisation 23
    Modern legal system 25
    Modern judicial system 30

PART II.—THE LAW OF PERSONS

4. STATUS AND CAPACITY OF INDIVIDUALS 53
    The royal family 54
    Chiefs 56
    Peasants 61
    Slaves 64
    Women 66
    Children 68
    Strangers 69
5. THE CLANS 72
6. MARRIAGE 77
    Types of marriage 78
    Capacity to marry 84
        Personal capacity 84
        Prohibited degrees 84
    Preliminaries of marriage 86
        Marriage negotiations 86
        Betrothal 90
    Marriage Payments 90
        Definitions 90
        Ancient marriage consideration 90

Chapter   Page

6. MARRIAGE—*contd.*

The draft native law, 1903   91
Modern marriage consideration   93
Marriage Ceremonies and Formalities   96
Customary marriage and the courts   100
Subsequent ceremony   102
Registration   103

7. FAMILY LAW   104
Husband and wife   104
Dissolution of marriage   107
    A.   By Divorce   107
          Grounds   107
          Procedure   109
          Effects   111
    B.   By Death   111
Parents and children   111
    Parental Control   111
    Duties of father   112
    Duties of mother   115
    Duties of children   116
    The ceremony of twins   117
Kith and Kin   119
    Responsibilities and avoidances   119
    Endobolo   122
    Abortion   122

PART III.—THE LAW OF PROPERTY

8. LAND   127
Tenure pre-1900   127
Butaka   128
Butongole   129
Bwesengeze   130
Peasant tenancy   131
The " Mailo " system   132
The Bataka problem   136
Registration of Titles   140
Position of landlord and tenant   141
Interest-holders   148
Kabaka's Mailo   150
Acquisition, transfer and extinction of interests   153
Common rights in land   163
Urban developments   166
The Busuulu and Envujjo Law   167
Jurisdiction in land cases   169

9. MOVABLE PROPERTY   171
Livestock   171
    Acquisition   172
    Okusibira ente   172
    Herding   176
    Rights of ownership   177

Chapter Page

9. MOVABLE PROPERTY—*contd.*
   Minor animals 177
   Other property 178
10. METHODS OF ACQUISITION 180
   Fishing 180
   Hunting 181
   War 182

PART IV.—THE LAW OF SUCCESSION

11. SUCCESSION 189
   Terminology 189
   Death and Burial 189
   Mourning 192
   Interim administration of estate 193
   Okwabya lumbe 193
   Categories of heritable property 194
   Law and jurisdiction 196
   Machinery of succession 209
   Choice of successor and distribution of estate 214
   Rights and duties of successor 221
   Debts for or against the estate 221
   Dispositive succession 222
12. GUARDIANSHIP 225

PART V.—MERCANTILE LAW

13. CONTRACTS 231
   Contracts creating or affecting status 231
   Contracts creating or transferring interests in property 231
   Barter 231
   Sale 232
   Loan 233
   Gift 234
   Contracts of service 234
   Contracts of guarantee 235
   Contracts of agency 236
   Modern developments 236
   Case-law 237
14. MARKETS 241
15. CORPORATIONS AND ASSOCIATIONS 244

PART VI.—THE LAW OF WRONGS

16. TORTS 259
   Injuries to property 260
   Physical injuries to the person 263
   Seduction 264
   Psychic injuries to person 266
17. CRIMES 268
   General rules as to criminal responsibility 269
   Offences against the Kabaka's authority 270
   Offences relating to the administration of justice .. 272

Chapter   *Page*

17. CRIMES—*contd.*

     Offences relating to religion   273
     Nuisances   273
     Defamation   274
     Offences against morality   274
     Offences against the person..   279
     Offences relating to property   281
     Malicious injuries to property   282
     Witchcraft   283

PART VII.—PROCEDURAL

18. PROCEDURE   287
     Ancient rules of practice   287
     Modern rules of practice   289
     Evidence   294
     Treatment of offenders   296
     Conflict of laws   297

APPENDICES

Appendix
1. Diagrams of judicial systems
     (a) pre-1940   301
     (b) 1940–1954   301
     (c) modern   301
2. List of clans   302
3. Chronological tables
     (a) Orders in council   304
     (b) Agreements   306
     (c) Native laws   307
     (d) Protectorate legislation not specified   313
     (e) Protectorate legislation specified   314
     (f) Protectorate legislation affecting Buganda courts   ..   317
4. The Succession Order, 1926   320
5. List of Ministers of Justice   332
6. Luganda proverbs connected with the administration of justice   333
7. Glossary of Luganda terms   335
8. Bibliography   336

INDEX

CITATION

In addition to the accepted method of citing English cases, the following abbreviations have been used:

E.A.C.A.	Reports of Decisions of Her Majesty's Court of Appeal for Eastern Africa.
E.A.	The Eastern Africa Law Reports (Butterworths series).
L.R.K.	Kenya Law Reports.
U.L.R.	Uganda Law Reports.
H.C.Cr.A.	High Court Criminal Appeal.
H.C.C.A.	High Court Civil Appeal
H.C.Misc.A.	High Court Miscellaneous Appeal.
H.C.Cr.R.	High Court Criminal Revision.
H.C.C.R.	High Court Civil Revision.
H.C.C.C.	High Court Civil Case.
H.C.Misc.C.	High Court Miscellaneous Cause.
P.C.R.O.	Provincial Commissioner's Revisional Order.
J.A.Cr.A.	Judicial Adviser's Criminal Appeal.
J.A.C.A.	Judicial Adviser's Civil Appeal.
J.A.Misc.A.	Judicial Adviser's Miscellaneous Appeal.
P.C.Cr.A.	Principal Court Criminal Appeal.
P.C.C.A.	Principal Court Civil Appeal.
P.C.Cr.C.	Principal Court Criminal Case.
P.C.C.C.	Principal Court Civil Case.
P.C.Misc.C.	Principal Court Miscellaneous Case.
C.L.R.	Customary Law Reports (of the Kingdom of Buganda).
Notes	Notes of Selected Decisions of Her Majesty's High Court of Uganda 1940–1958.
OIC	Order-in-Council.
O	Ordinance.
Rev. Edn.	Revised Edition of the Buganda Native Laws, 1957.
Supplement	The Buganda Native Laws Supplement 1957–1958.
J.A.A.	Journal of African Administration.
J.A.L.	Journal of African Law.
U.J.	Uganda Journal.
Bulletin	Monthly Bulletin of High Court Decisions (Cyclostyled).

TABLE OF LEGISLATION CITED

Adultery and Fornication Law, 1918 101
  s. 2 101
  s. 7 67
  s. 8 297
Africa Order in Council, 1889 .. .. 8, 25
  Art. 13 9
  Art. 16, 17 9
African Authority Ordinance 48
Buganda Agreement, 1894 65
  Art. 10 183
Buganda Agreement, 1955 .. ..27, 28, 41, 183
  Art. 1 (1) 65
  Art. 2 55
    (2) 54
  Art. 3 55
  Art. 8 .. ..: 39, 75
  Art. 10 19
  Sch. I 25, 27
Buganda Agreement (Allotment and Survey), 1913 135
Buganda Agreement (Native Laws), 1910 208
  Art. 1 .. .. 26, 27, 199
  Art. 4 .. .. 26, 36
  Art. 5 26
Buganda Births Registration Law, 1923 .. .. 23, 24
Buganda Courts (Defence Jurisdiction) Regulations, 1943
  Reg. 2 29
Buganda Courts Ordinance 48, 238, 254
  s. 2 .. .. 253, 255
  s. 3 (1) 42, 253
    (3) (a) 42
  s. 4 39
  s. 6 (1) 42, 53, 250
    (3) 54
  s. 7 .. .. 42, 250, 255
  s. 9 250
    (a) 42
    (e) 43, 199
  s. 10 30
    (b) 43
    (e) 239
  s. 11 30
    (1) 43, 169, 199
    (2) 43
      (a) 43
    (3) 169
  s. 12 .. .. 28, 29, 239
  s. 20 290
  s. 24 .. .. 43, 44
  s. 25 43

Buganda Courts Ordinance (*continued*)
s. 26 43
    (1) (a), (b) 43
    (3) 43
    (6) (a), (b) 44
Buganda Courts (Amendment) Ordinance, 1945 39
Buganda (Declaratory) Agreement (Native Laws), 1937 27
Bunyoro Agreement, 1933
  Art. 13 23
Busuulu and Envujjo Law, 1927 .. .. 61, 142, 167
  ss. 2–4, 6 168
  s. 8 168
    (2) 167
  s. 9 (a) 163
    (b) 242
  s. 10 168
  ss. 11, 12 .. .. 167, 168
  s. 15 168
  s. 16 .. .. 143, 167, 168
  s. 18A (b) 147, 168
Coming of Age Law, 1920 .. .. 197, 239
  s. 2 67
Constitution of Buganda
  Art. 4 .. .. 54, 55
  Art. 26 .. .. 27, 207, 297
  Art. 34 .. .. 25, 61
Courts Ordinance, 1911 (No. 12) 34
  s. 3 34
  s. 50 34
  s. 51 34
Courts Ordinance, 1919
  s. 3 35
  s. 13 35
  s. 39 35
  s. 43 36
Criminal Procedure Code, 1919 60
  s. 2 36
Diseases of Animals Ordinance 29
Divorce Ordinance, 1904 35
Emergency Powers (Defence) Act, 1939 (2 & 3 Geo. 6 C. 62) .. 29
Emergency Powers (Defence) Act, 1940 (3 & 4 Geo. 6 C. 20) .. 29
Evidence Ordinance, s. 2 30
Foreign Jurisdiction Acts, 1843–1878 8
Great Lukiiko (Election of Representatives) Law 24, 67
  s. 7 69
Guardianship Law 225
  s. 4 66
  s. 5 66
  s. 6 .. .. 66, 225
Income Tax Ordinance 254
Indian Contract Act, ... 239
Indian Criminal Procedure Code 36
Interpretation and General Clauses Ordinance (C.1) 27, 254
  s. 3 254
    (1) 54, 253, 254
    (4) 54
    (8) 253, 254

Interpretation (Definition of " Native ") Ordinance, 1945 254
Land (Agreements) Law, 1939 .. .. 157, 158, 161
  s. 3 (b) 158
Land Law, 1908 .. .. 197, 204
  s. 2 (f) 199, 206
Land Law, 1909 .. .. 141, 154
Land Law, 1912 141
Land Succession Law, 1912 .. .. 201, 203, 206, 227
  s. 2 227
  s. 3 .. .. 199, 206
Land (Survey) Law, 1909 134
Land Tax Law
  s. 2 68
  s. 3 .. ..68, 168
  s. 4 168
Law for Preventing Venereal Disease, 1913 23
Law for Selecting Non-Official Representatives to the Lower Councils 24
  s. 8 69
Law for the Establishment of Lower Councils in Buganda 24, 67
Law to Prevent Prostitution
  s. 3 (2) 67
  s. 5 66
Law to Prevent the Use of Indecent Language 118
Marriage Ordinance (C. 109)
  s. 30 102
Masters and Servants Ordinance
  s. 58 (1) 29
Native Courts Ordinance, 1905 (No. 10 of 1905) 32, 53
  s. 2 31
  s. 3, 4 31
  s. 14 31
    (ii) 32
  s. 15 31
Native Courts Ordinance, 1909 (No. 15 of 1909) 34, 53
  s. 14 (i) 53
Native Law Ordinance, 1919
  s. 4 36
Native Official Estates Ordinance (C. 122) 148
  s. 6 148
Order in Council, 1902 141
Partnership Act, 1890 (53 & 54 Vict. C. 39) 250, 251
Partnership Ordinance, 1950 250
Penal Code 268, 298
Poll Tax Ordinance, 1939 29
Possession of Land Law, 1908 .. .. 134, 136, 139
  s. 2 (b) 139
    (c) 139, 148, 161
    (d)–(f) 139
    (h) 163
  s. 4 139
  s. 5 .. .. 209, 228
  s. 6 148
Public Health Ordinance 29
Prevention of Abortion Law, 1904 123
Registration of Land Ordinance, 1908 .. .. 135, 140
Registration of Titles Ordinance, 1922 135
  s. 141 .. .. 203, 204
Registration of Titles Ordinance, 1924 140

Repatriation of Undesirable Foreigners Law
s. 2 67
Sale of Goods Ordinance 240
Sleeping Sickness Ordinance 29
Townships Ordinance, 1938 29
Transfer of Land Acts, 1915–16 (State of Victoria) 135
Uganda Agreement, 1900 .. .. 7, 18, 19, 20, 21, 24, 26, 27, 32, 39, 60, 61,
64, 67, 72, 132, 133, 137, 139, 148, 150, 169, 204, 296
Art. 5 .. .. 19, 21
Art. 6 .. .. 19, 20, 53
Art. 8 20
Art. 9 60
Art. 10 19
Art. 11 .. .. 19–21, 24
Art. 13 183
Art. 15 .. ..22, 133
Arts. 16–18 133
Uganda Agreement (Clan Cases) 1924 .. .. 26, 43, 75, 138, 195, 197,
199, 200, 205, 207
Uganda Appeal Ordinance, 1910 34
Uganda (Judicial) Agreement, 1905 .. .. .. 26, 28, 31, 39
Art. 3 31
Uganda Memorandum of Agreement (Forests), 1907 135
Uganda Muhammadan Marriage and Divorce Ordinance, 1906
s. 19 35
Uganda Order in Council, 1902 .. .. 25, 141
Art. 6 (1) 25
Art. 15 (2) 25
Uganda Order in Council, 1911 25
Uganda Order in Council, 1920 25
Uganda Succession Ordinance, 1906
s. 337 196
Vagrancy Law
s. 4 67
Wills Law, 1916 .. .. 223, 320, 321
Witchcraft Ordinance 29
Witchcraft Ordinance, 1957 .. .. 283, 298

TABLE OF CASES CITED

A

Aliziwangula v. Takantwa, P.C.R.O. 29 of 1926 (unreported)   283

B

Baganda Bus Coy. Ltd. v. Sewanaku, P.C.C.C. 25 of 1943, 1940–55
C.L.R.   245
Baganda Co-operative Society v. Mugwanya, P.C.C.C. 22 of 1944
(unreported)   246
Balikolamanyi v. Tonondola, P.C.C.C. 59 of 1949, 1940–55 C.L.R.   208, 226
Balikupu v. Mukasa, P.C.R.O. 27 of 1928 (unreported)   293
Balinevumagana v. Weraga, P.C.R.O. 25 of 1933 (unreported)   ..   293
Bamweyama v. Lukiko, H.C.Cr.A. 91 of 1952 (unreported)   43
Bangisibanno v. Lubogo, P.C.C.A. 74 of 1958, 1958 C.L.R. 87   167, 168
Basajabalaba v. Rex, H.C.Cr.A. (1911), 2 U.L.R. 29   279
Battabikere v. Kabadzi, P.C.R.O. 94 of 1928 (unreported)   158
Battabikere v. Kaggwa, P.C.R.O. 26 of 1930 (unreported)   159
Batulabudde v. Nalubowa and Another, P.C.C.C. 63 of 1958, 1958
C.L.R. 77   266
Bavunanyeki v. Mukasa, P.C.R.O. 17 of 1923 (unreported)   ..   261
Bawakanya v. Masembe, P.C.C.C. 405 of 1956, 1958 C.L.R. 103   ..   226
Bazekuketta v. Luswa, P.C.C.C. 264 of 1955 (unreported)   153
Baziwane v. Lukiko, H.C.Cr.A. 1 of 1944, Notes 11   294
Binagwa v. Muwonge, P.C.C.C. 119 of 1954 (unreported)   262
Binyogambwa v. Lweterima, P.C.R.O. 3 of 1935 (unreported)   ..   171
Bisaso v. Lukabwe, P.C.C.A. 177 of 1955, 1956 C.L.R. 71   147
Bosa v. Seba, P.C.C.C. 230 of 1955, 1957 C.L.R. 163   249
Botobewa v. Katumwa and Another, H.C.C.A. 31 of 1959, P.C.C.C.
102 of 1955 (unreported)   163
Buganda Growers and Agricultural Co-operative Society v. Mutanda,
P.C.C.C. 1 of 1945 (unreported)   246
Bugembe v. Kiwanuka and Others, H.C.C.A. 42 of 1951, Notes 47 ..   207
Bukenya v. Mutebi and Another, H.C.C.C. 826 of 1958, Bulletin 51/59   239
Buko v. Kiddu, H.C.C.A. 44 of 1951, Notes 51   239
Bukunja Traders Association v. Kibali, P.C.C.C. 198 of 1954, 1957
C.L.R. 137   148
Bulembe v. Lukiko, H.C.Cr.A. 500 of 1949, Notes 33   43
Busulwa v. Texas Co. (South Africa) Ltd., H.C.Misc.C. 10 of 1933,
5 U.L.R. 55   169
Buteraba v. Lukiko, H.C.Cr.A. 580 of 1949, Notes 31   293
Buza v. Lubega and Others, H.C.C.A. 71 of 1951 (unreported)   ..   228
Byandazo v. Nsubuga, P.C.C.C. 376 of 1956, 1957 C.L.R. 159   ..   221

C

Crown v. Alifairi Mahomed, H.C.Cr.C. (1909), 1 U.L.R. 67   78
Crown v. Anselmi Kiimba, H.C.Cr.R. (1910), 1 U.L.R. 79   61

D

Damulira v. Sekubunga, P.C.C.C. 174 of 1954 (unreported)   236
Ddamulira v. Mabirizi, P.C.C.A. 23 of 1958, 1958 C.L.R. 71   263

E

Ediyamu *v.* Lukiko, H.C.Cr.A. 50 of 1954, Notes 61 292
Ekibina kya Isiramu *v.* Nswemu, P.C.C.C. 34 of 1944, 1940–55 C.L.R. 246
Esugbayi Eleko *v.* Government of Nigeria AIR 1931, P.C. 253 and (1931)
    A.C. 662 .. .. 208, 269

F

Fazaldin Miranbux *v.* Simoni Lule, H.C.C.C. 79 of 1922, 3 U.L.R. 101 136,
    138

G

Galiwango *v.* Gavamukulya, P.C.R.O. 50 of 1930 (unreported) .. 244
Gavamukulya *v.* Kawesa, P.C.C.C. 88 of 1954, 1958 C.L.R. 69 .. 238
Gayaza Growers Society *v.* Kasenene Agricultural Growers Society,
    P.C.C.C. 52 of 1945 (unreported) 246
General Cattle Traders Co. *v.* Lule, P.C.C.C. 74 of 1945 (unreported) .. 246
General Cattle Traders Co. *v.* Matovu, P.C.C.C. 93 of 1945 (unreported) 246
Gingo Radio Ltd. *v.* Uganda Electricity, P.C.C.C. 224 of 1958 (un-
    reported) 255
Gulemye *v.* Mukasa, P.C.C.C. 113 of 1955 (unreported) 237
Gyotogendanga *v.* Sekabira, H.C.C.A. 5 of 1950, Notes 41 260

I

Iga *v.* O.C. Mengo Police, H.C.C.A. 90 of 1956, Notes 81 260
Itewala *v.* Sebugenyi, H.C.C.A. 46A of 1958, Notes 91 43

J

Jakana and Another *v.* Lukiko, (1957) E.A. 587 ix
Jumba *v.* Ssali, P.C.C.A. 98 of 1957, 1957 C.L.R. 119 114

K

Kabali *v.* Kalanzi and Another, H.C.C.A. 47 of 1950, Notes 61 .. 157
Kabalu *v.* Kabalu, P.C.C.C. 172 of 1947, 1940–55 C.L.R. 178
Kabangala *v.* Wakulira, P.C.C.C. 97 of 1952 (unreported) 264
Kabasanda Baganda Kwebera *v.* Sekanyo, P.C.C.C. 88 of 1945 (un-
    reported) 246
Kabazi *v.* Kibuka, H.C.C.A. 2 U.L.R. 9 .. .. 22, 32, 134, 139
Kabenge and Another *v.* Mulwanyi, P.C.R.O. 22 of 1932 (unreported) 138
Kabi *v.* Kiyimba and Others, H.C.C.A. 19 of 1947, P.C.C.C. 63 of 1946
    (unreported) 176
Kabusu *v.* Semugoma and Others, P.C.C.C. 38 of 1957, 1958 C.L.R. 107 222
Kaddu *v.* Kawesa, H.C.Conf.C. 13 of 1951 (unreported) 170
Kadumukasa, *Re* H.C.Misc.A. 13 of 1949 (unreported) 75
Kadumakasa, *Re* H.C.Misc.A. 8 of 1950 (unreported) 203
Kafero *v.* Kalulengwa, P.C.C.C. 43 of 1952, 1940–55 C.L.R. 224
Kafero *v.* Lukiko, H.C.Cr.A. 15 of 1943, Notes 7 293
Kaganda *v.* Katabazi, P.C.C.A. 151 of 1957, 1958 C.L.R. 1 70
Kaggwa *v.* Mukasa, P.C.C.C. 42 of 1944 (unreported) 159
Kaggwe *v.* Kalibala, P.C.C.C. 120 of 1956, 1956 C.L.R. 55 259
Kagimu *v.* Lukiko, H.C.Cr.A. 127 of 1949, Notes 25 43
Kagwa, *Re* H.C.Misc.C. 42 of 1952 (unreported) 200, 205
Kagwa *v.* Kasaja, P.C.R.O. 125 of 1928 (unreported) 291

Kagwa *v.* Parma, H.C.C.A. 14 of 1948, Notes 23 292
Kaika *v.* Buyingira, H.C.C.A. 11 of 1943 (unreported) 221
Kajubi *v.* Kabali, E.A.C.A. C.A. 2 of 1944 (1944) 11 E.A.C.A. 34 .. 68
Kajugujwe *v.* Mugwanya, P.C.C.C. 56 of 1954 (unreported) 293
Kajwala *v.* Lukiko, H.C.Cr.A. 75 of 1954, Notes 63 291
Kakembo *v.* Lukiko, H.C.Cr.A. 31 of 1953, Notes 57 295
Kakoza *v.* Kwerimba and Others, H.C.C.A. 91 of 1957, J.A.C.A. 12 of
  1957, P.C.C.C. 31 of 1955 (unreported) 157
Kakungulu *v.* Maweje, P.C.C.C. 129 of 1940, 1940–55 C.L.R. .. 237
Kalanzi *v.* Ntambi and Another, H.C.C.A. 43 of 1952, P.C.C.C. 89 of
  1952 (unreported) 160
Kalekezi *v.* Kakuba, P.C.C.A. 183 of 1955, 1956 C.L.R. 1 70
Kalekye *v.* Lulyambalyamba, P.C.C.C. 177 of 1949, 1940–55 C.L.R. ... 228
Kalenzi and Another *v.* Lukiko, H.C.Cr.A. 223 and 224 of 1955, Notes
  69 295
Kalibbala *v.* Nsubuga, P.C.C.A. 24 of 1955, 1956 C.L.R. 75 146
Kaliramujjira *v.* Banabakintu, P.C.C.C. 336 of 1956, 1957 C.L.R. 111 .. 168
Kaluba *v.* Kajaya, H.C.C.C. 20 of 1957, (1957) E.A. 312 298
Kalule *v.* Mulira, P.C.C.C. 347 of 1957, 1958 C.L.R. 73 .. ..68, 266
Kamulegeya *v.* Bossa, P.C.C.A. 146 of 1957, 1957 C.L.R. 105 .. . 168
Kamulegeya *v.* Omumbeja Alina Luwedde, P.C.C.C. 262 of 1950,
  H.C.C.A. 15 of 1954 (unreported) 116
Kamya *v.* Nakasinde, J.A.C.A. 40 of 1945, P.C.C.C. 38 of 1945 (un-
  reported) 160
Kanyalutale *v.* Lubega, P.C.C.A. 65 of 1956, 1956 C.L.R. 71 .. 146
Kapere *v.* Mumpi, P.C.R.O. 48 of 1936 (unreported) 96
Kasajja *v.* Nyanjabulye, P.C.C.C. 329 of 1957, 1958 C.L.R. 111 .. 221
Kasali *v.* Kaggwa, P.C.C.C. 171 of 1958, 1958 C.L.R. 95 .. 161, 238
Kasbante *v.* Kaira, P.C.R.O. 3 of 1911 (unreported) 136
Kasiga *v.* Kasiga, P.C.C.C. 107 of 1954 (unreported) 177
Kasirivu *v.* Kukulakwetta, P.C.C.A. 110 of 1956, 1957 C.L.R. 117 .. 168
Kasirye *v.* Mugema and Another, P.C.C.C. 157 of 1949, 1940–55 C.L.R. 147
Kasolo *v.* Sekubwa, H.C.C.A. 74 of 1957 (unreported) 293
Kasoma *v.* Lukiiko, P.C.Cr.A. 64 of 1958, 1958 C.L.R. 81 168
Kasozi *v.* Mukasa, H.C.C.A. 16 of 1945, Notes 17 .. .. ..43, 293
Kasozi *v.* Mukasa, H.C.C.A. 45 of 1949, Notes 41 261
Kasule *v.* Kato, H.C.C.A. 13 of 1951, Notes 47 263
Kasule *v.* Kiwanuka, P.C.R.O. 132 of 1934 (unreported) 237
Kasule *v.* Nakuya and Others, P.C.C.C. 58 of 1946, 1940–55 C.L.R. .. 96
Kasule *v.* Namunyaka and Another, P.C.C.C. 225 of 1955, 1956 C.L.R.
  65 221
Kasule *v.* Ntambi for Mengo Blue Gardens, H.C.C.A. 51 of 1958
  (unreported) 255
Kasule *v.* Sengendo, J.A.C.A. 22 of 1951, P.C.C.A. 5 of 1949 (un-
  reported) 147
Kasule *v.* Seputemba, P.C.R.O. 16 of 1923 (unreported) 262
Katabazi *v.* Mukasa, P.C.C.A. 72 of 1952, 1956 C.L.R. 57 263
Katambala *v.* Nsimbe, P.C.C.C. 139 of 1954, 1956 C.L.R. 61 .. 148
Katenda *v.* Mukasa, H.C.C.A. 45 of 1948, Notes 39 158
Katende *v.* Luyulu, P.C.C.A. 20 of 1958, 1958 C.L.R. 73 262
Katende *v.* Musigere and Another, H.C.C.A. 12 of 1946, Notes 19 .. 292
Katende and Another *v.* Kawuma, P.C.C.C. 135 of 1955 (unreported) 157
Kato *v.* Kasule, P.C.C.C. 223 of 1950, 1940–55 C.L.R. 237
Katongole *v.* Ddaki, P.C.C.A. 74 of 1957, 1957 C.L.R. 99 265
Katosi *v.* Kahizi, 1 U.L.R. 22 21
Katwe Cattle Dealers and Butchers Co. *v.* Mukasa and Others,
  P.C.C.C. 42 of 1946 (unreported) 247
Kaungu *v.* Ntambi, P.C.C.C. 165 of 1948, 1940–55 C.L.R. 159

Kawagga v. Lubega, P.C.C.A. 41 of 1957, 1957 C.L.R. 115 168
Kawesa v. Mbewadde, P.C.C.A. 67 of 1957, 1958 C.L.R. 89 147
Kawesi v. Lukiko, H.C.Cr.A. 92 of 1952 (unreported) 43
Kayolo v. Kayondo, H.C.C.C. 58 of 1945 (unreported) .. 250, 252
Kayongo v. Kiwanuka and Another, P.C.C.C. 162 of 1953, 1956 C.L.R. 53 .. .. 157, 238
Kayongo v. Lukiko, H.C.Cr.A. 361 of 1956, Notes 79 278
Kewaza v. Byandala, P.C.C.C. 53 of 1950 (unreported) 168
Kezimbira v. Nakalogo, P.C.C.C. 12 of 1956, 1956 C.L.R. 55.. .. 259
Kibalama and Another v. Basazemagya and Others, H.C.C.C. 6 of 1944, 6 U.L.R. 137 .. ,.. .. .. 250, 252
Kiberu v. Ba Bulemezi Bus Co., P.C.C.C. 217 of 1955 (unreported) .. 249
Kibuka v. Bertie Smith, H.C.C.C., E.A.C.A. C.A. 1 U.L.R. 41 .. 21, 22
Kibuka v. Lukwago and Another, P.C.C.C. 207 of 1954, 1956 C.L.R. 47 238
Kiggundu v. Mubiri, P.C.C.C. 39 of 1949, 1940–55 C.L.R. 223
Kigozi v. Lukiko, H.C.Cr.A. 149 of 1942, Notes 7 295
Kigozi v. Namubiru, P.C.R.O. 43 of 1938 (unreported) 101
Kigozi v. Walusimbi, H.C.C.A. 21 of 1947, P.C.C.C. 27 of 2946 (unreported) 134
Kigundu v. Lukiko, H.C.Cr.A. 69 of 1956, Notes 73 295
Kikonyogo v. The Kivuvu (Uganda) Rubber Co. Ltd., 2 U.L.R. 36 .. 157
Kikwata v. Nanungi, P.C.R.O. 26 of 17 (unreported) 136
Kimbowa v. Mayanja, P.C.C.C. 71 of 1948 (unreported) 236
Kirabira v. Lukiko, H.C.Cr.A. 248 of 1957, Notes 77 42
Kirama v. Serunkuma, P.C.C.C. 92 of 1945 (unreported) 159
Kirwaneire v. Ntwatwa, H.C.C.A. 29 of 1920, 3 U.L.R. 69 141
Kisalita v. Kabangala and Bros., H.C.C.A. 38 of 1949, Notes 37.. 148, 167
Kisasa v. Mivule, P.C.R.O. 8 of 1923 (unreported) 78
Kisitu v. Kitaka, P.C.C.C. 9 of 1950 (unreported) 261
Kitakule v. Nsimbe, P.C.C.C. 118 of 1954 (unreported) 261
Kitakuli v. Lukiko, P.C.R.O. 5 of 1912 (unreported) 136
Kiteteyirwano v. Byalugaba, P.C.C.C. 54 of 1944, 1940–55 C.L.R. .. 228
Kiuka v. Sekimwanyi, H.C. Matrimonial C. (1916), 2 U.L.R. 238 .. 78
Kiviri v. Damba and Another, P.C.C.C. 43 of 1950, 1940–55 C.L.R. .. 223
Kivu v. Lukiko, H.C.Cr.A. 125 of 1942, Notes 3 269
Kiwanuka v. Buganda Government, P.C.C.C. 183 of 1955 (unreported) 261
Kiwanuka v. Nakku, P.C.C.C. 46 of 1954 1956 C.L.R. 67 143
Kiwanuka v. Wasswa and Others H.C.C.C. 225 of 1958, Bulletin 34/59 42
Kiwesi v. Balinya P.C.C.A. 70 of 1956, 1957 C.L.R. 103 264
Kiyaga v. Lukiko H.C.Cr.A. 135 of 1940, Notes 1 293
Kubo v. Buganda Butchers Ltd., H.C.C.C. 194 of 1951 (unreported) .. 254
Kubo v. Kiwanuka, P.C.R.O. 160 of 1935 (unreported) 245
Kulikiri v. Lutalungibwa, P.C.C.C. 84 of 1955 (unreported) .. 226
Kyagulanyi v. Sebuliba, E.A.C.A. C.A. 16 of 1949, H.C.Misc.C. 10 of 1947 (unreported) 156
Kyakwambala v. Gyagenda, P.C.R.O. 22 of 1923 (unreported) .. 101
Kyazze v. Mukubira, P.C.C.C. 84 of 1952, 1940–55 C.L.R. 237
Kyewalabye v. Simwogerere, P.C.R.O. 56 of 1924 (unreported) .. 264
Kyeyune v. Sekayiba, P.C.C.C. 274 of 1955, 1957 C.L.R. 125 .. 157, 238

L

Loto v. Alata, P.C.C.C. 277 of 1950 (unreported) 248
Lubanga v. Kirunduga and Another, P.C.C.C. 44 of 1950, 1940–55 C.L.R. 143
Lubega v. Lukiko, H.C.Cr.A. 140 of 1954, Notes 65 42
Lubega and Others v. Lukiko, H.C.Cr.A. 63 of 1943, Notes 9 292
Luboyera v. Buganda Government, H.C.C.A. 27 of 1950, Notes 43 161, 167

Luboyera v. Musoke, H.C.C.A. 13 of 1942, Notes 3 　.. 　.. 　.. 　160
Luboyera v. Serunkuma, P.C.R.O. 161 of 1928 (unreported) .. 　.. 　291
Lugakingira v. Nakibuka, P.C.C.A. 42 of 1956, 1956 C.L.R. 71 　.. 　147
Luganda v. Kateregga, P.C.C.A. 130 of 1955, 1956 C.L.R. 53 　.. 　238
Luima v. Buganda Government, P.C.C.C. 31 of 1946 (unreported) 　.. 　261
Lukiko v. Bazanganengo and Another, P.C.Cr.C. 461 of 1958, 1958
　C.L.R. 101 　.. 　.. 　.. 　.. 　.. 　.. 　.. 　.. 　93
Lukiko v. Gavamukulya and Another, P.C.Cr.A. 91 of 1957, 1958
　C.L.R. 99 　.. 　.. 　.. 　.. 　.. 　.. 　.. 　.. 　238
Lukiko v. Kauwa and Others, P.C.R.O. 40 of 1917 (unreported) 　.. 　195
Lukiko v. Kibirango, P.C.R.O. 108 of 1934 (unreported) 　.. 　.. 　224
Lukiko v. Kigozi, P.C.Cr.C. 537 of 1958, 1958 C.L.R. 41 　.. 　.. 　190
Lukiko v. Kivu, E.A.C.A. Cr.A. 134 of 1942 (1942) 9 E.A.C.A. 82 　.. 　45
Lukiko v. Lwanga, P.C.R.O. 10 of 1912 (unreported) .. 　.. 　.. 　272
Lukiko v. Mayanja, P.C.R.O. 26 of 29 (unreported) .. 　.. 　.. 　57
Lukiko v. Mutabazi, P.C.CrC. 528 of 1957, 1957 C.L.R. 151 　.. 　.. 　109
Lukiko v. Namirembe and Another, P.C.Cr.C. 271 of 1958, 1958 C.L.R.
　45 .. 　.. 　.. 　.. 　.. 　.. 　.. 　.. 　.. 　109, 120
Lukiko v. Odima, E.A.C.A. Cr.A. 77 of 1941, (1941) 8 E.A.C.A. 54 　.. 　45
Lukiko v. Opeda, P.C.Cr.C. 554 of 1957, 1957 C.L.R. 1 　.. 　.. 　70
Lukiko v. Twase, P.C.Cr.A. 83 of 1957, 1957 C.L.R. 113 　.. 　.. 　168
Lukonzolwa v. Kakoba, P.C.C.C. 73 of 1954 (unreported) 　.. 　.. 　174
Lukwayo v. Singh and Another, H.C.C.C. 37 of 1957, Bulletin 7/59 　.. 　261
Lule v. Nakikulu, P.C.C.C. 10 of 1952 (unreported) 　.. 　.. 　.. 　261
Lumu v. Nsubuga, H.C.C.A. 6 of 1956, Notes 73 　.. 　.. 　.. 　239
Lutalo v. Kiddu, P.C.R.O. 85 of 1932 (unreported) 　.. 　.. 　.. 　245
Lutanzira v. Kichweka, P.C.C.A. 153 of 1956, 1957 C.L.R. 157 　.. 　221
Lutaya v. Kikasima and Another, P.C.C.C. 83 of 1954, 1940–55 C.L.R. 　224
Lutaya v. Mugambe, P.C.C.C. 216 of 1955 (unreported) 　.. 　.. 　237
Lutemesa v. Muwairoha, P.C.C.C. 128 of 1952, 1940–55 C.L.R. 　.. 　228
Lutuga v. Galiwango, H.C.C.R. 19 of 1935, 5 U.L.R. 147 　.. 　.. 　159
Lwanchwende v. Funga, H.C.C.A. 9 of 1941, P.C.C.C. 8 of 1941 (un-
　reported) .. 　.. 　.. 　.. 　.. 　.. 　.. 　.. 　172
Lwanga v. Makumbi, P.C.C.C. 269 of 1950, 1940–55 C.L.R. .. 　.. 　237
Lwasa v. Lukiko, H.C.Cr.A. 401 of 1949, Notes 27 　.. 　.. 　292, 293
Lwokya v. Bukunduga, P.C.R.O. 13 of 1923 (unreported) 　.. 　.. 　109

M

Magezi v. Mutegombwa and Another, P.C.C.C. 264 of 1956, 1957
　C.L.R. 143 　.. 　.. 　.. 　.. 　.. 　.. 　.. 　70, 94, 238
Magunda v. Bunnya, P.C.C.C. 18 of 1955, 1956 C.L.R. 75 　.. 　.. 　96
Makanga v. Kasana, H.C.C.A. 36 of 1951, Notes 45 　.. 　.. 　158
Makerere Builders and Concrete Pipe Manufacturers v. Lule, P.C.C.C.
　12 of 1952 (unreported) 　.. 　.. 　.. 　.. 　.. 　.. 　267
Male v. Kayongo and Another, H.C.C.A. 4 of 1949, Notes 29 　.. 　200
Malimbo v. Alideki, P.C.R.O. 10 of 1923 (unreported) 　.. 　..96, 109
Mambule v. Kavuma, P.C.C.C. 267 of 1957, 1958 C.L.R. 61 .. 　.. 　238
Masaba v. Kasoma, P.C.R.O. 3 of 1930 (unreported) .. 　.. 　.. 　161
Masajage v. Gweweyigira, P.C.R.O. 38 of 1936 (unreported) .. 　.. 　163
Masumbuko v. Lukiko, H.C.Cr.A. 198 of 1940, Notes 1 　.. 　.. 　293
Matovu v. Iga and Another, H.C.C.A. 30 of 1957 (unreported) 　.. 　143
Matovu v. Kalasi, J.A.C.A. 49 of 1947 (unreported) 　.. 　.. 　.. 　251
Matovu v. Manager of General Cattle Traders Co., P.C.C.C. 18 of
　1946 (unreported) 　.. 　.. 　.. 　.. 　.. 　.. 　.. 　247
Mayanja v. Bamulondere, P.C.R.O. 18 of 1929 (unreported) .. 　.. 　89
Mayanja v. Kulubya, P.C.C.C. 35 of 1947 (unreported) 　.. 　.. 　139
Mayanja v. Mukasa and Another, P.C.C.C. 173 of 1955, 1940–55 C.L.R. 　293

Mayanja *v.* Mwayi and Another, H.C.C.A. 8 of 1953, Notes 57 .. 158
Mayanja *v.* Rex, H.C.Cr.A. 1 of 1927, 3 U.L.R. 205 61
Mayanja *v.* Takirambudde, P.C.C.C. 36 of 1957, 1958 C.L.R. 93 .. 161
Mbazira *v.* Senkubuge, P.C.C.C. 135 of 1948, 1940–55 C.L.R.   .. 223
Mbowa *v.* Kaggwa, P.C.C.C. 197 of 1951, 1940–55 C.L.R. 261
Mengo Builders and Contractors Ltd. *v.* Kasibante, H.C.C.A. 77 of
    1958 (unreported) 53, 253
Mikando *v.* Mukezi, H.C.C.A. 29 of 1957, Notes 83 168
Mikulumya *v.* Waswa, P.C.R.O. 14 of 1925 (unreported)   262
Mubiru and Another *v.* Lukiko, H.C.Cr.A. 131 of 1949, Notes 25 .. 295
Mubito *v.* Senyanga, P.C.C.C. 31 of 1948, 1940–55 C.L.R. 248
Mufubyagenda *v.* Kabangala, P.C.C.C. 31 of 1941, 1940–55 C.L.R. .. 236
Mugabe and Another *v.* Senkubuge, P.C.C.C. 28 of 1941, 1940–55
    C.L.R. 160
Mugadya *v.* Namusoke and Another, P.C.C.C. 288 of 1955 (unreported) 266
Mugalasi *v.* Lubwama, P.C.R.O. 97 of 1937 (unreported)   245
Mugalu *v.* Nakabiri, H.C.Misc.C. 50 of 1958, Bulletin 30/59 42
Mugwanya *v.* Kajugujwe, P.C.C.C. 350 of 1926 (unreported)   .. 36
Mugwanya *v.* Sensuwa, H.C.C.A. 2 U.L.R. 207   ..   .. 135, 139
Mukasa *v.* Abdalla, P.C.C.C. 157 of 1953 (unreported)   249
Mukasa *v.* Buganda Government and Another, P.C.C.C. 185 of 1948,
    1940–55 C.L.R. 260
Mukasa *v.* Kasozi, H.C.C.A. 9 of 1946, Notes 19   157
Mukasa *v.* Kiggundu, H.C.C.A. 23 of 1951, Notes 47 158
Mukasa *v.* Kyalikyobulungi, H.C.C.R. 18 of 1948, Notes 83 43
Mukasa *v.* Luboyera, P.C.C.A. 190 of 1956, 1956 C.L.R. 51 238
Mukasa *v.* Lukiko, H.C.Cr.A. 72 of 1942, Notes 1   293
Mukasa *v.* Lwanga, P.C.C.C. 218 of 1957, 1957 C.L.R. 95 .. 162, 259
Mukasa *v.* Mukasa, P.C.C.C. 158 of 1949, 1940–55 C.L.R. 164
Mukasa *v.* Mulindwa, P.C.C.C. 119 of 1949 (unreported)   248
Mukasa *v.* Ziryawulamu, P.C.C.A. 38 of 1956, 1956 C.L.R. 73 168
Mukasa and Another *v.* Lukiiko, P.C.Cr.A. 54 of 1956, 1956 C.L.R. 59 264
Mukasa and Another *v.* Muguluma, H.C.C.A. 10 of 1952 (unreported) 154,
                                                                   228
Mukezi *v.* Mikando, P.C.C.C. 205 of 1956, 1957 C.L.R. 109   .. 168
Mukuye *v.* Sejongo, P.C.C.C. 19 of 1950 (unreported)   236
Mukwaba and Others *v.* Mukubira and Others, H.C.C.C. 50 of 1954
    (unreported) 22
Mukwenda *v.* Zavuga, P.C.R.O. 5 of 1916 (unreported)   272
Mulika *v.* Mohamed, E.A.C.A. C.A. 9 of 1949, (1949) 16 E.A.C.A. 51 152, 168
Mulindwa *v.* Musoke, H.C.C.A. 41 of 1951, Notes 49 239
Mulira and Another *v.* Lukiko, H.C.Misc.A. 10 of 1956, (1957) E.A. 584 293
Mulongosa *v.* Gowa, P.C.C.A. 1 of 1958, 1958 C.L.R. 79   149
Mulwanyi *v.* Alitubera, P.C.R.O. 52 of 1924 (unreported)   68
Musajjakawa *v.* Ddungu and Another, P.C.C.C. 24 of 1951 (unreported) 249
Musanje *v.* Lukambagire, P.C.C.C. 281 of 1956, 1956 C.L.R. 61 .. 157
Musema *v.* Katabazi, P.C.C.A. 17 of 1956, 1956 C.L.R. 49 238
Musigire *v.* Sebabenga, H.C.C.A. 26 of 1956, J.A.C.A. 92 of 1955,
    P.C.C.C. 19 of 1955, 1940–55 C.L.R. 167
Musoke *v.* Educational Secretary General, P.C.C.C. 158 of 1957, 1958
    C.L.R. 65 237
Musoke *v.* Kabazzi, P.C.C.C. 105 of 1955, 1956 C.L.R. 49 238
Musoke *v.* Kabi, P.C.C.C. 21 of 1943, 1940–55 C.L.R.   236
Musoke *v.* Kasaliko, P.C.C.C. 26 of 1941 (unreported)..   263
Musoke *v.* Kezala, P.C.C.C. 26 of 1954, 1940–55 C.L.R.   159
Musoke *v.* Kibuka, P.C.C.A. 6 of 1958, 1958 C.L.R. 79   148
Musoke *v.* Kintu, P.C.C.C. 42 of 1942, 1940–55 C.L.R.   245
Musoke *v.* Lukiko, H.C.Cr.A. 178 of 1946, Notes 17 292

Musoke *v.* Lukiiko, H.C.Cr.A. 98 of 1953, Notes 53 269
Musoke *v.* Luyombya and Another, H.C.C.A. 11 of 1944, Notes 13 .. 239
Musoke *v.* Mivule and Another, P.C.C.C. 251 of 1955, 1957 C.L.R. 131 261
Musoke *v.* Mpanga, H.C.C.A. 5 of 1953, Notes 59 .. .. 293, 295
Musoke *v.* Musoke, P.C.C.A. 54 of 1957, 1957 C.L.R. 121 147
Musoke *v.* Nakibinge, P.C.C.C. 124 of 1957, 1958 C.L.R. 91 161
Musoke *v.* Zavuga, P.C.C.A. 104 of 1955, 1956 C.L.R. 57 265
Musoke and Others *v.* Head of Nsenene Clan and Another, H.C.Misc.A.
    13 of 1949, Notes 35 200
Musulo *v.* Hyxinthe, H.C.C.A. 24 of 1946, 6 U.L.R. 149 54
Musuza *v.* Katanda, P.C.R.O. 190 of 1935 (unreported) 243
Mutasa *v.* Mukibi, P.C.C.A. 58 of 1945 (unreported) 263
Mutulakungo *v.* Kalibuggyawa, P.C.C.C. 140 of 1957, 1958 C.L.R. 63 238
Mutumba *v.* Ssonko, P.C.C.A. 142 of 1953, 1956 C.L.R. 53 238
Muwanga *v.* Lukiko, H.C.Cr.A. 214 of 1947, Notes 21 43
Muwanga *v.* Mukuta, P.C.C.C. 429 of 1956, 1957 C.L.R. 97 263
Muyinda *v.* Kitaka, H.C.C.A. 21 of 1932, 5 U.L.R. 19 224
Muzito *v.* Ngalombi, P.C.C.C. 62 of 1945 (unreported) 243
Mwamula *v.* Kasaja and Another, H.C.C.A. 94 of 1956, Notes 85 .. 43
Mwanje *v.* Mulindwa, P.C.C.A. 16 of 1957, 1957 C.L.R. 93 238
Mwanula *v.* Serruga and Another, P.C.C.C. 257 of 1955, 1956 C.L.R. 63 221
Mwaziza *v.* Kato, P.C.R.O. 28 of 1925 (unreported) 216
Mwenge *v.* Migade, H.C.Misc.C. 19 of 1933, 5 U.L.R. 97 138

N

Nabaggala *v.* Kasule, P.C.C.A. 190 of 1955, 1956 C.L.R. 69 143
Nabanja *v.* Kayinja, H.C.C.A. 39 of 1950, Notes 45 265
Nabyonga and Others *v.* Sewava, H.C.Misc.A. 9 of 1949 (unreported) ..75, 200
Nadiope *v.* Mwebe, E.A.C.A. C.A. 7 of 1939, (1939) 6 E.A.C.A. 44 .. 298
Naduli *v.* Serwanga, H.C.C.A. 28 of 1947, Notes 21 157
Nagadya *v.* Kiwanuka, J.A.C.A. 36 of 1956, P.C.C.C. 118 of 1955
    (unreported) 157
Nakabale *v.* Lukiko, H.C.Cr.A. 101 of 1952, Notes 49 295
Nakabugo *v.* Naddibanga, P.C.C.C. 112 of 1953 (unreported) .. 263
Nakabugo *v.* Nkoyoyo, H.C.C.A. 10A of 1947, Notes 19 .. 161, 223
Nakaka and Another *v.* Rex, H.C.Cr.A. (1909) 1 U.L.R. 60 279
Nakalema *v.* Kapalaga, P.C.C.C. 118 of 1940 (unreported) 261
Nakalyakani & Co. Ltd. *v.* Kulanima M. N. Musoke, H.C.C.A. 34 of
    1942 (unreported) 245, 254
Nakifuma Galyawamu Co. *v.* Lwanga and Another, P.C.C. 66 of 1954
    (unreported) 255
Nakityo *v.* Lukiko, P.C.Cr.A. 31 of 1957, 1957 C.L.R. 153 225
Nakkaka *v.* Kibuka and Brothers, P.C.C.C. 279 of 1950 (unreported) .. 248
Nakuzabasajja *v.* Kakembo, P.C.C.C. 85 of 1958, 1958 C.L.R. 109 .. 191
Nakuzabasajja *v.* Mukasa, H.C.C.A. 98 of 1957, Notes 81 293
Nakyaze *v.* Kitonto, H.C.C.A. 42 of 1952 (unreported) 43
Nalumenya *v.* Tabasima, H.C.C.R. 9 of 1948 (unreported) 44
Nalwanga *v.* Kyeyune, P.C.C.C. 116 of 1948, 1940–55 C.L.R. 106
Namatovu *v.* Mivule, P.C.C.A. 3 of 1944 (unreported).. 78
Namayanja *v.* Bamutta, P.C.R.O. 51 of 1931 (unreported) 291
Nambasa *v.* Kiddu, P.C.C.C. 139 of 1953, 1940–55 C.L.R. 157
Namirembe *v.* Kalembe and Others, P.C.C.C. 38 of 1949, 1940–55
    C.L.R. 228
Namuimba *v.* Lukiko, P.C.R.O. 6 of 1912 (unreported) 136
Namungona *v.* Mutyaba, P.C.C.C. 274 of 1950, 1940–55 C.L.R. .. 263
Namusoke, *Re* H.C.Misc.C. 62 of 1958, Bulletin 13 of 1959 158

B

Namutebi v. Nansbuga, P.C.C.C. 8 of 1955, 1956 C.L.R. 63 220
Nanfuka and Others v. Mpiso and Another, P.C.C.C. 5 of 1953 (un-
reported).. .. .. 221, 261
Nanfuma v. Mugwanga, P.C.C.C. 202 of 1947 (unreported) 247
Nanfumba v. Nyumba and Another, P.C.C.C. 97 of 1948 (unreported) 159
Nansibo v. Nsubuga, P.C.C.C. 199 of 1947, 1940–55 C.L.R. 237
Nantumbwe v. Kalibwani, H.C.C.A. 10 of 1955, Notes 69 293
Nantumbwe v. Kasozi and Another, P.C.C.C. 263A of 1950, 1940–55
C.L.R. 228
Ndagire v. Kasozi, H.C.C.A. 10 of 1941, Notes 5 293
Ndiwalana v. Katera, H.C.C.A. 84 of 1956, Notes 87 .. .. ..42, 291
Nduga v. Nkinzi, H.C.C.A. 1 of 1950, Notes 37 261
Ngubiri v. Semombwe, P.C.C.C. 403 of 1956, 1957 C.L.R. 139 .. 148
Njirwa v. Kagang'ama, 5 U.L.R. 146 ix
Nkalubo v. Mukibi and Another, P.C.C.C. 56A of 1945 (unreported) .. 263
Nkangoli v. Mugwanya, H.C.C.A. (1915) 2 U.L.R. 140 222
Nkeretanyi v. Gazanyawo, H.C.C.A. 90 of 1955 (unreported) .. 294
Nkeretanyi v. Kabanda, H.C.C.A. 25 of 1950, Notes 43 237
Nnamulondo and Others v. Musigire and Others, H.C.C.A. 17 of 1948,
Notes 23 228
Nnanfuka v. Kizito, P.C.C.A. 209 of 1955, 1956 C.L.R. 73 143
Nsimbe v. Kibirige, H.C.C.A. 8 of 1957, Notes 79 43
Nsobeddwa v. Kivumbi, P.C.C.C. 130 of 1953, 1940–55 C.L.R. 265
Nsubuga v. Kasozi, H.C.C.A. 11 of 1949 (unreported) 252
Nsubuga v. Nabbowa, P.C.C.C. 173 of 1956 (unreported) 159
Ntambi v. Jumba, H.C.C.A. 35 of 1958, Bulletin 35/58 293
Nunga v. Kibirango, P.C.C.C. 108 of 1949, 1940–55 C.L.R. 226
Nyanzi v. Bikanduse, P.C.R.O. 55 of 1934 (unreported) 245
Nyanzi v. Kayima, H.C.C.A. 67 of 1953, Notes 65 .. .. ..44, 292
Nyanzi v. Kiggundu, H.C.C.A. 8 of 1950, J.A.C.A. 1 of 1950, P.C.C.C.
97 of 1949 (unreported) 159
Nyonyintono v. Lukiko, H.C.Cr.A. 194 of 1952, Notes 51 278
Nyonyintono v. Sewanyaga and Another, P.C.C.C. 164 of 1950, 1940–55
C.L.R. 260
Nzalambi v. Ssonko, P.C.C.C. 468 of 1956, 1957 C.L.R. 103 265

P

Publishers of " Munyonyozi " v. Lukiko, H.C.Cr.A. 4 of 1923, 3 U.L.R.
124 274

R

Rex v. Kiyimba, H.C.Cr.R. 50 of 1935, 5 U.L.R. 124 278
Rex v. Mberebezi, H.C.C.R. 41 of 1921, 3 U.L.R. 79 295
Rex v. Mohamed, H.C.Cr.R. 100 of 1940, 6 U.L.R. 91 54
Rex v. Muigira, H.C.Cr.R. 42 of 1942, 6 U.L.R. 118 298
Rex v. Mukasa and Another, H.C.Cr.C. (1918), 2 U.L.R. 276 .. 282
Rex v. Ngobi, H.C.C.R. (1918) 2 U.L.R. 287 297
Rex v. Paulo and Others, H.C.C.R. 43 of 1922, 3 U.L.R. 98 .. 270, 292
Rex v. Salima and Another, 2 U.L.R. 182 102
Rex v. Sebbowa, H.C.Cr.R. 100 of 1935, 5 U.L.R. 128 278
Rex v. X.Y., H.C.C.C. 8 of 1926, 3 U.L.R. 202 273
Rex v. Yusufu, E.A.C.A. Cr.A. 132 of 1931 (1931) 13 L.R.K. 64 .. 37
Rusoke v. Ntambi and Others, P.C.C.C. 310 of 1956, 1957 C.L.R. 161 249

S

Sajjabi *v.* Kyadze, P.C.R.O. 102 of 1932 (unreported) 245
Sajjabi *v.* Musoke, P.C.C.C. 160 of 1950 (unreported) 262
Saku and Another *v.* Mugema and Others, H.C.C.A. 8 of 1945, Notes
15 .. ..43, 199
Sawabiri *v.* Serumaga, H.C.C.A. 12 of 1953, Notes 71 168
Sebaggala *v.* Rex, H.C.Cr.A. 64 of 1932, 5 U.L.R. 4 295
Sebanakirya and Others *v.* Lukiko, H.C.Cr.A. 300–304 of 1957, Notes
79 and 87 .. .. 43, 269, 281, 293
Sebugwawo *v.* Mundu, P.C.R.O. 30 of 1925 (unreported) 138
Sebuliba *v.* Gonzabato and Others, P.C.C.C. 29 of 1952, 1940–55 C.L.R. 236
Sebuliba *v.* Kamya and Others, P.C.C.C. 176 of 1946 (unreported) .. 222
Sebuliba *v.* Kyebatenda and Another, P.C.C.C. 33 of 1948 (unreported) 263
Sekinnemye *v.* Mmengo African Traders Ltd., P.C.C.C. 132 of 1951,
1940–55 C.L.R. 249
Sekkuma *v.* Lukiko, H.C.Cr.A. 505 of 1945, Notes 15 274
Sekubwa *v.* Kazibwe, P.C.C.C. 234 of 1950 (unreported) 248
Sekweyama *v.* Kabangala, P.C.C.A. 106 of 1956, 1956 C.L.R. 67 .. 168
Semalinte *v.* Mayanja, H.C.C.A. 3 of 1945, Notes 15 161
Sematimba *v.* Lupyazitta, P.C.C.C. 58 of 1940 (unreported) 169
Semijja *v.* Lukiko, H.C.Cr.A. 123 of 1950, Notes 35 281
Sempa *v.* Sempagama, P.C.C.C. 184 of 1946 (unreported) 247
Sempa *v.* Sewanyaga and Another, P.C.C.C. 187 of 1950, 1940–55
C.L.R. 260
Sempa and Another *v.* Wasswa and Others, H.C.C.A. 53 of 1955
(unreported) 252
Sendagire *v.* Kateregga, P.C.C.A. 42 of 1957, 1957 C.L.R. 123 .. 147
Sendi *v.* Sebuliba, P.C.C.C. 1 of 1953 (unreported) 160
Senfuma *v.* Lukiiko, P.C.Cr.A. 150 of 1958, 1958 C.L.R. 105 .. 225
Senfuma *v.* Mbago, P.C.C.C. 45 of 1946 (unreported) 263
Seninde *v.* Manager of Nakatema Store Co., Kampala, P.C.C.C. 180
of 1946 (unreported) 247
Sentongo *v.* Katende, H.C.C.A. 27 of 1948, Notes 23 293
Sentongo *v.* Kulazikulabe, P.C.C.C. 49 of 1949, 1940–55 C.L.R. .. 260
Serunkabidde & Co. *v.* Serunkabidde, P.C.C.C. 97 of 1947 (unreported) 247
Serunkuma *v.* Nandyose, H.C.C.A. 69 of 1956, Bulletin 12/59.. .. 293
Seruwagi *v.* Gitta and Others, P.C.C.C. 31 of 1953, 1940–55 C.L.R. .. 228
Serwada *v.* Mukasa, P.C.R.O. 23 of 1939 (unreported) 292
Sewalu *v.* Musajakawa, P.C.C.C. 167 of 1953, H.C.C.A. 40 of 1955,
Notes 71 .. ..96, 238
Sewava, *Re* H.C.Misc.C. 17 of 1951 (unreported) 205
Sewava *v.* Kawalya Kagwa and Others, E.A.C.A. C.A. 30 of 1954
(unreported) 200, 206
Shaku *v.* Bamuta, E.A.C.A. C.A. 15 of 1946, (1946) 13 E.A.C.A.48 .. 45
Ssango *v.* Lukiko, H.C.Cr.A. 263 of 1957 (1958) E.A. 265 295

T

Tibyasa *v.* Sempala, P.C.C.C. 165 of 1956, 1957 C.L.R. 99 263
Twalabekyo *v.* Gawede, P.C.R.O. 14 of 1921 (unreported) 174

W

Walusimbi *v.* Buganda Government, H.C.C.A. 62 of 1953, Notes 63 .. 259
Wamala *v.* Kusalakuzibu, P.C.C.C. 431 of 1956, 1957 C.L.R. 133 .. 146
Wamala *v.* Muguluma, H.C.C.A. 49 of 1952, Notes 53 228
Wamala *v.* Musoke, H.C.C.A. 2 of 1923, 3 U.L.R. 120 159

Wamala *v.* Ssessanga, P.C.C.A. 104 of 1957, 1957 C.L.R. 107 .. 168
Wamala and Another *v.* Lukiko, P.C.Cr.A. 4 of 1957, 1957 C.L.R. 49 .. 115
Waswa *v.* Bayitanomugumu, H.C.C.A. 12 of 1954 (unreported) .. 161
Waswa *v.* Lukiko, H.C.Cr.A. 220 of 1947 (unreported) 44
Waswa *v.* Lule, P.C.R.O. 144 of 1928 (unreported) 138
Waswa *v.* Sebuliba, H.C.C.A. 61 of 1951 (unreported) 200
Wasswa *v.* Lubega, P.C.C.A. 167 of 1956, 1956 C.L.R. 51 238
Wasswa and Others *v.* Sempa and Another, P.C.C.C. 82 of 1952
(unreported) 249
Wayononye *v.* Mwebe and Another, P.C.C.C. 169 of 1950, 1940–55
C.L.R. 248

Y

Yakuze *v.* Kitamirike, P.C.R.O. 88 of 1933 (unreported) 88
Yaye *v.* H.H. The Kabaka, H.C.C.A. 7 of 1942, P.C.C.C. 12 of 1941
(unreported) 172

Z

Zake *v.* Bazongere, P.C.C.C. 32 of 1941, J.A.C.A. 3 of 1942, H.C.C.A.
15 of 1942 (unreported) 29, 30, 44
Zake *v.* Bazongere, H.C.C.A. 35 of 1948, Notes 25 239
Zake *v.* Kasajja and Others, P.C.C.C. 187 of 1955 (unreported) .. 249
Zamwanguya *v.* Kabali and Another, P.C.C.C. 59 of 1948 (unreported) 223
Zirabamuzale *v.* Kiggundu, P.C.C.C. 159 of 1952 (unreported) .. 237
Zirimuwagabo *v.* Kasolo, P.C.C.A. 132 of 1957, 1958 C.L.R. 89 .. 147
Ziryawulamu *v.* Mayanja, P.C.R.O. 115 of 1932 (unreported) .. 61
Zzimbe *v.* Ssajjabi, P.C.C.A. 89 of 1957, 1957 C.L.R. 135 146
Zzimula *v.* Buganda Government. H.C.C.A. 107 of 1956, Notes 75 .. 292

INTRODUCTION

Terminology and Delimitation of Subject

Throughout this book the following terms have been employed to convey the meanings ascribed:

"law" a rule of human conduct which is recognised as being obligatory.[1]

"native law" a law enacted by the Kabaka with the advice and consent of the Lukiko and with the prior approval of the Governor, in accordance with Article 26 of the Constitution of Buganda.

"customary law" the native customary law prevailing in Buganda (vide subsection 10(b) of the Buganda Courts Ordinance), which expression is taken to include customs of the Ganda and other law from whatever source, which have not as yet been incorporated in written legislation but which have legal force or validity or both in the courts.

"custom" a custom of the Ganda, which has neither legal force nor validity in the courts, and which is a mere social convention.

As has been already indicated,[2] the aim in writing this book has been to trace the development of Buganda customary law and judicial institutions from the middle of the last century until the present day. We are then primarily concerned as regards law, not with the written but with the unwritten native law. Only brief mention will therefore be made of the more important provisions of Buganda native laws. A chronological list of all Buganda native laws enacted will be found in an appendix to this book. To turn to the other side of the

---

[1] A. L. Goodhart—"The Importance of a Definition of Law", J.A.A., Vol. III, No. 3, July 1951, p. 106; and J. H. Driberg, "The African Conception of Law", *Journal of Comparative Legislation and International Law*, 1934, Vol. XVI, p. 230.

[2] See above p. viii

canvas, we are likewise not concerned in this work with customs which are mere social conventions without legal force or validity. They are the concern of the sociologist and but form a background to the legal sanctions and judicial institutions of the Ganda.

As in Nigeria, so in Buganda

> " local laws and customs are not simply exceptions to the general body of law but are also the *fons et origo* of a substantial part of the entire law of the country."[1]

Indeed a greater part of all cases tried in Buganda are tried in the native courts and the majority of cases so tried are tried in accordance with customary law, until now largely unrecorded.

DESCRIPTION OF LAND AND PEOPLE

As a foundation to an introduction to the land and people of Buganda, the opening description of Bere, who was kind enough to introduce me to the country and people on my first arrival, can hardly be bettered:

> " The Kingdom of Buganda is one of the four provinces of the Uganda Protectorate and lies, astride the equator, on the north-west shores of Lake Victoria, having the Victoria Nile for its eastern border. Buganda is roughly square in shape and its boundaries to the north, east and west are contiguous with those of the other three Provinces of the Protectorate: to the South it touches the Lake Province of Tanganyika. The land area of the Kingdom is 17,381 square miles, just over one fifth of the total area of the Protectorate. . . ."[2]

The average elevation of Buganda is 4,000 feet and it is covered in the lacustrine region with flat-topped hills which inland from the Lake at a distance of about twenty miles give way to rounded hills. On the lower slopes of the flat-topped hills lies fertile cultivation and the wide valleys are partly filled with papyrus or forest. The vegetation in those lakeside areas is heavy. Inland the valleys contain scrub, while the hills are generally covered with short grass. The climate is equable with a mean annual temperature not less than 65°F. and the rainfall ample.[3]

---

[1] Elias, *Groundwork of Nigerian Law*, 1954, p. 14, and *pace* Julius Lewin in " The Recognition of Native Law and Custom in British Africa ", *Journal of Comparative Legislation and International Law*, 1938, Vol. XX, p. 18.

[2] R. M. Bere, " Buganda", *Corona*, October 1951, p. 383.

[3] J. W. Pallister, " The Physiography of Mengo District, Buganda ", U.J., Vol. 21. No. 1, March 1957, p. 16.

According to the 1959 census there are 1,834,128 Africans in Buganda of whom 1,006,101 are Ganda. Of the balance of 828,027 the majority are immigrants from Ruanda Urundi. The African population is mainly of agricultural pursuit and settlement is over the slopes of hills leaving the bare tops and swampy or afforested valleys uninhabited. A typical homestead consists of a house surrounded by a plantain garden, wherein is grown the staple basic crop (ettooke).[1]

The Ganda have an ancient history going back into the mists of mediaeval antiquity. The original stock was of Bantu cultivators but they were subjected to Hamitic and then Nilotic invasions.[2] Certainly the oldest settled areas of Buganda are the Ssazas of Kyaddondo, Busiro, Mawokota, Butambala and Busujju.[3] From time immemorial the Ganda have been ruled by a Kabaka and the present Kabaka, Mutesa II, is the thirty-sixth in direct succession. Since the advent of the earliest European explorers the Ganda have held the reputation of being one of the most intelligent and advanced peoples of Africa. During this century they have as small-scale peasant cultivators successfully developed the cultivation of cotton for export and more recently have engaged in the wide-scale cultivation of coffee.

This peasant cultivation is based on an individual system of holding land in freehold title which is without counterpart in Africa. Under this so-called " mailo " system inaugurated by the 1900 Agreement there has grown up a wealthy landowning class.

The political organization of the Kingdom and the social organization of the Ganda clans are described in the pages which follow.[4]

---

[1] J. E. Goldthorpe, *Outlines of East African Society*, 1958, p. 68.
[2] Bere, *loc. cit.*
[3] A. I. Richards, *Economic Development and Tribal Change*, p. 99.
[4] See Chapters 3 and 5 below.

PART I

CONSTITUTIONAL

SUMMARY

PAGE

CHAP. 1   The Nineteenth Century   3

CHAP. 2   The 1900 Agreement   18

CHAP. 3   The Twentieth Century   23

CHAPTER 1

THE NINETEENTH CENTURY

ANCIENT POLITICAL ORGANISATION

The dawn of history in Buganda and the rise of the chieftainships under the suzerainty of the Kabaka are for our purposes
most succinctly outlined by Lord Hailey:[1]

"Prior to the incursion of the Hamites into the country on the
northern shores of Lake Victoria, portions of the area which is now
Buganda were inhabited by a number of clans, some of whom, if
not all, had affinities with each other. The Hamites came from the
north-west in the fourteenth century, and tradition is agreed that
they were at the time under the leadership of Kintu, the titular
founder of the Buganda Kingdom. It is said that fourteen of the
Buganda clans came with them, though in their journey they had
doubtless gathered others in their train. . . . As a pastoral people
they no doubt wandered about in search of pasture, merging with
the population and adopting their habits and language.

During this period Busuju appears to have become part of the
territory occupied by them, if indeed it was not so already. Three
saza posts are mentioned in this period, Mugema (Busiro), Kago
(Kyadondo) and Kaima (Mawokota). It is possible that they
were then those of ' palace officials ', rather than territorial administrators. When the Hamites left the country or lost their
supremacy, the most important figure for a time was one of the
original inhabitants. Kimera, the first Kabaka of the present
dynasty then arrived in the country from Bunyoro, and Sebwana,
the autochthonous leader, fled to the Sesse Islands. This happened
possibly at the end of the fourteenth century.

As far as is known, Kimera appointed five saza heads, Mugema
and Kago and also Kasujju (Busujju), Mukwenda (Singo) and
Kangawo (Bulemeezi). This indicates that he added Southern
Singo and Southern Bulemezi to his realm or else appointed chiefs
over what had formed parts of other chiefdoms. The next extension
of Buganda did not occur till the reign of Katerega, the fourteenth
Kabaka, in the early seventeenth century. He added eastern Gomba
and Butambala by conquest and created two new posts, those of
Kitunzi (Gomba) and Katambala (Butambala). Later in the same
century Juko (sixteenth Kabaka) created the post of Sekibobo and

---

[1] Lord Hailey, *Native Administration in the British African Territories*, 1951,
Part I, p. 12.

presumably brought the greater part of Kyaggwe under administration. Late in the eighteenth century Junju (twenty-sixth Kabaka) conquered Buddu and created the post of Pokino, and in the early nineteenth century the generals of Kamanya (twenty-eighth Kabaka) conquered the northern part of Bulemezi, the southern portion of Bugerere and Buwekula. Southern Bugerere was administered from Kyaggwe and Buwekula became a ' gombolola ' of Singo."

For practical purposes the curtain rises on the death of Kabaka Suna and the accession of Mutesa I,[1] as it was about this epoch that important decisions, as will appear later,[2] were made on points of customary law and any precise knowledge of the Ganda begins.[3] It is, however, necessary with a view to getting the law and justice administered to the Ganda into perspective to appreciate the cruel nature of the tyranny of the Kabakas of the last century. A famous Ssaza Chief and man of affairs, Hamu Mukasa, born in 1871, thus describes[4] the initial cruelties and subsequent recantation of Kabaka Mutesa I, who was at first called Mukabya (the Groan-maker) and later earnt the name Mutesa (the Wise Councillor):

> " Then Mukabya became King of his country and ruled well. But afterwards having completed a period of four or five years he commenced, as you know youths will, to behave maliciously, wishing to follow the murderous habits of his father, killing people for nothing and such small offences as would nowadays, perhaps, be met by a punishment of two or three weeks' imprisonment. In such cases he just killed people, and attempted to kill very many people in an unthinkably cruel manner. Now in the year 1859 some Arabs arrived from Karagwe named Abdulla bin Hassan and Muhoya bin Saleh. These tried to convert the Kabaka to Mohammedanism. His servants and chiefs applied themselves to a study of their holy book the Koran and obstructed him strongly in his attempts to slaughter people without cause, endeavouring to replace execution by punishment and imprisonment, exhorting him thus: ' You Kings are God's representatives, you should not meet offences with death but rather with imprisonment and fines. That is the good custom of Kings and kind Kings are those whose lives last for many years.' Then he stayed his hand on account of these teachers."

Further evidence of these tyrannical acts of those Kabakas is

---

[1] Variously stated to be 1852 (by Sir Apolo Kagwa, *Ekitabo kye Bika bya Baganda*, p. 140) and 1857 (by Thomas and Scott, *Uganda*, p. 1).
[2] See pp. 10 and 217.
[3] Thomas and Scott, *op. cit.*, p. 3.
[4] " Some Notes on the Reign of Mutesa ", *U.J.*, Vol. I, 1934, p. 129.

to be found in the account of Dr. Carl Peters,[1] the German explorer:

" In Uganda we are within the limits of the dark despotism of Central Africa. The stranger marvels at the number of human beings he encounters who have lost one eye, or both ears, or their noses, or lips; but the missionaries have stories to tell of much worse things. Everything in the whole of this country belongs to the ruler above. He issues his command, and the people at once bring him their cattle, daughters and wives. He commands, and hundreds of his subjects are dragged off to the place of execution, and there put to death with fearful tortures. The limbs of the victims are hacked off one by one, roasted before the very eyes of the unfortunate sufferers, who are then forced to eat their own flesh. The mutilated trunk is then slowly roasted, and everything is done to prolong the agony as much as possible."

There was nevertheless some semblance of law and order even in those wild times for an early missionary, the Reverend R. P. Ashe, describes[2] the embryo Council of the Kabaka:

" The king has his council, or ' Lukiko ', answering roughly to our own Privy Council, of the chiefs (Pokino, Kangao, Sekebobo, Mukwenda, Kyimbugwe, Kasuju, Mugema, Kibare and Gabunga) with others of less degree. He himself appoints all the chiefs, called *aba-saza*, and all the officers of his court, or *batongole*. Besides these, he appoints the under officers in the households of these chiefs."

The chiefly system in Buganda in the nineteenth century was complicated with a variety of classes and ranks, of which more anon,[3] but the most intelligible and comprehensive description of that system is to be found in Mair's reconstruction[4] from whom I have no hesitation in quoting:

" Theoretically, the whole country and all that was in it was not only subject to the King's authority but actually belonged to him; hence his power of life and death, his right to the spoils of war, to tax his subjects, and make use of their labour. He made his will effective throughout his kingdom by the appointment of chiefs, of whom it may with equal truth be said that each controlled a certain area of land or that he controlled the whole population within that area. Formal acknowledgment of his authority and theoretical ownership was made, on the appointment of a new chief, by a payment of cattle from the chief himself, and cowries from every peasant in the village, to the King's messenger who installed him. Till that payment had been made only the royal representative

[1] Dr. C. Peters, *New Light on Dark Africa*, 1891, p. 414.
[2] R. P. Ashe, *Two Kings of Uganda*, 1889, p. 86.
[3] See Chapter 4.
[4] L. P. Mair, *op. cit.*, p. 159 *et seq.*

could have bananas cut for beer in the chief's plantation—the chief himself could not do so—and peasants who had come with the new chief could not begin cultivation.

The country was not divided into a fixed number of chieftainships. There were ten main divisions—*masaza*—whose heads were called *bakungu*, or great chiefs. These exercised a certain authority over the other chiefs in their divisions, though not in matters concerning the allocation of land to peasants. The number of these lesser chiefs, or *batongole*, was unlimited. These were appointed to office as a reward for services at court, or sometimes a peasant received this honour on the recommendation of his own chief, and to make the appointment the King might either fill a post left vacant by death or promotion, create a vacancy by deposing the holder, or make a new chieftainship. Every King created one new chieftainship after his accession to commemorate his reign."

And again Mair reconstructs[1] the political hierarchy:

" There was a definite hierarchy of rank among the chiefs, not, certainly, forming a symmetrical administrative pyramid like the modern system, but recognised and understood. The chieftainships fell roughly into three grades, and each chief was said to ' enter into ' his superior. The lowest rank comprised the *batongole*, and the *bataka* unless these were appointed by the King, as fairly often happened, to administer larger areas in addition to their ancestral land. In each ssaza there were a number of *bakungu* or great chiefs, whose authority extended over these inferior chiefs; there were also some ' great *batongole* ', who were too important to come under the authority of another *mukungu* but did not, like the bakungu, exercise authority over inferior chiefs. At the head of all these came the chief of the ssaza. The whole hierarchy culminated with the Katikiro, the King's chief minister, whose authority and dignities were almost equal to the King himself."

Of the *bataka*, heads of clans, that is kinship groups, who formerly lived together on clan land—*butaka*—a more precise definition will be made when describing the customary law of land.[2]

To revert to chronology for a moment—in 1884 Kabaka Mutesa I died and was succeeded by Mwanga whose reign was marked by religious wars. On the 3rd September, 1888 the Royal Charter was granted to the Imperial East Africa Company which was beginning to take an interest in Buganda affairs. That same year, 1888, saw two fresh Kabakas, Kiwewa and Kalema, succeeding to the Throne of Buganda within forty days of each other but on the 11th February, 1890 Mwanga returned

---

[1] *Op. cit.*, p. 174.
[2] See below, Chapter 8.

and finally drove Kalema from Rubaga and the throne. On 1st July the Anglo–German Agreement confirmed the inclusion of Buganda in the British sphere of influence and on 26th December the then Captain Lugard signed the first Treaty with Mwanga.[1]

We shall be considering that Treaty and others later in this chapter. Before doing so, let us round off the development of the political organisation of Buganda in the nineteenth century by considering further Lord Hailey's synopsis:[2]

> " In the 1890's, considerable additions were made to Buganda, largely with British help. Bugangadzi, Buyaga, Buruli, Northern Singo and Northern Bugerere were annexed at the expense of Bunyoro or Bunyoro's tributaries. Buvuma, hitherto independent, was conquered; Kabula and Mawogola, previously in the Ankole sphere of influence were annexed; the independent Kingdom of Koki joined Buganda by treaty, and Buwekula was erected into a separate saza. New saza posts were created as follows: Kiimba (Bugangadzi), Kyambalango (Buyaga), Kimbugwe (Buruli), Mugerere (Bugerere), Mbubi (Buvuma), Lumama (Kabula), Mutesa (Mawogola), Kamuswaga (Koki) and Luwekula (Buwekula).
>
> The position of the Sesse Islands had always been somewhat different from the rest of Buganda. The islanders had ties of some kind with the Baganda and at some unspecified period recognised the Kabaka's overlordship. Until the period under discussion, however, they had always controlled their own internal affairs with a Muganda hereditary chief (the Gabunga) on the mainland, acting as the Kabaka's emissary. Sesse now became a saza with a chief holding the title of Kweba. This completes the list of twenty sazas whose existence was ratified in the Uganda Agreement of 1900."

Early Legislation

Under this title I propose to review briefly the Imperial legislation governing Uganda or, as it was to all intents and purposes, Buganda affairs, the native laws in so far as they were recorded and the customary law, in the last century. In the first section of this chapter we left the chronology of events with the signing of the first treaty on the 26th December, 1890 between Kabaka Mwanga and Captain Lugard of the Imperial British East Africa Company. *Inter alia* that treaty (No. 75 of the Company in East Africa) provided:[3]

---

[1] Following chronology of Thomas and Scott, *loc. cit.*
[2] *Op. cit.*, p. 13.
[3] J. V. Wild, *The Story of the Uganda Agreement*, 1950, pp. 41–45.

> " With a view to carrying out the obligations into which they now enter, the Company engage to send to the Court of Uganda a fully accredited agent. His powers shall be as follows:—
>
> (a) All Europeans resident in Uganda shall refer all disputes and all differences or questions connected with their affairs to him as arbitrator, and his decision subject to appeal to the higher authorities of the Company shall be final."

From the first then Europeans were excluded from the jurisdiction of the native customary courts and this arrangement was further stabilized by the instructions of the Secretary of State dated 31st July, 1891, whereby the British sphere on the East Coast of Africa, within which fell Uganda, was constituted a local jurisdiction for the purposes of the Africa Order-in-Council, 1889, issued under the Foreign Jurisdiction Acts 1843–1878. On 30th March, 1892 Mwanga and Lugard entered into a second treaty which was for the most part a repetition of the treaty of 1890.[1] On the 1st April, 1893 the Chartered Company's régime in Uganda came to an end and on 29th May Sir Gerald Portal entered into a provisional agreement with Mwanga, having proclaimed a provisional British protectorate over Uganda. This Agreement, which superseded " all other Agreements or Treaties whatsoever made by Mwanga or his predecessors ", contained *inter alia* the following provisions:

> " 5. I fully recognise that so far as I, the King, am concerned the sole jurisdiction over Europeans and over all persons not born in my dominions and the settlement of all cases in which any such persons may be a party or parties, lie exclusively in the hands of Her Majesty's Representative.
>
> 6. In civil cases between my subjects, the Court of Her Majesty's Representative shall be a Supreme Court of Appeal, but it shall lie entirely within the discretion of the said Representative to refuse to hear such appeals.
>
> 7. In criminal cases where only natives are concerned it is left to the discretion of Her Majesty's Representative to interfere, in the public interest and for the sake of justice, to the extent and in the manner which he may consider desirable.
>
> 8. And I, Mwanga, the King, undertake to see that due effect is given to all and every decision of the Court of Her Majesty's Representative under Articles 6 and 7."

Thereby the jurisdiction of the Kabaka's Courts in civil and criminal cases between natives was recognised.

The Africa Order in Council, 1889, was applied to Uganda

---

[1] Wild, *op. cit.*, pp. 54–57.

on the declaration of a British Protectorate on 18th June, 1894 by Notification in the *London Gazette* of 19th June, 1894. Article 13 of that Order applied English law and procedure but Article 16 declared that the provisions of a treaty were to prevail over the Africa Order in Council or any English law. Article 17 is note-worthy:

> " Crimes, offences, wrongs and breaches of contract against or affecting the person, property, or rights of natives of Africa, or other foreigners as herein defined, committed by persons subject to this Order, are punishable or otherwise cognisable under the provisions of this Order, *with the consent of such natives or foreigners*, in the same manner as if they were committed against or affected the person, property or rights of British subjects."

Parts III and IV established Consular Courts and the pro-cedure of those Courts and Part XI provided that Queen's Regulations made by a Consul are to have effect.

On the 27th August, 1894, Colonel Colville and King Mwanga entered into a further Agreement ratifying Sir Gerald Portal's provisional Agreement with King Mwanga of the previous year. The charter of the Imperial British East Africa Company was revoked on the 1st July, 1895, and the East Africa Protectorate was constituted. Kabaka Mwanga finally fled from Mengo on the 6th July, 1897, and on the 14th August of that year Daudi Chwa, one year of age, was proclaimed King of Buganda.

As Mair rightly observes,[1] the royal council of Buganda was not, in the nineteenth century, either a deliberative or a legisla-tive body. Decisions were made by the Kabaka and the Katikkiro and were announced to it. A clear picture of the subservience of the Lukiko in those days and the penalties for deviating from the norm of its behaviour are to be found in Speke's eyewitness account[2] of this court just before the coronation of Mutesa I in January 1862:

> " It is the duty of all officers, generally speaking to attend at court as constantly as possible; should they fail, they forfeit their lands, wives, and all belongings. These will be seized and given to others more worthy of them; as it is presumed that either insolence or disaffection can be the only motive which would induce any person to absent himself for any length of time from the pleasure of seeing his sovereign. Tidiness in dress is imperatively necessary, and for any neglect of this rule the head may be forfeit. The

---

[1] Mair, *op. cit.*, p. 178.
[2] J. H. Speke, *Journal of the Discovery of the Source of the Nile*, 1863, pp. 255 *et seq.*

punishment for such offences, however, may be commuted by fines of cattle, goats, fowls, or brass wire. All acts of the King are counted benefits, for which he must be thanked; and so every deed done to his subjects is a gift received by them, though it should assume the shape of flogging or fine; for are not these, which make better men of them, as necessary as anything? . . .

In consequence of these salutations, there is more ceremony in court than business, though the King, ever having an eye to his treasury, continually finds some trifling fault, condemns the head of the culprit, takes his liquidation present, if he has anything to pay, and thus keeps up his revenue.

No-one dare stand before the King whilst he is either standing still or sitting, but must approach him with downcast eyes, and bended knees, and kneel or sit when arrived. To touch the King's throne or clothes, even by accident, or to look upon his women, is certain death.

To complete the picture of the court, one must imagine a crowd of pages to run royal messages; they dare not walk, for such a deficiency in zeal to their master might cost their life."

The customary law of the Ganda in the second half of the nineteenth century will be considered in the appropriate chapters. There are, however, a few laws of which the authenticity is vouched by contemporary or near-contemporary writers and which will now be quoted: after his recantation Kabaka Mutesa I made the following reforms *inter alia*:

   (i) it is wrong to kill people;

  (ii) selling of slaves is prohibited;

 (iii) slandering of chiefs is prohibited;

 (iv) drunkenness is prohibited—particularly among chiefs as thereby they are unable to settle the cases of their people;

  (v) the plundering of the Namasole's men, when the Kabaka was vexed with the Namasole, was abolished.[1]

Certain of Mutesa's prior and more tyrannical edicts are recorded by Ashe:[2]

". . . every man was to wear a bead on his wrist, on pain of losing his head; and every woman, a bead round her waist, on pain of being cut in half. . . ."

Cunningham adds a more humorous note:[3]

"The bald were banned and exiled to a special province, Kitongole, where they were doomed to remain till their hair grew. There was a special tax imposed on persons who had enlarged navels."

---

[1] Hamu Mukasa, "The Rule of the Kings of Buganda", *Bulletin of the Uganda Society*, 1944, p. 21.

[2] *Op. cit.*, p. 82.

[3] J. F. Cunningham, *Uganda and its peoples*, 1905, p. 232.

Sir Apolo Kagwa has recorded much of the customary laws of the Ganda in the last century in Chapter 23 of his great work on Buganda custom,[1] but those parts of the unwritten customary law will be considered in their appropriate chapters below.

The times, however, were ripe for a beginning to be made in recording native law and, as is to be expected, we find that that great administrator, Lugard, made such a start in February 1891:[2]

> " For I had established a ' statute-book ', in which to set down all decisions arrived at and all laws passed, as the Wagande set great weight on a written contract. . . .
> On the 27th I got the King to announce in baraza—
> ' (1) That on no account whatever should any chief evict any man from his shamba without the express order of the baraza, and if he did so he should be liable to lose his place.
> (2) That all the dwellers on any estate should do the work of the chief immediately over them, and he again of his superiors, providing the customary food or tribute, etc. entirely irrespective of creed or party.'
> Both sides emphatically approved of this law, which was entered in the newly instituted statute-book, and the Kimbugwe (F) made an admirable speech about it. . . ."

In the twenty-second chapter of his second major work,[3] Sir Apolo Kagwa records eighteen laws which were made by Mr. Jackson in 1895, as Her Majesty's Representative, but as these laws were made by the British power with the acquiescence of the Kabaka they cannot be regarded as truly native laws and the more important will therefore be reviewed not here but in the subsequent chapters according to their relevance.

Ancient Judicial System

We have the authority of a former Attorney General of Uganda for believing that in Buganda, at the time of the arrival of the European, the native system of administering justice was found to be in a surprisingly stable and advanced state, as was the whole organisation of that country.[4] Certainly ancient

---

[1] *Ekitabo ky'Empisa za Baganda.*
[2] Capt. F. D. Lugard, *The Rise of our East African Empire*, 1893, Vol. II, pp. 72 and 92.
[3] *Ekitabo kya Basekabaka beBuganda*, p. 199.
[4] H. R. Hone (now Sir Ralph Hone), " The Native of Uganda and the Criminal Law ", *U.J.*, 1938–39, Vol. VI, p. 1.

Buganda had a great variety of judicial tribunals connected in a pyramidal structure so that appeal lay from the minor chiefs through the great chiefs to the Katikkiro (Prime Minister) and thence to the Kabaka and rarely on final appeal from the Kabaka to ordeal by intoxication (amaduudu).

Disputes were usually settled by arbitral proceedings within the family, clan or relatives. Mair appears to be correct in her view:

> " It is also worth noting that the cases which came before him (*i.e.* a chief) were matters arising between persons not bound by close ties. Quarrels between members of one clan were settled by the senior clansman; matrimonial quarrels by the senior wife, or, if they became serious enough for the wife to run away by her near relatives."[1]

If those arbitral fora were inappropriate or inadequate for the settlement of the case then the parties had recourse to the village chief (omutongole).

> " Every chief, even a petty chief, with only a dozen followers, was able to hold a court and to try cases among his own people."[2]

Mair, whose researches were carried out a quarter of a century ago, describes[3] the rather loose arrangement that obtained in this lowest of judicial institutions in Buganda in the last century:

> " In the old days a case was discussed in the presence of all the peasants who happened to have come to pay their respects to the chief, and anyone might ask questions and express an opinion. Thus this was the aspect of the chief's authority which touched the peasants most closely and continuously.
>
> It is rather remarkable, however, that the chief's authority did not preclude the possibility of private revenge for admitted injuries, though informants differ in their view of the extent to which such action was independent of his approval. There seems to have been a good deal of difference in the extent of effective authority over their own subjects as between greater and smaller chiefs. In any case no chief's authority was developed to the point where he was himself responsible for bringing criminals to justice. That responsibility rested always upon the injured person or his relatives. . . .
>
> The chief's authority functioned essentially in cases where a crime was denied, where responsibility was disputed, or where there was a question of fixing compensation; this last seems to have been done always under the auspices of the chief, who received a large share of the amount handed over."

---

[1] *Op. cit.*, p. 187.
[2] Roscoe, *op. cit.*, p. 241.
[3] *Op. cit.*, pp. 184–187.

Any case which such a lesser chief (omutongole) was unable to settle,[1] or in which a party appealed from his decision,[2] was sent by that lesser chief to the superior chief (omukungu) and then if need be to the ssaza chief, whom Roscoe terms " the District-Chief ":

> " In the provinces the District-Chief was the principal magistrate, and he had his sub-chiefs to assist him in trying cases in their districts. . . . The sub-chiefs were also appointed by the King and by the Council (Lukiko) to their office and they could not be deposed except by the King's consent.
>
> In each district there was a supreme court, at the District-Chief's residence or near it; to this court cases were referred from the sub-chiefs, when the parties tried were dissatisfied with the decision."[3]

If the case was above the jurisdiction of the court of the ssaza chief or there was an appeal from his court's decision then the parties had recourse to the Katikkiro's court. For this court's composition and procedure and for a description of the Kabaka's own court's functioning in the last century we have a wealth of contemporary eye-witness accounts, but before reviewing the relevant passages it should be recalled that the administration of justice in the Kingdom of Buganda was a prime duty to the people of Buganda, which was impressed from the earliest times on each Kabaka at his accession[4] when he was required to promise to decide cases justly.[5] This undertaking by the Kabaka to his people was passed on by him to his Prime Minister (Katikkiro) when he installed the latter in his office by handing him the *Ddamula* (stick of office).[6]

The best account of the Katikkiro's court is to be found in the record of the missionary Ashe of what he himself saw about the year 1882:[7]

> " Passing through yet another gateway we came to the chief judge's court-house or " Kigango ". The chief judge or chancellor, like the chief whom we had just left, was seated on a mat and surrounded by a still greater crowd. On our approach he rose and came out to meet us, and received us very graciously; he was dressed in Arab costume, a snowy white gown of fine cotton, over

---

[1] Mair, *op. cit.*, p. 174.

[2] Roscoe, *op. cit.*, p. 249.

[3] Roscoe, *op. cit.*, pp. 240–241.

[4] Sir Apolo Kagwa, *Empisa*, pp. 6–24.

[5] *Ibid.*, p. 12.

[6] *Ibid.*, pp. 19 and 319. The word " Ddamula " is derived from *okulamula* = to administer justice.

[7] *Op. cit.*, pp. 54 *et seq.*

which he wore a long mantle or robe of rich black cloth, heavily embroidered with gold. . . .

I watched the great man as he listened to the counsel who were arguing the cases on which he was to give judgement, 'sala musango', 'cut judgement', he all the while playing the game of *Mweso*.[1] He was nevertheless listening carefully, though you would hardly think so to see his lithe fingers gathering up the counters with which he played and dropping them into their proper holes. He would eventually stop, arrange some small white sticks in order on the ground to mark the points of his summing up, and then give judgement, though the scale could be made to incline this way or that by a timely bribe. On hearing the verdict, both plaintiff and defendant and their supporters energetically thanked the judge. Kneeling before him and clasping their hands, they moved them up and down, crying out, ' Neyanze, Neyanze, Neyanzege ', or, speaking in the plural, ' Tweyanze, Tweyanzege ', We thank you."

Although the Katikkiro's court had separate jurisdiction and indeed did not necessarily decide every case in favour of the King,[2] the Katikkiro (called Kamala Byona = who decides everything) was under a duty to report to the Kabaka his decision

" who might either accept the verdict without any further hearing, or might direct the same case to be tried before his own court."[3]

Hamu Mukasa stated that it was very difficult to make an appeal to the Kabaka unless the appellant had someone of great influence to help him to do it.[4] Roscoe in fact recounts:

" The majority of appeals ended in the Katikkiro's court, which ranked next after the King's court; it stood facing the King's entrance. This court-house appears to have been a survival of an old custom, according to which the King sat under one of the sacred trees at the entrance of his enclosure and tried all cases brought to him. The Katikkiro tried the more important cases in person, but deputed an assistant to try others; the assistant had to report the result of his examination, and the Katikkiro then gave his decision."[5]

A former Minister of Finance in the Kabaka's Government

---

[1] *Mweso* is a Ganda game played on a partitioned board with beans as counters. See Roscoe, *op. cit.*, p. 78 for illustration. See also Sir Apolo Kagwa, *Empisa*, p. 7 for similar account.

[2] Mair, *op. cit.*, p. 177.

[3] Roscoe, *op. cit.*, p. 235.

[4] Hamu Mukasa, " The Rule of the Kings of Buganda ", *Bulletin of Uganda Society*, 1944, p. 21.

[5] *Op. cit.*, p. 260, and followed literally by Jules LeClercq, *Aux Sources du Nil*, 1913, p. 205.

and later a member of the Executive Council of the Protectorate, Owekitiibwa S. W. Kulubya, described the royal court thus:

> " Throughout history the Kings of Buganda have been the supreme tribunal for their people. There used therefore to be set aside days when they appeared to their subjects to hear and decide all matters, legal or administrative, and settle all disputes which were brought to them. The hut or house where the King usually heard these and cases which came from all parts of his country was known as Masengere. . . ."[1]

(The full title of this royal courthouse was " Masengeregansaze " which means " I have been met by ores ". The derivation of this title is given by Sir Apolo Kagwa as the cry of the convicted man as he was dragged bound by the executioners over the rough ground.[2]) Here it was the Katikkiro's duty to present the cases he had decided but those who appealed from the Katikkiro's decision were allowed to present their own cases.[3] In order to obtain a clear picture of this royal court in action in the last century we cannot do better than to refer again to Speke's eyewitness account:[4]

> " As to the minor business transacted in court, culprits are brought in bound by officers, and reported. At once the sentence is given, perhaps awarding the most torturous lingering death— probably without trial or investigation, and, for all the King knows, at the instigation of someone influenced by wicked spite. If the accused endeavour to plead his defence, his voice is at once drowned, and the miserable victim dragged off in the roughest manner possible by those officers who love their King, and delight in promptly carrying out his orders. Young virgins, the daughters of Wakungu, stark naked, and smeared with grease, but holding, for decency's sake, a small square of *mbugu* at the upper corners in both hands before them, are presented by their fathers in propitiation for some offence, and to fill the harem. Seizing-officers receive orders to hunt down Wakungu who have committed some indiscretions, and to confiscate their lands, wives, children and property. An officer observed to salute informally is ordered for execution, when everybody near him rises in an instant, the drums beat, drowning his cries, and the victim of carelessness is dragged off, bound by cords, by a dozen men at once. Another man, perhaps, exposes an inch of naked leg whilst squatting, or has his *mbugu* tied contrary to regulations, and is condemned to the same fate."

---

[1] Presidential Address to Uganda Society, 1942, *U.J.*, Vol. IX, p. 53.

[2] *Empisa*, p. 123; see also the translation in Edel, *The Customs of the Baganda*, p. 72.

[3] Sir Apolo Kagwa, *idem*, p. 318 and Edel, *op. cit.*, Chapter XXXVI.

[4] *Op. cit.*, pp. 257-258.

The composition of the Kabaka's court was said to be the Katikkiro, the Kimbugwe and the ten ssaza chiefs,[1] but in September 1895 fifteen separate batches of six greater chiefs were appointed to decide cases in the royal council and to satisfy themselves on behalf of that council that other cases had been properly tried.[2]

To recapitulate there were a number of courts in or about the Kabaka's palace (Lubiri) in the last century:

firstly there was Masengere, the royal court itself, wherein the Kabaka decided cases presented to him by the Katikkiro and his assistant;

then there was the Kigango, sometimes called Akagango K'Essanga, which, as the name suggests used to have an elephant's tusk in front of it, wherein the Katikkiro and the senior chiefs decided cases;[3]

thirdly there was the Gombolola, wherein since the reign of Mutesa I, another assistant of the Katikkiro, entitled Kisekwa, decided minor cases;[4]

lastly there appears to have been a domestic court wherein the chief Kibale, " the deputy of the Kabaka in the Palace " decided all cases arising in respect of internal Palace matters.

Before leaving the classification of the ancient courts in Buganda mention must be made of the two courts presided over by the two leading royal ladies—the Lubuga or Nnaalinnya, that is the Queen-sister, and the Namasole, that is the Queen-Mother. Roscoe describes these courts briefly, firstly that of the Lubuga:

> " She held her own court apart from that of her brother the King, though she consulted him in difficult cases, where other men beside her own people were concerned. She had powers of life and death, and did not hesitate to put a person to death if there was the slightest reason for doing so."[5]

The court of the Namasole he mentions and then records of both:

> " Both the Queen and the King's Mother tried cases among their own servants. But persons against whom any serious charges

---

[1] Roscoe, *op. cit.*, p. 233.
[2] Sir Apolo Kagwa, *Basekabaka*, p. 206.
[3] S. W. Kulubya, *loc. cit.*
[4] Sir Apolo Kagwa, *Empisa*, pp. 122 and 318.
[5] *Op. cit.*, p. 237.

were brought in these courts would not infrequently induce a relative, who was a wife of the King, to intercede for them, so that the King might transfer their case to his court, where a more lenient sentence would be pronounced than they would otherwise have received."[1]

[1] *Idem*, p. 266.

CHAPTER 2

THE 1900 AGREEMENT

For the last sixty years the Buganda Agreement, 1900, has regulated the relationship between the Kingdom of Buganda and the protecting power and in order to appreciate fully this treaty's importance it is necessary not only to examine its actual provisions but also to consider its historical setting and some of the more important case law which has been made on its basis.

Retracing our steps a little to the declaration of the British Protectorate on 18th June, 1894, we cannot do better than to consider the historical background etched by Thomas and Spencer:[1]

> " There followed five years during which the country continued to be the stage for successive excursions and alarms; the threat of Kabarega, the King of Bunyoro, in the northern provinces; the Muhummadam insurrections; the flight of King Mwanga of Buganda; and finally the mutiny of the Sudanese troops. As a result the net annual cost of occupation which Portal had estimated at £20,000 had by 1899 risen to over £300,000. Further, the maintenance of the British protectorate had rendered the construction of the Uganda Railway inevitable, and the British taxpayer had, before the close of the century, contributed in all a sum approaching six millions sterling towards an undertaking which, in its inception, was a concession to public idealism.
>
> It was in these circumstances and to an exhausted country that the Imperial Government despatched Sir Harry Johnston in 1899 as Special Commissioner. The ultimate purpose of his appointment was, in brief, to devise such measures as might be expected to render the local British administration in due course self-supporting.
>
> The Kingdom of Buganda was the focus of the British sphere, and, being almost the only portion provided with a native authority with which it was possible to conduct political negotiations, received first attention. Within three months of his arrival Johnston had prepared the Uganda Agreement, which, after weeks of discussion, was signed by the regents of the infant King and leading chiefs ' on behalf of the Kabaka (King) of Uganda, and the chiefs and people of Uganda ', on 10th March, 1900."

---

[1] H. B. Thomas and A. E. Spencer, *A History of Uganda Land and Surveys and of the Uganda Land and Survey Department*, 1938, p. 61.

The Buganda Agreement, 1900, or the Uganda Agreement as it was originally styled, has since been amended by Article 10 of the Buganda Agreement, 1955, but the first Article of the 1900 Agreement, which is germane to our present purpose is Article 5, which reads:

" 5. The laws made for the general governance of the Uganda Protectorate by Her Majesty's Government will be equally applicable to the Kingdom of Uganda, except in so far as they may in any particular conflict with the terms of this agreement, in which case the terms of this Agreement will constitute a special exception in regard to the Kingdom of Uganda."

That was the only provision dealing with legislation but there were many Articles which dealt with the political organisation of the Kingdom:

" 6 . . . . The Kabaka of Uganda shall exercise direct rule over the natives of Uganda, to whom he shall administer justice through the Lukiko, or native council, and through others of his officers in the manner approved by Her Majesty's Government.

9. For purposes of native administration the Kingdom of Uganda shall be divided into the following districts or administrative counties:—(there follows a list of the present 20 counties). At the head of each county shall be placed a chief who shall be selected by the Kabaka's Government, but whose name shall be submitted for approval to Her Majesty's representative. . . . When arrangements have been made by Her Majesty's Government for the organisation of a police force in the province of Uganda, a certain number of police will be placed at the disposal of each chief of a county to assist him in maintaining order. . . .

10. To assist the Kabaka of Uganda in the government of his people he shall be allowed to appoint three native officers of state with the sanction and approval of Her Majesty's representative in Uganda (without whose sanction such appointments shall not be valid)—A Prime Minister, otherwise known as Katikkiro; a Chief Justice;[1] and a Treasurer or Controller of the Kabaka's revenues. . . .

11. The Lukiko, or native council, shall be constituted as follows:—

In addition to the three native ministers, who shall be *ex officio* senior members of the council, each chief of a county (twenty in all) shall be *ex officio* a member of the Council. Also each chief of a county shall be permitted to appoint a person to act as his lieutenant

---

[1] Prior to this Agreement and since the Agreement between the rival Protestant and Catholic factions on the 7th April, 1893, there had been two Katikkiros, one for the Protestants and one for the Catholics. The appointments to these posts had to be approved by the Resident. (See Wild, *op. cit.*, p. 62). Under the 1900 Agreement the intention was, and in fact was implemented, that the Katikkiro should be a Protestant and the Chief Justice or *Omulamuzi* a Catholic.

in this respect to attend the meetings of the council during his absence, and to speak and vote in his name. The chief of a county, however, and his lieutenant may not both appear simultaneously at the council. In addition, the Kabaka shall select from each county three notables, whom he shall appoint during his pleasure, to be members of the Lukiko or native council. The Kabaka may also, in addition to the foregoing, appoint six other persons of importance in the country to be members of the native council. . . . The functions of the council will be to discuss all matters concerning the native administration of Uganda, and to forward to the Kabaka resolutions which may be voted by a majority regarding measures to be adopted by the said administration. The Kabaka shall further consult with Her Majesty's representative in Uganda before giving effect to any such resolutions voted by the native council, and shall, in this matter, explicitly follow the advice of Her Majesty's representative."

Finally the 1900 Agreement contained the following provisions in respect of the Kabaka's Courts and the system of appeals:

" (6). . . . The Jurisdiction of the native court of the Kabaka of Uganda, however, shall not extend to any person not a native of the Uganda province. The Kabaka's Courts shall be entitled to try natives for capital crimes, but no death sentence may be carried out by the Kabaka, or his Courts, without the sanction of Her Majesty's representative in Uganda. Moreover, there will be a right of appeal from the native courts to the principal Court of Justice established by Her Majesty in the Kingdom of Uganda as regards all sentences which inflict a term of more than five years' imprisonment or a fine of over £100. In the case of any other sentences imposed by the Kabaka's Courts, which may seem to Her Majesty's Government disproportioned or inconsistent with humane principles, Her Majesty's representative in Uganda shall have the right of remonstrance with the Kabaka, who shall, at the request of the said representative, subject such sentence to reconsideration. . . .

8. All cases, civil or criminal, of a mixed nature, where natives of the Uganda province and non-natives of that province are concerned, shall be subject to British Courts of Justice only.

(9). . . . To the chief of a county will be entrusted by Her Majesty's Government, and by the Kabaka, the task of administering justice amongst the natives dwelling in his county, . . .

(11). . . . The Lukiko, or a committee thereof, shall be a Court of Appeal from the decisions of the Courts of First Instances held by the chiefs of counties. In all cases affecting property exceeding the value of £5, or imprisonment exceeding one week, an appeal for revision may be addressed to the Lukiko. In all cases involving property or claims exceeding £100 in value, or a sentence of imprisonment exceeding five years, or sentences of death, the Lukiko shall refer the matter to the consideration of the Kabaka, whose decision when countersigned by Her Majesty's chief representative in Uganda shall be final. The Lukiko shall not decide any questions affecting the persons or property of Europeans or others who are not natives of Uganda. . . ."

The first reported decision of the High Court on the provisions of the 1900 Agreement was that of CARTER, J., on 11th December, 1908 in the original civil case of *Nasanairi Kibuka* v. *A. E. Bertie Smith*.[1] The subject of those proceedings related to the transfer of land, with which we are not presently concerned, but the question as to whether the Lukiko had legislative powers under the Uganda Agreement, 1900, was also for determination:

> "The Uganda Agreement is in the nature of a treaty whereby Her Majesty's Government agrees to recognise the Kabaka of Uganda as the native ruler of the Province of Uganda under Her Majesty's protection and overrule and by its Articles the powers of the ruler are limited in various ways. As I understand the Agreement it is not to be regarded as taking away any right or power of the Kabaka except by its express provisions, therefore whatever powers were his before remain with him, except so far as they are expressly taken away or limited. A sovereign state has undoubtedly the power of legislating and there is no Agreement with Uganda prior to the 1900 Agreement, so far as I am aware, which takes away this right; in the Agreement with Sir Gerald Portal, of 1893, Mwanga speaks of ' myself, my Government and people throughout my Kingdom of Uganda ', these words seem to imply sovereign rights and there is nothing elsewhere in that Agreement taking away legislative powers; nor can I find anything in the Uganda Agreement, 1900 providing that the Kingdom of Uganda is to lose its right of legislating for its people. Article 5 of the Agreement states that laws made by H.M.'s Government for the general governance of the Uganda Protectorate will apply to the Kingdom of Uganda except in so far as they may in any particular conflict with the terms of this Agreement. I do not find that this provision ousts the right of the Baganda to legislate for themselves, nor can the Uganda Order in Council take away any powers from the native Government, as the Order in Council must be read as subject to the Agreement.[2] I consider further that the words ' native administration ' in Clause 11 of the Agreement are not to be read in the narrow sense as merely the executive distinguished from legislative and judicial authority, but in the wider sense including all these three departments of the State, and that the Lukiko would be competent to forward resolutions which would have the force of law when given effect to by the Kabaka after the latter had consulted with and followed the advice of the Governor.
>
> I therefore hold that the native Government of Uganda has power to legislate for the subjects of the Kabaka after consultation with and following the advice of the Governor. . . .

[1] 1 U.L.R. 41.
[2] See also *Katosi* v. *Kahizi*, 1 U.L.R. 22.

As regards the promulgation of the law there is nothing in the Agreement laying down how native laws are to be promulgated and the Order in Council does not deal with native legislation, and although it would without doubt be convenient that laws passed by the native Government should be published in the *Gazette*, as is now being done, I do not find anything which requires that new native laws should be published or promulgated in any particular manner, any more than there is anything which requires that the native law which came into being before the date of the Agreement or the Order in Council and which still exists should be so published. The manner of publication would appear to be left in the hands of the native Government although H.M.'s Representative in Uganda has to be consulted and his advice followed before a new native law can have effect. I do not consider that the validity of the law is affected by the fact that the result of any consultation has not been notified in the *Gazette*, particularly in view of the fact that there is no necessity to promulgate the law in that manner."

On appeal from that decision of Carter, J., the Court of Appeal for Eastern Africa on 10th April, 1909 held:[1]

" We think that by the Agreement of 1900 the Kabaka of Buganda parted with his rights of legislation to this extent that the approval of H.M.'s Commissioner was thereafter necessary to complete the validity of his laws. . . . The appellant further argues that no law can have any force or validity until it is promulgated or otherwise officially notified. With regard to this point we agree with the observations of the learned Judge below and hold that the law is not invalid for want of promulgation or notification."

The next reported decision of the High Court on the terms of the 1900 Agreement mainly concerns the allotment of land to natives under Article 15,[2] and the other notable decision is so concerned with recent politics that it has been popularly termed " the Kabaka's case ".[3] Neither decision is relevant to our present survey.

---

[1] 1 U.L.R. 41.
[2] H.C.C.A. *Alipo Kabazi* v. *Jemusi Kibuka*, 2 U.L.R. 9.
[3] H.C.C.C. 50 of 1954, *S. K. Mukwaba and Others* v. *D. M. Mukubira and Others* (unreported).

CHAPTER 3

THE TWENTIETH CENTURY

MODERN POLITICAL ORGANIZATION

Those readers who live in Uganda will already be adequately acquainted with the modern political structure for the purpose of this legal study, and those who live elsewhere cannot fail to obtain a deep insight into the administrative organisation of both the Kingdom of Buganda and the Protectorate as a whole from Monsieur Bustin's recent detailed analysis.[1] I shall therefore confine my description to a mere outline account.

The 1900 Agreement had provided an administrative machine of the three Ministers, the Lukiko, and the twenty county chiefs. No mention was made therein of any lesser chiefs except in regard to the distribution of 8,000 square miles of land, but from the Note on Land Settlement and more particularly its accompanying document dated 25th July, 1900,[2] it is clear there were in addition to the ssaza (county) chiefs also " 2nd grade chiefs and other sub-chiefs ". There appears to be no formal recognition of the grades of chiefs in the earlier Buganda Agreements as is to be found in Article 13 of the Bunyoro Agreement, 1933, but by 1913 Buganda native law[3] was referring to " Ggombolola " chiefs and by 1923[4] to *muluka* chiefs and to the lowest grade of *mutongole* chief. Those three grades of chief still administer under the ssaza chiefs but the mutongole chief, although relied upon to perform the function of village constable and arbitrator is not paid a salary by the Kabaka's Government. There are at present (October 1959) 135 Ggombolola Chieftainships and 928 *muluka* chieftainships in the Kingdom of Buganda. The population to be found in units of the same grade vary enormously according to the density of the population in the areas in question.

---

[1] E. Bustin, *La Décentralisation Administrative et l'Évolution des Structures Politiques en Afrique Orientale Britannique*, 1958, *Livre Premier: l'Uganda*.
[2] *Laws of Uganda*, 1951, Vol. VI, p. 27.
[3] The Law for Preventing Venereal Disease, 1913.
[4] The Buganda Births Registration Law, 1923.

Each chief within a defined area has a title following a fixed series—Mumyuka, Ssabaddu, Ssabagabo, Ssabawaali, Musaale, Mutuba I, Mutuba II, etc. In this way the ssaza chief Kaggo of Kyaddondo being the chief of the metropolitan county traditionally ranks next after the Katikkiro in the order of chieftainships and so is entitled the Ssabaddu (*i.e.* the Ruler of all slaves) of Buganda.[1] And to carry the illustration further, each Ggombolola or sub-county chief in the ssaza or county of Kyaddondo has a title according to that series; each *muluka* or parish chief in each ggombolola also is entitled according to that series and finally each *mutongole* or village chief in each muluka is similarly given a title.

Before leaving the subject of chiefs mention must be made of the *omusigere* or lieutenant. Each chief of whatever grade has such a lieutenant and, of course, the *omusigere* of a muluka and *a fortiori* a *mutongole* chief is not paid from public funds. Both native law[2] and customary law have however recognised the *omusigere* as exercising all the powers and charged with all the responsibilities of the substantive chief in the latter's absence unless statutory provisions otherwise provide.

It will therefore be observed that the ancient administrative organisation of Buganda based on the *bitongole* and *butaka* land tenures, which we shall consider fully in Chapter 8, was swept away by the 1900 Agreement and the heads of clan (abataka) no longer had direct administrative recognition. The chieftainships were in the nature of dual offices, coupling responsibility for administering an area with personal service to a superior chief. The resulting chiefly system of rule thereby became extremely well-knit and well-disciplined.[3]

A native law[4] in 1945 inaugurated a system of election of non-official representatives of the Ganda people in the Councils. In 1951 a native law[5] was enacted regularizing the establishment of ssaza, ggombolola and miruka councils. This was followed in 1953 by a further law[6] which further regularized the democratic election of representatives to the Great Lukiko of Buganda.

The latest stage in the development of the political system

---

[1] M. B. Nsimbi, *Amannya Amaganda n'Ennono Zaago*, 1956, p. 70.
[2] See Article 11 of the Buganda Agreement, 1900, and the Buganda Births Registration Law, 1923.
[3] Goldthorpe, *op. cit.*, p. 70.
[4] The Law for Selecting Non-Official Representatives to the Lower Councils
[5] The Law for the Establishment of Lower Councils in Buganda.
[6] The Great Lukiiko (Election of Representatives) Law.

was reached in the 1955 Agreement and the First Schedule thereto, namely the Constitution of Buganda, whereby the conduct of the Kabaka's Government was entrusted to the Kabaka's Council of Ministers, those Ministers now numbering six. The constitution of the Lukiko laid down in the 1900 Agreement was preserved. The administrative division of Buganda into ssazas, ggombololas and miruka, each type of area being in the charge of a chief was preserved in Article 34 of the same Constitution.

MODERN LEGAL SYSTEM

The Africa Order in Council 1889 had been applied to the new-born Protectorate of Uganda in 1894[1] and thereafter four other Africa Orders in Council were applied to the Protectorate introducing Indian law.[2] All five of these Orders in Council were repealed with certain provisoes by the Uganda Order in Council 1902. That Order in Council, made on the 11th August, 1902, *inter alia* provided:

" 12(3). In making Ordinances, the Commissioner shall respect existing native laws and customs except so far as the same may be opposed to justice and morality.
20. In all cases, civil and criminal, to which natives are parties, every Court (a) shall be guided by native law so far as it is applicable and is not repugnant to justice and morality or inconsistent with any Order in Council or Ordinance, or any regulation or rule made under any Order in Council or Ordinance; and (b) shall decide all such cases according to substantial justice without undue regard to technicalities or procedure and without undue delay."

The Uganda Order in Council, 1902, in fact made Uganda Protectorate a British dependency and on the 1st April, 1905 responsibility for Uganda was transferred from the Foreign Office to the Colonial Office. On 27th June, 1908, the then Governor (H. Hesketh Bell) made a declaration under Article 6 (1) of the 1902 Order in Council to the following effect:

" Kingdom of Uganda, with the islands appertaining thereto, shall be known and described as Buganda. The whole Protectorate shall continue to be called the Uganda Protectorate."

There was a minor amendment of Article 15 (2) by the Uganda Order in Council, 1911, and more general revision by the Uganda Order in Council, 1920.

---

[1] See above p. 8.
[2] For list see Chronological Table in Appendix 3 (a), p. 304, below.

C

Turning from Imperial legislation to treaties, the first Agreement after 1900 of importance to our present purpose is the Uganda Judicial Agreement, 1905, which gave the Kabaka power, with the consent of the Commissioner to constitute native courts subordinate to the Lukiko other than the ssaza courts, provided for the rendering of monthly returns of cases tried by subordinate courts, for the transfer of cases from native courts to Protectorate courts[1] and included the following provision for appeal:

> " 4. There shall be an appeal to His Majesty's High Court of Uganda (1) in criminal matters, from the Courts established by or under this or the principal Agreement from the sentences of such Courts where a sentence of death or of imprisonment exceeding five years or of fine exceeding £100 or of whipping of over 24 lashes has been passed, and (2) in civil matters, in cases where the amount or value of the subject-matter of the suit exceeds £100; and nothing contained in the principal Agreement shall prejudice or affect such right of appeal as aforesaid."

A list of all Agreements made is to be found in a chronological table below,[2] but mention must here be made of the Buganda Agreement (Native Laws), 1910, which clearly owed its origin to the judgment of Carter, J., noted above.[3] Article 1 of that Agreement reads:

> " The Kabaka and Lukiko with the consent of the Governor have had and shall have power to make laws governing the Baganda in Buganda. . . ."

Article 5 required the Governor to submit such laws for the approval of the Secretary of State.

In 1924 was made the Uganda Agreement (Clan Cases) which has a far-reaching provision in succession matters.[4] This was:

> " Notwithstanding anything contained in the Uganda Agreement, 1900, or the Uganda Agreement (Judicial) 1905, no native Court shall take any cognisance of any case relating to the headship, membership or other matter affecting clans. In all such matters the respective Clan Councils shall lay their recommendations before the Kabaka and his Lukiko Council. The decision of the Kabaka shall be final and His Majesty's High Court of Uganda

---

[1] Employed on 5th November, 1931 to transfer three cases against the Baganda Cotton Co. (*i.e.* Yusufu Bamutta's Company) as non-native money involved.

[2] See Appendix 3 (b), p., 306 below.

[3] See pp. 21 *et seq.*, below.

[4] See p. 75, below.

shall not take cognisance of any appeal from or exercise any revisional jurisdiction over any decision given by His Highness the
Kabaka in clan cases."

It is now hardly necessary, apart from the purpose of historic
record, to refer to Buganda (Declaratory) Agreement (Native
Laws), 1937, since that Agreement was specifically revoked by
the Buganda Agreement, 1955. This 1937 Agreement did,
however, declare, doubts having arisen as to the right under the
Buganda Agreement (Native Laws) 1910, that:

> " The Kabaka and Lukiko, with the consent of the Governor,
> have had and shall have power to make laws binding upon all
> natives in Buganda."

That Agreement was further embodied in the Statute law[1]
and section 4 of the Ordinance validated all laws lawfully enacted
since the Uganda Agreement, 1900.

Article 26 of the Constitution of Buganda, contained in the
First Schedule to the Buganda Agreement, 1955, expressly empowered the Kabaka, with the advice and consent of the Lukiko,
to " make laws binding upon Africans in Buganda " providing
that such laws had been first approved by the Governor. That
Article further provided that such laws shall be published in the
Uganda Gazette. There were two further important provisions:

> " (4) The laws made for the general governance of the Uganda
> Protectorate shall be equally applicable to Buganda, except in so
> far as they may in any particular conflict with the terms of the
> Buganda Agreements, in which case the terms of the Buganda
> Agreements shall constitute a special exception in regard to
> Buganda.
> " (5) For the purposes of this article the expression ' African '
> shall have the meaning assigned to it by the Interpretation and
> General Clauses Ordinance of the Uganda Protectorate, as from
> time to time amended, or any Ordinance replacing that Ordinance."

As I indicated in the preface to this book, my main concern
is not with the native laws of Buganda, enacted with the approval
of the Governor, but with the customary law of Buganda, so far
unwritten. Since, however, 113 such native laws have been
enacted from 1904 until the present date a chronological table
of those laws will be found in an appendix.[2] The far-reaching
importance of some of these native laws is illustrated by contemporary missionaries' accounts[3] of the imposition of hut and

---

[1] Laws of Uganda, 1951, Chapter 71, Vol. II, p. 1044.

[2] See Appendix 3 (c), p. 307, below.

[3] C. W. Hattersley, *The Baganda at Home*, 1908, p. 38, and J. D. Mullins,
The Wonderful Story of Uganda, 1904, p. 115.

poll taxes in 1904 which caused Ganda to seek ways of earning
money both in Uganda and in Kenya, by the cultivation of the
new crop, cotton, and by porterage.[1]

It is convenient to digress at this point into the question of the
dominant language of the Buganda Agreements on the one hand
and the Buganda native laws on the other. The Uganda Agreement 1900 was done in English and Luganda but no mention is
made therein as to which version was to prevail. From extrinsic
evidence, however, to wit, its publication in English in the Laws
of Uganda and its translation (sic) into Luganda, it is clear that
the English version prevails. This point was confirmed in the
Uganda (Judicial) Agreement, 1905, in which Article 6 provides
that " in the construction thereof the English version shall prevail ". Subsequent Agreements up to but not including the
Buganda Agreement, 1955, followed suit. There can, however,
be no doubt that the English version of all Buganda Agreements
prevails.[2] The opposite position obtains, as one would expect
with legislation enacted by a native ruler, in regard to the native
laws of Buganda. The Luganda version of such a law prevails
and the English version is merely a translation, published for
convenience.[3]

From the latter years of the last century, certain Protectorate
legislation, although not strictly specified for administration by
the native courts of Buganda, has in fact been a potent influence
and has frequently been followed in their decisions of cases.
I refer to such legislation as the Gambling Regulations, 1901,
and the various Ordinances governing matrimonial affairs and
land. For convenience a chronological table of most of such
legislation is given in an appendix.[4]

Provision was included in section 12 of the Buganda Courts
Ordinance, 1940, for jurisdiction to be conferred, by order in
the *Gazette* or in the warrant, upon a Buganda court to administer or enforce the provisions of a specified Ordinance subject
to any restriction or limitation that might be imposed by such

---

[1] *Economic Development and Tribal Change*, 1954, ed. A. I. Richards, Chapter II,
" The History of Migration in Uganda ", by P. G. Powesland.

[2] See Explanatory Note of the then Solicitor General to Vol. VI of the
Revised Edition of the Laws of Uganda, 1935.

[3] And was so marked at all times except when the English versions were
reprinted in the Laws of Uganda, 1951, Vol. VII; but that reprint is wno
replaced by the *Revised Edition of Native Laws of Buganda*, 1957, under Legal
Notice 138 of 1958.

[4] See Appendix 3 (d), p. 313, below.

order or warrant. By the first warrants establishing ssaza and ggombolola courts on the 1st September, 1940 the following six Ordinances were so specified:

the Poll Tax Ordinance, 1939;

the Witchcraft Ordinance;

the Diseases of Animals Ordinance;

the Public Health Ordinance;

the Sleeping Sickness Ordinance; and

the Masters and Servants Ordinance, section 58(1).

Further, the ggombolola court of the Kibuga, which had extended powers in view of its metropolitan area, had jurisdiction conferred in respect of this other piece of Protectorate legislation:

The Townships Ordinance, 1938.

The specifying of Protectorate legislation for administration by the Buganda courts was given an impetus by " the interests of defence, and, the more efficient prosecution of the war "[1] and:

> " For the purposes of section 12 of the Buganda Courts Ordinance, 1940, the word ' Ordinance ' shall be deemed to include regulations, orders and rules made under the authority of the Emergency Powers (Defence) Acts 1939 and 1940."[2]

Thereafter, and indeed until 1956, many pieces of Protectorate legislation, as indicated in an appendix,[3] were specified for administration by the Buganda courts.

Finally the Buganda courts do not administer English Law. The authority for this statement is the judgment of a former Acting Judicial Adviser, the present Chief Justice of Uganda, Sir Audley McKISACK:[4]

> " The Principal Court does not administer English Law, and is therefore not bound by, nor does it have the assistance of, the rules of English Law applicable to a case of this nature, such as those which govern the admissibility of evidence or the interpretation or variation of written documents. As I understand the position created by the Buganda Courts Ordinance, the duty of the Principal Court in cases like this is to decide what were the true facts on any evidence which it may consider relevant, and then to determine the rights and liabilities of the parties according to what the court thinks just in relation to these facts. In accepting or rejecting evidence the court is bound by nothing but its own discretion.

---

[1] Preamble to Legal Notice No. 88 of 1943 of 26th March, 1943, Buganda Courts (Defence Jurisdiction) Regulations, 1943.

[2] *Ibid.*, Regulation 2.   [3] See Appendix 3 (e), p. 314, below.

[4] J.A.C.A. 3 of 1942, P.C.C.C. 32 of 1941, *Petero Zake* v. *Samusoni Bazongere* (unreported).

(Section 2 of the Evidence Ordinance makes it clear that that Ordinance does not apply to native courts.) Again, in deciding as to the rights and liabilities of the parties in cases tried under section 11 of the Buganda Courts Ordinance, *i.e.*, cases relating to mailo land, the Principal Court is not concerned with the English Law relating to land. The laws which that court may administer are restricted to those which are set out in section 10. I do not think it possible to read into section 11 the meaning that in dealing with mailo cases the Principal Court is to apply English Law. Yet in many questions which arise in these cases there is no other law applicable. There is no Protectorate legislation, no law enacted by the Kabaka and no customary law. These cases can only be tried in one court, and that court is unable to apply the only law applicable to such cases. I can only conclude, therefore, that it was intended that the Principal Court should decide such cases without reference to any law; that their decision should be based solely upon what they consider fair and proper in each case."

That decision was subsequently upheld by the then Chief Justice of Uganda, Sir Norman WHITLEY.[1]

MODERN JUDICIAL SYSTEM

In this section we shall review the developments which have taken place in the Kabaka's courts since the 1900 Agreement until the present year. Clearly the most practical way of making such a review is year by year, and although such a method may at times lead one off the real path, nevertheless it has been followed as thereby over the years the true pattern more readily appears.

Before getting involved again in legislation let us consider a passage from an address by a former Attorney General of Uganda already cited:[2]

" Firstly, it must be most emphatically stated that with the inauguration of a system of British Courts, the native system was not swept away holus-bolus and an alien system substituted in its place. . . . The native courts and the ancient powers in the chiefs to adjudicate upon their people were preserved from the outset either formally or tacitly in so far as the jurisdiction they exercised was not repugnant to natural justice and morality or to the specific laws of the Protectorate. These courts have continued uninterruptedly to exercise both civil and criminal jurisdiction and have been fostered and encouraged throughout the period of our administration."

---

[1] H.C.C.A. 15 of 1942 (unreported).
[2] H. R. Hone, " The Native of Uganda and the Criminal Law ", *U.J.*, Vol. VI, 1938–39, p. 1.

The more important provisions of the Uganda Judicial Agreement, 1905, have already been considered[1] and Article 3 of that Agreement regarding the transfer of cases was forthwith employed in respect of divorce cases between natives of the Kingdom of Uganda.[2] That early concern with the dissolution of marriage between Ganda may explain why the Divorce Ordinance, a Protectorate Ordinance never administered by the Kabaka's Courts, was printed in both original English text and in a Luganda translation which appeared in a publication of legislation about the year 1909.[3]

In the same year, 1905, the Native Courts Ordinance (No. 10 of 1905) was enacted. The main provisions of this Ordinance were:

(i) section 2 empowered the Commissioner to apply the Ordinance by Proclamation;

(ii) section 3 established a district British Native Court with full civil and criminal jurisdiction over all natives of the district and with concurrent jurisdiction with any native courts established or recognised therein;

(iii) section 4 stipulated that the Collector of any district should preside over the British Native Court.

Later came the important sections 14 and 15:

" 14. (i) Nothing herein shall affect the power of the Commissioner to recognise the jurisdiction of a tribal Chief over the members of his tribe, or the exercise by such tribal Chief of such authority as may be lawfully vested in him, or may be granted to him by the Commissioner.

(ii) The Collector may transfer to any recognised tribal Chief in the district the determination of any suit or proceeding in a British Native Court.

(iii) The Collector may take such steps as he thinks fit to enforce the orders of any such recognised tribal Chief.

15. The Collector shall exercise supervision over, but shall not unduly interfere with, the procedure, orders, or punishments of any tribal authority within the district, except where such procedure, orders, or punishments are contrary to justice or morality, or the laws in force for the time being within the Protectorate."

That this piece of legislation was largely experimental is

---

[1] See p. 26, above.

[2] Direction of Acting Commissioner with consent of Regents of Buganda, dated 23rd January, 1905.

[3] *Endagano Zona Ezalaganibwa ne Gavumenti ya Bangereza na Baganda mu Buganda.*

evidenced by the High Court Circular of 27th December, 1905 signed by both Judges and approved by the Acting Commissioner:

" Jurisdiction under this Ordinance is concurrent with any other native jurisdiction in the District, and experience will show whether natives prefer to be tried by British officers or by native chiefs. No application by a native of the District for the exercise of jurisdiction by a British Native Court should be refused. Nothing in this instruction is to be taken to prevent Collectors from exercising the power of transfer given them by Section 14 (ii) of the Ordinance."

On the 29th January, 1909, the Native Courts in Buganda Proclamation under the Native Courts Ordinance 1905, was published and the native courts in Buganda organised.[1] The objects of this Proclamation are most conveniently set out in the preamble:

" Whereas it is expedient and has been agreed by the Kabaka, Chiefs and People of Buganda:—

(1) That the Native Courts in Buganda should be organised and recognised, and their powers and jurisdiction defined;

(2) That the supervision of the Native Courts by His Majesty's Government should be defined;

(3) (a) That all natives of Buganda charged with committing offences within the Township of Entebbe, and that part of the Township of Kampala known as Nakasero Hill, and the Crown Land on Kampala Hill shall be tried by British Courts;

(b) That certain native cases in which Buganda servants of the Government are parties, and other cases at the request of native Chiefs shall ordinarily be brought before British Courts;

(c) That any breaches of any special law (*e.g.* Arms, Game, Forest, Fiscal, Mining etc.) committed by natives of Buganda shall ordinarily be tried by British Courts; "

Sir Henry Hesketh Bell, the then Governor of Uganda, thereby declared and proclaimed:

" That the following Native Courts have been established in Buganda with powers and jurisdiction following, that is to say:—

A. The Court of the Lukiko, consisting of a committee of any 7 or more members of the Lukiko as constituted by The Uganda Agreement, 1900, presided over by the Kabaka or one of the three Native Officers of State (Katikkiro, Mulamuzi and Mwanika) with full jurisdiction in Buganda (original, appellate and revisional), except as mentioned hereafter, in all cases in which all parties are natives of Buganda;

---

[1] H.C.C.A. *Alipo Kabazi* v. *Jemusi Kibuka*, 2 U.L.R. 9.

B. The Courts of the Abamasaza as hereinafter mentioned presided over by the Saza Chief of the County, or his Deputy (Mubaka), or, failing them, by a person (Musigire) appointed by the Saza Chief, sitting with any two or more of the following Sub-Chiefs of the Saza, namely the Mumyuka, the Sabadu, the Sabagabo, the Sabawali, the Mutuba (one or more), the Musale or their Deputies (Babaka); or, failing them, any two or more of the wise men or elders of the Saza, with jurisdiction in the Saza, except as hereinafter mentioned, to hear and decide the cases and revise the proceedings of the Courts of the Sub-Chiefs.

(I) All cases in which a native of Buganda is accused of an offence; provided always that a greater punishment than 6 months rigorous imprisonment, or fine of Rs. 30/– or whipping of 24 lashes shall not be imposed by a Saza Court.

(II) All cases between natives of Buganda in which the amount or value of the subject matter in dispute does not exceed Rs. 75/–.

(III) Appeals from the Courts of the Sub-Chiefs.

C. The Courts of the Sub-Chiefs as hereinafter mentioned presided over by the Sub-Chief or his Deputy (Mubaka); or, failing them, by a person (Musigire) appointed by the Sub-Chief, namely the Mumyuka, the Sabadu, the Sabagabo, the Sabawali, the Mutuba (one or more), the Musale or their Deputies (Babaka); or, failing them, any two or more of the wise men or elders of the district of the Sub-Chief, with jurisdiction in the administrative district of the Sub-Chiefs, except as hereinafter mentioned, to hear and decide.

(I) All cases in which a native of Buganda is accused of an offence, provided always that a greater punishment than one month's rigorous imprisonment or fine of Rs. 10/– or whipping of 10 lashes shall not be imposed by any such Court.

(II) All cases between natives of Buganda in which the amount or value of the subject matter in dispute does not exceed Rs. 35/–.

and by section 2(b):

" The District Commissioner shall exercise the following powers of supervision over the Native Courts, but shall not unduly interfere with their proceedings:—

(1) A power to call for records or to make any enquiry as to proceedings.

(2) A power to stay all proceedings where they appear illegal or improper, or where the sentence is excessive or inhumane.

(3) A power to direct the re-hearing of any case by the court whose proceedings are being supervised, or to refer the case for revision to the next highest Native Court.

(4) A power in any case in which it appears that the Court of the Lukiko, Saza or Sub-Chief has no jurisdiction to annul the proceedings and refer the case for hearing to a court having jurisdiction.

The ' Provincial Commissioner ', or in his absence the ' District Commissioner ' or any Magistrate at the request of the Provincial Commissioner, shall have power to revise the proceedings of the Court of the Lukiko."

In 1909 the Native Courts Ordinance (No. 15 of 1909) was enacted amending the 1905 Ordinance in certain particulars and from that year to 1911 several amending Proclamations and Directions[1] regarding appointments of presidents of Native Courts were made. The Uganda Appeal Ordinance, 1910, prohibited any further appeal to the Court of Appeal *inter alia* when a decree or order was given by the High Court on appeal from the native courts. The next major piece of legislation was, however, the Courts Ordinance, 1911 (No. 12 of 1911) which repealed both the 1905 and the 1909 Ordinances but saved the existing Proclamation until other provision be made. Section 3 of the Ordinance provided that native courts subordinate to the High Court might be constituted by or under that Ordinance and Part IV contained detailed provisions governing such native courts, of which sections 50 and 51 are of particular note. The former limited jurisdiction to offences other than those punishable with death or transportation for life and the latter preserved the jurisdiction and authority of the tribal chiefs or councils of elders by tribal custom except where the native court's jurisdiction extended.

From 1912 to 1917 various minor amendments to the Courts Ordinances and to the Proclamation were made but the next major enactment was the Native Courts in Buganda Proclamation, 1917 (General Notice 412 of 27th October, 1917). The main provisions of this new Proclamation, which distinguished it from the 1909 Proclamation, which it cancelled, were as follows:

(i) both in ssaza and in sub-chief's courts the personal jurisdiction was widened to

a native of the Protectorate, except when the complainant is a non-native of the Protectorate

(1(a) B I and C I);

---

[1] For chronological list of Protectorate legislation affecting the Buganda courts see Appendix 3 (f), p. 317, *post*.

(ii) the native courts in Buganda must conform with such procedure practice and rules as may be from time to time specially or generally prescribed by the High Court (1(d));

(iii) all cases in which a person is charged with an offence in consequence of which death has resulted must be tried by British Courts (2(1));

(iv) the High Court must hear and decide all causes in Buganda between natives of the Protectorate of a like nature to the causes which would come before the said Court in the exercise of its jurisdiction under the Divorce Ordinance, 1904, or under section 19 of the Uganda Muhammadan Marriage and Divorce Ordinance, 1906 (3);

(v) power conferred on the British Courts to transfer any case other than one before the Lukiko Court in which any party not a native of Buganda to a British Court (4(a) (5));

(vi) power conferred on the Provincial Commissioner or his representative to revise proceedings of the Lukiko Court (4(b) (1));

(vii) powers of the Provincial Commissioner and District Commissioner conferred on the High Court (4(1)); and

(viii) in any original case, whether civil or criminal, tried before the Lukiko, in which the accused, the complainant or any of the parties are not natives of Buganda there must be an appeal from the Lukiko to the High Court (5).

The amending Proclamation 1918 added a cattle limit to the monetary limit of the civil jurisdiction of the Ssaza and subchief's courts.

The year 1919 saw the passage of three Protectorate Ordinances which were of importance to the administration of justice in Buganda. First came the Courts Ordinance, 1919, section 3 of which provided *inter alia* that native courts were constituted subordinate to the High Court and section 13 that no appeal should lie from the High Court acting in an appellate capacity from native courts. Part V of that Ordinance provided for the detailed establishment and running of the native courts. We need only note two particular provisions:

(i) section 39 to the effect that practice and procedure in civil matters should be that followed by tribal authorities subject to supervision and until prescribed by the High Court;

(ii) section 43 to the effect that the Governor could recognise tribal authority except in so far as the jurisdiction of any native court extended.

Secondly came the Criminal Procedure Ordinance, 1919, and by subsection 2 (1) thereof the Indian Criminal Procedure Code ceased to apply to Uganda. Chapter II, B of that Ordinance contained specific provisions in regard to native courts. Lastly section 4 of the Native Law Ordinance, 1919, saved the powers of " the Kabaka and chiefs of the people of Buganda " to make laws, under Article 4 of the Buganda Agreement (Native Laws), 1910, " governing the Baganda in Buganda ".

By a Proclamation of 30th April, 1925, the Special Native Court of Bombo was established with jurisdiction in petty civil and criminal cases and marriage under Nubian custom over Nubians and Sudanese within ten miles of Bombo cantonment.

A judgment of the Lukiko Court dated 25th November, 1926,[1] which happens to be preserved, indicates that the Court comprised two Ssaza chiefs, deputising for the Omulamuzi and Omuwanika respectively, and seven other Ssaza chiefs and eight Ggombolola chiefs. Three years later, in 1929, three permanent members were appointed to the Lukiko Court, namely the Assistant to the Omulamuzi and two permanent representatives of the Lukiko,[2] the Court's quorum being the Omulamuzi or his substitute and these three new members. The same Proclamation empowered the Kabaka, with the approval of the Governor, to appoint a special court of ssaza chiefs to try cases of an exceptional nature, where the ordinary mode of trial would be undesirable. The first Assistant to the Omulamuzi was Omulangira J. T. K. Ggomotoka, Ssabalangira, a Catholic and the two permanent members of the Lukiko were Mikaeli Kawalya, a son of Sir Apolo Kagwa, a Protestant and later himself destined to be a Katikkiro of Buganda, and Abdullah Kironde, a Muslim chief.[3] This constitution of the Lukiko Court was, however, of short life. In 1931, in the *cause célèbre* when Yusufu Bamutta was tried for rape of a Princess of the Buganda Royal Family, the Omulamuzi's minority decision, against the majority decision of his Assistant and the

---

[1] P.C.C.C. 350 of 1926, *Stanislasi Mugwanya* v. *E. M. Kajugujwe* (unreported).

[2] Native Courts in Buganda Proclamation of 23rd January, 1929.

[3] Ggomotoka, *op. cit.*, p. 68.

two permanent members, was confirmed on revision by the High Court and not disturbed by the Court of Appeal for Eastern Africa.[1] The outcome was that in 1932 came the Native Courts in Buganda Proclamation of 22nd September, 1932 (Legal Notice 111 of 1932, with effect from 1st January, 1933) which substituted for the permanent members three members of the Lukiko appointed for one year, a quorum being the Omulamuzi or his representative and two of the three members.

The combined total of cases entered in the register of the Lukiko Court for the year 1930 was 404; that number dropped in 1931 to 298 cases. For the next three years the original are separated in the register from the appellate proceedings, and there is for the first time a distinction between criminal and civil original cases:

Year	Original		Appeals Combined
	Criminal	Civil	Criminal and Civil
1932	381	182	133
1933	277	75	109
1934	468	258	180

This steep rise in proceedings of every type which came before the Lukiko Court in 1934 resulted in an amending Proclamation of 12th June, 1934 (L.N. 86/34) empowering the Kabaka with the Governor's approval to appoint a special court

" additional to the Court of the Lukiko and with similar powers to sit for such period as may be considered necessary to hear appeals on behalf of the Court of the Lukiko whenever it appears that the number of appeals pending is such that that Court cannot deal with the accumulation in an expeditious manner. Such Special Court shall consist of three members[2] appointed temporarily by the Kabaka, subject to the approval of the Governor, of not less rank than that of Ggombolola Chief and shall be presided over by one of their number who shall be of not less than that of a Ssaza Chief."

It is convenient to turn aside for a moment from the study of actual legislation in order to consider the assessment of the development of the native administration of justice over the fifty years past made by the then Attorney General of Uganda in 1938.[3]

" It would be idle to suppose that the business performed by the native courts of the present time is comparable in any way to that

---

[1] Cr.A. 132 of 1931, *Rex* v. *Yusufu s/o Bamutta* (1931) 13 L.R.K. 64.

[2] Altered retrospectively to " not less than three or more than four members " in an amending Proclamation of 26th September, 1934.

[3] Hone, *loc. cit.*

transacted before this country was administered by the British. The same factors which influenced the development of the English System of law, *viz*, violent political changes and the force of public opinion, have been at work here. The great political change was, of course, contact with European ideals and institutions, while the main force of native public opinion is now unquestionably directed to the acceptance and emulation of European codes of commerce, legislation and justice. The result of these influences, coupled with the almost entire absence of any arresting or retrogressive factors over the period of the last fifty years, in regard to the development of native courts and the native system of justice has been remarkable. In the first place, the result of the systematisation of the jurisdiction of the various courts and the definition of their powers according to their capacity, has resulted in the natives becoming fully acquainted with the nature and jurisdiction of the native courts to which they have access, and, having regard to the supervisory powers of the British administrative officers, the recognition by the populace of the enforceability and the general impartiality of native justice. Further, the procedure and panoply of the courts are becoming settled and uniform. The judges sit on a bench; a witness box and a dock are provided; the onus is on the plaintiff or prosecutor to begin; cross-examination of the witness is a familiar feature of the trial; the defendant answers the case against him; the judgement of the court, in which the case of each side is discussed and weighed one against the other, is decorously delivered. In many of the superior courts, printed case files are in use and a full record of the proceedings is written—and indeed often typed. Even the questions and answers in cross-examination are frequently scrupulously recorded ' verbatim '; questions are often disallowed or questions and answers are discounted in the judgement as having nothing to do with the point at issue. In the inferior courts, a summary, at least, of the case and the decision is recorded."

About this time the then Governor, Sir Philip Mitchell, had proposed to the Secretary of State that a specialist officer be appointed to advise the Buganda courts. This proposal was favourably received and the first Judicial Adviser, Buganda[1] was appointed—the first such appointment made in the British Empire. A Proclamation of the 11th January, 1939 bestowed on the Judicial Adviser inspectorate and revisional powers. The first major task entrusted to the Judicial Adviser was to draft a Bill governing the constitution and jurisdiction of the Kabaka's courts and the administration of justice therein. This Bill found its way into the Statute Book as the Buganda Courts Ordinance, 1940, which, amended in 1945 and 1946, is still the governing

---

[1] Mr. C. Mathew, later Sir Charles Mathew, C.M.G., Chief Justice of Malaya, was the first Judicial Adviser, Buganda.

Ordinance.[1] The Lukiko Court retained full jurisdiction over natives and permanent judges of varying degrees were made its members by the 1945 amending Ordinance. By the 1940 Ordinance the Judicial Adviser took over from the High Court and the Resident the power of revision. The rights of appeal set out in the Buganda Agreements 1900 and 1905 were preserved and the Judicial Adviser became the appellate authority for certain lesser appeals.

The style of the Court of the Lukiko was changed by the Regents of Buganda, with the approval of the Governor, on 16th June, 1941 to " The Principal Court of His Highness The Kabaka of Buganda ".[2] This change of style was reflected in the Buganda Courts (Amendment) Ordinance, 1945.

By section 4 of the 1940 Ordinance the Kabaka, with the consent of the Governor, was empowered, by the issue of a warrant, to establish courts subordinate to what was then the Lukiko Court, now the Principal Court. The jurisdiction and powers of such courts were therein defined subject to the provisions of the Ordinance. Warrants were issued on the 1st September, 1940, the date when the Ordinance came into operation, establishing ssaza and ggombolola courts throughout the Kingdom. The territorial jurisdiction of each was limited to the area ruled by the chief in question. He and two of his immediately inferior chiefs (ggombolola or muluka as the case may be) or their lieutenants and an unofficial representative were the court. A quorum was the chairman (the chief or his lieutenant) and two other members. Appeal lay to the Lukiko Court and then to the Judicial Adviser in all cases originating in the ssaza courts but cases originating in the ggombolola courts were appellable to the ssaza court then to the Lukiko Court and only subsequently on third appeal to the Judicial Adviser if the case concerned the Busuulu and Envujjo Law.[3] The civil jurisdiction of the ssaza court was limited to subject matter of six hundred shillings or twenty-five head of cattle or less. That of the ggombolola court was limited to two hundred shillings or ten head of cattle. In criminal cases the ssaza court was empowered to inflict sentences of imprisonment not exceeding twelve months, fines or compensation not exceeding six hundred shillings and whippings not

---

[1] Cap. 77 in Vol. II of *Laws of Uganda*, 1951, and Article 8 of the Buganda Agreement, 1955.

[2] L.N. 170/41.

[3] See below p. 167.

exceeding twenty-four strokes. The penal powers of ggombolola courts were limited to imprisonment not exceeding three months, fines or compensation not exceeding two hundred shillings and whippings not exceeding twelve strokes.

The Court of the Ggombolola of Omukulu we Kibuga, the metropolitan area, was given jurisdiction mid-way between that of an ordinary ggombolola and a ssaza: civil jurisdiction wherein the subject matter did not exceed five hundred shillings or fifteen cattle; and criminal jurisdiction where the sentence did not exceed nine months' imprisonment, a fine or compensation of five hundred shillings, or whipping of eighteen strokes.

Those powers of the ssaza and ggombolola courts were increased in 1951[1] as follows:

(i) the civil jurisdiction of ssaza courts was increased to include subject matter valued at two thousand shillings or twenty-five head of cattle and criminal powers to impose sentences of imprisonment not exceeding two years, fines not exceeding one thousand two hundred shillings or whippings not exceeding twenty-four lashes;

(ii) the civil jurisdiction of ggombolola courts was increased to include subject matter valued at six hundred shillings or ten head of cattle and criminal powers to impose sentences of imprisonment not exceeding six months, fines not exceeding five hundred shillings and whippings not exceeding twelve strokes; and

(iii) the civil jurisdiction of the Court of Omukulu we Kibuga was increased to include subject matter valued at one thousand five hundred shillings or fifteen head of cattle and criminal powers to impose sentences of eighteen months' imprisonment, fines not exceeding one thousand shillings and whippings not exceeding twelve strokes.

From 1950 onwards the numbers of cases filed in the Principal Court increased greatly. In 1955 the total number of original cases criminal and civil tried by the Principal Court exceeded 1,000 and there were a further 370 appeals heard in addition. It was fortunate therefore that in October of the previous year, 1954, the number of courts of the Principal Court had been raised from the former 3 to 5 in accordance with the re-organisation plan approved by the Kabaka in September 1953 and by the Governor twelve months later. Financial provision was included

---

[1] See the Omulamuzi's Circular No. 5/1951 of 20th March, 1951.

for this re-organisation in the financial year beginning 1st July, 1954.

Not only was the Principal Court re-organised but fundamental changes were made in the organisation of the subordinate courts; an attempt was made as far as possible to separate the judiciary from the executive. Financial limitations prevented the full attainment of the ideal but during 1954 and the next three years the re-organisation was accomplished throughout the Kingdom. Ssaza courts were abolished and subordinate courts, with identical powers as those formerly held by Ssaza courts, were set up and presided over by a full-time itinerant magistrate who sits with two non-official court members chosen from a panel of worthies in each ggombolola. Generally ggombolola courts were reduced to petty criminal jurisdiction only but in certain outlying areas, notably the Islands, the ggombolola courts retained their former powers. In 1956 the total number of criminal and civil cases tried by the Kabaka's courts throughout Buganda rose to over 21,000. At this time the number of permanent judges of varying grades in the Principal Court had under the re-organisation risen to 16 sitting in benches of three and the number of magistrates to 33. The number of lay court members exceeded 800, 6 or 8 being appointed in each ggombolola.

There were certain other salient points involved in the re-organisation:

(i) the Omulamuzi ceased to sit as a Judge (in fact his predecessors in office had not done so for about ten years previously) and became the political Minister of Justice which the Buganda Agreement 1955 envisaged; the post of the former deputy to the Omulamuzi was transformed into the post of the permanent head of the Buganda judiciary entitled the Chief Judge, Buganda; the former multiplicity of appeals was cut down to one appeal from subordinate courts to the Principal Court and no right of appeal at all, merely petition for revision, from the petty criminal jurisdiction of ggombolola courts;

(ii) a concomitant of the scheme of re-organisation which was insisted upon was that the trial judges and magistrates themselves recorded the proceedings in their own handwriting thereby dispensing with clerks who had tended to slow down trials previously;

(iii) two so-called " clerks of court " were also appointed as an experiment to assist the trial of cases in the Principal Court but this experiment was not a success and the posts were abolished in June 1959.

Before leaving the matter of this re-organisation of the Kabaka's courts, mention must be made of the systems of legal training introduced. Even the judges and magistrates had very little legal knowledge. None were professionally qualified. They had been recruited from the ranks of chiefs, ex-inspectors of police and court interpreters. Courses of legal instruction run both locally in Buganda and on a Protectorate basis helped during 1955 and subsequent years to raise the standard of legal knowledge not only of these permanent full-time members of the Buganda judiciary but also of the court members and chiefs of every degree in every ggombolola throughout the Kingdom.

The Buganda Courts Ordinance has been the subject of interpretation on many occasions by Her Majesty's Judges and it may be useful to set out some of the more important decisions here:

It has been held:

(i) under section 3(1) that the Principal Court has full original jurisdiction which cannot be taken away by a directive of the Kabaka;[1]

(ii) under section 3(3)(a) that if the same judges have not heard all the evidence then the proceedings are a nullity and there must be a re-trial;[2]

(iii) under section 6(1) that the High Court had no power to prevent the Principal Court from determining a dispute between two Ganda;[3]

(iv) under section 7 that the High Court was bound to transfer to the Principal Court a case, in which, after a non-African (a Bank) had been dismissed from the suit, all remaining parties were Africans;[4]

(v) under section 9(a) that the words " in consequence of which death is alleged to have occurred " refer to an allegation which is contained in the charge itself;[5]

---

[1] H.C.Cr.A. 140 of 1954, *Lubega* v. *Lukiko*, Notes 65.
[2] H.C.C.A. 84 of 1956, *Ndiwalana* v. *Katera*, Notes 87.
[3] H.C.Misc.C. 50 of 1958, *Mugalu* v. *Nakabiri*, Bulletin 30/59.
[4] H.C.C.C. 225 of 1958, *Kiwanuka* v. *Wasswa and Others*, Bulletin 34/59.
[5] H.C.Cr.A. 248 of 1957, *Kirabira* v. *Lukiko*, Notes 77.

(vi) under section 9(e) that jurisdiction granted under section 11(1) must be read not only in conjunction with the Buganda Agreement (Clan Cases), 1924, but also in conjunction with this section;[1]

(vii) under section 10(b) that it is preferable to allege a contravention of customary law without any reference to the Ordinance;[2]

(viii) under section 11(2) that confirmation is not necessary before an appeal can be filed against the decision of the Principal Court;[3]

(ix) under section 11(2)(a) that there is no right of appeal against a confirmation order;[4]

(x) under sections 24–26 that the High Court has no revisionary powers under the Ordinance;[5]

(xi) under section 26 that the appellate jurisdiction of the High Court is limited to cases originating in the Principal Court;[6]

(xii) under section 26(1)(a) that the High Court was unable to entertain an appeal where the sentence on any one count did not exceed five years' imprisonment;[7]

(xiii) under the same section 26(1)(a) that it is at least doubtful whether an appeal lies to the High Court when compensation in excess of Shs 2,000/– has been ordered as there is no mention of compensation in that section of the Ordinance;[8]

(xiv) under section 26(1)(b) that the value of the subject matter as stated in the plaint is *prima facie* decisive for the purpose of this section;[9]

(xv) under section 26(3) that there is no right of appeal to the High Court from a decision of the Judicial Adviser given in his revisional jurisdiction or refusing an application for revision;[10]

---

[1] H.C.C.A. 8 of 1945, *Saku and Another* v. *Mugema and Others*, Notes 15.

[2] H.C.Cr.A. 127 of 1949, *Kagimu* v. *Lukiko*, Notes 25, and H.C.Cr.A. 300–304 of 1957, *Sebanakirya and Others* v. *Lukiko*, Notes 87.

[3] H.C.C.A. 8 of 1957, *Nsimbe* v. *Kibirige*, Notes 79.

[4] H.C.C.A. 94 of 1956, *Mwamula* v. *Kasaja and Another*, Notes 85.

[5] H.C.C.R. 18 of 1958, *Mukasa* v. *Kyalikyobulungi*, Notes 83.

[6] H.C.C.A. 42 of 1952, *Nakyaze* v. *Kitonto* (unreported) and H.C.Cr.A. 214 of 1947, *Muwanga* v. *Lukiko*, Notes 21.

[7] H.C.Cr.A. 500 of 1949, *Bulembe* v. *Lukiko*, Notes 33.

[8] H.C.Cr.A. 91 of 1952, *Bamweyama* v. *Lukiko* (unreported) and H.C.Cr.A. 92 of 1952, *Kawesi* v. *Lukiko* (unreported).

[9] H.C.C.A. 16 of 1945, *Kasozi* v. *Mukasa*, Notes 17.

[10] H.C.C.A. 46A of 1958, *Itewala* v. *Sebugenyi*, Notes 91.

(xvi) under section 26(6)(a) that the power to hear additional evidence on appeal must be judicially exercised in accordance with well recognised principles;[1]

(xvii) under section 26(6)(b) that the Judicial Adviser is intended to have the power to review the whole decision in a criminal appeal and to make it conformable with justice.[2]

Before leaving decisions of the High Court it may be of value to refer to another decision made on revision from an original case in the Busoga District Native Court,[3] as it would appear that the basis of that decision is equally applicable to the like power of revision in section 24 of the Buganda Courts Ordinance. It was therein held that the revisional authority on complaint being made to him must apply his mind to the question whether or not something has been brought to his notice sufficiently serious to justify him in sending for the record of the subordinate court with a view to inspecting it.

Finally an important passage occurs in a judgment of an Acting Judicial Adviser to which I have already referred[4] which has a bearing on all the judicial functions of the Judicial Adviser:

> " Now when a mailo case comes before the Judicial Adviser on appeal or revision or for confirmation it seems to me that he is in much the same position as the Principal Court in this respect. It is not for him to quash or vary a judgment on the ground that its decision does not accord with the English law relating to land cases that the evidence has not been dealt with in accordance with the Evidence Ordinance. His function is merely to see that the court correctly weighed the value of whatever evidence was taken, that its findings of fact were in accordance with the evidence so weighed and that its decision was fair and proper and capable of being carried out. If the court's judgment does not in his opinion comply with these principles, then he must substitute a judgment which does so comply."

and which was confirmed and held to be equally applicable to the High Court sitting on appeal by the then Chief Justice of Uganda.[5]

The Court of Appeal for Eastern Africa has held repeatedly that no appeal lies to it from an appellate decision of the High

---

[1] H.C.C.A. 67 of 1953, *Nyanzi* v. *Kayima*, Notes 65.
[2] H.C.Cr.A. 220 of 1947, *Waswa* v. *Lukiko* (unreported).
[3] H.C.C.R. 9 of 1948, *Nalumenya* v. *Tabasima* (unreported).
[4] See p. 29 above.
[5] H.C.C.A. 15 of 1942, J.A.C.A. 3 of 1942, P.C.C.C. 32 of 1941, *Zake* v. *Bazongere* (unreported).

Court of Uganda in proceedings originating in the Principal Court of Buganda.[1]

To descend abruptly from the highest to the lowest, it is convenient at this point to consider the place of arbitral proceedings in the Ganda system of justice. There have in fact from time immemorial been arbitral tribunals before which disputes were taken in Buganda. Mair[2] writes a quarter of a century ago:

> " It is also the landlord's duty to bring to justice any criminal who is a tenant. Moreover, though a landlord has now no legal competence whatever, a case between two of his tenants is always taken first to him, and sent on by him to the *muruka*, one of his personal chiefs, going with the parties to ' introduce ' the case. To omit this preliminary would be an unthinkable insult to his dignity; and it serves a useful purpose for quarrels which prove to be entirely without substance are often smoothed down here.
>
> The *muruka* also, though he has no authority to inflict penalties, often effects an amicable settlement in cases of brawling or petty theft by persuading the guilty party to compensate his victim with a fowl, beer, or a few shillings ' to tie up his head ', and questions of debt can be settled here if the debtor does not refuse to pay up."

Southall and Gutkind, two sociologists, carried out surveys of two parishes of the metropolitan ggombolola of the Kibuga in recent years[3] and have produced valuable independent material of the volume and place of arbitral proceedings in Buganda's judicial structure. Of Mengo parish in 1953, when the parish council was visited every Saturday afternoon, Southall writes:[4]

> " Over a third of the cases were for debt, half being debts for rent, and half from other causes. Four cases arose from disputes over property resulting from the separation of couples who had been cohabiting in free unions. Three cases of fighting were dealt with, three cases of failure to fulfil contracts to build or make furniture, three cases of eviction in which the lodger resisted the houseowner's right to serve notice, and three applications for permits to build. There were two cases of theft, two of obscene abuse, and two concerning the renewal of trading permits. Other cases related to the price of water, the guardianship of two girls, damage to crops by children, encroachment on another's land, control of the hours of water selling and of beer selling, property damaged in a dispute over the distillation of spirit (waragi), failure

---

[1] Cr.A. 77 of 1941, *Lukiko* v. *Odima* (1941) 8 E.A.C.A. 54; Cr.A. 134 of 1942, *Lukiko* v. *Kivu* (1942) 9 E.A.C.A. 82 and C.A. 15 of 1946, *Shaku* v. *Bamuta* (1946) 13 E.A.C.A. 48.

[2] Mair, *op. cit.*, p. 200.

[3] A. W. Southall and P. C. W. Gutkind, *Townsmen in the Making—Kampala and its Suburbs, East African Studies*, No. 9, E.A.I.S.R., Kampala, 1951.

[4] Southall and Gutkind, *op. cit.*, p. 196.

to report cases of smallpox, refusal to allot a plot as promised, official bribery, the finding of stolen property, overcharging for and misappropriating sugar, violence by a usually harmless lunatic, failure to turn out for planting anti-erosion grass bunds, and a demand for wages by a woman whose lover had brought in a rival.

These were the cases heard by the parish court during its regular Saturday afternoon sessions during the 38 weeks on which it was observed. Though these were the majority, there were a number of other cases heard by the parish court on other occasions. Sometimes cases of theft or violence were brought straight to the chief and dealt with at once if he happened to be present. Other cases were heard at odd times because of the failure of witnesses to appear at the Saturday courts. Others again were settled on the spot, when the chief decided to visit the scene of a dispute over land or housing, or deputed a headman to do so. The exact number of these cases heard at odd times cannot be stated, but was not very large. Besides these, some cases were heard by the headman on their own. They have no official power to do this, but in some cases of theft or violence a headman who is available nearby is applied to direct and may succeed in settling a dispute on the spot through his arbitration.

The total number of cases heard within the parish in all these ways cannot exceed 300 at the most in the course of a year. This is not a very large number, but when repeated in the other parishes of the sub-country of the Kibuga, they represent a very important saving of the time of the Kibuga Court. Of the 60 cases recorded, 11 had to be referred to the Kibuga Court in the end, after preliminary hearing in the parish. Three other cases of theft involved the police and were sent to them. The number of cases heard by the Kibuga Court varies from year to year. At the five year intervals 1943, 1948 and 1953, the numbers were 1,306, 2,536 and 1,527 respectively. It would appear from this that if all cases at present heard by parish authorities had to go to the Kibuga Court its work might become unmanageable."

Such arbitral courts, as the same sociologists point out,[1] have no official recognition nor any legal powers of enforcement. This is an important point and leads to the next topic we must consider:

" The parish chief and his staff have the duty of enforcing the law, but at the parish level they have no legal sanctions to assist them, since the court of the parish cannot impose fines or imprisonment. This may account for the rather pompous way in which admonitions are given in the court, though it must be clear to all present that such admonitions are very unlikely to be heeded. Short of arresting a person and sending him straight to the chief of the Kibuga this is all that the parish authorities can do, and from this seems to have evolved a technique of attempting to curb the

---

[1] Southall and Gutkind, *op. cit.*, p. 197.

grosser excesses in law breaking, so that although many regulations are broken with impunity, this should not be done so flagrantly as to make strong deterrent action unavoidable. It is this flexible approach which offers such wide scope for the giving and receiving of gifts to influence the precise manner in which the law is applied."[1]

It is satisfactory to observe that twenty-five years ago an independent sociologist opined:[2]

> " It is conceivable that a ssaza chief might attempt to make a good thing out of the corruption of justice—though the ample salaries which they receive probably constitute the best safeguard against this—but the litigants in a ggombolola chief's courts are so poor that this would hardly be worth his while, and certainly all those I attended showed a most painstaking determination to get at the truth of the matters before them. Certainly there is no dissatisfaction on that score among the people at large."

Corruption in fact is hardly ever to be found in the modern courts of Buganda. It is probable that Mair was to some extent whitewashing the chiefly courts of the past on that score. There is, however, frequently voiced public satisfaction with the propriety of the present magisterial courts and the Principal Courts in this respect.

Before concluding this chapter on the modern judicial system mention must be made of the successors to the royal courts of the past in the Lubiri. The Royal Court House, the Masengere, is still to be found in front of the Old Twekobe Palace but because of the change in the judicial system it is no longer used as the Royal Court. This change may be traced in the Presidential Address of Owekitiibwa S. W. Kulubya to the Uganda Society in 1942,[3] to which I have already referred:[4]

> " In the Royal Court House, the Masengere, the King used to appear as often as he chose to do so, and the place where he actually sat was roped off. This house was looked after by members of the Mbogo (buffalo) clan. All his subjects came hither to pay homage to their King. A house or hut called by his name is still maintained and is looked after as in days past. Some time back, during comparatively recent times, the King ceased to make his appearances in Masengere and deputed the duty to the Katikkiro who. henceforward heard cases in which an appeal had been made to the King. There was still, however, an appeal from him to the King."

Nowadays in fact the Kabaka decides the clan cases, the only

---

[1] Southall and Gutkind, *op. cit.*, p. 199.

[2] Mair, *op. cit.*, p. 283.

[3] *Loc. cit.*

[4] See above, p. 15.

class of case which is submitted to him personally for final decision, in his office.

The second royal court, Akagango K'Essanga, is still to be found in front of the New Twekobe Palace, though it no longer sports an elephant's tusk, and is still used for petty arbitration and the trial of minor domestic offences among the staff of the Palace. Its president is the Omukulu W'Olubiri and its members are the Sabakaki, who controls the Kabaka's Pages, and the Officer Commanding the Bodyguard. This court in fact is the modern counterpart of the ancient court of Kibale in the Lubiri.[1]

The Ggombolola, the Katikkiro's court, was handed over by the Katikkiro to the chief appointed to control the metro-politan area of the Kibuga, and first entitled " Omusolowoza W'Ekibuga ",[2] in the period of the First World War. This chief at first heard cases in the Katikkiro's compound in front of the Lubiri until he moved his court to the site of the present head-quarters of Omukulu we Kibuga.

The Court of the Lukiko used to sit, until the opening of the Courts in the New Bulange at the end of 1955, at the side of the Old Bulange (" mu mbirizi ") and was, of course, until fairly recent times, presided over by the Omulamuzi, the Minister of Justice in person.[3]

Finally mention should be made of the legal publications in Luganda and English which have been produced in the last two years and which have undoubtedly improved the machinery of justice in the Kabaka's Courts. Thanks to the confidence placed in this project by the Kabaka's Government and the enthusiastic response from the Ganda themselves, whose thirst for law in their native language appears unlimited, by early 1960 all the present native laws,[4] and translations[5] of the specified Pro-tectorate legislation and other relevant Protectorate legislation[6] together with customary law reports of the Principal Court over the last twenty years[7] and notes of selected decisions of the High

---

[1] See above, p. 16.
[2] The tax-collector of the Kibuga.
[3] See p. 19, above.
[4] The Native Laws of Buganda, Revised Edition, 1957, and Supplement 1957–58.
[5] Translations in Luganda of certain Protectorate Legislation, Vols. I, II and III.
[6] *E.g.* The Buganda Courts Ordinance, The African Authority Ordinance and the Registration of Titles Ordinance.
[7] Customary Law Reports, 1956, 1957, 1958, 1940–1955 and 1959.

Court over the last nineteen,[1] will have been published. These are by no means the first publications of legislation in Luganda, indeed as far back as 1909,[2] in the period of the First World War[3] and subsequently, notably in 1941,[4] there were small booklets published. It can, however, properly be claimed that the whole field of law within the jurisdiction of the Kabaka's Courts has now at last been covered by the various series of publications issued or prepared in the last two years.

---

[1] Notes of Selected Decisions of Her Majesty's High Court of Uganda, 1940–1958.

[2] See p. 31, above.

[3] See p. ix, above.

[4] *Native Laws of Buganda*, Revised Edition, 1941, and *Directions for Trial of Cases*—see below p. 289.

PART II

THE LAW OF PERSONS

SUMMARY

			PAGE
CHAP. 4	Status and Capacity of Individuals	. . .	53
CHAP. 5	The Clans	72
CHAP. 6	Marriage	77
CHAP. 7	Family Law	104

CHAPTER 4

STATUS AND CAPACITY OF INDIVIDUALS

By Article 6 of the Uganda Agreement, 1900, the jurisdiction of " the native Court of the Kabaka of Uganda " did not extend to any person " not a native of the Uganda province ". That personal jurisdiction was extended by intermediate steps,[1] and then by the Native Courts in Buganda Proclamation, 1917, to " natives of the Protectorate ", that is, any natives of any tribe on the confines of the Protectorate, who had been resident in the Protectorate for a period of at least one year, and also included any Sudanese or Nubian, without any restriction as to period of residence. With minor variations,[2] that definition of a person subject to the laws[3] and the native courts of Buganda continued until the Buganda Courts Ordinance, 1940, came into force. Thereupon by subsection 6(1) the courts of Buganda were empowered to exercise

> " jurisdiction over all causes and matters where, in proceedings of a civil nature, all parties are natives, or where, in proceedings of a criminal nature, the accused is a native."

A " native ", under the interpretation section of the same Ordinance, means " any person whose tribe is a tribe of the Protectorate or of the Colony and Protectorate of Kenya, the Tanganyika Territory, Nyasaland, the Sudan, the Belgian Congo or the mandated territory of Ruanda-Urundi, and includes a Swahili". It will be observed that that definition of a legal person subject to the jurisdiction of the Buganda courts, while it is not as wide as the definition of an " African " to be found in the Interpretation and General Clauses Ordinance (Cap. 1),[4] is at any rate much wider than the previous definition of such a

---

[1] The Native Courts Ordinances, 1905 and 1909, particularly section 14 (i) of the latter.
[2] Native Courts in Buganda Proclamation of 3rd June, 1940. (L.N. 117/40).
[3] Buganda Native Laws (Declaratory) Ordinance, 1938.
[4] See judgment of McKISACK, C. J., in H.C.C.A. 77 of 1958, *Mengo Builders and Contractors Ltd.* v. *K. M. L. Kasibante* (unreported) and Chapter 15 below.

person.[1] Section 6(3) of the Buganda Courts Ordinance provides that when any person claims that he is not justiciable by a Buganda Court, the court shall refer the matter to a Protectorate magistrate to decide. No doubt such a magistrate, there being no guiding section in the Buganda Courts Ordinance, would take into consideration subsections 3(1) and (4) of the Interpretation and General Clauses Ordinance and the order of Francis, J., in High Court Criminal Revision No. 100 of 1940, *R.* v. *Ibrahim Mohamed*[2] which applied " a reasonable and common-sense meaning to the word (native) " having regard to the following considerations:

    " 1. The descent of the persons affected;
       2. Their place of residence;
       3. Their personal appearance; and
       4. Their mode of life."

On the question of whether the personal jurisdiction of the Kabaka's courts embraces juristic persons in the shape of companies, partnerships, societies and associations, reference is invited to Chapter 15 below.

To sum up then, a legal person amenable to the jurisdiction of the courts of Buganda is an African of East Africa or the Belgian Congo or trust territories, male or female and in view of the provisions of Clause 12(e) of the Succession Order, 1926,[3] would appear to include a child in the womb. Certainly by custom, when a pregnant woman dies, the foetus is extracted and buried separately, usually in a second grave next to its mother but possibly in the father's clan (butaka) land. There are however no funeral rights for such foetus.

The Royal Family

The Royal Family of Buganda consists of the descendants of the former Kabaka Mutesa I[4] and the members of that Royal Family by virtue of Article 4 of the Constitution of Buganda

    " shall enjoy all such titles and precedence as they have heretofore enjoyed."

---

[1] See judgment of Pearson, J., in H.C.C.A. 24 of 1946, *Yosamu Musulo* v. *Hyxinthe*, 6 U.L.R. 149.
[2] 6 U.L.R. 91.
[3] See Chapter 11 below and Appendix 4, p. 320, *post*.
[4] Buganda Agreement, 1955, Article 2(2).

The Royal Family of Buganda, " Abaana b'engoma ",[1] retain their importance through their relationship to the Kabaka and because from their number the next Kabaka is selected by the Lukiko under Article 2 of the Buganda Agreement, 1955.

In ancient times indeed there was no fixed rule of succession to the Kabakaship; the issue was settled at a meeting of chiefs or fought out between rival princes.[2] Now, however, the selection and recognition of the Kabaka are regulated by Articles 2 and 3 of the Buganda Agreement, 1955. Thereafter, by virtue of Article 4 of the Constitution,

> " the Kabaka shall enjoy all the titles, dignities and pre-eminence that attach to the office of Kabaka under the law and custom of Buganda."[3]

The special relationship of the King's Mother (Namasole) to the Kabaka is recorded by Sir Apolo Kagwa.[4] The Namasole was in truth the protectress of the Kabaka against potential rebels among his chiefs. For this powerful aid and in recognition of her special position it was taboo for a Kabaka to order the Namasole's palace to be plundered[5]—a method of punishment employed against other offenders among the chiefly ranks. Roscoe records:

> " The King's Mother (Namasole) also had estates in each district, and held her own court; she was a woman who, in virtue of being the King's Mother, was raised to power and given great honour in the land."[6]

In early times the custom was for the Nnaalinnya or Lubuga, Kabaka's Sister, to be celibate but this custom was abolished by Kabaka Mutesa I.[7]

Roscoe describes the powerful status of these two royal ladies:[8]

> " There were the Queen (Lubuga) and the King's Mother (Namasole), whose offices were superior to those of the chiefs. These ladies ranked below the King, yet their powers over their own people and estates were absolute, and both took the title of Kabaka like the King."

Formerly the Princes, Abalangira, held property and lived in

---

[1] " Children of the Drum ".
[2] Goldthorpe, *op. cit.*, p. 72.
[3] For crimes against the Kabaka's authority see Chapter 17 below.
[4] *Empisa*, p. 121.
[5] Hamu Mukasa, *Bulletin of Uganda Society*, 1944, p. 21.
[6] Roscoe, *op. cit.*, p. 237.
[7] Hamu Mukasa, *loc. cit.*
[8] *Op. cit.*, p. 236.

different parts of the country. Their estates were managed and their private affairs were regulated by a chief entitled the Kasuju.[1] Indeed until the advent of the British, the Princes were generally in hiding to escape the Kabaka's usually murderous attention.[2] Nowadays, however, they go free about their private affairs with, of course, the prestige of the Royal Family to support them. Abalangira follow their mother's totem.

Likewise the Princesses, Abambejja, used to enjoy an unenviable lot. Ashe records:[3]

> "The Bambeja are an important body of women, often very numerous. They are condemned to perpetual virginity. . . . They often use every blandishment, and even force, to secure some young peasant, the unhappy object of their affection; but, should he be discovered with them, he must meet the awful fate of death by fire, the common capital punishment in Buganda."

Today like other members of the Royal Family, the Princesses usually have an independent income from their estates and apart from the prestige springing from their royal blood go about their affairs like other ladies of the land. It is said that they do not want to marry as they do not wish to be ruled by a peasant husband (omukopi). This has not prevented them, however, from having love affairs and their children—*serwava*, if a boy, and *nawava*, if a girl follow their paramour father's clan.

Before leaving the topic of the Royal Family, mention must be made of the royal tombs (amasiro). These tombs of former Kabakas and Princes are situated on land belonging to the Kabaka, Princes or Princesses and the Ssabalangira, the Head of the Princely clan, controls the tombs in their names. If any dispute arises over the tombs it is decided in the clan. But if a criminal offence is committed at a tomb, the offender is tried in the ordinary courts of law.

CHIEFS

The ex-Ssabalangira Ggomotoka[4] and the White Father Gorju[5] both detail the hierarchy of the chieftainships in the mid-

---

[1] Roscoe, *op. cit.*, p. 256.
[2] Goldthorpe, *op. cit.*, p. 73.
[3] *Op. cit.*, p. 87.
[4] *Op. cit.*, p. 24.
[5] *Op. cit.*, p. 137.

nineteenth century and though there are minor variations in their lists the general picture was as follows:

(i) the Katikkiro;
(ii) Kimbugwe, the Guardian of the Kabaka's umbilical cord.
(iii) the ten ssaza chiefs or *bakungu*;
(iv) the *batongole*—the favourites—great chiefs who controlled large areas;
(v) the *miruka* chiefs who controlled small areas within the large estates of the *bakungu*;
(vi) the lesser *batongole* or village chiefs;
(vii) the archaic chieftainship of *omutongole ow'ensimu*. This kind of *mutongole* chief gave personal service to the Kabaka but controlled no peasants.[1] " A Mutongole who holds his chieftainship by right of grant to his ancestors during the era when all land was regarded as belonging to the Kabaka, is so known."[2]

There were three main types of chieftainship operating side by side and each in its separate way under the control of the Kabaka. Firstly there were the *bakungu* or great chiefs who had wide political power; then there were the *batongole* or favourites given office by the Kabaka in certain areas; and lastly there were the *bataka* or heriditary heads of clanlands. These three types of chieftainship in juxtaposition enabled the Kabakas to maintain balance and control.[3]

The *bakungu* have already been described[4] and the *bataka* will be more fully described below[5] but it is opportune to define at this point the offices of the *batongole*. These were the Chief Porter (Mulamba), the Head Cook (Kawuta), the Head Brewer (Seruti), the Head Drummer (Kawula), the Guardian of the Sacred Fire (Omusoloza), the Chief Herdsman (Sebalijja), the Controller of the Royal Household (Sabakaki) and many others.[6] As a recompense for their duties in the Palace, these officials were given estates by the Kabaka in various parts of the Kingdom.

This chiefly system did not recommend itself to the early British administrators and it is of value to consider a passage from a despatch from Sir Gerald Portal to the Earl of Roseberry,

---

[1] Ggomotoka, *loc. cit.*
[2] P.C.R.O. 26/29, *Lukiko* v. *Ali Mayanja* (unreported).
[3] The delicate equilibrium is well described by Gorju, *op. cit.*, pp. 140–142. For a more elementary but contemporary description see Ashe, *op. cit.*, pp. 88–94.
[4] See Chapter 1, above.
[5] See Chapter 8 below.
[6] Gorju, *loc. cit.*, and Sir Apolo Kagwa, *Mpisa*, pp. 317–318.

D

dated 24th May, 1893, a year before the Protectorate was declared:

> " Uganda is divided into ten provinces, each of which is under the nominal governorship of a Chief. Under these Governors again are an immense number of minor Chiefs, one below the other in a complicated system of transmitted authority. For instance, if we take the Province of Chagwe, lying along the left bank of the Nile, we find that the Governor of Chagwe transmits his orders to four sub-Governors of different districts, who exercise a doubtful control over eighteen minor Chiefs and these, in their turn, are the direct superiors of twenty-three others, under whom again are a large number of Headmen of villages. In theory, at first sight, this organisation would appear to be not a bad one; in practice, it has proved to be the cause of a vast system of oppression and robbery. The unfortunate peasantry are forced to toil for the support and glory of an immense number of useless and idle petty Chieftains, who would think it beneath their dignity to do a stroke of any sort of work from one end of the year to the other. In recent times, even the smaller Chiefs had powers of life and death over the peasants, and although this has been stopped, there can still be no doubt that cruelty and oppression in various forms are rife throughout the provinces.
>
> Economically, the present system is as bad a one as could be devised; certain taxes in kind have to be paid to the King from each province; these taxes are levied solely from the lowest classes, but as they have to pass through the hands of a long gradation of chiefs, the amount which ultimately reaches the King does not represent more than a fifth part of what has been paid by the villagers. Besides the taxes in kind, every province is forced to contribute annually a certain number of men to work for the King without payment. They are employed chiefly in building new houses for the King and his numerous women. . . .
>
> In each province, again, there are many semi-independent estates or separate divisions which are not under the authority of the Governor or any of his satellites. The King, his mother, sister, the Katikkiro or Vizier, the Commander of the Soldiers, the Chief of the Canoes, and several others, each possess, *ex officio*, estates in every province, with all the organisation of sub-Chiefs as in the Provincial Government, and with great numbers of slaves, peasants, and farmers, who owe allegiance only to their own immediate superior."

It would be untrue, however, to hold out the chief's position in the last century as a sinecure. Roscoe gives a clear picture of the chief's subjection to the whims of the Kabaka:

> " The District-Chiefs (Basaza) were appointed by the King, though he generally left the Katikiro and the District-Chiefs to nominate some person to a vacant post; if their choice pleased him, he confirmed it; if not, they had to select someone else. If the King

wished to depose any person from a chieftainship, he could do so summarily; usually, however, he would trump up some charge against the man, imprison him, and then depose him, instructing the Council (Lukiko) meanwhile to nominate someone else. When a chief was deposed, he was not allowed to remove any property, but might only take his wives and cattle. But if he was deposed because he had been accused of some misdemeanour, the King also captured his wives and cattle, provided that he could find them. The wives and family would at once flee to places of safety when they knew that the Chief had been deposed; and they would take away as much of his property as they could remove without being caught."[1]

and again:

" The King often brought a spurious charge against a chief who was becoming rich, and fined him heavily, or sent him to prison, intimating to him that he must pay a handsome sum if he wished to be freed; failing that, he would be cast into the stocks, where he would be so much ill used, that he would be glad to pay any fine to escape the torture and the danger of being put to death."[2]

Sir Apolo Kagwa has recounted[3] how bakungu chiefs were fined for their short-comings by the Kabaka, how the Kabaka's messenger was sent to collect the fine decreed and how the chief was bound to satisfy the fine forthwith, if necessary by calling on his lesser chiefs to assist him in supplying the women, cattle, goats, barkcloths, salt and other things exacted.

Notwithstanding these risks attendant on chiefly office there were certain lasting rewards which Mair has described:

" Conversely, satisfactory service was rewarded by promotion to the control of larger and larger areas. This constant change was a very marked feature of Baganda life. It was every Muganda's ambition to rise in this way, and there are still old men alive who have held nine or ten different chieftainships. Thus the chiefs neither had nor desired permanent tenure of any one position. The only definite security which a chief had was that he would never revert altogether to the status of a peasant; however deep his disgrace, he would at least be left in control of some ten or twenty men. Moreover, a chief's heir would normally succeed to his father's position, and only in case the heir to an important chief was a child would he be given a lesser area or taken into court service with a view to finding a place for him later."[4]

Further, certain great chiefs were exempt by custom from the Kabaka's power to put his subjects to death. They were:

---

[1] *Op. cit.*, p. 238.
[2] *Ibid.*, p. 259.
[3] *Empisa*, pp. 167–168.
[4] *Op. cit.*, p. 160.

    (i) the Katikkiro;

   (ii) the Kimbugwe;

  (iii) the Kaggo, Ssabaddu of Buganda;

  (iv) the Mugema, styled " the parent of the Kabaka ";

   (v) and the Kasujju, styled " the chief nurse of the princes ".[1]

A chief's duties were manifold:

    (i) he must keep his official estates in good order;[2]

   (ii) he must attend the Kabaka's council for months at a time on pain of being suspected of treachery;[3]

  (iii) he must build the King's houses in the royal enclosure;[4]

  (iv) he must rule and remain popular with the people in his area through his lesser chiefs and keep abreast of events there;[5]

   (v) he must decide cases brought to him;[6]

  (vi) he must maintain the roads in his area;[7]

  (vii) he must remit taxes punctually;

 (viii) and he must be a brave leader in war.[8]

The Agreement of 1900 had the effect, as observed above,[9] of unifying two of the types of chieftain—the *bakungu* and the *batongole*—and of over-riding the whole position of the third—the *bataka*.[10] Sub-chiefs or ggombolola chiefs entered the hierarchy below the various Palace officials but above the miruka chiefs, being directly responsible to the ssaza chiefs.[11]

The duties of chiefs laid down in Article 9 of the 1900 Agreement have already been mentioned.[12] A legal duty was laid upon all chiefs under the Criminal Procedure Code, 1919, to communicate to the nearest Magistrate or Police Officer any information which he may possess or obtain respecting:

    (a) the permanent or temporary residence of any notorious thief, receiver or vendor of stolen property in any area of which he is a chief;

    (b) the resort to any place within or the passage through

---

[1] Sir Apolo Kagwa, *Empisa*, p. 146.

[2] Roscoe, *op. cit.*, pp. 239 and 269.

[3] Roscoe, *op. cit.*, p. 246, and Mair, *op. cit.*, p. 177.

[4] Roscoe, *op. cit.*, p. 269.

[5] *Ibid.*, p. 257.

[6] *Ibid.*

[7] P. MacQueen, " *In Wildest Africa* ", 1910, pp. 354–355.

[8] Mair, *op. cit.*, p. 160.

[9] See Chapter 2 and Gorju, *op. cit.*, p. 142.

[10] See below, Chapter 8.

[11] Ggomotoka, *op. cit.*, p. 71 and Chapter 3.

[12] See Chapter, 2 above.

such area of any person whom he knows or reasonably suspects to be a robber, escaped convict, or proclaimed offender;

(c) the occurrence in or near such area of any sudden or unnatural death under suspicious circumstances, or the discovery of a corpse in or near such area in circumstances which lead to a reasonable suspicion that such death has occurred;

(d) any matter likely to affect the maintenance of order or the prevention of crime or the safety of person or property respecting which a Magistrate by general or special order has directed him to communicate information.

More recently Article 34 of the Constitution of Buganda has charged ssaza chiefs with responsibility under the Katikkiro for the administration of their ssazas and for the collection of taxes. Ggombolola and Muluka Chiefs are therein charged to assist the Ssaza Chiefs.

In conclusion regard must be had to certain decisions of the courts as to the status of chiefs in Buganda:

(i) a chief is, under the Uganda Agreement, bound to give information to the British authorities respecting the Hut and Poll Tax;[1]

(ii) a ssaza chief is not a servant of the British but of the Native Government and is triable by the Lukiko;[2]

(iii) and it is established custom in Buganda that natives opposing the authority of a chief are arrested and punished.[3]

Peasants

The word " peasant " is the best translation of the Luganda " omukopi " and I, therefore, propose to employ it in describing those Ganda who were not chiefs (abaami) in the last century and the first forty years of this. Nowadays the term " omukopi " has acquired under culture contact a derogatory flavour and this has been reflected in legislation wherein the palliative " omusenze " or " tenant " is now employed.[4] But this modern substitute born of class-consciousness has not the significance of the time-honoured term " omukopi " and I shall not accordingly use it now.

---

[1] H.C.Cr.R. (1910), *Crown* v. *Anselmi Kiimba*, 1 U.L.R. 79.
[2] H.C.Cr.A. 1 of 1927, *Nasanairi Mayanja* v. *Rex*, 3 U.L.R. 205.
[3] P.C.R.O. 115 of 1932, *Ziryawulamu* v. *Mayanja* (unreported).
[4] See Busuulu and Envujjo Law.

When the customary law of land comes to be considered,[1] we shall have to revert to a more detailed discussion of the relationship of the peasant to his landlord, that is his chief, but here I propose to mention briefly the salient points in his status, powers and duties.

As Mair observes:

> " Every Muganda was the subject of some chief, from whom he obtained the land where he built his house and his wives grew their crops, and his tenure of this land depended entirely on the goodwill of the chief."[2]

It was, however, for the peasant to choose his chief (okusenga) and, if he became dissatisfied with his chief, he could by stealth remove himself to another's protection (okusenguka). But Ashe records:[3]

> " It is not always a safe thing to do. One of my friends, a Muhuma herdsman, who kept the Katikiro's cattle, left the chancellor's service to enter that of the King. On some lying pretext he was seized, his ears cut off, and his eyes put out, as a warning that the imperious chancellor would allow none of his servants to prefer anyone else to himself, not even the King."

The first duty of a peasant was to follow his chief to war,[4] formerly the national pursuit of wealth, but he had other duties and responsibilities both towards his chief and towards the Kabaka. Mair describes:[5]

> " A peasant could be called on at will by his chief to build his houses and the high fence which surrounded them, or to send food to the chief when the latter was in the capital, and he was obliged to send the chief a gourd of beer from every brew (perhaps one-eighth of the total quantity). Specialists had to supply their wares free on demand, and itinerant traders—principally hawkers of fish—since during the time they stayed in the village they were subject to the chief's authority, were taken to him and gave him a portion of anything they were selling.
>
> Peasant's services to the King, which were organised by means of the authority of the chiefs, consisted in building the houses and fencing of the royal enclosure, weeding the paths all over the country to keep communications open, hunting wild animals, and fighting. Both war and work in the capital might take the peasant from his home for months at a time."

---

[1] See Chapter 8, below.
[2] *Op. cit.*, p. 132.
[3] *Op. cit.*, p. 95.
[4] Ashe, *loc. cit.*
[5] *Op. cit.*, p. 132.

Roscoe tells us that:

> " Peasants did not care to live long in the capital because food was scarce and because the danger of being seized and put to death was great; they only went when they were obliged to do so to perform some work and they returned to the country as soon as they were free to do so."[1]

Sir Apolo Kagwa mentions one particular hazard for a peasant—to look on the royal ladies was death.[2]

There is no doubt that the system of labour for chiefs or for the Kabaka was forced. Roscoe records:

> " When a house (in the royal enclosure) required to be re-built, the King appointed an overseer, and the latter went to the District-Chief concerned, and settled with him how many men would be required for the work; the overseer then collected the men from the sub-chiefs according to the arrangements with the District-Chief, commenced the building, and fined those who did not work or who did their work badly."[3]

And again:

> " Every person called to do any State-work had to pay the overseer a sum of cowry-shells; . . . If the workman had not the sum to hand, he was required to give something else, such as a barkcloth or an equivalent in food or beer. Until this had been paid, no workman was allowed to begin his work, but unless he made a start within a given time, he was fined. If he was unable to obtain the amount by barter, or to borrow it and still delayed making a start, his wife or some other member of his family, would be taken as hostage, until he should bring the necessary sum; the woman or child thus taken would be required to work for the chief during the time of detention. This same custom held good with all State-labour."[4]

During this century this ancient system of State-work had its successor in the dreaded " Kasanvu " system, which was designed by a former Governor, Sir Hesketh Bell, in December 1908 to ensure a supply of compulsory paid labour for Government purposes. During the period of the First Great War 1914–1918, " Kasanvu " became much hated and was abolished with effect from 1st January, 1922.[5]

---

[1] *Op. cit.*, p. 246.
[2] *Basekabaka*, p. 124.
[3] *Op. cit.*, p. 246.
[4] *Op. cit.*, p. 241.
[5] P. G. Powesland, Chapter II, " The History of the Migration in Uganda ", at p. 20 in *Economic Development and Tribal Change*, ed. A. I. Richards.

But we have run ahead without considering the benefits which accrued to the peasant from his relationship with the chief. As we shall observe below,[1] the peasant was generally assisted in settling in his new abode by the chief and his men. For his services the chief would give the peasant a wife or two;[2] and in general the chief would act as his protector and patron.

This relationship of chief and peasant began to suffer severe shocks under the impact of the economic activity in the first quarter of this century. The landlords, whose chieftainship had often suffered as a result of the political reorganisation under the 1900 Agreement, were in the 1920's activated by self-interest and attempted more and more to obtain a share of the wealth produced from their land by their tenants.[3] The tenant cultivators felt insecure and so began to cast off the remnants of the old system of peasantry and to acquire smallholdings of from 10 to 30 acres, thus establishing a class of free peasant proprietors.[4]

SLAVES

Until the last decade of the last century slavery was a widespread institution throughout the Kingdom of Buganda. The first British administrators made the abolition of slavery one of their prime objectives and so it is that we find that Article 10 of the Treaty between Kabaka Mwanga and Captain Lugard for the Imperial British East Africa Company reads:

> " 10. Slave-trading or slave-raiding shall be declared illegal and punishable by law. The import or export of slaves is prohibitied."[5]

This provision was repeated, as has been noted above,[6] in the 1892 Treaty between the same parties.

Clause 15 of the Provisional Agreement between King Mwanga and Sir Gerald Portal on 29th May, 1893 was more explicit:

> " 15. Slave-trading or slave-raiding, or the exportation or importation of people for sale or exchange as slaves, is prohibited. I, Mwanga, also undertake, for myself and my successors to give due effect to such Laws and Regulations, having for their object

---

[1] See below, Chapter 8.
[2] Ashe, *loc. cit.*
[3] Mair, *op. cit.*, p. 132.
[4] Powesland, *op. cit.*, p. 35.
[5] Wild, *op. cit.*, pp. 41–45.
[6] See p. 8, above.

the complete ultimate abolition of the status of slavery in Uganda and its dependencies, as may be dictated by Her Majesty's Government."

That clause was repeated in the Buganda Agreement, 1894, between Mwanga and Colville and is still in force.[1]

To enforce these provisions in the treaties, Mr. Jackson, Her Majesty's Representative, prohibited the seizing of slaves and plundering in his very first order of the 31st March, 1895.[2]

Ashe, however, writing in 1889 gives a contemporary account of slaves:

> " The slaves have no rights. . . . The slaves in Buganda are drawn from the surrounding countries, chiefly Bunyoro and Busoga, a few from Busagora, Ihangiro, Buzongora and Buzinja. They fetch ten thousand to twenty thousand cowrie shells, equivalent to between three and six pounds in English money, according to description. A beautiful Muhuma woman will fetch far more."[3]

The slaves, mainly boys and women, were obtained, of course, in the raids on neighbouring tribes and indeed were the main object of those warlike excursions.[4] Such slaves (myandu) consisting of males (abaddu) and females (abakazi banyage) were if in excess of their master's requirements bartered for cattle or later, after the advent of the Arabs, in the reign of Kabaka Suna II, were sold for cowrie shells. A slave sold was whether male or female called " envuma ". However, if a man sold a wife whom he had married as a slave he was prosecuted and fined.

Roscoe's definition of their status reads as follows:

> " A slave was deprived of his freedom, . . . neither his wife nor her children were his own and . . . his life was at his master's disposal. On the other hand if a man married his slave girl, and she had children, she became free, and her children were acknowledged by the clan."[5]

The master was entitled to one or two of a slave's children as *endobolo* (lit.= percentage).[6] The male slave could, however, purchase the redemption of himself, his wife and all his children but one, who remained with the chief as his *endobolo*.[7]

---

[1] See preamble and Article 1(1) of the Buganda Agreement, 1955.
[2] Sir Apolo Kagwa, *Basekabaka*, p. 199.
[3] *Op. cit.*, p. 97.
[4] Powesland, *loc. cit.*, and Hattersley, *op. cit.*, p. 114.
[5] *Op. cit.*, p. 14.
[6] *Res fructificat domino*, as Gorju aptly remarked, *op. cit.*, p. 300.
[7] Gorju, *op. cit.*, p. 300.

Mair's reconstruction[1] of their status is the most complete:

> " Captured women were taken at once as wives, and except that they had no relatives to go to in case of ill-treatment or their husband's death their different status ceased to have much importance: girls might marry into their master's family or might marry other slaves; the latter on marriage set up their own houses, described themselves as members of their master's clan, and observed its practices. They differed from ' free men ' in that they could not leave him and that they could not inherit from a real member of the clan. Their children would be indistinguishable from their neighbours, except that it was the duty of heads of clans, who kept track of genealogies, to know that they had not the rights of genuine members as regards inheritance, and that they were debarred from becoming chiefs—a position reserved for people who could prove that they were Baganda by tracing their ancestry back to the original founders of the clan."

For good services slaves could be freed and accepted into their master's clan. In such case their heirs would be clansmen.

Recent cases of slavery will be considered under the Law of Crimes.[2]

WOMEN

In Chapter 7 we shall be considering in detail a woman's relationship in the past and in present times with her family, her husband, his family and their own children. It will suffice, therefore, if in this chapter we consider the status and legal rights of women under the native laws of Buganda.

By section 4 of the Guardianship Law[3] a girl is in the custody of her mother until she is eighteen years of age or until she is married; if her mother is dead, her father or uncle take charge of her and she in any case passes to the custody of her father, under section 5 of the same law, on reaching the age of eighteen or until she is married. If the father is dead, she remains with her mother; and if both are dead she passes to the custody of her uncle. Under section 6 of the same law the Principal Court has power to give any order it thinks fit in respect of the guardianship of any child brought before it.

By section 5 of the Law to Prevent Prostitution,[4] it is an offence, subject to certain exceptions, for any unmarried girl

---

[1] *Op. cit.*, p. 33.
[2] See below Chapter 17.
[3] Rev. Edn., pp. 24–25.
[4] Rev. Edn., pp. 8–9.

under the age of twenty years to enter any employment or to engage in any kind of work which takes her away from the home of her parents or guardians at night. Further if any unmarried girl under the age of twenty years elopes then her parents or guardians may by virtue of section 7 of the Adultery and Fornication Law sue for her restoration.[1]

The courts have powers to order the repatriation of women convicted of prostitution,[2] convicted of crimes of moral turpitude and sentenced to imprisonment for two years or more, if they are foreigners,[3] or declared to be vagrants.[4]

A girl comes of age on attaining twenty years and thereafter can bind herself in contract and is entitled to be put in possession of her property.[5] In the last century, of course, such a provision would have had little importance as only the Princesses of the royal blood, prior to the 1900 Agreement, owned land. But after that Agreement and the subsequent legislation, notably the Possession of Land Law,[6] any woman was empowered to acquire the ownership of land by gift, purchase or inheritance.[7] *A fortiori* women acquired the right of residence as tenants of mailo land under the Busuulu and Envujjo Law.[8]

The status and capacity of a Ganda woman in marriage and in divorce are considered below.[9]

As to political franchise, while a woman has no right to vote in the election of representatives to the Great Lukiiko, she nevertheless can be elected as either a ssaza or a Ssaza Council Representative.[10] No Ganda woman has to date ever been so elected. Again under the Law for Selecting Non-Official Representatives to the Lower Councils, women have no vote nor can they be directly elected but can be selected to sit on ssaza councils as non-official notables, on ggombolola councils as non-officials of good standing or on miruka councils as land-owners or residents of the Muluka chosen by the other members.[11]

---

[1] Rev. Edn., pp. 4–5.
[2] The Law to Prevent Prostitution, section 3(2).
[3] The Repatriation of Undesirable Foreigners Law, section 2.
[4] The Vagrancy Law, section 4.
[5] The Coming of Age Law, section 2.
[6] Rev. Edn., pp. 154 *et seq.*
[7] See below, Chapters 8 and 11.
[8] Rev. Edn., pp. 168 *et seq.*
[9] See below, Chapter 7.
[10] Great Lukiiko (Election of Representatives) Law.
[11] The Law for the Establishment of Lower Councils in Buganda.

Finally women have no liability under the Graduated Tax Law[1] or under the Education Tax Law[2] but are liable to pay land tax if they own or occupy mailo land.[3]

CHILDREN

The detailed relationships and customary law governing children within the family will be considered in Chapter 7 and children's rights in succession in Chapter 11. I shall but briefly now deal with the status of a child.

The first great maxim of Ganda customary law is that all children begotten by one man on several women are equal in rank whether they were conceived in lawful marriage or not. A child born in adultery ranks *pari passu* with a legitimate child and can succeed to property whether boy or girl.[4]

If on the death of her husband, a woman admits that her child was born of an adulterous union then the adulterer having paid agreed compensation to the clan heads of the deceased husband's clan, may take the child to rear as his own but such a claim is sometimes contested.[5]

On divorce the children of the dissolved marriage remain in their father's home and are equal in rank with any children which may be born to him by a subsequent marriage (omusai ogumu, *i.e.* " of one blood ").

A step-child is brought up in his step-father's home but cannot succeed to his step-father's property.[6]

Responsibility for the costs of rearing and educating a child fall on the natural father. The mother's father or brother may, if need be, sue the natural father for those expenses and this legal right can also be enforced against the seducer of an unmarried girl. Formerly in such cases the courts used to rely mainly on the mother's evidence but nowadays regard is had also to medical evidence of potential paternity.[7]

---

[1] Rev. Edn., pp. 196 *et seq.*
[2] Rev. Edn., pp. 214 *et seq.*
[3] The Land Tax Law, sections 2 and 3.
[4] E.A.C.A.C.A. 2 of 1944, *Kajubi* v. *Kabali* (1944), 11 E.A.C.A. 34.
[5] P.C.R.O. 52 of 1924, upholding Lukiko Court Case 279 of 1924, *Mulwanyi* v. *Alitubera* (unreported).
[6] See Chapter 11, below.
[7] See P.C.C.C. 347 of 1957, *Rebecca C. Kalule* v. *Enoka E. K. Mulira*, 1958 C.L.R. 73.

STRANGERS

The Ganda have never been xenophobes. As mentioned above, large numbers of the neighbouring tribes were absorbed into Ganda families in the last century as slaves, and during the last thirty years large numbers of immigrants, particularly from Ruanda and Urundi, sometimes whole family units, have been absorbed into Ganda villages as labourers and later as tenants. In some areas in Buddu ssaza near Masaka, 40% of the African population is of immigrant origin.

When a stranger arrives in a village in Buganda, it is the duty of the peasant with whom he first stays to introduce him immediately to the village chief (omutongole) and the latter in his turn must pass the information through the muluka chief to the ggombolola. It is an offence under customary law punishable with a fine to omit to introduce a newly arrived stranger in that manner.[1]

Providing the stranger is of good behaviour and fulfils his tax obligations, he is absorbed into the community and enjoys the full franchise.[2] He is in fact counted as a Ganda for all purposes except clan matters.

Mukwaya, a sociological research worker and himself a Muganda observes:

> " Again, there is no evidence to show that the immigrants are not receiving fair treatment in the Buganda Courts. In no case was a complaint made by an immigrant voluntarily or on questioning about the Buganda Courts as Courts. And most of the informants who are immigrants stated that they lived peacefully with the Ganda who treated them well."[3]

This statement of an independent enquirer is reassuring particularly in view of the fact that in October 1945 the then Minister of Justice found it necessary to issue a circular instructing all Buganda courts to treat foreigners impartially as though they were Ganda.

Lewin has stated the general rule of conflict of tribal laws as follows:

---

[1] See Resolution IX of the Lukiko in April 1916, approved by the Provincial Commissioner, *Akatabo Ke Biragiro na Mateka Ebyatesebwa Olukiko Olukulu olwe Buganda okuva* 1916 *okutusa* 1919, p. 3.

[2] Great Lukiiko (Election of Representatives) Law, section 7 and the Law for Selecting Non-Official Representatives to the Lower Councils, section 8.

[3] A. B. Mukwaya, " The Immigrants and the Law ", p. 191 in *Economic Development and Tribal Change*, 1954, ed. A. I. Richards.

" It is submitted that the rule is that Natives are deemed to
follow the custom prevailing in the place where they live, regardless
of their own tribal origin.

And if they live in different places then that prevailing at the
defendant's home.

Notwithstanding that they both may be of different tribes from
each other and from the place of their residence."[1]

Gutkind thought that the high proportion of non-Ganda
(40%) who brought cases to the parish chief of Mulago to be
arbitrated upon was " suggestive of the fact that immigrants
whose own legal and administrative authorities have been left
behind look to Ganda customs and procedures for the arbitra-
ment of their affairs. This appears to be part of their training
in Ganda custom."[2]

While there is much truth in that suggestion, immigrants often
particularly in cases involving family law such as marriage and
inheritance cling to the customs of their country of origin and
what is particularly noteworthy is that the Principal Court has
repeatedly permitted proof of, recognised and applied foreign
customary law in the trial of cases. A short passage in one judgment will suffice to make the attitude of the judges of that Court
clear:

" In our view both litigants are of one tribe, namely Banyaruanda.
So, although they are within the Kingdom of Buganda, they are
at liberty to follow the customs of their country and in particular
that which affects marriage; for it is unjust merely to force them
to follow the Buganda custom when both should be able to remain
with their own custom. For example, we Baganda class it as an
abomination to sleep with our children in a house when they have
been married. This however you will find other nations do not
regard with disgust."[3]

Before concluding this chapter, it is convenient to consider
blood-brotherhood (okutta omukago). This practice was originally of frequent occurrence between Ganda of the highest and
lowest degree:[4] Kabakas used to make blood-brotherhood with
their Katikkiros and every father attempted to arrange such a

---

[1] Julius Lewin, *Studies in African Native Law*, 1947, Chapter VI.

[2] Gutkind, *op. cit.*, p. 201.

[3] P.C.C.A. 183 of 1955, *Kalekezi* v. *Kakuba*, 1956 C.L.R. 1. See also
P.C.Cr.C. 554 of 1957, *Lukiiko* v. *Tomasi Opeda*, 1957 C.L.R. 1; P.C.C.A. 151
of 1957, *Kaganda* v. *Katabazi*, 1958 C.L.R. 1: and the cases concerning Bahima
succession customs reported in 1957 C.L.R. 157–162; but Ganda customary
law applied in P.C.C.C. 264 of 1956, *Magezi* v. *Mutegombwa and Another*, 1957
C.L.R. 143 where husband/plaintiff was Ganda and wife/defendant Ruanda.

[4] See Sir Apolo Kagwa, *Empisa*, Chapter 25, pp. 249 *et seq.*

compact for his son. The object of such an arrangement has been described by Mair:[1]

> " The value of such a relationship was that it provided security against all possible risks, including those resulting from the commission of a crime. A blood-brother could refuse a man no request of any kind, from a drink of beer or safe keeping for his cattle to a wife, the payment of a heavy fine or debt, or the concealment of a fugitive from justice. The relationship took precedence of kinship, in that a murderer might count on finding refuge with a blood-brother even if the latter was a relative of his victim, and one informant said that the blood-brother might even give himself up to be killed in the place of his friend."

Mair in 1934 observed that the greatly increased opportunities of getting into debt would make any man hesitate before undertaking unlimited responsibility for a friend and indeed that the need for blood-brotherhood had died out in the greater security of the times.[2]

While Mair's observation still holds true between the Ganda, the custom of blood-brotherhood has been practised occasionally in recent years between Ganda and foreigners, usually their herdsmen.[3] The advantages accruing to each party are that the Ganda cattle-owner safeguards his cattle by entrusting them to his blood-brother and the foreigner obtains usually an education for his children. Blood-brothers must help each other's children in the provision of funds for their marriage; and on the death of one of the two blood-brothers the children of the other must inherit some portion of the estate.

---

[1] *Op. cit.*, p. 71.
[2] *Op. cit.*, p. 73.
[3] The Ex-Ssabaganzi informed me he entered into blood-brotherhood with his herdsman Lwabuteera in 1939; in 1945 at any rate chiefs in Buweekula ssaza did so with their herdsmen; and a young Muganda had done so with a Munyoro herdsman in South Buddu in 1957.

CHAPTER 5

THE CLANS

Before considering in detail the various branches of Ganda family law, it is necessary to review the composition and general functioning of the social groups into which every Ganda is born, that is, to review the clan system of Buganda.[1]

A clan (ekika) is a social group each of whose members trace their descent through the male line[2] from a common ancestor. A wife adopted her husband's totems but at the same time retained her own.

A clan has two totems, the first (omuziro) from which the clan takes its name and the second (akabbiro) less generally known. Both totems are held sacred by the members of that clan who cannot injure, consume or destroy them.

Every clan has clan estates (butaka) in which are the burial grounds for members of that clan. Until the 1900 Agreement these estates were in the physical possession of the heads of clans but since the mailo distribution the clan lands are now generally in private ownership.[3]

Each clan has a set of names for its male members and a separate set for its female members. It is, therefore, possible to ascertain a Ganda's clan on hearing his name.

A clan has its special drum-beat which, although formerly a means of assembling clansmen in emergency, now has only a ceremonial usage.

Clans in ancient times had their own temples and shrines to their special deity usually situated on clan land.

Most clans[4] have an official duty to perform towards the Kabaka as Ssabattaka, the head of all clans, for example, the

---

[1] For general descriptions see Roscoe, *op. cit.*, Chapter VI, pp. 133 *et seq.*, Mair, *op. cit.*, pp. 33 *et seq.*, Sir Apolo Kagwa, *Ekitabo Kye Bika bya Baganda*, 1949, and CARTER, J.'s " The Clan System, Land Tenure and Succession among the Baganda ", 1 U.L.R. App.

[2] Except the Princely clan.

[3] See Chapter 8, below.

[4] Exceptions are the Leopard and Lion Clans, being royal clans, Roscoe, *op. cit.*, pp. 140–142.

members of the Lung-fish Clan are the Kabaka's canoe-builders and sailors and those of the Buffalo Clan carriers of his person on their shoulders or under modern conditions his chauffeurs. Clans also supplied levies of children both boys and girls for service in the Palace of the King,[1] and vied with each other in this duty, as a child of the clan who was favoured with royal preferment brought prestige and power to the whole clan.

> " The members of a clan were bound together by the rule of exogamy,[2] by a general obligation of mutual aid, to a certain extent by collective responsibility for the misdeeds of their members, by participation in the various ceremonies which marked significant events in a member's life, and by the fact that inheritance was kept strictly within the clan."[3]

The number of clans varies as new clans can be created and former clans can disappear.[4] To obtain the privilege of forming a separate clan the would-be members must establish firstly that they are a considerable body of persons and secondly that they have separate clan lands (butaka) available. Roscoe in 1911 listed 36 clans,[5] whereas Sir Apolo Kagwa listed 31 clans possibly four years earlier,[6] and certainly there are 49 clans in existence today.[7] The disappearance of clans in ancient times generally occurred when a clan incurred a Kabaka's wrath. If a member of a clan offended the Kabaka then the punishment was liable to fall on the whole clan. The heads of clan would suffer the plunder of their goods and members of that offending clan might be ordered to be slain. It was not unnatural in those circumstances, therefore, that members of such a clan would forthwith pretend to belong to other clans into which they were temporarily absorbed to reappear sometimes years later when the coast was clear. Examples are the Bush-buck Clan (Engabi) which took refuge with the Monkey Clan (Enkima) and the Elephant Clan (Enjovu) which under threat of extermination by Kikulwe joined the Civet Cat Clan (Ffumbe) for a period,

---

[1] Mair, *op. cit.*, p. 173.

[2] See Chapter 6, below, for exceptions.

[3] Mair, *op. cit.*, p. 33.

[4] For some examples see Appendix 2, p. 303, below; others are: the Rainwater Clan, which is now losing its identity in the Edible Rat Clan; the Red Ant Clan, a splinter group from the Buffalo Clan; two further splinter groups from the main Bird (Nnonyi) Clan now in the process of formation—the Parrot (Enkusu) and the Small Red Finch (Akasanke).

[5] *Loc. cit.*

[6] *Op. cit.* (The last year in the historical review on p. 153 is 1907).

[7] See Appendix 2, p. 302, below.

until in Muteesa I's reign, when the Namasole (Queen Mother) was Muganzilwaza of the Elephant Clan, her clansmen deemed it safe to reappear again with separate entity.

Each clan has a head of clan (ow'akasolya) formally chosen by its members but hereditary. He is styled the ancestor of the sub-clans (jjajja w'essiga). The sub-clan (essiga) is a group tracing their descent to one of the sons of the founder of the clan. To quote Mair again:

> " Membership of the ssiga was important in practice through the recognition of the authority of its senior member, a direct descendent of the original head, who settles disputes on matters of inheritance or clan status, debts or injuries committed by clansmen, and through whom such questions as a levy on clansmen to pay a fine for one member were settled."[1]

The head of the sub-clan (essiga) is styled the ancestor of the consanguinity (jjajja w'omutuba). The consanguinity (omutuba) is a group tracing their descent to one of the grandsons of the founder of the clan. To refer to Mair again:

> " Beyond the fact that each *mutuba* had its own lands, this division seems to have had little importance."[2]

The head of the consanguinity (omutuba) is styled the ancestor of the sub-consanguinity (jjajja ow'olunyiriri). The sub-consanguinity (olunyiriri) is a group tracing their descent to one of the great-grandsons of the founder of the clan. This head of sub-consanguinity has many detailed duties to perform, particularly in respect of succession, as he is styled the ancestor of the deceased. Immediately under him in the hierarchy comes the head of the courtyard (ow'oluggya), that is, the head of the household.

It will be appreciated that the clan heads must have a widespread organisation to perform the various duties and functions in the social lives of their members. Each clan head has his Katikkiro (chief minister) who is to be found in or near the Kibuga, the native metropolis, if the head of clan resides in the country. There are also clan councils both the principal one and inferior ones, succinctly described by Mair:

> " There was also a clan council consisting of the head of the whole clan and the *ssiga* heads, and at the present time there is an inferior council in every ssaza consisting of a representative chosen

---

[1] *Op. cit.*, p. 35.
[2] *Ibid.*

by the members of the whole clan living in each ggombolola. The clan council is a final court of appeal in disputes between members; the local councils appear to serve mainly as a means of promulgating its decisions. Nowadays, these councils keep type-written records."[1]

Disputes or matters which cannot be settled in the clan are referred to the Ddiiro which is the Standing Committee of the Lukiko, presided over by the Katikkiro or his Assistant, consisting of the Heads of Clans and Ggombolola Chiefs on duty at Mmengo, and appointed by the Kabaka to deal with clan cases and to advise him. Its authority stems from the absolute authority of the Kabaka in such cases.

It appears from approved Resolution 7 of 1919 of the Lukiko[2] that at any rate at that time the ladder of appeal in clan cases was from the Clan Council to the local Ggombolola Chief having jurisdiction over the Clansmen, where the aggrieved sued the Clan, and thence an appeal to the Ssaza Chief and finally to the Kabaka, in the same manner as ordinary cases. That procedure appears to have been only ephemeral for in Resolution 13 of October 1923[3] the Lukiko resolved that the Kabaka should finally decide clan cases himself. At any rate by the Uganda Agreement (Clan Cases), 1924, that is, in the following year, native courts and His Majesty's High Court of Uganda were excluded from jurisdiction in

" any case relating to the headship, membership or other matter affecting clans. In all such matters the respective clan councils shall lay their recommendations before the Kabaka and his Lukiko Council. The decision of the Kabaka shall be final. . . ."

That exclusion has been included in the statute[4] governing the Kabaka's Courts and has been again ratified in an Agreement.[5]

What exactly constitutes " other matter affecting clans " has caused courts some uneasiness from time to time[6] but it is well established[7] that that term includes succession matters and it also includes breaches of the rule of exogamy. " Membership "

[1] *Op. cit.*, p. 35.
[2] *Akatabo ke Biragiro na Mateka ebyatesebwa Olukiko Olukulu olwe Buganda okuva 1916 okutusa 1919*, p. 59.
[3] *Amateka ne Biragiro ebyatesebwa Olukiko Olukulu okuva 1922–1923*, p. 11.
[4] Buganda Courts Ordinance, 1940, section 9 (e).
[5] The Buganda Agreement, 1955, Article 8.
[6] See judgment of AINLEY, J., in H.C.Misc.A. 13 of 1949, *In re Kadumukasa* (unreported).
[7] See decision of PEARSON, J., in H.C.Misc.A. 9 of 1949, *Nabyonga and Others* v. *Sewava* (unreported).

cases comprise *inter alia* expulsion from a clan (okuboola) and the enticement of members away from their sub-clan to another sub-clan by its head or from one consanguinity to another, although all within the same clan. This latter activity is a fertile source of clan cases as the heads of the clan divisions thereby endeavour to enrich themselves. An example of a case relating to the headship of a clan is that of the Kibaale, the Head of the Oribi Clan, who sided with the then Katikkiro and was dismissed from his headship for contempt of the Lukiko in the Namasole affair in 1941.[1]

The various matters in which clans are interested namely family, land and succession affairs are dealt with in the subsequent chapters.

---

[1] See Bustin, *op. cit.*, pp. 162–163.

CHAPTER 6

MARRIAGE

Speke, on information supplied apparently by the then Namasole, wrote:

> " There are no such things as marriages in Uganda; there are no ceremonies attached to it."[1]

Were that so, my task would lighten considerably. In fact, marriage by natives in Buganda is one of the most important branches of customary law as it is elsewhere in Africa.[2] It is not, therefore, surprising to find that one of the two subjects with which the early administrators of the Uganda Protectorate were pre-occupied was the marriage of natives, as a glance at the chronological list of Protectorate legislation not specified to be administered by the Buganda courts[3] will illustrate. And the problems created by the confusion and complication of the laws and customs governing marriage of Africans in the Protectorate are still matters of the greatest public concern as the leading articles by the Bishop of the Upper Nile, published in 1958 in the local press, bear witness.[4]

Naturally in a book concerned with Ganda customary law it would be inappropriate to attempt to review also the Protectorate legislation governing marriage by statute.[5] As, however, there is a widespread misunderstanding among the Ganda and indeed among Africans generally as to the powers and authority of the Churches in matrimonial matters it may be salutary to refer to a passage in a revisional decision over twenty years ago:

> " It would perhaps be as well to point out that although it may be a common practice for proselytes of the Missions to submit their matrimonial differences to the arbitration of the Church authorities,

---

[1] *Op. cit.*, p. 361.
[2] Lewin, *op. cit.*, Chapter II.
[3] Appendix 3 (d), p. 313, below.
[4] *Uganda Argus* of 4th, 7th, 10th and 11 June, 1958.
[5] See caps. 109, 110 and 111.

their submission to such arbitration is entirely voluntary. The Church authorities have, of course, no legal jurisdiction, and no decision given by them would be legally binding on the parties."[1]

Marriage in a Church is governed by Protectorate legislation and the Protectorate courts alone have jurisdiction in respect of proceedings arising therefrom. Similarly marriage and divorce by Africans under Islamic law is the concern firstly of the Muslim Religious Council at Kibuli, near Kampala, " which has certain rather nebulous functions ",[2] and in the last resort such cases go to the Protectorate courts under the Ordinance.[3] The only points worthy of note for our present purposes are that the Kabaka's courts are in the habit of sending matrimonial disputes between African Muslims, arising from marriages contracted under Islamic law, to the Council at Kibuli, and that all questions of inheritance, and guardianship arising out of such marriages are governed by customary law.[4]

Further, since this book is concerned with the customary law of one African people, I shall leave to more general treatises on comparative African law such topics as the desirability of the marriage state, the prime object of the procreation of children, the subordinate role of the marriage relationship, the non-equality between the sexes and the ease of dissolution in African marriage.[5]

TYPES OF MARRIAGE

Ganda customary marriage appears always to have been and still is polygamous,[6] but polygynous never polyandrous. Within that general category of polygynous marriage there have in the past been various types of Ganda customary marriage. The two

---

[1] P.C.R.O. 55 of 1938 upholding Lukiko Court Case 10 of 1938.
[2] J. N. D. Anderson, *Islamic Law in Africa*, p. 154, and H.C.Cr.C. (1909), *The Crown* v. *Alifairi Mahomed*, 1 U.L.R. 67; H.C. Matrimonial Cause (1916), *Abaidi Kiuka* v. *Abdulla Sekimwanyi*, 2 U.L.R. 238; P.C.R.O. 8 of 1923, *Masudi Kisasa* v. *Asumani Mivule* (unreported) and P.C.C.A. 3 of 1944, *Aisa Namatovu* v. *Abudalahamani Mivule* (unreported).
[3] Cap. 110.
[4] Anderson, *loc. cit.*
[5] See Chapter 7, below.
[6] Although there is a tradition, possibly inspired by Missions, that monogamy was the rule in the reign of the first Kabaka Kintu, that polygamy increased with contact with the Arabs in the last century and that, of course, since the advent of Christianity it has been reduced again.

main authorities on this subject are the White Father Gorju[1] and the Ex-Ssabalangira Ggomotoka.[1] Gorju writing in 1920 lists seven or eight main types of ancient Ganda marriage. Ggomotoka writing in 1934 lists only three main types. The decrease in varieties mentioned in those fifteen years is marked, even though Gorju is clearly describing institutions current at the end of the nineteenth century. For reasons which will soon become apparent there are nowadays at least two types of Ganda customary marriage.

The first type of customary marriage described by Ggomotoka[2] is marriage of choice (obufumbo obwesimire), that is truly legal marriage under customary law (obufumbo obwa Nnakateka). This type Gorju[3] also describes, calling it marriage by engagement (okwogereze or *mariage de fiancailles*). This has always been the predominant type of Ganda customary marriage and it remains so to this day. This type of marriage was in ancient time only possible between free Ganda, not between free and captured slave.[4]

The second type was in general a marriage of a girl by gift without her consent. Gorju subdivides this type in two—a donation by a chief to one of his peasants (obufumbo obuwumirize)[5] and secondly a gift by the girl's brother to a friend (okugabirwa).[6] There is some confusion here between the authorities because Ggomotoka[7] does not mention marriage by donation of a chief but does describe the second subdivision of this type, marriage arranged by the father or brother of a girl without her consent but styles it by the title which Gorju uses for the first subdivision, *obufumbo obuwumirize* (lit.= marriage by giving a girl to a man not her owner). The strong culture contact between the Ganda and Europeans and the consequent emancipation of Ganda women has caused this type of customary marriage in general to disappear.

The third type of customary marriage was termed by Ggomotoka[8] slavegirl's marriage (obufumbo obw'envuma) and was

---

[1] *Op. cit.* In the descriptions which follow I have added fresh material to their two accounts from my own researches.
[2] *Op. cit.*, p. 28.
[3] *Op. cit.*, p. 303.
[4] Ggomotoka, *ibid.*
[5] *Op. cit.*, p. 300.
[6] *Op. cit.*, p. 302.
[7] *Op. cit.*, p. 30.
[8] *Op. cit.*, p. 30.

subdivided by him into three, with which subdivisions Gorju[1] was in agreement.

The first subdivision consists of marriage by purchase (obugule). Even a free Ganda girl (omwana ow'ekika) could be so sold by her parents to satisfy a debt or a fine, although they might indicate their intention of buying her back in due course in which case she would be a mere pledge to the purchaser. Sometimes a girl would be sold by her brother without any stipulation but the true vendor was usually the kindred on the mother's side.[2] Ashe described this type of marriage as " the easiest way for an ordinary man to obtain a wife ".[3]

The second subdivision was the straight-forward capture of a wife by plundering (okunyaga), either captured by the intending spouse or given to him by the leader of the expedition.

The third subdivision was the kidnapping and taking to wife of a girl found in a forest or by a spring (okuwuya). Accordingly in ancient times a woman never left the confines of the village unescorted or she might be seized by the first comer (kukwata mmomboze). Her family might ransom her by giving her captor a she-goat or her clansmen might combine together and raid her ravisher's village.

All these three variations of slavegirl's marriage (obufumbo obw'envuma) have now become extinct although Ggomotoka records that wives who had been kidnapped were still to be seen in the reign of the late Kabaka Chwa.

This is a convenient point to mention, not another type of marriage as Ggomotoka[4] would have us think, but a method by which a woman married as a slavegirl by one of three variations just mentioned could convert her marriage into a marriage of choice (obufumbo obwesimire), the first type described above and, as Ggomotoka explains, more highly respected than any other type of marriage. The method of conversion, which is also referred to by Gorju,[5] is termed treating one's relatives-in-law with disrespect (okuweebuula obuko), and took effect in the following manner: if the woman discovered her relations, she would leave her husband and return to them for a while. Then

---

[1] *Op. cit.*, p. 299.
[2] Gorju, *ibid.* See Chapter 7, below, for explanation of the custom of *endobolo.*
[3] *Life in Uganda*, p. 285.
[4] *Op. cit.*, p. 30.
[5] *Op. cit.*, p. 299.

if both parties wished to convert the marriage into one of choice (obufumbo obwesimire), the man would take a gourd of banana beer, the traditional gift, to the woman's brethren and the usual ceremony[1] and the payment of marriage consideration (ebintu by'obuko) would follow. Thereafter the wife was no longer a slave (envuma) but free.

The remaining four types of marriage are described by Gorju, but not by Ggomotoka, and are as follows:

The fourth type of customary marriage was marriage by abduction (endola)[2] and while it is similar to the third sub-division of a slavegirl's marriage already described, namely kidnapping and taking to wife a girl (okuwuya), is to be distinguished in that a girl married in that manner was a slave (envuma) while a girl abducted was free. Such a marriage took place when the girl's relatives and in particular her father opposed the marriage. The suitor would lie in wait for her with a band of his friends and carry her off. The girl was treated as an affianced bride and was repeatedly anointed with butter as a proper bride is treated. Her brother could drag her back but rarely did so, for often the girl had been abducted with his connivance. The usual practice was for the youth then to place cowrie shells (nsimbi nganda) on the doorstep of the girl's parents to indicate she had been abducted and then her parents and his consulted together and fixed the marriage consideration. This type of marriage has long since disappeared.

The fifth type of customary marriage was marriage by inheritance (okusikira),[3] that is, the leviratic remarriage of the deceased's wives by the heir. Prior to an edict of Muteesa I,[4] the heir used to be the deceased's brother and he invariably succeeded to all the deceased's wives and had the pick of the deceased's slavegirls (envuma), the rest being apportioned among his family. The deceased's wives *ipso facto* became the heir's wives under customary law without any further ceremonies. After Muteesa's edict that the heir was to be selected from among the children of the deceased, it would have been an act of abomination (kivve) for the son who inherited to marry any wife of his deceased father who had borne children as under universal African custom she stood in the relation of mother to

---

[1] See below, p. 88.
[2] Gorju, *op. cit.*, p. 301.
[3] *Ibid.*
[4] Of which more anon in Chapter 11, below.

him. Accordingly thereafter the heir only took to wife those of his father's wives who had not borne children. This type of marriage is obsolescent not the least for economic reasons.

The sixth type of customary marriage is that which occurs on the death of a wife who had borne her husband children.[1] The deceased woman's kindred substituted a younger sister or other female relative to be the widower's wife and to assist him to rear the children. This custom of marrying the deceased's younger sister or female relative arose from oral or later written testament of the deceased whereby she chose the girl to succeed her as her heiress and instructed her to take her place as wife of the widower and as guardian of her children. No bridewealth was paid nor were any matrimonial ceremonies performed but the husband could afterwards give the traditional gourd of beer and presents to his brother-in-law. Even if there was no direction to that effect in the deceased's testament her heiress often married the widower in this manner. Alternatively the family of the deceased may assist the widower to get himself a wife in their clan but in that event the normal ceremonies take place and bridewealth, albeit possibly reduced, is paid. This type of customary marriage still obtains.

The seventh type of customary marriage is termed by Gorju additional marriage (okwongerwa).[2] This type of marriage took place when the father or brother of the first wife gave the husband *de cursu temporis* another wife. It might also occur, Gorju states, when a brother-in-law violated his sister-in-law.

So much for the various types of Ganda customary marriage which have existed and in a few cases still do exist. It will be convenient to deal with three other kinds of sexual union.

Firstly concubinage is said to have started in Buganda at the beginning of the nineteenth century on introduction by Luzige, a chief of Buddu.[3] Foreign slaves became his concubines (abazaana). The institution rapidly spread but, of course, disappeared with the abolition of slavery at the end of the same century. The female children of concubines were classed as slavegirls (envuma).

The second institution is that of lovers (abaganzi or emikwano). There was an ancient institution whereby a man could have a permissible love affair with an estranged wife who had returned

---

[1] Gorju, *op. cit.*, p. 301.
[2] *Op. cit.*, p. 302.
[3] Gorju, *op. cit.*, p. 303.

to her family. The procedure was for the would-be lover to give the woman's brother the traditional gourd of beer, which in this connection was given the special name of " Kigula luggi " (lit. = it opens the door). The lover was then accepted by the woman's family; any children born of the union ranked equally with his other children; and the affair was terminable on either side, more particularly if the woman remarried another man. In such an event the *kigula luggi* (gourd of beer) was not, of course returnable. It was open to the lovers to legalize their relationship by a subsequent marriage under customary law but in such an event the usual ceremonies took place and marriage consideration was paid. Nowadays such irregular unions are as common if not more so than before.[1]

Lastly two persons married under Ganda customary law but then divorced may subsequently reunite but their reunion takes the form of resuming a love affair. No new marriage consideration is paid even if it had been returned on the divorce, and no ceremonies mark the reunion. It is usual, however, for the man to give his former brother-in-law the traditional gourd of beer and a cock.

Finally certain special procedures were followed in the case of marriage of chiefs and *a fortiori* of the Kabaka. Chiefs' courtyards in ancient Buganda served as educational establishments. A peasant sent a boy or girl to " the chief's fence " (ekisakaate) to be educated in wisdom and good manners. Later if such a girl as she grew up took the chief's fancy he would marry her but paid no marriage consideration. He would send presents to her parents in the shape of a goat, a *kanzu* (white cotton robe for a man) and a barkcloth (olubugo—woman's traditional attire) and the girl became his wife.

> " When the Kabakas wished to marry in the accepted sense, they went through the usual routine of first of all making an offering of beer to the girl's parents."[2]

Not so Roscoe,[3] who describes how the King married certain wives for various offices, often from among the princesses, but was not expected to take them to his couch and other wives from any clan that he desired, without going through the marriage ceremonies.

---

[1] See Southall and Gutkind, *op. cit., passim.*
[2] J. F. Cunningham, *Uganda and its peoples*, 1905, p. 232.
[3] *Op. cit.*, pp. 84–87.

CAPACITY TO MARRY

Personal Capacity

A youth has the capacity to marry under Ganda customary law on reaching the age of puberty (olutuula lw'ekirevu). It is Ganda custom to reckon a girl's age by the development of her breasts:

at 12 to 13 years the breasts appear (amabeere gasuna);

at 14 to 15 years the breasts are like fists (amabeere ga bikonde);

at 16 years the breasts appear kneeling down (amabeere gafukamira);

and soon thereafter the breasts hang down (amabeere gabunduka).

In ancient times a girl was put in a man's charge as his servant at 8–10 years of age but the man did not marry her until her breasts appeared (amabeere gasuna). He then could bring the traditional gourd of beer to the girl's paternal aunt (ssenga) with a view to betrothal. The proper age for a girl to marry was when her breasts were like fists (amabeere ga bikonde). It was an abomination (kivve) to have sexual intercourse with a girl before her puberty.

Prohibited degrees

The general rule prohibiting endogamy within the clan has already been mentioned.[1] The only authorised exceptions are princes and princesses who marry within the Princely (Ekirangira) Clan if they wish, though not within the same family, and the Lungfish (Mmamba) Clan, which was so large that a prohibition of endogamy on a clan basis was too onerous, and marriages between persons belonging to different sub-clans (amasiga) within that clan have been always permitted. It is sometimes said that other clans practised endogamy and the Bush-buck (Ngabi) and Civet Cat (Ffumbe) are mentioned. The explanation in the case of the Bushbuck Clan appears to be that many of the surrounding tribes have the same totem and a Ganda of that clan could marry a Nyoro or Soga of the same totem with impunity. Again an apparent endogamy within the clan would often be a marriage between persons of different clans which had joined together.[2] Roscoe tells us that:

" Sexual intercourse with a member of the same clan (kive), or with a woman of the mother's clan, was punished by the death of

---

[1] See p. 73, above.
[2] See list in Roscoe, *op. cit.*, p. 140.

both parties, because they were considered to have brought the god's displeasure on the whole clan."[1]

It does appear, however, that often a man who knowingly had sexual intercourse with a woman of his clan was expelled from the clan as he was shown to intend to expel her from their clan.[2]

Nowadays endogamy within a clan has been practically eliminated but when on rare occasions it occurs and is tried by the clan council the offender is usually fined six hundred shillings.

In the last passage quoted from Roscoe above it is stated further that not only was endogamy within one's own clan, that is one's father's clan, prohibited but also a man was forbidden to marry a woman of his mother's clan.[3] The reason is summed up in the Ganda proverb:

Ebikoja bo teva wa luvovo—Everyone who comes from there you call mother.
This restriction still has validity.

> " If a man had sexual relations with his father's sister (Sengawe), or with women termed his Kizibwewe, or called Mwana, he was called Kive, and put to death."[4]

In other words that restriction was, and is, on marriage of a man with his paternal aunt (ssenga) or with that aunt's daughters (Kizibwewe) or with any member of the extended family who stood in the relation of a child to him, such as his step-daughter or his wife's sister's daughter. He could, however, marry and often did his wife's sisters even in his wife's lifetime but not his mother-in-law nor his wife's paternal aunt.

The Ganda count it incestuous to have sexual relations with one's mother, sister[5] or daughter and always have done.[6]

A man can marry his brother-in-law's daughter but as his first wife is her paternal aunt (ssengawe) the second wife cannot use the same basin or bed as the first or even enter her room.

A man cannot marry a wife from the same family as that from which his son married a wife.

---

[1] Roscoe, *op. cit.*, p. 262.
[2] *Pace* Mair, *op. cit.*, p. 79.
[3] See also Roscoe, *op. cit.*, p. 128, Gorju, *op. cit.*, p. 279 and Sir Apolo Kagwa, *Empisa*, p. 178.
[4] Roscoe, *op. cit.*, p. 132 and Gorju, *ibid.*
[5] *Pace* Mair, *op. cit.*, p. 79.
[6] See below, Chapter 17.

The institution of blood-brotherhood brought in a restriction additional to the restrictions of consanguinity and affinity listed above. A blood-brother kept his original totem but acquired a second one thereby restricting his possibilities of marrying into his blood-brother's clan. Apparently this restriction applied in the main to the blood-brother's paternal aunt; it was permissible to marry his sister; and the children of the blood-brothers could intermarry.[1]

There were no professional restrictions on marriage.

PRELIMINARIES OF MARRIAGE

Marriage Negotiations

In ancient times the first step in any marriage was a consultation between the families of the potential spouses. The agreement of both families to the marriage was of paramount importance for the parties themselves were only consulted much later at the betrothal.[2]

In the nineteenth century in Buweekula Ssaza in particular and up to the present time in Buganda generally child betrothal (that is marriage by agreement of the parents of minor children), has been and is still practised. The marrige consideration is not fixed in those negotiations and therefore is not paid at the time. Some presents are usually sent by the father of the boy to the family of the girl with attention to the girl's upbringing. If one of the children dies then all fails and presents are not returned (bya mpuna).

Betrothal

It is difficult, if not impossible, to dissect the various elements of negotiations, consents and betrothal into separate sections and I accordingly propose to describe the ancient, recent and modern methods of betrothal in Ganda customary marriage, drawing attention to departures in practice which have been evolved with the years.

Ancient betrothal started, as explained above, with a consultation between the parents of the prospective parties. If this consultation went well, the youth was sent to do some tradi-

---

[1] Gorju, *op. cit.*, p. 279.
[2] *Pace* Mair, *op. cit.*, p. 78.

tional services for the girl's father, such as cutting wood, brewing beer or lighting his pipe, to show that he was properly brought up, of good manners and obedient. If that test was successfully completed, the girl's paternal aunt and the youth's father consulted together and thereafter two or three sureties (abayima) were demanded of the youth's family by the girl's father to consult together to ascertain whether there was any blemish in the youth which might vitiate the marriage. If those sureties were not obtained, the negotiations broke down. If they were obtained, they undertook that the youth would defend the girl from attack. Finally the youth sent a complete goat quartered in baskets to the girl's father to share with his future relatives-in-law.

In the recent period, that is, in this century, the man having met the girl of his fancy sent four letters, containing his proposal of marriage and enclosing money, to the girl's father (15/– to 20/–), and to her paternal aunt, to her brother and to her mother (10/– each). If the girl's father, after consulting with his sister, accepted the letter and cash he was understood to have accepted the man as his prospective son-in-law. Sometimes the man then sent 20 lbs. of meat, 10 lbs. of sugar, 4 lbs. of salt and 1 lb. of tea to the girl's father in a large basket by hand of one of his friends. The man then went to one of the girl's paternal aunts, selected by the girl, and introduced himself and gave her a present of a kind that was likely to please her. He also gave presents to the girl's brother and paternal uncle. The paternal aunt and brother of the girl then selected a day on which to introduce the man to the girl's parents. Thereafter the man sent his bride-to-be her trousseau consisting of a cloth garment (suka or bodingi), a hip-cloth (kitambi), a length of cloth about three yards long (kitambala), all comprising the native dress (bisuti), a vest, a handkerchief and a bar of soap. Finally the man went to be introduced to his prospective relatives-in-law taking with him two or three or more calabashes of beer, valued at ten shillings each, of which one was given to the girl's brother together with a *kanzu*, a second was given to the girl's father and possibly a third to her mother. The presents given by the man to the various relatives of the girl varied according to their particular tastes and might be in the form of a cash substitute (*e.g.* to Muslims who do not drink intoxicants).

It will be observed on comparing the above two procedures that in ancient times there was no introduction of the youth to the girl's parents for he was well-known to them before they took the first step of consulting with his parents. Girls were not in those days married to youths of unknown families. The second important difference is that sureties were not demanded in the recent method but instead each party had a friend as his sponsor (mujulirwa) who was called upon to relate each party's previous habits and to bear some responsibility in time of dispute. The third important development was the substitution of letters enclosing cash for the quartered goat, although sometimes recently the man provided meat and other edibles for the girl's family. Finally the provision of the girl's trousseau by the youth was unknown in ancient times.

To resume the description of the recent method of betrothal, the introduction of the man to the girl's family was the main ceremony. The man went along with his calabashes of beer to the girl's home, where her relatives were gathered. The girl's paternal aunt introduced the youth. The relatives then asked the girl if they should drink and on her agreeing poured out the beer. The girl's paternal aunt then offered some beer to the prospective bridegroom who drank and handed the cup to the girl. If the girl drank and handed it to her brother saying " Drink this beer " (Omwenge guguno munywe) she showed herself agreeable to the marriage. Afterwards all drank, thereby giving their formal consent to the match, while the girl herself left her father and brother to fix the marriage consideration.

The beer-drinking ceremony was the formal act of betrothal and was also legally binding.[1] To this act the husband would refer back in after life, if there arose any question as to the legality of the marriage.[2]

The recent method of betrothal just described, which originated early in this century, is still practised, although there is a modern innovation in the number of letters sent by the man, the addresses to whom he sends them and the amount of cash enclosed with each. Nowadays three letters are sent by him— the first to the girl herself enclosing a sum in cash ranging from twenty to one hundred and fifty shillings, the second to her paternal aunt with ten to forty shillings cash and the third to her brother with ten to thirty shillings.

A new method of betrothal has arisen in modern times whereby

---

[1] P.C.R.O. 88 of 1933, Lukiko Court Case 194 of 1933, *Yakuze* v. *Kitamirike* (unreported) (in which two Ministers gave evidence of the significance of this act of betrothal).

[2] Roscoe, *op. cit.*, pp. 88 and 97.

the youth who is attracted to a girl asks her if she will agree to marry him. If the girl is agreeable, she tells her paternal aunt or her brother or her elder sister and they tell the girl's father. Meanwhile the youth tells his own father and relatives. If the girl's father agrees, the girl's father or her aunt summon the youth through the agency of the girl to go to see the girl's father. The youth then goes with his paternal aunt to a meeting with the girl's father, mother, brother, paternal aunt and the girl herself. They pay their visit and return home. Thereupon the girl's family take counsel and either approve or reject the youth. If they approve, the girl tells the youth to bring the first presents which consist of a basket of meat and a packet of salt (1–5 lbs.) and sometimes curry-powder and sometimes sugar. The girl's relatives ask her if they should eat. If the girl signifies in the affirmative, she thereby shows that she still wants to marry the youth. The girl's family partake of the food brought and the youth thereby learns that he has been accepted as a prospective bride-groom. He returns home and writes the letters enclosing the cash, as recounted above.

Then the girl and the youth consult as to the day for his formal introduction to the girl's family and the youth either buys the girl the native dress (bisuti) as described above but with the addition of a tablet of bathsoap, as well as the bar of washing soap, or gives her eighty to one hundred shillings for her to buy her trousseau herself.

On the day of introduction, the youth and his friends go to meet the girl's brother at the latter's home where he waits with his friends and where the girl sits at one side with her paternal aunts. One of the girl's paternal aunts catches hold of the youth and introduces him to the girl's brother saying " This is the man whom I am going to marry." The girl's brother replies " Give me beer." One of the two gourds of beer is brought from the side where they had been left. The girl's brother drinks and then asks for beer for the girl's father; the youth supplies at least one more gourd of beer but often many more.

After betrothal the girl's brother is responsible to the pro-spective bridegroom for the wellbeing of his sister and must exercise precautions to ensure that his sister retains her virginity until the marriage.[1] Should the girl become pregnant by another man after betrothal the match can be dissolved.

---

[1] P.C.R.O. 18 of 1929, *Mayanja* v. *Bamulondere* (unreported).

E

MARRIAGE PAYMENTS

Definitions

It will be as well to define the terms about to be employed:[1]

" marriage consideration " means the amount fixed in the marriage contract for payment by the man to the girl's family before the marriage can take place. (The old terms used to describe this item were " bride-price " or " bride-wealth ");

" collateral gifts " means gifts of lesser items given under custom by the man to members of the girl's family whether before or after the marriage ceremony;

" reciprocal gifts " means gifts given by members of the girl's family to the bridal pair.[2]

Ancient marriage consideration

The first account that we have of the financial implications of a Ganda customary marriage is given by the missionary Ashe, writing in 1889:

> " Indeed matrimony in Buganda is not generally an affair of much romance, but rather a question of driving a bargain. The parents receive in return for their daughter, purchase money or ' Kasimu ', which usually consists of cows or cowrie shells or other barter goods; and the bridegroom also provides quantities of banana cider and goats' flesh for the wedding feast. If the Kasimu has been duly paid, there is no further difficulty, and after the feast the bridegroom takes his wife to his own home. The rich and powerful are not, as far as I am aware, obliged to pay any Kasimu. Sub-chiefs and peasants are only too happy to give their ' bawala ' (daughters) for nothing to a powerful patron, and woe betide them if they neglect to do so."[3]

The fixing of the marriage consideration in fact took place immediately after the betrothal ceremony but in the absence of the girl. Roscoe recounts:[4]

> " The next step was to call together some of the clan, and to settle with them what amount the suitor should pay in dowry for the girl. They might demand any sum from one to ten goats, or even ask a cow. In addition to the animals, ten pots of beer and several barkcloths were demanded. The animals and cowry-shells were difficult to obtain, and represented a large sum to a poor person so that it took him a long time to collect them."

---

[1] The first two terms were coined by Dr. A. N. Allott.

[2] One might have used the term " dowry " in this connection but it has so deep a European association and has so often been used as a synonym for bride-wealth that I have used another expression.

[3] *Op. cit.*, p. 285.

[4] *Op. cit.*, p. 88.

In fact it has always been the girl's brother who has acted as the agent for the girl's father in fixing the marriage consideration.[1]

It is Ggomotoka[2] who first makes the clear distinction between the two parts of the marriage consideration: there were firstly the gifts for the relatives-in-law (ebintu by'obuko), consisting of the calabashes of beer and three barkcloths, being one each for the girl's father, paternal aunt and mother, salt and goat's flesh, and secondly the sum in hard cash (then termed " akasimo "). Ggomotoka states that in the days of florins—in the first quarter of this century—a poor man would pay one hundred florins and a rich man or a chief as much as one thousand florins. Both Ggomotoka and Sir Apolo Kagwa agree that the custom was for the parents of the girl to return part (generally the major part) of this cash payment to the man to indicate that their girl, the bride, was free and not a sold slave-girl.

By the 1930's the cost of the gifts to the girl's relatives, according to Ggomotoka, had been increased to one hundred to three hundred or more shillings as compared with their overall cost of twenty shillings twenty years before.[3] The same author states[4] that the goods that the husband had to pay on conversion of the marriage from the slave-girl type to the marriage of choice (okuweebula obuko),[5] which consisted of two calabashes of beer, a large goat and two good barkcloths cost, presumably in the early 1930's, thirty-four to forty-five shillings on the basis that a calabash of beer cost two shillings, such a goat twenty shillings and barkcloths five shillings a piece.[6] Harking back a century and a half, Gorju[7] recounts that in the reign of the Kabaka Kamanya (1800–1810) a Ganda woman was valued at sixty cowry shells.

The draft native law, 1903

This appears to be a convenient point to mention a draft native law, which was revised and passed by the Lukiko at

---

[1] Sir Apolo Kagwa, *Empisa*, p. 172 and *pace* Mair, p. 81, I am informed that 97 out of 100 educated Ganda did not leave the fixing of the marriage consideration to the suitor's inclinations.

[2] *Op. cit.*, p. 25.

[3] For a comparison of costings in actual cases see p. 96 below.

[4] *Op. cit.*, p. 30.

[5] See above, p. 80.

[6] Compare modern prices below p. 93.

[7] *Op. cit.*, Footnote to p. 306.

Mengo on the 18th March, 1903, on the subject of marriage customs and procedure. Its main provisions were:[1]

Clause 1. The procedure for introducing the man to the girl's family and for the fixing of the brideprice; procedure when wife deserts.

Clause 2. The procedure for the return of " dowry " (= marriage consideration) and dissolution of marriage.

Clause 3. Marriage consideration fixed for chief when he married and rights of such a wife to leave stated.

Clause 4. Rights of peasants to desert stated.

Clause 5. Monogamy declared the rule and a monetary scale substituted instead of marriage consideration according to man's status.

Clause 6. The registration of marriage and its effects stipulated as regards an absconding wife.

Clause 7. Exceptions in respect of Muhammadan marriage defined.

Clause 8. Fine to be paid for paying excess marriage consideration or penalty of forfeiture for demanding exorbitant marriage consideration but permitting free gifts to the wife's relatives after some time as sign of affection.

Clause 9. Men not to marry under twenty years of age and girls to be at least seventeen years of age and virgins at marriage.

This draft native law never received official sanction and so never acquired the force of law.[2] For the most part the draft does not state Ganda customary law but is rather in the nature of a statement of the Lukiko's opinion as to what that law ought to be. It appears that the principal object of this draft law was to reduce and stabilise the amount of marriage consideration paid. Prior to 1900 the usual amount had been three or four rupee's worth of cowry shells but after the imposition of hut tax the parent of a marriageable daughter put the amount up to fifteen or twenty rupees. The amount of marriage consideration for a peasant proposed in the draft law was ten rupees in all or thirteen shillings and four pence sterling.[3]

---

[1] See J. F. Cunningham, *Uganda and its Peoples*, 1904, pp. 148 *et seq.*, where the full text of the English translation is given.

[2] Cunningham, *op. cit.*, p. 164 but *pace* MacQueen, *In Wildest Africa*, p. 343.

[3] *Ibid.*

Modern marriage consideration

The time for the fixing of the marriage consideration is still immediately the formal betrothal has been made by the drinking of beer and the bride's brother is still the relative who is charged by her father with the duty of fixing the amount.[1] In reality the girl's father may select a mere friend of the family to do this task and style him " the girl's brother " (mwanyina w'omuwala). Generally the girl's father gives his appointed agent instructions in this matter.

The modern marriage consideration, as the ancient, is divided into two parts—the gifts for the girl's relatives (ebintu by'obuko) and the sum in hard cash (now called " omutwalo ").[2] The gifts (ebintu by'obuko) are standardized as follows:

one prime goat	@	150/–
barkcloth for girl's mother	@	80/–
kanzu for girl's father	@	70/–
kanzu for girl's brother	@	50/–
barkcloth for girl's paternal aunt	@	30/–
2–4 gourds of beer @ 10/– ea, say		20/–
	at least	400/–

There is no limit to the amount of cash (omutwalo) which can be demanded and the social position of the parties does not affect the rates sought. Usually it is a sum between one hundred and fifty and three hundred shillings. The whole marriage consideration, that is the gifts (ebintu b'obuko) and the cash sum (omutwalo), is rather confusingly termed itself " omutwalo ".

Thereupon, immediately the marriage consideration has been fixed, on the same day a marriage contract (endagaano) is drawn up containing:

the names of the parties;
the names of the parents of the girl;
the marriage consideration;
the time limit for payment;
the names of witnesses;
the signature of the girl's brother;
the signature of the witness of the girl's family;
the signature of the man;
the signature of the man's witness.

---

[1] P.C.Cr.C. 461 of 1958. *Lukiko* v. *Bazanganengo and Another*, 1958, C.L.R. 101.

[2] The term " akasimo " now is used of the live goat sent by the bridegroom to the bride's parents as a collateral gift in gratitude for finding her a virgin—see p. 98 below.

Then there is a consultation between those present at the signing of the marriage contract as to responsibility for paying certain incidental expenditure to be incurred at the marriage ceremony. It is the invariable rule that the bridegroom shall pay the photographer who is engaged to photograph the bridal pair. There is, however, no fixed rule as to who pays for the bride's conveyance (okusiba mugole) which head of expenditure involves the provision of at least one vehicle and the decking of and presents for the bridesmaids (emperekeze).[1] The bridegroom may undertake to pay particularly if he is a rich young man who wishes to do it in style, or, if the girl's family are wealthy, they may undertake responsibility in the matter. It remains nevertheless the bridegroom's responsibility to provide the bride with her trousseau which nowadays consists of a western-style dress (ekiteeyiteeyi). Also it is usually the bridegroom's lot to foot the bill for the wedding feast unless the bride's father is rich and undertakes to do so.

If a dispute arises subsequently concerning the marriage consideration and that dispute comes before the Kabaka's courts, the practice now is to follow strictly the terms of the written marriage contract as regards any return of marriage consideration and if the gifts to the girl's relatives (ebintu by'obuko) are not written into that contract then they are not ordered to be returned.[2] The marriage contract can be sued upon by the man if the girl's family refuse afterwards to allow the marriage but cannot be sued upon by them if the marriage consideration remains unpaid within the period fixed, usually three months. In such an event, unless the girl's family see fit to extend the period, the marriage contract is avoided. The practice is for the father of the girl to summon the man and if the latter confesses himself unable to pay then the girl's family return him his presents and the value of the beer.

A man can be exempted from the payment of marriage consideration, and such exemption occurs frequently if he is a well-mannered youth or a friend of the girl's family or on the grounds that the woman has already borne his children in a love affair.

A youth was usually helped by all his relatives in ancient times to collect the marriage consideration (okumuzimbira amaka =

---

[1] Usually there are two or three bridesmaids who get a traditional present of a " simoni " (= 50 cents) but nowadays they usually receive two shillings each.

[2] P.C.C.C. 264 of 1956, *Magezi* v. *Mutegombwa and Another*, 1957, C.L.R. 143.

lit. to build him a home) but was never so assisted by them or by his blood-brothers after his first marriage.[1] Nowadays his father or his brother may help him as regards his first marriage if they see fit. Likewise if a landlord has a tenant of good behaviour whom he likes he may assist him to pay the marriage consideration. It is, however, only the bridegroom himself who can sue for the return of the marriage consideration, not the person who assisted him nor the bridegroom's heir.

The bridegroom may take the marriage consideration himself or may send it by hand of a friend (kibona muko) in which case the bearer becomes his witness. There is no ceremony of handing over the marriage consideration but the girl's father endorses the marriage contract as paid and a definite date for the marriage is thereupon agreed.

The marriage consideration is received by the girl's father and he distributes it as he sees fit to the girl's relatives, particularly the maternal uncles. If the girl's father is dead, then his heir stands in his shoes as regards receipt or return of marriage consideration.

Either party may renounce the other after betrothal without giving reasons and thereupon presents given are returned. Sorcery was the main but not the only reason which justified a girl formerly in breaking off her betrothal.[2] Other grounds were that the youth was a thief or, of course, that the marriage consideration was not paid. If the man or the girl dies after part payment of marriage consideration, whatever has been paid is returned to the bridegroom, if bereaved, or his family, if he died. If the girl becomes pregnant by another man subsequent to the marriage contract but before the marriage, then the man can sue for the return of all the presents given by him to that date; and formerly this was the only ground on which he could get the presents back. It is, in fact, unusual for him to carry on and marry the girl.

For completeness, mention should again be made[3] of the customary law to the effect that an heir who married the deceased's widow does not pay a second marriage consideration. Nor can an heir sue for the return of the marriage consideration if the deceased's widow chooses to return to her family.

---

[1] *Pace* Mair, *op. cit.*, p. 83.
[2] *Pace* Mair, *op. cit.*, p. 81.
[3] See p. 81 above.

If either spouse dies, there is no return of the marriage consideration. If a wife becomes mad or incurably sick in body then the husband cannot reclaim the marriage consideration.

The question of ordering the return of marriage consideration has come before the Buganda courts from time to time and the following selection of cases may indicate the trend of the decisions:

order for return of part of marriage consideration owing to refusal of conjugal rights (total of Florins 71/60 allowed);[1]

order for return of presents after girl declined to marry (total of Shs. 73/50 allowed);[2]

order for return of money spent on preparations for marriage and for return of marriage consideration after bride declined three days before marriage due to be solemnized in Church (total of Shs. 860/75 allowed);[3]

order for recovery of expenses incurred on refusal of betrothed girl to marry;[4]

refusal of order for return of expenses incurred for conveying bride to church and in preparing marriage feast after bride refused to marry man before priest.[5]

The remaining collateral and reciprocal gifts will be described in the following section as they occur in the ceremonies.

MARRIAGE CEREMONIES AND FORMALITIES

The wedding day usually takes place about two to three weeks after the payment of the marriage consideration, but during the week prior to the wedding the ceremony of " smearing the bride with butter " is performed (okumusiiga omuzigo). The girl's sister or paternal aunt smears her with butter and then washes her. The girl is then decked in barkcloth by her paternal aunt and is called " omugole " (bride). During this period the bride is fed on the best food—such as meat and mushrooms—and is supplied with all requisites—such as soap. At this time she must not speak to any man outside her family.

On the evening of the day before the wedding day the man takes a calabash of beer to the girl's home called " kasuze katya "

---

[1] P.C.R.O. 10 of 1923, *Malimbo* v. *Alideki* (unreported).

[2] P.C.R.O. 48 of 1936, *Kapere* v. *Mumpi* (unreported).

[3] P.C.C.C. 58 of 1946, *Kasule* v. *Nakuya and Others*, 1940–1955 C.L.R.

[4] P.C.C.C. 167 of 1953, *Sewalu* v. *Musajakawa*, mainly upheld by SHERIDAN, J. in H.C.C.A. 40 of 1955, see Notes, p. 71.

[5] P.C.C.C. 18 of 1955, *Magunda* v. *Bunnya*, 1956 C.L.R. 75.

(good morning to you), and returns home. It is intended to ease the parting of the girl from her parents. This custom has now somewhat changed for teetotal-cum-religious reasons and often money or a four gallon tin of paraffin and a couple of boxes of matches are substituted for the beer.

That night the appropriate clan drum-beat (omubala) is beaten on the drums. The bride's mother goes and cuts grass for the floor of the house (etteete). She also ties pieces of thorn tree (akasaana) in the grass and puts one such log (kasiki) in the fire-place and lights it. Another she places in the doorway (ak'omuziziko) for people to step over. Thereafter there is dancing and singing of ribald songs (ennyimba z'abalongo).

On the wedding morning the bride fetches water and wood for her parents. Afterwards her father and mother sit in the living-room and she sits first on her father's knees and is told to be faithful. She then sits on her mother's knees and is advised in her wifely duties (okubulirira empisa z'obufumbo). Then there is a feast partaken of by all relatives and friends and consisting of simsim, mushrooms and ntuula (a kind of egg plant). The bride is thereupon smeared with butter and leaves home for the last time.

The bride's brother and paternal aunt take her in the company of many friends and to the drumming of the *omubala* to the man's house on foot very slowly. The parents of the bride stay at home and drink beer, including the *kasuze katya*, with friends. In olden times the bridal procession used to set out in the evening but nowadays it usually takes place about 2 p.m. and sometimes as early as 10 a.m. Two bridesmaids (emperekeze), usually her sisters or friends, accompany the bride.

The bridegroom too has a party of friends and relatives who set out slowly to meet the bridal procession. As the parties approach each other, emissaries are sent from each side to pay respects.

When the parties have met the bride's brother demands a cock (mpanga) from the groom. The groom's best man (katikkiro w'omulenzi) hands the bridegroom a cock or a ten-shilling note in lieu to give to his future brother-in-law. The latter warns the bridegroom not to strike the bride but to take any dispute between them to himself to settle. The bride thereupon kneels down (okufukamira). The bride's brother then with his right hand joins the right hands of the bridegroom and bride. The bridegroom then raises up the bride and they enter their home amid general clapping and escorted by the bride's paternal aunt, who is distinguishable by her slung barkcloth and the knife which she carries. The brother-in-law joins the feast in the temporary booth that is customarily erected (kidaala) and there is applause, dancing and rejoicing on all sides. Nowadays the bride usually sits outside for a bit but in ancient times the bridegroom's sisters used to take her, accompanied by the paternal aunt, straight to the bridal chamber.

Apart from the cock (mpanga) the brother-in-law also receives a calabash of beer as a present from the bridegroom. The bridegroom also gives the bride's paternal aunt a barkcloth.

After the feast all depart leaving the newly-wed pair, except the bride's paternal aunt who stays the night to check that the bride is a virgin and the bridegroom potent. In the morning the aunt examines the bed-linen and if she finds it blood-stained she folds it up and goes to show the girl's parents that their daughter was a virgin. It was the custom, if the bride was not a virgin, to cut a hole in the barkcloth on the bed and send it to the bride's parents; but not so now. The stained bed-clothes become the aunt's property.

If his bride is a virgin, the bridegroom takes a young she-goat (embuzi enduusi etezaalangako) as a present to the girl's parents and ties it up in the corner of their courtyard; he shouts " Thank you for looking after your daughter so well " and runs away without being seen. The bride's parents take the goat and eat it with the family elders (abakulu b'oluganda) on that very day and without salt. If they do not finish eating that goat that day, the residue must be hung up outside the house on a plantain until the morrow.

If the bridegroom is impotent, the bride leaves him and goes back to her family with her aunt. The bridegroom cannot in such circumstances reclaim the marriage consideration which is lost to him and the girl is free to marry again, the first marriage under customary law being null and void.

The allegation that the bridesmaid stayed with the bridal pair for four days and could sleep with the bridegroom and become pregnant by him without disgrace is completely untrue.[1]

After a period varying from six days to a month in the seclusion of her new home, the bride accompanied by her groom's sister returns to her parents carrying butter in a barkcloth. This

---

[1] *Pace* Mair, *op. cit.*, pp. 85–86.

is the ceremony of " restoring the butter " (okuzzayo muzigo). This ceremony is essential to the validity of the marriage:

> " Ce kudzayo omuzigo est d'absolue rigueur. Sans cette cérémonie préalable et ses rites, ni la mariée ni son époux ne sont admis à franchir le seuil de la hutte du père, et la mort éventuelle des enfants qui naîtront de ce mariage sera infailliblement attribuée à l'omission de ce rite: ' Elle n'a pas reporté le beurre '."[1]

The bride's parents meanwhile have collected a goat or a cow, chicken, plantains (matooke), mushrooms, simsim, groundnuts, salt and fish, if available, and give these foodstuffs to the bridegroom who goes home with his brother-in-law acting as the parents' emissary and his friends. Often these foodstuffs are more than three times the value of the marriage consideration paid. A bunch of plantains (Nakitembe) with the cock, bought by her mother, and mushrooms strapped on top is placed on a circular pad (nkaata) on the bride's head to carry to her new home. Her sister may lend her assistance on the way. On the bride's arrival at her new home, the bridegroom gives her a few cents and then, only he, lifts off the bundle from her head. She kneels down and with both hands gives the cock to her seated husband. The bride hangs on to the pad (nkaata) and fights for it against the bridegroom's brothers who eventually take it from her; the meaning being that the bride is now a prisoner and must not elope. The bridegroom must hand the cock to his brothers and they must cut its throat immediately—it cannot be allowed to sleep. The food is then cooked. The bridegroom eats of the cock and plantains boiled in their skin (empogola) first; his brothers help him finish the cock; the women eat the mushrooms. The bridal couple retire to bed and she then becomes his *mukyala* (lady).

The following morning the husband takes a cock to his brother-in-law and a feast takes place there.

Four or five days later the husband's father summons the young wife to cultivate. She goes with her husband's sister and cultivates. After a while her father-in-law takes some cents to her for the piece (lubimbi) of his plot which she has cultivated and they return together to his house. There he gives her a she-goat, a barkcloth and a hoe; her mother-in-law a knife and a basket. Thereupon they take food together and then she returns home.

---

[1] Gorju, *op. cit.*, p. 321.

The young wife's parents then prepare other reciprocal gifts and, when all is ready, send word or write to their son-in-law telling him to bring his wife " to come to fetch the wedding gifts " (okuddukira eby'okufumba). They go accompanied by the husband's sisters and brother. The wife's parents give the latter a cock and he eats it there. The prepared gifts consist of plantains, a goat castrated, which had produced kids or barren (ndawo, mugongo or nsata) but not a billy-goat, one without horns nor one with glands on the neck (ennume ey'ekirevu, ya mpumpu, or erina butunga), a cage of chickens, a full basket of meat, mushrooms, simsim, salt and beans. Again the cock (sseggwanga) is placed on the young wife's head that she may give it to her husband. Her parents say goodbye to her on the doorstep of their house. Her paternal aunt is mistress of this ceremony (omukulu w'omukoro ogwo). Her brother, aunt and many others accompany her to her husband arriving at night. The same ceremony as before of delivering the cock takes place and it is eaten the same night.

In the morning it is the husband's turn to give some more collateral gifts. First he gives his brother-in-law another cock and there is another feast there. Then he puts twenty to thirty shillings in the baskets in which the foodstuffs were brought from his wife's parents and returns them thither—if he is happy. His parents-in-law distribute that money to those who carried the wedding gifts to the young couple's home.

The last ceremony is when the bride's mother summons her daughter to her and buys a goat, simsim, salt and mushrooms which she sends to her new son-in-law. These gifts are called " envunulabibya ". Thereupon the girl becomes his legal wife.

Gutkind comments from his survey of Mulago village:

> " These marriages traditionally calling for elaborate ceremonial are to-day practised with a less conscious effort to maintain the traditions of the past."[1]

Customary marriage and the courts

The Buganda courts for many years did not recognise in full the capacity of any African, who had not contracted a subsisting marriage under Protectorate legislation, to contract a marriage under customary law. Indeed a circular, issued by the Minister of Justice in 1919, stated that a pagan (*sic*) who married under

---

[1] *Op. cit.*, p. 154 and see also p. 155.

native custom could invoke the provisions of the Adultery and Fornication Law, 1918.[1] What was happening, of course, was that professing Christians were marrying one wife under Protectorate legislation with Christian rites in a Church and were subsequently and bigamously contracting several customary marriages as the circular of the next Minister of Justice in 1923 makes clear.[2] In that very year indeed a plaintiff had the effrontery to sue for the return of marriage consideration paid in respect of his " marriage under native custom " of a second wife, who had deserted, when at the time of that second marriage he was living with his first wife whom he had married by Christian rites (*i.e.* under Protectorate legislation).[3] In 1930 the Minister of Justice went further and quite illegally tacked on to section 2 of the Adultery and Fornication Law a requirement that customary marriage must be legalised by registration before a District Commissioner.[4] It is hardly surprising, therefore, that in 1938 we find a magistrate opining:

> " The possession of baptismal names has apparently been taken as presumptive proof that the parties are professing Christians, and a marriage by native custom between such persons has been regarded as no marriage.
> The latter has long been the accepted interpretation of the law, in Buganda at least, and I am not prepared to interfere with it, though the presumption that a ' Christian ' name implies Christian beliefs does not appear to me to be a very safe one."[5]

Nor is it surprising that Mair in 1940 writes:

> " The wording of this law (*i.e.* the Adultery and Fornication Law) makes it applicable both to Christian and native customary marriages, but it is the definite policy of the native government to apply it only to the former."[6]

Following in this train Southall more recently wrote:

> " It is important for present purposes to note that tribal customary marriages are not recognised either in Buganda or Protectorate courts."[7]

---

[1] Circular of Omulamuzi Stanislaus Mugwanya, 6th May, 1919, approved by P.C. Buganda on 23rd April, 1919, paragraph 5.

[2] Order of Omulamuzi Andereya Kiwanuka of September 1923, approved by the Ag. P.C. Buganda and published in *Amateka ne Biragiro ebyatesebwa Olukiko Olukulu okuva* 1922—1923.

[3] P.C.R.O. 22 of 1923, *Kyakwambala* v. *Gyagenda* (unreported).

[4] Omulamuzi's Circular PF.69/30 of 6th September, 1930.

[5] P.C.R.O. 43 of 1938, *Kigozi* v. *Namubiru* (unreported).

[6] Native Marriage in Buganda, 1940, p. 8.

[7] *Op. cit.*, p. 68.

His co-author, Gutkind, took up a half-way position:

> " The bulk of the population contract tribal marriages which are recognised by native law but not by Protectorate law."[1]

In the face of all these administrative circulars and sociological opinions it is fitting to consider the decision in 1915 of BARRETT-LENNARD J., a Judge with West African experience also, when exercising criminal revisional jurisdiction in respect of a case arising in Busoga:[2]

> " The unions usual between heathen natives of tropical Africa, although generally described as marriages, are not such according to English or International law. They are polygamous in character and create only a casual relation which either party can terminate at pleasure subject to the obligation of making money payments.
>
> These unions are, however, recognised by the British Courts of tropical Africa whenever a question of status arises.
>
> This Court is required to accord such recognition as well by the terms of the Charter which created it, as by expressions contained in the local Ordinances."

In the last quinquennium the Kabaka's Courts also have come to appreciate that their previous attitude, due to religious influence, was erroneous and now recognise marriage under customary law.

Subsequent ceremony

Although for the last eighteen years at any rate no-one has taken advantage of the provision in the Marriage Ordinance[3] to convert a customary marriage into a marriage under Protectorate legislation, nevertheless many Ganda married under customary law nowadays for religious reasons go through a second ceremony in Church or Mosque, as the case may be. Such second ceremony may take place ten or even fifteen years after the original marriage of the parties under customary law. Before the second ceremony occurs, the woman's father may ask for a second marriage consideration of one hundred shillings. Either he or the woman's brother or both must sign a written agreement to the second ceremony which is then taken to the religious authority. There are no other formalities.

There is never an unofficial customary ceremony after a marriage under Protectorate law.

---

[1] *Op. cit.*, p. 154.
[2] *Rex* v. *Salima d/o Salimu and Another*, 2 U.L.R. 182.
[3] Cap. 109, section 30.

Registration

As has already been mentioned,[1] Clause 6 of the draft native law of 1903 proposed the registration of customary marriages. The procedure was to be for

> " every man to take his wife to the Owesaza, to be written down with her in the register of the Lukiko, so that she should not leave her husband. Every woman thus registered, if she leaves her husband and he brings the matter before the Lukiko, and the Lukiko sees she was properly registered, is compelled by it to return to her husband."[2]

Clause 8 went on to provide that if the woman's relatives

> " demand a greater price than that laid down in these laws, they shall be deprived of the amount to which they would have been entitled, and the Lukiko shall use this money for the work of the country; and the woman shall be written down with the man she wishes to marry, and shall be married to him. . . ."[3]

As has been already stated, that draft native law never reached the statute book and so the Lukiko's proposal for the registration of customary marriages was never implemented.

The matter was again raised in the Lukiko in 1948 by the then Katikkiro, Owekitiibwa M. E. Kawalya-Kagwa, when he proposed the registration at the Ggombolola level of native customary marriage between parties, Christian or non-Christian, who had never been married previously. A resolution was passed but never approved.

---

[1] See p. 92, above.
[2] Cunningham, *op. cit.*, p. 158.
[3] *Ibid.*, p. 162.

CHAPTER 7

FAMILY LAW

Husband and Wife

In ancient times the division of domestic authority and labour between husband and wife was much more distinct and detailed than it is to-day. The husband was responsible for waging war, barkcloth-making, hunting, working metal, building, cutting reeds and poles, making the chief's woven fence, brewing, cutting logs for the fire and sweeping the courtyard. The wife on the other hand was responsible for cultivating, cooking, fetching water, picking up firewood, collecting grass to strew in the house, cutting grass for the brewing of beer, threshing millet and pounding sponges of plantain stem.

Nowadays the husband as head of the household has entire domestic authority. He has to protect his wife and treat her kindly. He must provide her with a house, food, clothing and maintenance. If these basic amenities are not provided the wife waits at her parents' home until they are or if she has left there previously returns.

If a visitor comes to the house at night it is the wife's duty to call out asking him what he wants. But if an alarm is sounded. it is the husband's duty to answer it not the wife's.

The beating of wives was a time-honoured Ganda tradition[1] and among the more conservative families some of the customs connected with it still survive. In the nineteenth century the husband was expected to beat his wife if she failed in her domestic duties. Indeed if he did not beat her he was considered to spoil her and if she became pregnant before her husband had beaten her, her parents would say that the husband had not treated her properly. The Ganda proverb runs:

Okukuba omukazi si kumugoba—To beat wife is not to expel her.

If the wife was not beaten by her husband, she used to think

---

[1] See Sir Apolo Kagwa's statement at p. 26 of *Akatabo ke Biragiro na Mateka ebyatesebwa Olukiko Olukulu olwe Buganda okuva* 1916 *okutusa* 1919.

her husband did not love her. After being beaten by him, she next morning cooked plantains (ttooke) and mushrooms (butiko) for him as a special treat. However, if the wife ran away when her husband was about to beat her, the husband must not pursue her and if she retreated behind the hearth-stones the husband must throw down his stick. It is an abomination (omusango gw'ekivve) for the husband to get angry and strike his wife while she is preparing food. And if he does so strike her, he must make amends by buying her sprats (nkejje) and a barkcloth; the wife, to put an end to the affair must bring a mushroom (akatiko) and cook food which they eat together.

It was a matter of masculine honour never to admit being injured by one's wife. The husband must not be beaten by his wife. If she did so and drew blood on her husband then she must go to her parents and bring back a present of a cock (sseggwanga) and until she did she could not partake of food with her husband. A husband so beaten was called " ekikere " (a frog) by his fellows and was not allowed to appear thereafter, until his death, before the Kabaka or even a chief.

There were also conventions regarding the establishment of a polygynous household. The husband must tell his first wife (Kaddulubaale) when he was going to have a second wife (Kabejja) and if he failed to do so he was held to have scorned her. When the husband intended to take to himself a third wife (Nnasaza) or a fourth (Musubika) he had only to tell his first wife (Kaddulubaale) not the others. Wives did not receive a share of the reciprocal gifts on the marriage of their husband with subsequent wives but only partook of the wedding feast. The husband was not under a duty to tell his first wife about his lovers (abaganzi) unless he intended bringing them home. Captured women (abakazi abanyage) were distributed by the husband among his wives to help them with their work. If the husband wanted to have sexual intercourse with one of those slave women he had to obtain the permission of the particular wife who had charge of that woman.

In ancient times in a chief's home the first four of his wives each had her own house in his courtyard but in a peasant's home all the wives lived in the one house but in partitions separated by barkcloth screens. Nowadays all wives live in the one house but they must each have a separate room. It was and is possible for the husband to have separate homesteads for each wife but the Ganda proverb runs:

Nnamakabirye n'afa enjala—The man with two houses dies of hunger.

Each wife has her own field (ennimiro) and plantain garden (lusuku) to cultivate but there is only one kitchen in which each takes a turn at cooking. The wives in fact combined together in the work of the home and the husband must assist all his wives.

If the husband moves house (okusenguka) the wife must go and settle with him.[1] If the husband goes on a visit abroad, the wife must stay at home. If a wife wishes to go on a visit she must obtain her husband's permission to do so.

The husband, as has been mentioned above, has *inter alia* economic responsibility for his household. A wife can possess her own property but must consult her husband before dealing with it. Further consideration of a wife's property rights will be made in Chapter 9.

A wife must first consult her husband before suing in her own right but could not and cannot be sued except when the husband had been consulted. Even a criminal charge against a wife was in olden days first referred to her husband but nowadays such a charge is laid directly before the chief. Both in ancient and in modern times the husband is responsible for paying fines and compensation on behalf of his wife except in respect of proceedings arising outside his domestic responsibility—for example, in connection with his wife's private estate, when she would pay herself.

As regards sexual rights and duties it is a *sine qua non* that a wife must not have sexual relations with men other than her husband. A wife must sleep with her husband if so required except that the husband cannot ask her to do so during her menstruation. If a wife goes on a visit of a week or so's duration and on return refuses her husband sexual intercourse, it is understood that she has acquired a lover and she is usually beaten. If indeed the husband does not have sexual intercourse with his wife, she may think he does not still love her and may leave him. In such a case the husband is considered to be at fault.

In the first November after their marriage, the wife is expected to go and collect edible grasshoppers (enseenene). When she brings them home her husband must give her a goat and a barkcloth. After the husband has eaten the grasshoppers, he has sexual intercourse with his wife. If her husband is away

---

[1] P.C.C.C. 116 of 1948, *Nalwanga* v. *Kyeyune*, 1940–1955 C.L.R.

from home on a visit when the grasshoppers appear, his wife cannot go and catch them (okukuza enseenene) on pain, tradition says, of her child's death.

If a wife appears to be sterile, her husband takes her to a Kiganda doctor, or in the olden days to a Lubaale (Divinity) also, in order to obtain an appropriate potion (oluzaalo derived from okuzaala = to produce a child). If such medicine fails then the husband usually marries again but his sterile wife remains with him in his home and cannot be driven away as the Ganda do not consider sterility is anybody's fault. If the wife is particularly devoted to her husband and if he agrees she may fetch a younger sister, never an elder as that would be taboo, from her family to be her husband's second wife.

Impotence will be considered in the next section as it is a ground for the dissolution of marriage. The customary law governing adultery will be reviewed in Chapter 17 as will the customary law of incest.

DISSOLUTION OF MARRIAGE

A. By divorce

A wife married under Ganda customary law may be divorced (okugattululwa) but in ancient times there were two kinds of wife who were under that law denied the capacity to be divorced; firstly a girl who was given by her father in a marriage of donation (okugabirwa) might be given for life and become a " wife of the worn-out hoe " (omukazi w'ensimu) and secondly a slave wife (omuzaana). Either of those kinds of wife were their husband's absolute property and could be arrested and retrieved by him if they eloped.

Indeed Roscoe tells us that in the last century:

> " A man did not trouble to divorce his wife, if she was unfaithful; he merely neglected her by not inviting her to share his couch, and reduced her to the status of a slave, often leaving her with very scanty clothing."[1]

Grounds

There is only one ground on which a husband may obtain a divorce from his wife under customary law and that is when the wife refuses to return to the marital home. It should be particularly noted that adultery by either spouse is not a ground for

---

[1] *Op. cit.*, p. 97.

divorce. The wife may obtain a divorce by leaving her husband and refusing to return. The real point at issue in such cases is whether or not the marriage consideration is to be returned to the husband by the woman's family. The husband's brother-in-law, who arbitrates in such matters, as will be described in the next section, will decide against the return of the marriage consideration to the husband in the following cases:

(a) if after trial of a week or so the newly-wed bride finds her bridegroom to be impotent;

(b) if the husband has consorted with loose women;

(c) if the husband has committed an abomination (omu-sango gw'ekivve), *e.g.* incest, endogamy, sodomy, bestiality;

(d) if the husband is a wizard (omulogo), and more particularly so if he is of the class of wizards who run about naked at night (omusezi);

(e) if the husband is a thief;

(f) if the husband has deserted the wife;

(g) if the husband has expelled the wife;

(h) if the husband has repeatedly (*i.e.* about thrice) neglected his wife;

(i) if the husband has been cruel to the wife several times; (The cruelty must take the form of threatening to kill her or wounding her with a knife, not just the customary beating of the wife, and further such cruelty must have been committed against her on more than one or two occasions previously. On those first occasions the husband has merely to pay his wife compensation in the shape of a garment, formerly a barkcloth nowadays a dress, or a goat.)

(j) if the husband continuously delivers serious abuse (okuvuma) to his wife;

(k) if there is incompatibility. (Such incompatibility is best explained by quoting a passage from Mair:

" The husband is expected to explain at the outset the household routine which he wants to have observed—times for meals, his favourite relishes, and so forth. Once laid down, this is not varied; if he attempts to make innovations later, or fails to come to meals at the agreed times, his wife is justified in leaving him. Other just grounds of offence are that he does not give her enough clothes, or that he does not provide the fowl which custom demands when her male relatives visit her. The duties to which the husband attaches most importance are that his wife should wash his feet every night, that she should never cook him a meal without any relish, and that when she goes away from home she should not stay away longer than the time fixed by him."[1]

The girl's family are, however, duty bound to return the marriage consideration (okumirulula omutwalo)[2] in the following circumstances:

(a) if the bride after a few weeks of the marriage is found to be incapable of sexual intercourse (ow'olwazi = like a rock);

(b) if the wife refuses her husband conjugal rights for physical reasons[3] or because her husband infected her with venereal disease;[4]

(c) in any other case in which the husband is not to blame for the breakdown of the marriage.

If either spouse becomes insane or sick the other spouse has a duty to care for the sick one or to arrange for treatment. Such illness of body or of mind is no ground for divorce.

Sterility likewise whether in the wife, as described in the previous section, or in the husband is no ground for divorce.

A wife was not allowed under customary law to desert a husband who had been imprisoned (okuteekebwa mu nvuba), as the proverb runs:

Muko mubbi talamula bba—The wife of a thief does not administer justice to her husband.

Procedure

It is well established that any domestic disputes between husband and wife, which cannot be resolved in the home, for example, by the arbitration of the first wife (Kaddulubaale) if a subsequent wife is involved, are taken to the wife's brothers (bako or bakkodomi) for settlement.[5] Not only are minor disputes taken there to be arbitrated upon but also that is the tribunal when a wife leaves her husband.

The procedure is that the husband must go in search of his wife when she disappears and find her before he can institute proceedings before his brothers-in-law. It matters not to which

---

[1] *An African People in the Twentieth Century*, p. 96.

[2] This procedure is said to have been copied by the Ganda from the Nyoro and Arabs when the amount of the marriage consideration increased in the last century.

[3] P.C.R.O. 10 of 1923, *Malimbo* v. *Alideki* (woman sexually small, husband the reverse) (unreported).

[4] P.C.R.O. 13 of 1923, *Lwokya* v. *Bukunduga* (unreported).

[5] P.C.Cr.C. 528 of 1957, *Lukiiko* v. *Mutabazi*, 1957 C.L.R. 151 and P.C.Cr.C. 271 of 1958, *Lukiiko* v. *Namirembe and Another*, 1958 C.L.R. 45.

particular relative she goes on leaving her husband, it is desertion (okunoba) all the same. If, of course, he finds her with another man, then the husband can arrest both as adulterers (obwenzi) even though there is only evidence that the man hid the wife from her husband. If she is found with another woman, the latter is counted as having abducted her (obusiguze) even though she may not have persuaded the wife to join her at all. If the husband fails to go in search of his absconding wife, the wife's family may charge him with failure in his duty.

The husband, having located his wife, goes to her family bearing the traditional calabash of beer.[1] Both sides plead their case and the wife's brothers-in-law give their decision. If the husband disagrees with the decision of his in-laws, then the dispute is referred to the village chief (omutongole) and, if he fails to settle the matter, to the parish chief (omuluka). If the parish chief fails to bring about a settlement the matter is referred to the Kabaka's Courts.[2] During such proceedings, if either spouse falls sick, the hearing is adjourned, and if either spouse dies, the proceedings come to an end.

An order for the return of the marriage consideration may be made irrespective of the period of the marriage which has elapsed and of the number of children born of the marriage.

Usually the marriage consideration itself is alone returned, not collateral prior or later gifts, but the express terms of the marriage contract nowadays prevail.[3] The goods given by the woman's parents in the ceremony of " returning the butter " (okuzzayo omuzigo) are unaffected by divorce and remain with the man.

Each side brings witnesses in the shape of brothers and neighbours to the return of the marriage consideration.

Even though a husband receives a decision in his favour regarding the return of the marriage consideration, the husband may let his brother-in-law off paying by omitting to press for collection.

If the woman's family fail to return the marriage consideration, when due on request, then they are compellable, if need be, in the courts of law.[4]

---

[1] Sir Apolo Kagwa, *Empisa*, p. 175, and Clauses 1 and 2 of the Draft Native Law, 1903, which closely follow that text; see Cunningham, *op. cit.*, p. 150.

[2] *Pace* Mair, *Native Marriage in Buganda*, p. 20.

[3] See p. 94, above.

[4] *Pace* Mair, *An African People in the Twentieth Century*, p. 99.

Effects

If the decision is that the marriage consideration is to be returned, then the date of return is the legally effective date of the divorce. If the marriage consideration is not to be returned, then the decision of the woman's family is the date when the divorce becomes legally operative.

A woman is not free to marry another man until her divorce has become legally effective. If she does so prematurely, she may be prosecuted for adultery.

If the woman's family accepted a second marriage consideration from another man before they had returned the first, in ancient times they would have been charged with the notorious offence of " eating two chicken " (okulya enkoko ebiri) and fined. Although nowadays they are not fined, it is not permitted under customary law to pay back the first marriage consideration out of the second in respect of the same woman. The return of the marriage consideration can stand as a debt but the woman cannot contract another marriage until the debt is satisfied.

On divorce the wife takes her own property,[1] that is:

what she took with her to the marital home;

what she inherited;

what she bought with her own money;

and what had been given her including gifts from her husband during marriage.

She cannot however remove any household utensils nor any standing crops. The children of the marriage stay with their father after divorce without exception. The woman's relatives are responsible for looking after her after the divorce. There is no system of registration of divorce under customary law.

B. By death

The death of either spouse dissolves the marriage. The marriage consideration is not returnable in such circumstances but a surviving widow is free to marry again. Substitute marriage for the dead wife has already been described above as has the leviratic marriage of widows.[2] The position of the widows in succession is considered in Chapter 11.

Parents and Children

Parental control

In the nineteenth century a child grew up under the control

---

[1] See also Chapter 9, below.
[2] See pp. 82 and 81, above.

of both parents. Indeed all the villagers in that village had control of the child to the extent of beating the child to teach him good manners.

The paternal grandfather had special authority in relation to all his grandchildren. The child's father consulted him as to the name to be given to the child (" omuganda ayagala okufuna erinnya ") and a son was taken to the grandfather after three months and a daughter after two and half months so that the grandfather might teach him to sit down (okumutuuza) and tie beads round his neck to make it erect (okuzingirira). Later the child was taken to his grandfather's to be educated in good manners and a trade. And although, of course, schools nowadays have made a great change in the education of Ganda children, this custom is still found. This close connection between paternal grandparent and grandson was cemented in ancient times by the grandson succeeding to the grandfather's estate on the latter's death. The grandson was in fact treated by the grand-father and his household as the owner of the grandfather's property even in the latter's lifetime.[1] This custom has largely been upset by the Kabaka's decision that a grandson even though brought up in the grandfather's home is not to succeed to the grandfather's estate while the father is alive.

The maternal grandparents have no authority over grand-children on their daughter's side.

The father has a particular control over his sons and the mother over her daughters in sexual matters (obuvunaanyizibwa obw'ekyama).

Sons were brought up to herd goats and were also taken on campaigns by their father to carry coverlets of barkcloth. A son was also taught the names of his brethren, how to beat barkcloth and how to cut trees for house-building and to weave them into a house-frame (okulaasa kasolya). Daughters stayed at home with their mother and learnt to cultivate, to collect firewood, to peel plantains and to cook.

Avoidances between parents and children are dealt with later in this chapter. The guardianship of children will be considered in Chapter 12 and seduction under the law of torts in Chapter 16.

Duties of father

The father has the following responsibilities in respect of his children:

---

[1] See p. 214, below.

   (i) to arrange the customary ceremonies;
  (ii) to provide food and clothing;
 (iii) and to educate them.

The first ceremony in the child's life is the teaching of the child to sit down by the paternal grandfather (okutuuza omwaana).[1] Only the paternal grandfather or the paternal aunt can perform this ceremony, being of the child's clan, not the paternal grandmother as she is of a different totem.[2] For special reasons this ceremony, usually performed at the grand-parents' home, may be performed at the child's home as Mair states.[3]

If a child fell ill during the period of suckling, the Ganda believed it was due to the father having committed adultery and a ceremony of propitiation (okukansira) had to be performed by the husband and the adulteress at the child's home.[4]

The next ceremony is again of ancient origin but is still customary:[5] it is the ceremony of naming the child (okwalula omwaana). The ceremony consists of placing the child's umbilical cord (akalira) in a basket and pouring thereon beer, water and butter. If the cord does not float on the concoction then the child is shown as of that clan. If the cord floats, the child is declared not to be of the father's clan, that is that it is an adulterous child.

In the case of a child of the Royal Family, the midwife, Nabikande, performs a similar ceremony using a concoction of beer, milk and butter in the presence of the Queen-Mother (Namasole) and the Kabaka. Afterwards it is the job of a woman, Mubisi, to drink the concoction and she is rewarded with villages and formerly with slave-girls (abazaana) to serve her.[6]

---

[1] See p. 112, above.

[2] *Pace* Mair, *An African People in the Twentieth Century*, p. 54.

[3] *Ibid.*

[4] See Gorju, *op. cit.*, p. 334.

[5] *Pace* Mair, *op. cit.*, p. 57.

[6] It may be of interest to record the treatment accorded subsequently to the Kabaka's umbilical cord. It is taken to his grandfather's where the cord is entitled " Kabaka Sebukule ". It is then decorated by " *bagirinnya* " who are liberally victualled meanwhile. The cord is then taken to the Namasole where there is a feast and finally to the Royal Tombs at Kasubi where a Namasole wa Sebukule is appointed. Formerly the *mukungu* Kimbugwe was charged with the function of looking after Kabaka Sebukule but that function is now the Nnaalinnya's (Queen-Sister's). Kimbugwe used to carry Kabaka Sebukule whenever the Kabaka made an appearance in his Lukiko. I understand from the ex-Ssabaganzi, who supplied me with this information, that the reigning Kabaka's umbilical cord was recently so decorated in South Buddu.

To revert to the ordinary ceremony itself, the child is then placed on the main verandah (kifugi) and if it did not die, it was counted of that clan and given its important name. That night the child's father and mother perform the rite of " *okubuka* " (= lit. jumping but in fact sexual intercourse) which had in this ceremony the particular title of " *okumala ekizadde* " (completing the birth celebrations).[1] This rite confirms the child is theirs because it was firmly believed that if the child was not it would thereby die. The following morning there is a very merry feast of sprats, mushrooms and simsim.

Each clan has its own test to ascertain whether a child is of their clan; for example, the Sprat Clan (Ab'Enkejje) throw the child in the Lake and the Genet Clan (Ab'akasimba) put the placenta up a tree.

When his son reaches puberty, the father must ensure that the boy is potent and if after examination of the boy's private parts he finds otherwise the father must obtain native medicine for his son to put the matter right. About this time the boy in ancient times changed his residence from his parent's house to a small separate one in their courtyard.[2] But this custom is not strictly followed nowadays. Previously when a boy reached puberty he was taken to his paternal grandfather's home and given a goat-skin to wear. The grandfather then supervised the boy, who herded cattle from the grandparent's home, and ensured that he did not wander about at night.

The next main ceremony in the boy's life was his betrothal by being sent to his prospective bride's parents' home to do certain work, a procedure which has been already described.[3] The final test was to see whether, after the boy had brewed beer and the girl's father had offered him a calabash of it, the lad respectfully declined on the grounds that he brewed as a courtesy. If he passed that test he was considered to have grown up sufficiently to look after the girl (okukema).

It is the father's responsibility to see that his sons and daughters are married off in good time. The elder son or elder daughter usually marries first. This custom is followed by an elaborate pretence if the marriage of a younger child in fact precedes that of an elder. If a younger sister is to be married, then the elder

---

[1] Gorju, *op. cit.*, p. 336.
[2] P.C.C.A. 98 of 1957, *Jumba* v. *Ssali*, 1957 C.L.R. 119.
[3] See p. 86, above.

unmarried sister first leaves the courtyard. If a younger son is to be married then the elder brothers pretend to marry their sisters the night before by providing the traditional calabash of beer.

The father has a duty to give his sons their property and to supply gifts to his daughters on their marriage. He must also tell his children, particularly his elder sons, matters affecting the home.

A child cannot sue or be sued without reference to his father, who in fact sues or is sued in the child's name. Usually, however, any dispute in which a child is involved is the subject of arbitration first at the parents' home. If it is a domestic dispute, that is between children or between a wife and a child, the father settles the issue, possibly consulting the grown-up members of the family;[1] if it involves people outside the family, the father consults his neighbours. If the father cannot resolve the dispute, then it is referred to the village chief (omutongole). If the son seduces a girl or commits another shameful act (okuwemuuka), then the father is under a duty to pay compensation on his son's behalf (amawemuukirano). If the dispute is between the father and one of his children, then the adult members of the family (ab'oluganda) arbitrate between them.

Duties of mother

In ancient times it was the mother's duty to take her daughter when she reached twelve years of age (amabeere nga gasuna), in company with her elder sisters, in secret to the bush to explain to her the facts of life (okukyalira nsiko). There never has been any circumcision ceremony in Ganda custom.

When the girl first menstruates on reaching puberty at thirteen years of age, her paternal aunt performs the second ceremony variously entitled " okuzza mukono emabega " or " okwekuba akagere ". This ceremony in fact consists of the paternal aunt taking the girl aside and in private checking on her menstruation (amubalirira ebizizi). Thereafter the girl is no longer allowed to reside in the same house as her parents but goes to live with her brothers in a smaller house in the same compound.

The mother further has the responsibility of periodically examining her daughter to ascertain that she is still a virgin until

---

[1] P.C.Cr.A. 4 of 1957, *Wamala and Another* v. *Lukiiko*, 1957 C.L.R. 49.

the time comes for the girl's paternal aunt to take her to her bridegroom.

The mother has no right to be consulted regarding the girl's marriage. She can only give her opinion in private to her husband. She does however receive a present of a barkcloth from the prospective bridegroom.[1]

A woman has no right to supervise her daughters-in-law.

Even a divorced woman still has responsibilities in the various ceremonies performed in relation to her children at her former husband's home and indeed visits them from time to time.

Duties of children

In ancient times children had a duty to support their parents and help in the home but nowadays that duty is not universally observed.

If a son is rebellious, his father calls the family (ab'oluganda) together to arbitrate and if the proceedings go against the son he is fined a goat, gourd of beer, barkcloth and a cock.

A child who hits his father commits an abomination (kivve) and has to be expelled from the clan—there is no other remedy. When a child is small it is permitted to beat its mother, as the proverb goes:

Omwaana okuyiga okukuba ayigira ku nnyina—A child learns to beat on its mother.

When the child grows up, it is fined if it strikes its mother and the mother is compensated.

When a Ganda was elevated to a chieftainship he gave his parent the ownership of a piece of land on his estate. This parent was entitled " Nnakazadde ". The parent could dispose of the land given or could leave it to his own heir. This customary donation of land to one's parent on assuming a chieftainship still continues but only the tenancy of a plot (kibanja) can be donated on official mailo land. The full ownership can still be given on private mailo, although it does not necessarily pass when a plantain garden is given to a parent by a chief for food without payment of rent.[2]

---

[1] See p. 93, above.
[2] P.C.C.C. 262 of 1950, *Kamulegeya* v. *Omumbeja Alina Luwedde* (upheld by BENNETT, J., in H.C.C.A. 15 of 1954) (unreported).

The ceremony of twins[1]

On the birth of twins the midwife tells the father who thereupon climbs on to the roof of his house and says:

"Nzadde abalongo Mukasa ampadde ezadde."—I have begotten twins, the god Mukasa has bestowed on me the parentage.

The father of twins (Ssalongo) then goes to fetch an old clan elder (mutaka musajja mukulu) in the village. This elder shuts the doors of Ssalongo's house and then cuts a hole in a door through which to pass. For his pains the elder is given a present of money.

The Ssalongo goes to the blacksmiths and gets two bodkins (enkatto) and takes them to his father's home at night. He puts them on his father's doorstep, announces that he has begotten twins and makes off. Ssalongo's mother picks up the bodkins and ties them with barkcloth to the main pole of the house near the fire-place.

After two days Ssalongo returns to his father and asks him to give him one of his other sons or brothers and the father of twins then returns to his home with whoever is chosen by his father. That person becomes " the Great Father of Twins " (Ssalongo Omukulu) and the real father of twins is called " *Ssalongo Omuto* " (the lesser father of twins).

Ssalongo Omuto then sends a messenger to his wife's (Nnalongo's = mother of twins) father and asks for one of her sisters to be the " *Nnalongo Omukulu* " (The Great Mother of Twins).

As soon as Nnalongo Omukulu arrives she and the real mother of twins, now styled Nnalongo Omuto, have licence to collect free whatever foodstuffs they like anywhere in the village and no legal liability attaches to such foraging. Both have adorned themselves with a wild vine (ebbombo).

The two fathers of twins array themselves in barkcloths

---

[1] The ceremony, which takes place on the birth of twins, has been described by Sir Apolo Kagwa (*Empisa*, Chapter XIX, p. 189), Roscoe (*op. cit.*, pp. 64 *et seq.*), Gorju (*op. cit.*, pp. 350 *et seq.*) and Mair (*op. cit.*, p. 44). I also give an account, practically word for word as that which was given to me at a meeting of chiefs and court members at Ssissa in South Busiro on the 14th August, 1959, partly because the previous account was written a quarter of a century ago and, as Mair suspected, appears to have been censored by her informant who had missionary connections, and partly because it is difficult to understand the legal consequences of certain acts without the background. This account was given me stage by stage with the agreement of a father of twins who was present. And, *pace* Mair, *op. cit.*, p. 47, the ceremony is still observed.

knotted on both shoulders and each carries two drinking cups (enseke) and as they wander round the village everybody gives them free beer. They may make love to any woman they like, married or unmarried, and no proceedings can be taken against them. Throughout their travels in these ceremonies the parents of twins, real and imaginary, sing " *Kuru, Kuru, Kuru. . . .*" One greets them with " *Gauga, Gauga* ".

People who meet the parents of the twins give them money (ebigali).

Ssalongo Omukulu has the right of sexual intercourse (oku-kandula bbombo) with the real mother of twins (Nnalongo Omuto) during the ceremonies which may take several months, and if she becomes pregnant by him no proceedings are taken against him. Likewise the real father of twins (Ssalongo Omuto) has the right of sexual intercourse with Nnalongo Omukulu (*i.e.* his wife's sister). On the other hand, if they wish the pairs can just perform the *okubuka* rite ceremonially. During the ceremonies also the young men of the paternal line have sexual relations with the girls of the maternal line freely (okukandula bbombo).

The real father of the twins then produces two goats and two chicken (each equivalent to the sexes of the twins), together with sprats and mushrooms. The neighbours all come and a feast is prepared. Each Ssalongo dips matooke (cooked plantains) in the mushroom sauce and gives it to his Nnalongo and she then does the same for him. Whenever the parents of twins, real and imaginary, eat food, they first eat plantains cooked unpeeled (mpogola). Then all feast and later sing:

> " Nnyinnimu mwali atamanyi kuboola nganda."—The owner
> of the house is here who knows not how to expel his clansmen.

and other songs including indecent ones against which the ordinary legal sanctions[1] do not apply (okuzina balongo). As they sing they decorate the umbilical cords of the twins with barkcloth and beads (okusiba balongo).

After that they go to the house of the paternal grandfather of the twins who kills two goats and two chicken (the sexes of these creatures being according to the sexes of the twins) and supplies sprats and mushrooms. A string of dried banana leaves is tied across the courtyard from plantain to plantain (lwaliro) and the

---

[1] The Law to Prevent the Use of Indecent Language, Rev. Edn., pp. 20–21.

paternal grandparents of the twins defend the string against the real parents. They struggle against each other until the string is broken (okumenya olukanda). Then all sing indecent songs with impunity. At the feast which follows the paternal grandfather gives plantain dipped in sauce to the Ssalongo Omukulu and then the real (minor) Ssalongo. The paternal grandmother then does the same for Nnalongo Omukulu and then the real mother of twins. They start feasting but when the food is half eaten, all stand up and trample in the feast. Then the paternal grandfather of the twins brings beer and washes the umbilical cords of the twins with the beer and shaves off part and puts it on one side (okumwa balongo). The cords are washed again in beer. The paternal relatives of the twins bring money and throw it on the umbilical cords (okuwa ebigali). Then the parents of the twins, real and imaginary, return to the twins' home in the daytime.

After a few days they go to the maternal grandfather's home and perform a similar ceremony (okumenya olukanda).

Then they tie the umbilical cords together in a bundle and whenever such a ceremony recurs in that village, the cords are taken along. If any person has eaten lung-fish recently (olya mmamba) he cannot touch the umbilical cords.

If a twin commits an offence, the father punishes both. When a male twin marries a girl, the other male twin enters into an imaginary marriage with her sister.

KITH AND KIN

Responsibilites and avoidances

As well as imposing certain responsibilities kinship in Buganda involves certain imperative avoidances. The most convenient point at which to start tracing these rules which regulate behaviour is the completion of the marriage ceremonies with the despatch of the gifts (envunulabibya) by the girl's mother to the bridegroom.[1]

After some time the bridegroom summons his parents-in-law to come and eat a meal at his home. They come accompanied by friends to this feast. Immediately the avoidances begin to be observed strictly: the mother-in-law does not cross her son-in-law's courtyard but skirts it and, though she enters his house she

---

[1] See p. 100, above.

gazes steadfastly downwards (so as not to look into the bed-room). She eats separately from her son-in-law and only food cooked separately and above all must never touch him.[1] They can however share water, beer or a pipe. At this feast the father-in-law is given a *kanzu*, which he dons, and then a cock (sseg-gwanga) which he eats. The mother-in-law is given a barkcloth, which she puts on, and then partakes of a goat given to her. They are also given a calabash of beer, plantains cooked in their skins (empogola) and mushrooms. In earlier times the mother-in-law never approached her son-in-law unless veiled but this practice is rarely followed nowadays.

There are said to be two exceptions to the rules of avoidance between a man and his mother-in-law:

(i) at a funeral in either family;

(ii) in ancient times, when his mother-in-law had been taken as a slave, the man if he wanted to redeem her, could say she was his wife and thereafter he could touch her. There-upon the mother-in-law provided and cooked a cock and a spotted Ganda mushroom (akatiko akaganda akekibala) together with sprats, which the man provided, and they ate this meal together.

A like avoidance obtains between the bride and her father-in-law. She cannot cross his courtyard when visiting his home nor can she eat with him although she can partake of the same food cooked together with his. Above all they must not touch each other. (When a child is born to the marriage, the mother holds one of the child's arms and her father-in-law the other). If he happens to touch her, he commits an abomination (omu-sango gw'ekivve) and is fined a female goat and a barkcloth.

Other avoidances are:

(i) the two mothers-in-law cannot live in the same house; (but the fathers-in-law can);

(ii) the elder sister does not visit a younger married sister, nor an elder brother a younger married brother (omukulu azira = the elder is taboo);

(iii) between cousins of opposite sex (bakizibwe) and between a man and his cousin's wife;[2]

---

[1] See P.C.Cr.C. 271 of 1958, *Lukiiko* v. *Namirembe and Another*, 1958 C.L.R. 45 *et seq.* and Gorju *op. cit.*, p. 283.

[2] Gorju, *op. cit.*, p. 284.

(iv) between a man and his paternal aunt (ssenga) whom Gorju describes as " *tyran féminin* "[1] in Ganda society.

If a male relative of the wife, for instance her father or brother, visits the married couple's home, the husband must provide him with a cock to eat and must place it alive in his hands. The visitor returns it saying " Genda ogitte " (Go and kill it). That is done and when cooking the bird, the gizzard (oluguve) must be placed underneath a smoked banana leaf (luwombo). If that method is not followed, another cock must be given (okuzirula) and cooked as it is taboo for the visitor to eat otherwise.

If a quarrel arises between husband and wife, then, whenever either his or her relatives visit them, they have authority to arbitrate between the two and settle the dispute.

If the quarrel is not settled and the wife elopes, the husband, as has been explained already,[2] must go to his brothers-in-law to fetch her back, taking a calabash of beer or its money equivalent with which to pay them for arbitrating, whether he wins or loses the case. When the wife returns to her husband, she takes from her relatives a cock as a present to him.

If his wife falls ill, the husband must go and tell her family. The husband also must announce any death in the marital home to his brothers-in-law on pain of a fine of a goat. When such a death occurs the brothers-in-law must bring barkcloths.

Similarly the husband must take a barkcloth and afterwards a calabash of beer to his brothers-in-law if there is a death in their family. If either actual parent of his wife dies he must also give his wife a garment, formerly a barkcloth now usually a dress.

A wife counts a death in her husband's family as a loss to herself.

Children have certain kinship obligations towards their parents, as have already been mentioned,[3] and among themselves. The eldest child whether a son or a daughter controls the rest of the children. An elder brother controls and protects his younger brothers and an elder daughter likewise her younger sisters. Sisters usually have feminine responsibility for performing jobs for their brothers, like mending clothes, when they are living together in the home before marriage. In the last century brothers and sisters used to help a younger brother to marry by giving

---

[1] *Op. cit.*, p. 285.
[2] See p. 110, above.
[3] See p. 116, above.

F

him goats, barkcloths and cash, but this custom is falling into disuse, although parents usually still help a dutiful son.[1] After her marriage a brother has responsibility for his sister as *omuko* (brother-in-law). If he succeeds as his father's heir, he has the responsibility of marrying off his sisters who still remain unmarried.

There are also certain avoidances between parents and their children. Mention has already been made of their separate residence on the children attaining the age of puberty.[2] Such children must also have their separate water supply. No grown-up child can enter his parents' house further than the front dining-room and more particularly must keep away from the bedroom.[3]

Endobolo

In theory the brother-in-law who gave the husband his wife is entitled to all the children of the marriage. This right, far from being obsolete under mission influence,[4] is still followed to this day. It is a customary right of ancient origin,[5] and consists of the redemption of each child from his brother-in-law's power by gifts sent by their father. If the gifts are not sent, the brother-in-law can come and claim the child as his endobolo (share)[6] when it has been weaned. It is open to the father to redeem the child subsequently by sending the required gift. The principal misfortune, which results to the child from remaining with its father's brother-in-law, is that it is thereby cut off from its own clan.

Abortion

In ancient times if a wife was found to have aborted herself or to have submitted to an abortion being performed upon her, the husband's brothers and paternal aunt charged the wife before her parents. A settlement was sought, not the payment

---

[1] See p. 95, above.
[2] See pp. 114 and 115, above.
[3] See Gorju, *op. cit.*, p. 284.
[4] *Pace* Mair, *op. cit.*, p. 62.
[5] See Ashe, *op. cit.*, p. 285 and Gorju, *op. cit.*, pp. 299–300.
[6] In ancient times this word was employed in respect of two other kinds of children—firstly a child belonging to a seducer who had failed to pay compensation was confiscated by the girl's father as his *endobolo* and sold into slavery; secondly the child of a slave was his master's *endobolo* for disposal (see above, p. 65).

of a fine nor of compensation. Such cases were rare as the women tended to abort themselves and dispose of the foetus in secret. But if the woman was questioned and admitted the offence, she was so charged.

Any person encompassing an abortion by the administration of a drug was called a wizard (omulogo) and was punished by being made to pay a fine, called " eggozi ", usually of a goat, and by being placed in the stocks (envuba).

If the child died at birth, the husband's relatives blamed the wife and attributed the death to one of the following three causes:

   (i) syphilis, anciently called " omunnyo ", now " kaboo-tongo ";

  (ii) promiscuous sexual excess (amakiro), for which she might sometimes be punished by her husband's sisters beating her and making her cut and carry home logs (okutema bisiki) and at other times she would be treated as for an illness;

 (iii) overlaying the child (okumutuulira) out of nervousness, for which she was beaten.

The customary law of abortion was superseded by one of the first native laws to be enacted, the Prevention of Abortion Law, 1904.

PART III

THE LAW OF PROPERTY

SUMMARY

			PAGE
CHAP. 8	Land	127
CHAP. 9	Movable Property	171
CHAP. 10	Methods of Acquisition	180

CHAPTER 8

LAND

Immovable property, that is land and what is affixed thereto in the shape of buildings and trees, is a most important part of Ganda customary law as the subject-matter of approximately one half of the original civil cases filed in any year in the Principal Court concerns land.[1] A brief description of the land and its economic determinants has already been given.[2] I propose now to outline the land tenure systems which obtained in Buganda in the last century. There is no need to dwell long on this part of the subject for on the one hand its relevance to modern litigation is infinitesimally small and on the other the ground has already been well covered by Mr. Justice Morris Carter in 1910,[3] Mair in 1932,[4] Thomas and Spencer in 1938[5] and more recently, but more comprehensively and certainly more easy of access, Mukwaya in 1953.[6]

TENURE PRE-1900

There is one matter on which all the authorities unhesitatingly agree and that is that in days prior to the arrival of the European in Buganda all land belonged to the Kabaka and no holding of land was recognised unless it had been conferred or agreed by him.[7] Such a system of land tenure was natural for the land had been acquired by conquest. In his person the Kabaka united the three main categories of land tenure which existed side by

---

[1] Based on the statistics of cases for the years 1953, 1954 and 1955.

[2] See pp. xxxviii and xxxix, above.

[3] " The Clan System, Land Tenure and Succession among the Baganda ", 1 U.L.R. Appendix, reprinted from the *Law Quarterly Review*, Vol. 25 (1909), p. 158 based on African No. 869, 1906, *Report on Land Tenure in the Kingdom of Buganda.*

[4] Mair, *Baganda Land Tenure, Africa*, Vol. VI, p. 187 and *An African People in the Twentieth Century*, pp. 154 *et seq.*

[5] Thomas and Spencer, *op. cit.*, pp. 63 *et seq.*

[6] A. B. Mukwaya, *Land Tenure in Buganda*, 1953.

[7] Carter, *op. cit.*, p. 107, Roscoe, *op. cit.*, p. 238, Mukwaya, *op. cit.*, p. 19.

side—*butaka, butongole* and *bwesengeze*.[1] Possession of land for a long period, even for generations gave no prescriptive title to the land only to its occupation.[2] Indeed there was never any conception of land as a negotiable possession; the chief or individual held it from the Kabaka and had no power to sell or otherwise dispose of it without the Kabaka's assent.[3] Proof of the Kabaka's ownership of the land is to be found in the tithe of produce which he exacted.[4] Lastly there was, despite the greater population in the last century, no shortage of land and boundaries were only recognised in general terms as following natural features.[5]

BUTAKA

The tenure of clan lands, *butaka*, by the hereditary " fathers of the soil ", *obataka*, was certainly the oldest category of the three and had origin before the Hima dynasty consolidated its power over Buganda.[6] This origin is reflected in the undoubted laxity of control which Kabakas exercised over this category of land, their title being recognised merely by the supply of labour and the payment of tax.[7] Not all clan tenures, however, were in existence in pre-Hima times and the Kabaka's position as head of all the clans (Ssabattaka) was recognised in that he alone had power to create and grant new *butaka*.[8] Moreover, in respect of such lands already existing there is no doubt that from the earliest times it was one of the Kabaka's prerogatives to confirm the clan's choice of a successor to the clan lands.[9]

The clan lands were primarily for the residence of the head of clan and secondarily for the burial of clansmen.[10] Indeed one of the main ways in which new *butaka* appears to have been created was by the burial in land of three to five generations of clansmen.[11]

It sometimes happened that out of clan lands the Kabakas

---

[1] See below for descriptions.
[2] Carter, *loc. cit.*
[3] Mair, *An African People in the Twentieth Century*, p. 155, and Thomas and Spencer, *op. cit.*, p. 63.
[4] See Chapter 9, below.
[5] Mair, *op. cit.*, p. 161.
[6] Thomas and Spencer, *op. cit.*, p. 63.
[7] Roscoe, *op. cit.*, p. 238 and Thomas and Spencer, *op. cit.*, p. 64.
[8] Carter, *op. cit.*, p. 109.
[9] Roscoe, *ibid.*, Mair, *Baganda Land Tenure*, p. 191, and Mukwaya, *op. cit.*, p. 19.
[10] Thomas and Spencer, *ibid.*
[11] Roscoe, *op. cit.*, p. 134, Thomas and Spencer, *loc. cit.*

carved areas to grant to other chiefs or favourites (butongole)[1] but in general the clan's *butaka* was respected.[2] If a mutaka (" father of the soil ", *i.e.* head of clan) was expelled from his lands, he would go to the Kabaka as of right and explain his position and would invariably be reinstated.[3]

The wars of the second half of the last century and Portal's religious settlement of the country in 1893 by the allocation of spheres of influence led to re-distribution of the population on sectarian lines and in the re-shuffle the tenure of clan lands became obscured.[4] It is however well-established that even before those tumultuous times, the majority of peasants inhabiting any clan land were in fact non-clansmen.[5]

Before leaving the subject of butaka tenure, the powers of the clan head over the people inhabiting clan land must be considered. Carter writes:[6]

> " The mutaka was in the position of a feudal lord with power of life and death over the people on his land, the collector of taxes, and the owner of the soil, with peasants under him, often of a different clan from his own, whom he could eject at his pleasure from his estates."

The Princely Clan (Ekirangira) never had butaka but the individual princes (abalangira) and princesses (abambeja) received land from the Kabaka at his pleasure through the Ssabalangira, head of clan.[7]

BUTONGOLE

The lands held by officials (obutongole)[8] were official estates (ebitongole) held by chiefs and officials as tenants-at-will of the King. Their tenure was uncertain and revocable by the King.[9] If the holders were fortunate, they held for life but these estates were not heritable.[10] The *batongole* may be taken to include the

---

[1] See below.

[2] Thomas and Spencer, *ibid.*

[3] Mair, *Baganda Land Tenure*, p. 191, and *An African People in the Twentieth Century*, p. 164.

[4] Thomas and Spencer, *op. cit.*, p. 64 and Goldthorpe, *op. cit.*, p. 76.

[5] Mair, *ibid.*, and Thomas and Spencer, *ibid.*

[6] *Op. cit.*, p. 111.

[7] See Carter, *op. cit.*, p. 113.

[8] Derived from *okutongola*—to become an official.

[9] Lugard, *The Rise of our East African Empire*, 1893, Vol. II, p. 645.

[10] Carter, *op. cit.*, p. 108.

great chiefs (abakungu) as well as the true " batongole " who
were favourites or officials of the Kabaka with duties to perform
for him.[1] The great chiefs (abakungu) consisted of the Katikkiro,
the Ssaza Chiefs and other chiefs, some of whom had been sent
as captains to guard and govern the large fiefs marching on the
borders of the Kingdom.[2] Each chief also had a " town house "
in the capital at Mmengo and spent most of his time there
leaving his estates in the country to be managed by a steward
(omusigere).[3] The favourites and officials not only include
palace officials but also the King's relatives of high and lesser
degree who had official estates scattered over the country consisting of various villages. Female commoners were not possessed of land but the ladies of the Royal Family such as the
Queen Mother (Namasole), the Queen Sister (Lubuga) and
Princesses held estates of the King. Certain divinities—at any
rate the two war-gods Kibuka and Nnende—had such estates
allocated for their temples.[4]

These official estates (ebitongole) were held with the respective political, military, palace or royal offices as emoluments
of that office.[5] The responsibilities carried by the holders of
these estates were to organise the peasantry so placed under
their authority for building palaces for the King, road-making,
hunting and war and to collect the taxes on behalf of the King.[6]
The Ganda saying sums up the position of these *batongole*:

Tafuga ttaka afuga bantu—He does not rule land he rules people.

In return for the discharge of these responsibilities towards the
King, the chief or official received service, both on domestic
works and on military expeditions, food, beer, barkcloth and
other commodities from the peasants.[7]

BWESENGEZE[8]

Lugard[9] had observed seven years before the end of the last
century:

---

[1] See above, p. 57.
[2] Roscoe, *op. cit.*, p. 238; Mukwaya, *op. cit.*, p. 11.
[3] M. J. Hall, *Through my spectacles in Uganda*, 1898, p. 61.
[4] Mair, *An African People in the Twentieth Century*, p. 161.
[5] Thomas and Scott, *op. cit.*, p. 99.
[6] Mair, *Baganda Land Tenure*, p. 191.
[7] A. I. Richards, *op. cit.*, p. 119.
[8] Derived from the word *okwesengeza*—to cause oneself to settle.
[9] *Loc. cit.*

" In Uganda the individual does acquire land and cultivate it for his own use and profit. . . ."

These individual grants were based on long occupation of one particular holding confirmed by the King, or on an original grant of one holding or one small estate to an individual chief or peasant by the King himself. Mukwaya explains:[1]

" Both chiefs and peasants who had some access to the King, availed themselves of the same opportunity to have a permanent claim to one particular piece of land recognised. It was common for a chief early in his career to choose one holding for his personal use as distinct from the holding for his official use. The former was called *ekibanja eky'obwesengeze* and the latter *ekibanja eky'obwami*. The personal claims were confirmed by the King sending a special messenger to plant a barkcloth tree on the holding or estate. This would then become a permanent piece of evidence of the claim to that land."

Mukwaya goes on to explain that such tenure consisted only of smallholdings, without political rights or duties but also without peasant service and, most important of all, inheritable.[2]

PEASANT TENANCY

A peasant (omukopi) occupied and cultivated a plot (ekibanja) of land at his chief's pleasure.[3] His plot was of an unspecified size with no formal boundaries unless there were near neighbours; he occupied " as much as he could cultivate ".[4] As the Ganda proverb runs:

Enkumbi tebba—The hoe does not steal.

In those days it was the tenants who were important not, as now, the land. Then landlords wanted tenants and far from the peasant having to give the landlord presents it was the latter who made available amenities to the new tenant. Tenants flocked to a generous landlord.

Their relationship was in fact a very personal one.[5] The peasants, instead of rent, used to render personal service to their master at the latter's home. Hence the proverb:

---

[1] Mukwaya, *op. cit.*, p. 12.
[2] *Op. cit.*, p. 13.
[3] Mair, *Baganda Land Tenure*, p. 191.
[4] Mair, *An African People in the Twentieth Century*, p. 155, and A. I. Richards, *loc. cit.*
[5] A. I. Richards, *loc. cit.*

Asenga omwami tagayala, akola kisakate—The man who joins a new master does not idle, he builds a chief's reed fence.

There were not fixed duties but as work became necessary the village chief (omutongole or nnanyini kyalo) would allocate parts of the work to his sub-chiefs for their people to perform. This duty might when the chief was on duty at Mmengo take the form of carrying food there for him (okugemula). Again, from time to time the peasant was expected to give his master a present of a chicken, a goat, a barkcloth or a calabash of beer (okutona). As long as the peasant performed that personal service and gave the customary gifts, he enjoyed the tenancy of his plot and his lord's protection and assistance. But if he failed, then he was liable to be punished by his lord: either death by the spear (okuzinda), plundering (okunyaga) or a fine (okutanza).

Peasants could however establish rights by long occupation, say by living on the same site for two or three generations and burying their ancestors in the plot, so that succeeding landlords would recognise their claim to remain undisturbed.[1] A plot could pass to the peasant's heir on his death.[2]

The " Mailo " System[3]

The background to the land clauses in the Uganda Agreement, 1900, is succinctly described by Thomas and Scott:

> " During Mwanga's later years and the infancy of his successor the reins of power were largely in the hands of the chiefs, foremost among whom was that strong man of affairs, the Katikiro or prime minister, the late Sir Apolo Kagwa. To these chiefs fell the task of negotiating the Uganda Agreement, 1900, with Sir Harry Johnston. Land settlement was perhaps the most contentious of the subjects dealt with, and inevitably the claims of the chiefs then in office received paramount consideration."[4]

Sir Harry Johnston had just previous to 1900 promoted a system of individual land tenure among natives in Nyasaland.[5]

---

[1] Mair, *Baganda Land Tenure*, p. 194.

[2] Mair, *An African People in the Twentieth Century*, p. 159.

[3] The classic record of the development of the system of land registration in Buganda is Thomas and Spencer's work but a more recent account is to be found in *Land Registration in Buganda*, by T. N. N. Brushfield and A. J. Relton (1955).

[4] *Op. cit.*, p. 99.

[5] Lugard, *loc. cit.*

It was not therefore surprising, indeed it was intended, that the principal architect of this 1900 Agreement should develop a similar system in Buganda. The effects, however, do not appear to have been clearly realised by either party:

> " But the result of the settlement was that, whereas under the old regime the usufruct of land—in fact the sum of the food and services provided by its occupiers—was available to the ruling authority, the King, for the recompense of those who were doing the King's work in the government of the country, under the new dispensation these land holdings were recognised as the private possession of those chiefs, great or small, who happened to be in the van at the time of the Uganda Agreement. These quasi-freeholdings, now supported by documentary titles guaranteed by the British Government, are the Mailo lands of Buganda, and constitute, as between the British Government and the natives, a definite partition of the land of Buganda.
>
> By succession and sale these Mailo lands now become transmissible to other natives who might not be attracted to, or might be unfitted for, the duties of chieftainship. The tribute—busulu—of the occupiers was gradually transformed into a money rent due to private landowners and no longer available for the support of those who were engaged in the native government of Buganda. Bataka claimants, except in so far as they happened to be active chiefs, were ignored, and, as for the peasant occupiers, whose case no one seems to have considered, their customary rights of cultivation were degraded to tenancies at will from private landlords."[1]

Articles 15, 16, 17 and 18 are the relevant clauses of the 1900 Agreement. Out of an assumed total area of the Kingdom of 19,600 square miles, and apart from land brought under the control of the Uganda Administration or allotted to the three missionary societies, 350 square miles were allotted to the Kabaka, 148 square miles to members of the Royal Family of Buganda, 320 square miles to ssaza chiefs, 140 square miles to the Regents and other important chiefs and 8,000 square miles to 1,000 chiefs and private landowners who were to

> " receive the estates of which they are already in possession, and which are computed at an average of 8 square miles per individual."

(Article 15). There were important reservations to Her Majesty's Government of rights to construct certain public works without compensation for the land, of forests and of mineral rights.

The Lukiko prepared allotment lists but soon found, after satisfying all claims, that 1,200 square miles out of the 8,000

---

[1] Thomas and Scott, *loc. cit.*

square miles " for chiefs and private landowners " remained undistributed.[1] Accordingly 1,000 square miles of that undistributed balance was allocated under a memorandum of the 25th July, 1900;[2] and meanwhile the Regents had obtained a further 45 square miles for their own acquisition under a memorandum of the 13th February, 1900.[3]

These allotments on paper were converted into claims for actual land by the majority of allottees under the rough demarcations and record made by the Lukiko's commissioners.[4] When a final settlement was effected in 1905 it was found that some 3,700 persons had become owners of mailo land instead of the 1,000 chiefs and private landowners contemplated by the Agreement.[5]

Survey, of course, could not start immediately but in 1902 it was appreciated that it was not going to be the " one man's job " originally thought.[6] The mailo survey commenced in October–November 1904.[7] It was, however, the rough diagrams of the Lukiko's Commissioners, mentioned above, which were endorsed by the Regents, and attached to the Provisional Certificates of Claim, issued by the Protectorate Government, which form the root of title to mailo land.[8] By a native law[9] any application for a provisional certificate lodged after 31st December, 1909, was barred.

In 1907 a committee, set up to consider land tenure, recommended that mailo tenure should be defined in a native law,

> " thus showing an appreciation of the fact that mailo land had never been vested in the Crown."[10]

The result was the Land Law, 1908.[11] The Committee had also recommended that for both mailo and other land a system of registration of title with a guarantee of indefeasibility on the lines of the Torrens System should be introduced to replace the

---

[1] Thomas and Spencer, *op. cit.*, p. 66. See H.C.C.A., *Kabazi* v. *Kibuka*, 2 U.L.R. 9.

[2] Laws of Uganda, 1935, Vol. VI, p. 1385.

[3] *Ibid.*, p. 1387.

[4] Thomas and Scott, *op. cit.*, p. 103.

[5] Thomas and Spencer, *loc. cit.*

[6] *Ibid.*, p. 10.

[7] *Ibid.*, p. 18.

[8] *Ibid.*, p. 67.

[9] The Land (Survey) Law, 1909. See H.C.C.A. 21 of 1947, *Kigozi* v. *Walusimbi*, upholding P.C.C.C. 27 of 1946 (unreported).

[10] Thomas and Spencer *op. cit.*, p. 53.

[11] Now entitled the Possession of Land Law, Rev. Edn., pp. 154 *et seq.*

then current system of registration of documents. To quote Thomas and Spencer:

> "Accordingly a short ordinance, The Registration of Land Titles Ordinance, 1908, was enacted in time to embrace the registration of the first final mailo grants issued in 1909, and this Ordinance, though only a provisional measure, under which the registration of new titles alone was compulsory, established the important principle that all land upon registration, must be identifiable by a satisfactory plan. Registration of new titles to land under Documents Registry thereupon ceased. This Ordinance gave way to the current comprehensive Registration of Titles Ordinance, 1922 (founded largely on the Transfer of Land Acts, 1915–16, of the State of Victoria), which came into force on 1st May, 1924."[1]

The Uganda Memorandum of Agreement (Forests), 1907, regulated the inclusion of small or isolated pieces of forest in native estates;[2] but the Buganda Agreement (Allotment and Survey), 1913, had such a radical effect on the mailo land distribution that it is worth referring to the actual words of the classic authorities:

> "The position had arisen in certain cases that a chief, assuming that his principal family estate covered two square miles, had obtained a Provisional Certificate of Claim for that area. Upon survey this holding might be found to cover three square miles, and he was then called on to cut off the extra square mile, which would revert to the British Government. The chiefs asked that they might be permitted to surrender equivalent areas from other of their less desirable claims and thus to retain the ascertained excess. This seemed not unreasonable, but the draftsmen of the Buganda Agreement (Allotment and Survey), 1913, in their endeavour to meet all the implications arising from the original proposition, can hardly have foreseen the abuses which were legalised when the Lukiko, in addition to the rights which had been sought over ascertained excesses or 'surplus estates', was given very wide powers in regard to the redistribution of unsurveyed land, not only in satisfaction of any deficiency ascertained upon survey to exist in respect of the area shown in a provisional claim, but in exchange for other unsurveyed claims. Thus a Provisional Certificate of Claim, which originally purported to recognise a chief as entitled to a certain piece of land 'by occupation and cultivation' became to a large extent a letter of credit for land negotiable where and when desired."[3]

---

[1] *Loc. cit.*
[2] See Thomas and Spencer, *op. cit.*, p. 74.
[3] *Ibid.*, pp. 67–68. See also H.C.C.A., *Mugwanya* v. *Sensuwa*, 2 U.L.R. 207.

THE BATAKA PROBLEM

The 1900 Agreement had played havoc with the *butaka* and *butongole* land tenures which had existed in Buganda in the previous century. It was as if those two categories of tenure had been fused and then converted into something approaching the third category of *bwesengeze* tenure which had obtained. Be that as it may, it soon became clear that the hereditary " fathers of the soil " (abataka) had been deprived of most of their ancient rights.[1] That the Protectorate Government appreciated this situation by 1908 at any rate is evidenced by the first draft of the Land Law, 1908, but the members of the Lukiko by then were determined to maintain their vested interests in the new system of land tenure.[2]

Not unnaturally disputes concerning what was previously *butaka* land began to come before the courts and the first case found among the available records is of 1911.[3] A summary of the more important early decisions on this subject is as follows:

  (i) that Kaira, Head of the Buffalo Clan, had first right to mark out all land allotted to him in area of clan's " butaka ";[3]

 (ii) that the appellant, who had bought from a stranger in 1909 *butaka* land of his clan (Scaly Ant-Eater) under an arrangement with the clan to subscribe was properly prevented by the Lukiko when, the clan having omitted to refund the purchase price, he attempted to sell the land to a European;[4]

(iii) that no appeal lies after 8 years against the confirmation of the Lukiko of the heir to the Head of the Otter Clan;[5]

 (iv) that a suit in respect of the sale of the *butaka* of the Sprat Clan is a clan case and should be tried by the full Lukiko with the Katikkiro as President and with appeal from the decision to the Kabaka.[6]

What was to become a leading case for many years came before GUTHRIE SMITH, J., in 1922.[7] After reference to the Native Chief Justice and the Lukiko Court as to the meaning of " butaka "

---

[1] See Goldthorpe, *op. cit.*, pp. 76–77.
[2] Thomas and Spencer, *op. cit.*, p. 69.
[3] P.C.R.O. 3 of 1911, *Kasbante* v. *Kaira* (unreported).
[4] P.C.R.O. 5 of 1912, *Kitakuli* v. *Lukiko* (unreported).
[5] P.C.R.O. 6 of 1912, *Namuimba* v. *Lukiko* (unreported).
[6] P.C.R.O. 26 of 1917, *Kikwata* v. *Nanungi* (unreported).
[7] H.C.C.C. 79 of 1922, *Fazaldin Miranbux* v. *Simoni Lule*, 3 U.L.R. 101.

and the rights and powers connected therewith, the following certificate was received by the High Court:

" (a) 1. *The meaning of butaka land.* The *butaka* is land held by right of birth, which is in the gift of the Kabaka to a certain person, where are buried the remains of the fore-fathers, ancesters, members of the clan, brothers and children; it comprises hills, rivers and forests according to its boundary, and also some hills are given the names of the children who are born on that land, such as Gingo the children of the place are named Gingo.

(b) 2. *The right Kabaka has.* He is the supreme ruler of Bataka, and is the one who allots the land to a person.

(c) 3. *The power Kabaka has.* He is the one who allots the land to a certain person, and is the guardian of the *butaka* land; and to-day if a person wants to sell *butaka* land, he (Kabaka) stops him from doing so.

(d) 4. *The right the owner of land has.* He has the right on the *butaka* land to look after it, to receive rents from persons on the land, to sell trees which are there, and the fruits and things found therein.

(e) 5. *The power the owner has.* He is the one who settles all disputes arising in that mile.

(f) 6. *The power the members of clan have.* The members of clan have power to select the successor of the *butaka* land, they select the very person among the descent of the very line as they did in the case of Simoni Lule to succeed the *butaka* of Gingo, and if they find out that their brother (the successor) offered that land for sale to other people who are not the descendants of that line, they can bring their complaint before the Lukiko. If Lukiko find out that he was offering for sale that land privately, the Lukiko would order the members of clan to redeem their *butaka* land by giving another mile in exchange or in money; and also they have the right to bring the bodies of the members of the clan who have met their death elsewhere to be buried on that land.

(g) 7. *The power the owner of mile has to sell.* If the mile is not *butaka* Land the owner can sell it, but if it is *butaka* land he has no power to sell it to the people who are not members of that clan born on that land.

(h) 8. The whole of Gingo is *butaka* land, *butaka* of Ngeye clan throughout the extent of its boundaries.

Signed. APOLO KAGWA,
Katikiro.
Signed. ANDELEYA KIWANUKA,
Omulamuzi.
Signed. HAMU MUKASA,
for Omuwanika of Buganda."

The learned trial judge accordingly held that any portion of land in Buganda which had been held as *butaka* of one of the clans from time immemorial and had been allotted under the Uganda Agreement, 1900, to a member of the clan, was to be regarded as subject to the customary law of *butaka* and could not be sold out of the clan and therefore could not be taken in attachment.

There followed a series of further cases, of lesser authority, but during the period when " the *bataka* problem " was being aired most vigorously. It is no part of our present purpose to go into the details of that agitation.[1] The more important of those cases can be summarized as follows:

   (i) that a deposition of *butaka* at will was entirely contrary to Buganda custom and that until the clan exercises its right to deprive a clan chief of his office and its per-quisites for good cause he remains a clan chief;[2]

  (ii) that the mere statement of some person claiming to be a representative of the clan that the land is *butaka* is not sufficient proof that it is *butaka* but that the Omulamuzi must approach the Katikkiro with a view to obtaining an authoritative ruling from the Kabaka as to whether the land is *butaka*;[3]

 (iii) that a decision of the Katikkiro's Court upholding the clan's interest in *butaka* wherein were the clan's burial grounds must be upheld, in accordance with the Uganda Agreement (Clan Cases), 1924, against would-be pur-chasers.[4]

Then came a leading decision of GRAY, Ag. J.,[5] which criticised the decision in the Miranbux case in the following terms:

> " I will assume for present purposes that the land in question is *butaka*, by which I mean that it is the ancestral burial ground of members of the defendant's clan, and for that reason was by the ancient custom of the Buganda not alienable to persons who were not members of that clan. *Fazaldin Miranbux* v. *Simoni Lule* (3 U.L.R. 101) is an apparent authority for saying that such land is still inalienable outside the clan, but I am strongly of the opinion that that decision calls for reconsideration. One has only to look at the land legislation passed by the Baganda themselves to see that more than considerable doubt is thrown on the correctness of the decision.
>
> If the provisions of any law are repugnant to the continued existence of any custom, that custom must be treated as abrogated and destroyed, even if the law does not expressly abrogate it in so many words. Examination of the land legislation passed by the

---

[1] See, however, Thomas and Spencer, *op. cit.*, pp. 70–72.

[2] P.C.R.O. 30 of 1925, *Sebugwawo* v. *Mundu* (unreported).

[3] P.C.R.O. 144 of 1928, *Waswa* v. *Lule* (unreported).

[4] P.C.R.Q. 22 of 1932, *Kabenge and Another* v. *Mulwanyi* (unreported).

[5] H.C.Misc.C. 19 of 1933, *Timoni Mwenge* v. *Serwano Migade*, 5 U.L.R. 97.

Native Government of Buganda for the Baganda of Buganda clearly shows to my mind that customary *butaka* tenure no longer exists.

By the Uganda Agreement, 1900, a certain area of land was allotted to official chiefs of Buganda as ' official estates '. Other land was allotted to ' chiefs and private landowners ' as private estates. The right of the British Government to acquire any of this land—' public or private '—compulsorily for purposes of public utility was expressly recognised. No provision was made that any particular class of land should be exempt from such acquisition. The actual allotment of land was left to the Lukiko and their decision on the point was final and not appealable. (*Alipo Kabazi* v. *Jemusi Kibuka*, 2 U.L.R. 9.) From the report of *Stanislaus Mugwanya* v. *Lui Sensuwa* (2 U.L.R. 207) it would appear that the Lukiko did not always allot *butaka* land to members of the clan.

In 1908 the Buganda Native Government passed a Land Law. By Section 2(b) the owner of a mailo was permitted ' to sell his land to another man or to give it him as a gift, or to will it to him in writing, or to hand it to him in any other manner not in conflict with this or any other law '. No restriction was imposed by this law on the alienation of any particular class of land. The sole restriction on alienation is that contained in Section 2(c) and (d), which deals with alienation to non-natives of the Protectorate and religious or other societies.

Again, by Section 2(e) it is re-affirmed that ' the owner of a mailo will be permitted to dispose of his mailo by will in writing to people of the Protectorate ', but not to non-natives or religious or other societies. It is only in the case of an intestacy that ' a successor will be ascertained according to the rules of the law of succession of the Baganda ' (Section 2(f)) and in such cases if ' there is no one to succeed him as directed by law . . . the mailo shall be in the hands of the Governor and the Lukiko to have and deal with as trustees of the Baganda '. (Section 4). The Land Law, therefore, does not impose any restriction on the right of the landowner to alienate his land by will outside the clan.

It is perfectly clear from the Land Law of 1908 that, subject to certain restrictions imposed upon alienation to non-natives and to religious and other societies, a Muganda Landlord has been granted the unrestricted right to alienate his land—no matter of what customary tenure it may formerly have been held—to any person he chooses. Such right of alienation is repugnant to the continued existence of any customary tenure, which makes such land inalienable outside the clan. The plaintiff therefore has a right to this land whether it was once of *butaka* tenure or not. . . ."

That decision has been followed ever since and although cases concerning *butaka* have come subsequently before the courts,[1] no further case law was made.

---

[1] *E.g.* P.C.C.C. 35 of 1947, *Mayanja* v. *Kulubya* (unreported).

Registration of Titles

It is no part of our present purpose to examine in detail the steps taken to register the titles to mailo land. Indeed the recent account[1] by two officers of the department primarily responsible makes sorry reading so many have been the lost opportunities and failures over the years:

(i) the omission to translate the Registration of Titles Ordinances 1908 and 1924 into Luganda;[2]

(ii) the inadequacy of survey facilities;

(iii) the omission to establish district registries;

(iv) the omission to provide landowners with an official transfer form, which resulted in the unregistered Lukiko Endagaano (Agreement);[3]

(v) the dealing in abstract areas of land unidentified at the time by survey.

Most of these matters have now been set right and that is fortunate as the fragmentation of the original mailo estates, involving consequential subdivision surveys, has increased each year since the end of the First World War.[4] Out of the original 3,700 allottees in 1905, there were about 20,000 in 1935,[5] between 50,000 and 75,000 in 1950, of whom 25,004 were registered holders,[6] and about 120,000 in 1958, of whom on the 12th April, 1958 only 46,060 were holders of registered titles.[7] The ownership of land bringing with it security and social prestige has certainly come within the reach of a peasant's ambition.[8] At the present time one in every five or six male adult Ganda owns land.

In the light of that confused position one can sympathise with the opinion expressed by Guthrie Smith, J., thirty years ago:

" It is much to be regretted that when the authorities saw fit to endow the natives of Buganda with the blessings of private ownership of land they did not provide a sensible and simple method of carrying out their beneficial intention. They have allowed a sort

---

[1] T. N. N. Brushfield and A. J. Relton, *Land Registration in Buganda*, 1955, pp. 10 *et seq.*

[2] Now rectified by the Kabaka's Government in Volume II of the Translations of Protectorate Legislation (published September 1959).

[3] See below.

[4] Thomas and Spencer, *op. cit.*, pp. 80 and 90.

[5] Thomas and Scott, *op. cit.*, p. 103.

[6] Lord Hailey, *Native Administration in the British African Territories*, 1951, Part I, p. 7.

[7] Figures provided from memorandum of Registrar of Titles.

[8] Goldthorpe, *op. cit.*, p. 77.

of dual control to grow up which in time will provide a fruitful crop of disputes and litigation. Put shortly the system followed is that the Lukiko issue a provisional certificate for a given area of land and the grantor then marks out that area on the ground as nearly as he can, and then when the surveyor arrives on the scene he cuts the boundaries to the correct acreage and a final certificate is issued. Since the survey has been going on for 20 years and will last at least as many more, it is obvious that people will die and dealings with the land will occur. As there was no means whereby the Land Office could trace such changes of ownership the Lukiko were asked to pass the Land Laws, 1909 and 1912. These laws are intended to facilitate the task of the Land Office in issuing final certificates in the proper names after survey. The word valid can only mean valid for the purpose of issuing final certificates, but they do not interfere with the right of native owners to deal with their land, and do not affect equitable rights or the duty of the Court under the Order in Council 1902 to decide native cases according to substantial justice. Disputed rights cannot possibly be determined either by the Land Office or the administrative Lukiko. They can only be determined in a Court of Law."[1]

POSITION OF LANDLORD AND TENANT

The transition of the landlord from the pre-1900 system of land tenure to the mailo system is summed up by Richards:

" By the new mailo system introduced in 1900 the King and a number of the existing " landlords ", to use the term in its original sense, were granted a kind of freehold over the estates they happened to be occupying. They ceased to be dependent on the King's pleasure and obtained permanent security of holding, together with the quite new right to buy and sell land and to pass it on to their heirs. Their rights extended to enormous stretches of land from one square mile to eight or even more. The chiefs, now commonly referred to as landowners, retained much of their old power, their rights to allocate land, their authority over their ' men ', now described as tenants, and their position in the political councils of Buganda. They could still demand services from their peasants, and when cotton was introduced at the beginning of the century and peasants asked for extra land on which to grow the new crop, they began to levy toll on the cotton grown under the title of envujo. They seem also to have made other demands considered excessive."[2]

The economic pressure which the mailo owners began to put on their tenants during and after the First World War is described in detail by Thomas and Spencer:

---

[1] H.C.C.A. 29 of 1920, *Nasanaire Kirwaneire* v. *Masiale Ntwatwa*, 3 U.L.R. 69.
[2] *Op. cit.*, p. 127.

" The imposition of a rent on cultivators was a simple evolution arising from the commutation into money of the services traditionally due by a peasant to his overlord. By 1918 this rent had been generally fixed at 10 shillings a year for each peasant's garden, occupying usually one or two acres, but signs were not wanting in succeeding years of a desire on the part of certain landowners to increase this figure. A few thousand fortunate landowners were entitled to the rents of several hundred thousand tenants; but there was no security of tenure nor formal recognition of tenant's rights.

From the earliest days it had been a custom of the peasant to give to his chief periodical presents in kind—a bunch of bananas, a goat, or a pot of beer from each brew. When, during and after the war, peasant cotton production became a considerable industry, this tribute in kind, known as ' *nvujo* ', was magnified by landowners into a demand for a substantial proportion of the tenant's crop. As much as one out of every three bags of seed cotton was said in certain cases to have been levied."[1]

The Protectorate Government began then to appreciate that the rights of the peasantry had not been defined in the 1900 Agreement.[2] This realisation was driven home by the Bataka agitation of the early '20's. When announcing its decision on that problem on the 7th October, 1926:

" The British Government at the same time declared its intention of insisting upon the passage of legislation to ensure security of tenure to native occupiers and for the limitation and regulation of rents and tribute in kind.

This clear guidance met with a loyal response from the Native Government. Subordinating the narrower interests of its individual members to considerations of the common welfare, it eventually passed, in July, 1927, the Busulu and Nvujo Law, 1927, which, while safeguarding the peasant cultivator, gave reasonable regard to the claims of the landowner. This law is probably the first instance of a rent restriction act in tropical Africa."[3]

That Busuulu and Envujjo Law remains on the statute book with minor amendments to this day,[4] and while it is the charter between landlord and tenant of mailo land in Buganda it is not within the scope of this book to examine that native law in detail.[5] The social effects of that notable piece of legislation were described by Mair five years afterwards as follows:

" In law the security of the peasant is greater than it was before, since he is protected against arbitrary eviction; the chief can no

---

[1] *Op. cit.*, p. 69.
[2] Richards, *ibid.*
[3] Thomas and Spencer, *op. cit.*, p. 72.
[4] Rev. Edn., pp. 168 *et seq.*
[5] See below at p. 167 for notes of decisions on that law.

longer plunder his possessions, and his obligations are defined by a law which fixes the landlord's share of economic crops at a much smaller amount than that which some chiefs had previously demanded. At present some landlords go to the limits of their legal rights, but many of the older chiefs do not exact their full dues. Peasants who complain of oppression usually say that it would be no use moving because all landlords are alike; but others will tell one that they have left a landlord who ' treated them badly ', and on inquiry the ill-treatment will prove to have been a pressing demand for rent. One hears the advantages of living on Government land, where the annual rent is the only obligation, weighed against the fact that there a man who fails to pay his rent is evicted at once."[1]

The powers and liabilities of owners of mailo land are generally set out in the Possession of Land Law[2] and the Busuulu and Envujjo Law.[3] Subject to those native laws, the landowner has other rights springing from the nature of his tenure, which have come to be recognised as part of the customary law.

The landowner has power to allot holdings on his mailo.[4] Eviction of a tenant, of course, under the procedure laid down in the Busuulu and Envujjo Law, is an exercise of the powers of ownership.[5] The landowner has the right of reversion to a plot on his land.[6] He also has the right to establish his official residence (embuga) on each of his estates and such a residence may be resited by a new owner within the estate.[7] But in establishing his embuga the landowner must have regard to the preservation of the rights of his existing tenants as far as possible.[8] The official residence on each estate is left in the charge of the landowner's steward (omusigere) who usually lives nearby on his own plot (kibanja).

The part played by the landowner and his steward at this official residence has been aptly explained by Mukwaya:

" In fact it is not only the stability of the society that is dependent on the landowner or his steward. In order to keep law and order in the country, the Government is dependent on him to an extent greater than is often admitted. The landowner keeps peace

---

[1] *Baganda Land Tenure*, p. 167.
[2] Rev. Edn., pp. 154 *et seq.*
[3] Rev. Edn., pp. 168 *et seq.*
[4] H.C.C.A. 30 of 1957, *Matovu v. Iga and Another* (unreported).
[5] P.C.C.C. 44 of 1950, *Lubanga v. Kirunduga and Another*, 1940–1955 C.L.R.
[6] P.C.C.C. 46 of 1954, *Kiwanuka v. Nakku*, 1956, C.L.R. 67.
[7] Busuulu and Envujjo Law, section 16.
[8] P.C.C.A. 190 of 1955, *Nabaggala v. Kasule*, 1956, C.L.R. 69 and P.C.C.A. 209 of 1955, *Nnanfuka v. Kizito*, 1956, C.L.R. 73.

in his area and will arbitrate between his tenants in all the petty cases. The muruka chief who is usually a landowner or the steward of a landowner considers it his duty and right to arbitrate in all cases. It is only when the case is considered serious, or if the complainants will not accept the muruka chief's decision, that it is taken to the gombolola court, which is the lowest officially constituted court in the country."[1]

The steward organises the collection of the rents and dues from the tenants on the estate and usually takes 10% of the amounts collected, 5% being retained by the actual collector and the balance of 85% going forward to the landowner.

Landlords, however, have for some years past become dissatisfied with the return from their tenants permitted by the law especially in areas where land values have risen. If tenants occupy their land, the landowners cannot evict them without the order of a court and so cannot develop their land to the full.[2] The landowners in general have retaliated by exacting a premium from anyone desirous of taking up a plot. This is now a practice so widespread and of such economic importance that it is worth digressing for a moment to trace its origin.

In the last century plots (ebibanja) were not sold nor was a premium demanded. As has been already observed,[3] chiefs were keen to attract tenants to their area in order to increase their own prestige and to gain manpower with which to enrich themselves in war. A chief would even give his new tenant assistance firstly by sending his men to bring the new tenant's property from his former abode and paying them with a goat to feast upon and secondly by giving his new tenant part of a plantain garden, until his own was established, spears, a wife and a hoe. Sometimes, of course, the chief was brought presents of a calabash of beer and a cock on the occasion when his peasant wanted to introduce an unmarried brother with a view to the latter becoming the chief's servant and thereby, it was hoped, eventually obtaining a plot, wife and livestock.

The cultivation of cotton and then of coffee also accelerated the breakdown in the old economic relationship. The tenants began enriching themselves and the landowners felt that rent (obusuulu) of Shs. 8–50 cents was quite insufficient as a return

---

[1] " The Immigrants and the Law ", at p. 193 in *Economic Development and Tribal Change*, 1954, ed. A. I. Richards.

[2] Richards, *op. cit.*, p. 128; and see below p. 166, on the subject of urban land in the Kibuga.

[3] See p. 64, above.

on their land. This reaction by the landowners came at a time when in the years 1942 to 1946 ex-askari were returning home with their pockets lined with substantial gratuities. My information is that the practice of exacting a premium for a plot was first seen in Buddu and Kyaggwe, spreading to Bugerere in 1945, Kyaddondo in 1946 and to the rest of Buganda by 1948.[1] In Bugerere the practice increased with the influx of Ruanda settlers.

The premium is variously referred to as the landowner's *kanzu* (cotton garment), " eky'emisana " (lunch) or " enkoko " (chicken) and is of no fixed amount. It is assessed on the general condition of the plot and its situation. A plot on virgin bush or in forest or swamp is allocated for anything up to Shs. 500/– and a plot under cultivation may call for Shs. 2,000/– as premium or even Shs. 4,000/– for a 7–10 acre plot in the rich soil of Bugerere.[2]

The tenants themselves have been quick to follow their landlord's lead. An outgoing tenant now demands up to two thousand shillings from an incoming tenant allegedly for improvements to the plot and growing crops.[3] On being paid the outgoing tenant then introduces the incoming tenant to the landlord with the fiction " I have brought my brother " (ndeese omuganda wange). The landowner then exacts his premium. The outgoing tenant, of course, may well apply what he gets in payment of premium for a new plot elsewhere.

The only exception to this practice is said to be an heir succeeding to a plot (kibanja) and he merely takes to his landlord the traditional calabash of beer when he is introduced to him.[4]

My information is that this practice is only to be found on private mailo and that any chief on the Kabaka's mailo who connived at the practice would be sacked.

It is said that there are similar kinds of payments made:

 (i) by an incoming tenant to the landowner's steward (omusigere) who after the landowner's acceptance of the tenant took him to the plot allotted—the money is called *ensambakandi*;

---

[1] Compare Richards, *op. cit.*, p. 129, who gives place of origin as Bulemeezi.
[2] Prices have obviously risen in the last five years—compare Richards, *loc. cit.* (Shs. 50/– to 1,000/– in 1954).
[3] I was informed that Shs. 2,000/– had in fact been exacted by an outgoing tenant for five acres of coffee at Kyengera, Busiro.
[4] See Chapter 11, below.

(ii) by a lodger in the Kibuga, the key-money consists of nine cowries or a chicken or a *simoni* (50 cent piece), and is called *kiwejjowejjo*; and

(iii) by an intending buyer to prevent sale of an article to another—the gift being called *tonvamu*.

The landowners and tenants who practise these methods are clearly ignoring the provisions of the Busuulu and Envujjo Law but it is well-established that if a plot is leased at a higher rent than Shs. 10/– per annum then that Law does not apply. It is therefore possible to contract out of the provisions of the Law. Cases concerning premium do not, understandably enough, come to the courts but Richards has written as follows on the legality of the practice:

> " The entry money is thus not illicit in the sense that there is any legal prohibition of such individual arrangements between land-lord and tenant, but it is often discussed as though it were an ' under the counter ' transaction. Few cases of dispute over *Kye musana* payments come to court as the custom is not covered by the Busulu and Envujo Law or its amendments. The transactions are also usually made without witnesses. Foreigners who do not know the whole history of the evolution of the *kibanja* system simply talk of ' buying ' plots."[1]

It is usually in respect of plots used for commercial purposes that a lease outside the terms of the Busuulu and Envujjo Law is to be found,[2] but also in respect of residential plots particularly in urban areas.[3]

As with the owners of mailo land, so with the tenants their present rights and duties are mainly embodied in the two native laws.[4] There are other rights and limitations of tenancy which apply under customary law to plots governed by the Busuulu and Envujjo Law.

The tenant, of course, must pay his master *busuulu* (rent) and *envujjo* (dues) under the Law but if his plot lies on the lands of two or more owners legal complications arise.[5] The decision usually followed is that of the Judicial Adviser in a 1949 case wherein he ruled that the tenant should only pay *busuulu* to the

---

[1] *Loc. cit.*
[2] *E.g.* P.C.C.A. 24 of 1955, *Kalibbala* v. *Nsubuga*, 1956 C.L.R. 75, P.C.C.C. 431 of 1956, *Wamala* v. *Kusalakuzibu*, 1957 C.L.R. 133 and P.C.C.A. 89 of 1957, *Zzimbe* v. *Ssajjabbi*, 1957 C.L.R. 135.
[3] See p. 166, below.
[4] See p. 143, above.
[5] P.C.C.A. 65 of 1956, *Kanyalutale* v. *Lubega*, 1956 C.L.R. 71.

landlord on whose land the tenant's house stood and *envujjo* alone to those on whose land he had crops but no buildings.[1] The landlord or his steward usually allots boundaries to his tenant's plot but plots vary greatly in size.[2] Those boundaries usually enclose an area of uncultivated bush which the tenant may later develop,[3] and even though the tenant may not cultivate therein he can prevent others from doing so. A new custom is coming into vogue whereby a landlord can, with his tenant's permission, lease part of that tenant's bush to another but on the expiry of the lease that portion cultivated reverts to the tenant. The rent from the lease, of course, goes to the landlord.

A plot does not usually extend over streams[4] nor onto another owner's land.[5] A plot in fact ends with the cultivation (ekibanja kikoma w'alimye) unless other boundaries have been defined to include uncultivated bush. But cultivation includes land lying fallow (ebisambu). Formerly a peasant could let a friend cultivate his fallow land temporarily surplus to his own requirements in return for a present out of each crop. He was entitled to take back the land at any time.[6] Such a seasonal letting of fallow by the tenant is no longer permissible in view of the general prohibition on subletting in section 18A (b) of the Busuulu and Envujjo Law.

A tenant, then, may in respect of his cultivation on his plot prevent all outside interference. He may shut off his fallow land and prevent herding of livestock there. As to his bush, he may prevent cultivation but not herding, the collection of firewood or the cutting of grass or reeds.

Despite the growing practice of extracting a premium already noted,[7] a tenant certainly has no right to sell his plot to another without his landlord's approval of the incoming tenant.[8]

As regards the rights and liabilities of a tenant on a leased plot which is outside the provisions of the Busuulu and Envujjo Law,

---

[1] J.A.C.A. 22 of 1951, P.C.C.A. 5 of 1949, *Kasule* v. *Sengendo* (unreported) and see Mukwaya, *Land Tenure in Buganda*, p. 56.

[2] P.C.C.A. 42 of 1956, *Lugakingira* v. *Nakibuka*, 1956 C.L.R. 71.

[3] P.C.C.A. 177 of 1955, *Bisaso* v. *Lukabwe*, 1956 C.L.R. 71, P.C.C.A. 132 of 1957, *Zirimuwagabo* v. *Kasolo*, 1958 C.L.R. 89 and P.C.C.C. 157 of 1949. *Kasirye* v. *Mugema and Another*, 1940–1955 C.L.R.

[4] P.C.C.A. 54 of 1957, *Musoke* v. *Musoke*, 1957 C.L.R. 121.

[5] P.C.C.A. 42 of 1957, *Sendagire* v. *Kateregga*, 1957 C.L.R. 123.

[6] Mair, *An African People in the Twentieth Century*, p. 156.

[7] See p. 145, above.

[8] P.C.C.A. 67 of 1957, *Kawesa* v. *Mbewadde*, 1958 C.L.R. 89.

the High Court has tended to follow the general principles of the English common law and equity.[1]

The other rights of tenants will be considered below in the section dealing with common rights in land.[2]

INTEREST-HOLDERS

It is convenient at this point to consider the various groups of interest-holders in mailo land at the present time.

Taking ownership first, there are the political interest-holders, to wit the Ministers and Ssaza Chiefs who hold official mailo out of the original allotments to their predecessors in office under the 1900 Agreement. Of the eight square miles that each Ssaza chief was allotted,[3] he has allocated 49 acres to each of his ggombolola chiefs as his official estate, upon which his headquarters are built. These official estates of the chiefs are liable to be utilized for buildings put up by the Kabaka's Government in the area and for the residences of Government employees but otherwise the chief during the tenure of his office enjoys the usufruct from his official estate in the same manner as a private landowner. Official estates, as has been mentioned above, are also held by certain members of the Royal Family of Buganda[4] and quite the largest holder of official mailo is the Kabaka himself with his 350 square miles (I propose dealing with the special situation to be found on the Kabaka's mailo in the succeeding section). Official mailo estates are not only subject to the general legislation whether native law or Protectorate Ordinance governing mailo land but also to the special provisions of section 6 of the Possession of Land Law and the Native Official Estates Ordinance (Cap. 122).

The latent interest of the clans in the former *butaka* land has already been described.[5] Section 2(c) of the Possession of Land Law militates against social groups holding an interest in mailo land, but commercial and even religious societies appear to do so of late.[6] Those social groups, including the clans, and joint

---

[1] See judgment of AINLEY, J., in H.C.C.A. 38 of 1949, *Benwa Kisalita* v. *Yokana Kabangala and Bros.*, Notes 37 (alteration of building).

[2] See p. 163, below.

[3] See also P.C.C.C. 139 of 1954, *Katambala* v. *Nsimbe*, 1956 C.L.R. 61.

[4] *E.g.* P.C.C.A. 6 of 1958, *Musoke* v. *Kibuka*, 1958 C.L.R. 79.

[5] See above p. 128.

[6] *E.g.* P.C.C.C. 198 of 1954, *Bukunja Traders Association* v. *Kibali*, 1957 C.L.R. 137 and P.C.C.C. 403 of 1956, *Ngubiri* v. *Semombwe*, 1957 C.L.R. 139.

registered proprietors, of whom more anon, are the only examples of community rights over land in Buganda.

The individual Ganda interest-holder in the ownership of mailo land we have considered at some length already but the position of strangers requires separate mention. Non-Ganda Africans may certainly hold mailo land or an interest therein but Richards, who conducted a detailed study of the immigrants position in Buganda, writes:

> " In fact, however, the sale of land to non-Ganda is comparatively rare. Land ownership is still associated with political rights and social status and hence there is considerable feeling against a foreigner becoming a landowner (mutongole) in his own right."[1]

Land can belong to the dead until transferred to the heir.

To turn to holders of tenancies, there are official plots occupied by servants of the Kabaka and Royal Family[2] and also by the stewards of mailo estates.[3]

Individuals we have already considered but a special word must be said of non-Ganda immigrants. The majority settle as ordinary customary tenants on mailo land under the provisions of the Busuulu and Envujjo Law:

> " In the villages studied in Busiro, 65.2 per cent of the immigrants were settled on customary plots, in Kyagwe 61.9 per cent and in Buddu 55.8 per cent."[4]

There are, however, two other types of status that an immigrant may acquire on mailo land:

(i) he may be a jobbing porter (omupakasi akola lejjalejja) who pays 50 cents to one shilling a month to the landlord for the right to dwell in temporary grass-huts (nsisira) on the land;[5] these lodgers (abasuze) are prohibited from growing food crops around their dwellings;[6] or

(ii) he may rent a plot for either one, two or even three successive seasons (omweyazize atalina kibanja) in order to grow cotton, usually building a temporary grass hut only and omitting to cultivate a regular food garden he works as a jobbing labourer for food (okusaka busasi).

---

[1] *Op. cit.*, p. 132.
[2] P.C.C.A. 1 of 1958, *Mulongosa* v. *Gowa*, 1958 C.L.R. 79.
[3] See p. 143, above.
[4] Richards, *op. cit.*, p. 130.
[5] *Ibid.*, p. 119.
[6] Southall, *op. cit.*, p. 31.

" When he has gathered his cotton he pays dues on a share-cropping basis, the share usually being fixed at one bag of cotton per plot (worth Shs. 45 at the time of survey) or in some areas two bags of cotton and additional dues. . . . This type of tenancy is based on purely commercial considerations on each side. It carries with it none of the rights of permanent occupation which customary tenants enjoy and it is not governed by laws enforceable in the courts of Buganda, as is the holding of customary plots. It is not clear when this practice of renting land became common. It was evidently considered a very usual practice in 1937. . . ."[1]

KABAKA'S MAILO

The system of land tenure in the last century has already been described.[2] The estates of the batongole were either named after the Kabaka who created that estate (ekitongole), and it was the custom and still is of each Kabaka to create one such estate on his accession,[3] or after the work or attributes of the first chief of the estate (ow'ekitongole).[4]

On the allotment of mailo under the 1900 Agreement the Kabaka received official estates totalling 350 square miles of which 150 square miles are situated in Kyaggwe and the balance mainly in the four ssazas of Kyaddondo, Bulemeezi, Busiro and Buddu.

When some of his chiefs of estates became ggombolola chiefs in the early years of this century, the Kabaka replaced them as chiefs of his official estates.[5] Other of the Kabaka's former chiefs of estates obtained ggombolola status on their own lands under the mailo distribution.[6]

The chain of control on the Kabaka's estates under the new system, starting at the bottom, runs as follows:

    (i) the village chiefs (abatongole);

    (ii) the parish chiefs (ab'emiruka);

    (iii) the chief of the estate (ow'ekitongole);

    (iv) the Katikkiro of the Villages of His Highness the Kabaka (Katikkiro we Byalo bya Ssabasajja Kabaka);

---

[1] Richards, *op. cit.*, p. 130.

[2] See above pp. 127 *et seq.*

[3] *E.g.*, Kiteesa, Kichwa, Kisuna, Kyanga, Kikabya, Kimanya.

[4] *E.g.*, Kimaasa (Happy One), Kiwunge (Earless One), Kisonyi (Tailor).

[5] *E.g.*, Mukabya became Mutuba III Kyaggwe at Kyampisi.

[6] *E.g.*, Mukusu at Nakisunga, Nafumbambi at Mpumu, Namutwe at Msinde, Katenda-eziba at Masiki and Mubito at Ntenga.

(v) the Private Treasurer to His Highness (Omuwanika we Nkuluze);

(vi) the Minister of Finance (Omwanika); and

(vii) His Highness the Kabaka.

It is necessary to examine this chain of control in detail:

The village chiefs (abatongole) are very numerous, for example on the estate Kiteesa alone in Kyaggwe, there are 53 such chiefs. They, like batongole chiefs, elsewhere in the Kingdom receive no salary from the Kabaka's Government. For their work they receive an allowance from the Kabaka in the form of a percentage of the *busuulu* and *envujjo* which they collect in their village. This allowance is not fixed, indeed the Kabaka from time to time varies it by order, but it is now about one fifth, that is, the village chief receives the rent and dues of 2 tenants for that of every 10 collected—or Shs. 17/– and more.

The parish chief (Ow'omuluka) on the Kabaka's mailo may or may not be also a muluka chief recognised by the Kabaka's Government for work under the Ggombolola Chief of the area. In 1916 the Lukiko, with the approval of the then Provincial Commissioner acceded to the Kabaka's request that as far as possible the chiefs on his estates should be given muluka chieftainships as Government chiefs also.[1] This policy has been implemented in those areas where the Kabaka's mailo is concentrated. For example, on the same estate Kiteesa, three out of the nine parish chiefs (ab'emiruka) are recognised and paid by Government. Where the Kabaka holds fragmented estates intermingled with private mailo his estate chiefs are not usually also recognised and paid by the Kabaka's Government. The parish chief (ow'omuluka) on the Kabaka's mailo has his own group of tenants to collect rent from, usually more numerous than those under the village chief's authority, and he receives a percentage allowance at the same rate.

There are forty-two chiefs of estates (ab'ebitongole) and they receive a percentage allowance on the rents of a certain allotted number of tenants, usually more numerous than those under the parish chief's authority, but at the same rate.

In administrative matters the chief of estate (ow'ekitongole) refers to the Katikkiro we Byalo but in financial matters the chief of estate refers direct to the Private Treasurer (Omuwanika we Nkuluze) without passing through that Katikkiro.

---

[1] *Akatabo ke Biragiro na Mateka ebyatesebwa Olukiko Olukulu olwe Buganda okuva* 1916 *okutusa* 1919, p. 3.

The Katikkiro we Byalo is a salaried post which was created to relieve the Private Treasurer of administrative work in respect of the Kabaka's estates. In fact there is, of necessity, the closest co-operation between them in the administration of the estates. Such consultation extends to the recommending of names to the Minister of Finance and so to the Buganda Appointments Board for the appointment of chiefs on the estates but does not extend to the settlement of disputes arising from the arbitral tribunals on the estates.[1] The Katikkiro has a council composed of usually 20 or 22 representatives of the chiefs of the larger estates to assist and advise him.

The Private Treasurer (Omuwanika we Nkuluze) is also a salaried official and he is responsible to the Minister of Finance for the management of these estates and, of course, of the Kabaka's privy purse.

Under a new system introduced two years ago, to prevent the abuse of the exaction of premia, the application of a would-be tenant on the Kabaka's mailo is introduced by the chief of the estate in question (ow'ekitongole) to his council of subordinate chiefs and an allotment is then made. Alternatively the Kabaka may order that a certain individual receive a plot (ekibanja) on one of his estates and this order passes through the Katikkiro we Byalo to the chief of estate selected.

As has already been observed, the Possession of Land Law and the Busuulu and Envujjo Law[2] apply to tenants on the Kabaka's mailo. The principal differences between such tenants and tenants on private mailo are:

  (i) they have a special obligation to provide a bunch of plantains (ettooke) every month, and banana leaves and fibre when required;[3]

  (ii) they have a much greater security of tenure as there is no likelihood of sale, fragmentation or distribution of the land, although there is a slightly increased but still very remote risk of eviction for public purposes.

Finally there is a special arbitral system for the settlement of disputes arising on the Kabaka's estates. Arbitration is first undertaken by the village chief (omutongole). Neither at this stage nor at any later stage are fees paid. If the dispute cannot

---

[1] See below.
[2] See E.A.C.A., C.A. 9 of 1949, *Zedi Mulika* v. *Ismail Mohamed* (1949) 16 E.A.C.A. 51.
[3] Mukwaya, *op. cit.*, p. 46.

be settled by the village chief, arbitration is then undertaken by the parish chief (ow'omuluka). If he fails to settle the matter, it is referred to the chief of the estate (ow'ekitongole) and his council. If their decision is disputed, a case file is opened and is sent to the Katikkiro we Byalo, who hears the case sitting with his council. The register of cases kept by the Katikkiro we Byalo shows that he deals with about one hundred such cases a year, originating from about 31,000 tenants.[1] If the decision of the Katikkiro we Byalo is disputed, the case file is referred to the Minister of Finance (Omuwanika) for decision. Should his decision be disputed and should the case concern custom, the case file may be referred to the Kabaka for decision. Sometimes the Katikkirö we Byalo, the Minister of Finance or the Kabaka if the aggrieved party is not satisfied with the decision of these administrative tribunals may send the matter to the courts of law for trial.[2]

Acquisition, Transfer and Extinction of Interests

The procedure for acquiring, transferring and being evicted from the tenancy of a plot (ekibanja) have already been considered but the acquisition, transfer and extinction of ownership of mailo land calls for especial study.

At the time of the final allotment in 1905, the transferable wealth obtained in mailo was not appreciated by the Ganda, who at first merely distributed pieces from their allotment to relatives. With the advent of cotton cultivation in 1906, the need for land and then for money were felt and the sale of mailo started. In that year and for the next few years, the sales were comparatively few and the price was exceedingly low, being merely a few rupees. It appears to have been the heirs of the original allottees, who had died meanwhile, who first began to realise their wealth.

In the beginning the agreements to sell land were verbal, often a square mile would be sold for a few cows. Thereupon both parties went before the Katikkiro, Sir Apolo Kagwa Gulemye, who confirmed the price or reduced it. This confirmation by the Katikkiro had early been seen to be necessary in view of the sharp practice which began to develop. The situation that then existed has been described by AINLEY, J.:

---

[1] See Mukwaya, *loc. cit.*, for number of tenants.
[2] *E.g.*, P.C.C.C. 264 of 1955, *Bazekuketta* v. *Luswa* (unreported).

G

" The very obvious difficulties of transaction in land while the land was still the subject of these so called Provisional Certificates was fully recognised early on in the history of land settlement in Buganda. To meet the difficulty the Land Law of 1909 was made, and amended in 1912.

A perfectly simple and wise scheme was devised, of which the Baganda occasionally took advantage. The law began by saying ' The words which are herein written are the words which shall govern every owner of land before the Government have surveyed his land and have finally recognised that the land is his.' Then followed direction that no transactions in ' such land ' should be valid unless verified by the Lukiko. Thus the ' Lukiko endagano ' came into being. Then the method whereby the beneficiary of a transaction in ' such land ' could achieve absolute and final title to it was not lost. The Lukiko was to issue what became known as a ' Certificate of Ownership to the beneficiary ', and on the strength of this the Final Certificate could be issued to the beneficiary, that is the ' purchaser ' or ' donee '."[1]

So widely employed was the " Lukiko endagaano " and such an important factor in the confusion that resulted in the registration of mailo titles that it is worth examining its actual wording, of which this is a translation:

" KINGDOM OF BUGANDA   LUKIKO MAILO No. 3
                        Agreement to sell land.

No.

I   of

have sold my land entered below, which I obtained in the manner described below. ·

I have sold it to   of

to be his very own and of his children who shall succeed him. For it he has given me those shillings recorded below. And we have made out this Agreement to confirm that we have completed this transaction, and we have appended hereto our signatures to be evidence of our transaction. And if when the surveyor surveys the land in question, these acres which are the subject of this our transaction are found to be missing, then all the balance of those acres I will pay to him out of my other land.

The Parties	*Witnesses*
I the vendor	
	I confirm that that is his very own signature.
	I confirm that that is his very own thumb print.

---

[1] H.C.C.A. 10 of 1952, *Hamu Mukasa and Another* v. *Muguluma* (unreported).

I the purchaser

I confirm that that is his very own
signature.
I confirm that that is his very own
thumb print.

Name of Landowner	Area of land which is sold, the number of the certificate, village, ssaza, how he received it and its boundaries	Amount for which the land is sold	Name of the person who buys the land

We of the Lukiko have carefully checked that the land stated
above is the property of   indeed, and
that he received it in that manner recorded above. Therefore we
have without dispute appended our signatures hereto giving him
permission to sell it.

Mengo

19   Katikiro ⎫
                              ⎪   Ministers
            Omulamuzi ⎬   of
                              ⎪   the Lukiko "
            Omuwanika ⎭

It will be observed that such a " Lukiko endagaano " is not a
contract to sell but is a memorial of a sale that has already taken
place. Although such " agreements " were filed at Entebbe in
the Office of Titles they were not instruments registrable under
the Registration of Titles Ordinance and consequently landowners and would-be purchasers were misled as to the true state
of the land in question and unprotected as to their transactions.
Quite a few such agreements were protected by caveats placed
on the register by the purchaser or by the Registrar of Titles but
in general there was insufficient staff to convert these " agreements " into registrable instruments of transfer and to clear the
caveats.[1] In 1955 it was estimated that there were 40,000 such

---

[1] See the account of Brushfield and Relton, *op. cit.*, pp. 13–16, and statistics
on p. 140, above.

unregistered documents lying in the Office of Titles; fortunately that number had been reduced to 18,000 by the end of 1957, to 16,600 by April 1958 and to 10,000 by 1959.[1] On the setting up of the branch registries in 1955, no more such agreements were accepted for deposit and vendor and purchaser were henceforth required to execute a proper registrable instrument of transfer.

So much for the problem of those concerned with the actual registration of such transactions, but the aftermath has caused and still causes the courts great difficulty. The best exposition of this difficulty is that of AINLEY, J., sitting as a Puisne Judge on the Court of Appeal for Eastern Africa:

> " Here there is a striking example of a phenomenon very common and indeed inevitable in Buganda. The transactions of the Lukiko have resulted in the creation of a title recognised by the Native Courts but which is not founded upon any transaction which the Registration of Titles Ordinance recognises. The Lukiko by granting a Certificate of Succession to the Respondent have declared him ' to be entitled according to Law to have possession of and to sell ' the land in question ' according to the custom of succession of the Baganda '. But the man whom the Respondent succeeded was never upon the Register at all and from him no title could flow either by way of transfer or by way of succession according to the law which governs title to land in Uganda. It seems to me then that this Certificate of Succession was worthless to effect any change upon the Register or to confer upon the Respondent the status of Registered Proprietor, although in practice the Registrar normally accepts Certificates of Succession as a justification for effecting a transfer by succession. . . .
>
> The appellant sought to discharge this onus by proving that Banalaba died four years before the execution of the document. I think that upon what is before this Court he did establish that fact as a probability. How then, he asks can this document be otherwise than a forgery. The question might be unanswerable were we not dealing with a transaction taking place in Buganda a few years after the idea of individual ownership of land was introduced to the people. There is little doubt that at that time perfectly honest transactions in land appeared on paper in forms which would horrify an English conveyancer and to this day the representative of the estate of a deceased man, even the representative of a living man, will honestly use the name of the deceased or of the living person whom he represents."[2]

The courts have, however, made some important decisions on sale of mailo land and this is a convenient point to review them:

---

[1] Figures abstracted from memoranda by the Registrar of Titles.
[2] E.A.C.A. C.A. 16 of 1949, *Kyagulanyi* v. *Sebuliba*, H.C.Misc.C. 10 of 1947 (unreported).

(i) the maxim of *caveat emptor* obtains;[1]

(ii) a verbal sale of land is valid[2] (though written agreements are more usual);

(iii) a written agreement of sale, however, speaks for itself and cannot be upset by a subsequent verbal agreement;[3]

(iv) an agreement of sale in which a witness did not actually witness the signature of the parties but signed subsequently is invalid;[4]

(v) an agreement of sale may contain a condition precedent;[5]

(vi) where a purchaser buys a number of acres out of the bulk of an estate without specific description or stated boundaries, he must be satisfied with that number of acres anywhere within the estate;[6] (or as another Judge put it seven years later:

" The buyers know, or should know that there can be no transfer of particular acres by a man who has not a registered title to particular acres. If they choose to bet on the chances of the vendor eventually getting a title to the land sold, and they lose their bet, that is their own look out."[7])

(vii) if a man wishes to protect by caveat a particular bargain he must specify the precise boundaries of the land which is the subject of the bargain;[8]

(viii) all disputes between joint registered proprietors of estates must be decided with reference to what can be proved of their title;[9]

(ix) the maxim *qui prior est tempore potior est jure* obtains between rival purchasers, that is, the first to buy shall be allowed to survey his portion first;[10]

(x) it is the practice for the vendor or his representative to be present when land sold is being surveyed to confirm the boundaries agreed;[11]

---

[1] P.C.C.C. 162 of 1953, *Kayongo* v. *Kiwanuka and Another*, 1956 C.L.R. 53.

[2] H.C.C.A., *Adamu Kikonyogo* v. *The Kivuvu (Uganda) Rubber Co. Ltd.*, 2 U.L.R. 36 and P.C.C.C. 135 of 1955, *Katende and Another* v. *Kawuma* (unreported).

[3] P.C.C.C. 139 of 1953, *Nambasa* v. *Kiddu*, 1940–1955 C.L.R.

[4] P.C.C.C. 118 of 1955, *Nagadya* v. *Kiwanuka* (upheld in J.A.C.A. 36 of 1956) (unreported).

[5] P.C.C.C. 274 of 1955, *Kyeyune* v. *Sekayiba*, 1957 C.L.R. 125.

[6] H.C.C.A. 9 of 1946, *Mukasa* v. *Kasozi* (*per* PEARSON, J.), Notes 19.

[7] *Per* AINLEY, J., in H.C.C.A. 45A of 1953 upholding P.C.C.C. 39 of 1951 (unreported).

[8] H.C.C.A. 47 of 1950, *Kabali* v. *Kalanzi and Another*, Notes 61.

[9] H.C.C.A. 28 of 1947, *Naduli* v. *Serwanga*, Notes 21.

[10] P.C.C.C. 31 of 1955, *Kakoza* v. *Kwerimba and Others* (upheld in J.A.C.A. 12 of 1957 and H.C.C.A. 91 of 1957) (unreported) but see below p. 158 for effect of the Land (Agreements) Law.

[11] P.C.C.C. 281 of 1956, *Musanje* v. *Lukambagire*, 1956 C.L.R. 61.

(xi) a tenant who purchases land from his landlord is likely to bargain for land surrounding his homestead;[1]

(xii) a purchaser has a contractual right against the vendor's successor in title;[2]

(xiii) the proper course for the purchaser to adopt, should he suppose that there was a danger of collusion between the vendor and other parties, is to intervene in the suit brought to attack the title of the vendor, not to file a separate action against the vendor.[3]

To deal with the chaotic accumulation of transactions in mailo an attempt was made in 1939 to lay down a rule of priorities of agreements but the legislation—the Land (Agreements) Law—was bungled in the drafting: it was enacted as a native law and so did not bind the Registrar of Titles; nor did the Law make provision for what was to be done with agreements already lodged in the Office of Titles. The effect of the law was that all informal land transactions were brought to the Registrar of Title's notice and a rule of priorities was provided which was workable until there was an oversale. Unfortunately most of the disputes which come to court involve oversale of mailo. Section 3 of the Law does not state that an unregistered instrument shall have no validity at all, nor does it apply to documents relating to title by succession.[4] But where a vendor has made agreements to sell the same land to two different purchasers, and one purchaser only has lodged his agreement with the Registrar of Titles as required by subsection 3(b) of the Law, that purchaser alone has a right to insist upon the preparation and registration of an instrument of transfer.[5]

In 1928 a magistrate, who was later to be Provincial Commissioner, Buganda, observed:

> " The present land tenure in Buganda being an alien institution and mortgages of this nature a modern innovation, there can be no customary law applicable."[6]

Five years previously indeed the High Court had occasion to draw the attention of the Lukiko Court to the applicability of the doctrines of the Court of Chancery in matters relating to a

---

[1] H.C.C.A. 8 of 1953, *Mayanja* v. *Mwayi and Another*, Notes 57.

[2] H.C.C.A. 45 of 1948, *Katenda* v. *Mukasa*, Notes 39.

[3] H.C.C.A. 23 of 1951, *Mukasa* v. *Kiggundu*, Notes 47.

[4] H.C.Misc.C. 62 of 1958, *Re S. Namusoke*, Bulletin 13 of 1959 (February).

[5] H.C.C.A. 36 of 1951, *Makanga* v. *Kasana*, Notes 45.

[6] A. H. Cox in P.C.R.O. 94 of 1928, *Battabikere* v. *Kabadzi* (unreported).

mortgage of mailo land.[1] It is pleasing therefore to observe that in 1930 when the same Battabikere, who had been before the Provincial Commissioner in the other case in 1928, attempted to obtain the actual plot of land, which secured the debt, the Lukiko Court refused his application and gave the mortgagor a certain time to pay and failing that, ordered the plot be sold in public auction to satisfy Battabikere's claim.[2]

A mortgage may be made originally by word of mouth and later confirmed in writing.[3] There grew up, however, a regrettable practice of evidencing a mortgage by a document in the form of an agreement of sale. Sometimes such agreements, at any rate in Bulemeezi fifteen years ago, were in three parts:

(1) an agreement of loan secured by a mortgage of land to a fixed date;

(2) an agreement of the same loan secured by the same mortgage to a later fixed date;

(3) the outright sale of the land mortgaged for the sum loaned on a later fixed date.

Naturally such agreements proved fertile soil for litigation and not only did mortgagees pretend agreements of mortgage were outright sales,[4] but vendors pretended that contracts of sale were really mortgages.[5] In deciding such cases the Principal Court looked to the actual wording of the document, to extraneous even verbal evidence[6] and to the vendor's silence for 20 years without suing the other party for refusing to accept repayment of the alleged loan.[7]

The same court has held that where there was nothing in a mortgage agreement stipulating that rents from the land in security were to be applied to pay off the capital loan the mortgagee was entitled to repayment of the full sum loaned.[8] And that while interest on a loan was allowable, 36% per annum was

---

[1] H.C.C.A. 2 of 1923, *Erieza Wamala* v. *Musa Musoke*, 3 U.L.R. 120 (*per* GUTHRIE SMITH, J.). See also H.C.C.R. 19 of 1935, *Lutuga* v. *Galiwango*, 5 U.L.R. 147.

[2] P.C.R.O. 26 of 1930, *Battabikere* v. *Kaggwa* (upholding Lukiko Court Case 35 of 1930) (unreported).

[3] P.C.C.C. 173 of 1956, *Nsubuga* v. *Nabbowa* (unreported).

[4] *E.g.*, P.C.C.C. 42 of 1944, *Kaggwa* v. *Mukasa* (unreported).

[5] *E.g.*, P.C.C.C. 97 of 1948, *Nanfumba* v. *Nyumba and Another* (unreported), and P.C.C.C. 165 of 1948, *Kaungu* v. *Ntambi*, 1940–1955 C.L.R.

[6] P.C.C.C. 97 of 1949, *Nyanzi* v. *Kiggundu* (upheld in J.A.C.A. 1 of 1950 and H.C.C.A. 8 of 1950) (unreported).

[7] P.C.C.C. 26 of 1954, *Musoke* v. *Kezala*, 1940–1955 C.L.R.

[8] P.C.C.C. 92 of 1945, *Kirama* v. *Serunkuma* (unreported).

too high a rate to allow over a period of 23 years (sic),[1] although 9% was permissible.[2]

The extreme difficulties involved in cases concerning mortgages of property on mailo land are typified by a case which came before the High Court in 1942.[3] The circumstances were that the appellant had been unsuccessful before the Principal Court in claiming damages against the respondent for pulling down his house and carrying off his iron sheet roofing and other belongings on the grounds that the seizure had been in accordance with an agreement which purported to be one of sale of the house but contained a proviso that the vendor (the appellant) should retain possession for a month and might redeem within that time by repaying the cash advanced. PEARSON, J., held:

(a) that this was not a *bona fide* sale and purchase, but a mortgage or pledge under the form of sale;

(b) that a proviso to the agreement, wherein it was agreed that the purchaser might seize the premises and the vendor purported to renounce his remedy for seizure of any goods in the house though not included in the agreement, was a clog or fetter on the equity of redemption and void;

(c) that this form of moneylending contract should not be countenanced by the Court, not only because it is harsh and unconscionable but also because the pulling down of a house arbitrarily is likely to cause a breach of the peace and is against public policy.

Leases of plots of mailo outside the provisions of the Busuulu and Envujjo Law, as has been already observed, are common particularly in urban areas or for purposes other than residence elsewhere, *e.g.* for shops. The Principal Court has on occasion made an order for rent due and for immediate possession (of the Blue Bar, Kibuye).[4] Rent is usually payable in advance.[5] Failure by the lessor over a period of 14 years to protest at a breach of a lease and his continued acceptance of rent constituted acquiescence of the breach by the tenant to the time when the rent next fell due and the lease was not forfeit until after notice

---

[1] P.C.C.C. 38 of 1945, *Kamya* v. *Nakasinde* (upheld in J.A.C.A. 40 of 1945) (unreported).

[2] P.C.C.C. 28 of 1941, *Mugabe and Another* v. *Senkubuge*, 1940–1955 C.L.R.

[3] H.C.C.A. 13 of 1942, *Donezio Luboyera* v. *Semu Musoke* (Manager, " Agenda yalaba " Co., Moneylenders, Wandegeya), Notes 3.

[4] P.C.C.C. 89 of 1952, *Kalanzi* v. *Ntambi and Another* (upheld by GRIFFIN, C. J., in H.C.C.A. 43 of 1952) (unreported).

[5] P.C.C.C. 1 of 1953, *Sendi* v. *Sebuliba* (lease of house for use as dance-hall) (unreported).

the tenant should fail to conform with the terms of the lease within a reasonable time.[1]

Land may also be given. Gifts of mailo, as has been mentioned already, took place first immediately after the original allotment in 1905. And such gifts are valid and it matters not whether the land in question was previously *butaka* and the donee is a member of another clan.[2] A gift, however, made during the lifetime of the deceased donor, which was not subsequently mentioned in his will and in respect of which no instrument of transfer was registered, was incomplete.[3] As regards revocation of a gift SHERIDAN, J., opined:

> " In giving judgment for the appellant the Principal Court gave as its reason that where someone has made a gift he cannot go back on it and take it away. This reasoning did not commend itself to the Judicial Adviser, and unless this accords with native customary law prevailing in Buganda, it does not commend itself to me. In English law if a person makes a gift which is not supported by valu(abl)e consideration, there is nothing in law to prevent the donor from changing his mind and withdrawing the gift. It would be otherwise, of course, if the donee had already dealt with the gift by disposing of it to a third party. In his Plaint before the Principal Court the appellant stated that in accordance with the Land (Agreement) Law he sent the agreement to the Registrar of Titles within a month of the date on which it was made. The Principal Court made no finding on this, but if the appellant took this step before he received the letter of withdrawal then it would appear that the letter was too late to be of any effect."[4]

It is interesting to note that four years later the Principal Court held that a donor can under customary law revoke a gift of land in respect of which no transfer has been registered.[5] Land may not be given to a Church under section 2(c) of the Possession of Land Law.[6]

The statutes of limitation do not apply to tenures by native custom nor is there any prescriptive right to land by native custom.[7]

---

[1] H.C.C.A. 27 of 1950, *Luboyera* v. *The Buganda Government*, Notes 43. See also P.C.C.C. 171 of 1958, *Kasali* v. *Kaggwa*, 1958 C.L.R. 95.
[2] P.C.R.O. 3 of 1930, *Masaba* v. *Kasoma* (upholding Lukiko Court Case 249 of 1929) (unreported).
[3] H.C.C.A. 10A of 1947, *Nakabugo* v. *Nkoyoyo*, Notes 19.
[4] H.C.C.A. 12 of 1954, *John Waswa* v. *Danieri Bayitanomugumu* (unreported).
[5] P.C.C.C. 36 of 1957, *Mayanja* v. *Takirambudde*, 1958 C.L.R. 93.
[6] P.C.C.C. 124 of 1957, *Musoke* v. *Nakibinge*, 1958 C.L.R. 91.
[7] H.C.C.A. 3 of 1945, *Semalinte* v. *Mayanja*, Notes 15.

The acquisition of land and interests in land by inheritance will be considered in Chapter 11.

During the last ten years, a practice has grown up of leasing a plot of coffee or of beer bananas (mbidde) in order to obtain money to pay a debt. Sometimes a plot of coffee is mortgaged as security for a debt on the understanding that the proceeds of the sale of the coffee will go to pay off the debt. Sometimes the owner of a coffee plot, usually a new heir, hires the crop out in order to avoid the trouble of harvesting. Plots of permanent economic crops are leased in this manner for two, three or even four years running. The agreement is usually for a term of years, not just in respect of a single harvest, as coffee crops twice a year. Always the owner of the plot, the lessor, is responsible for the cultivation of the coffee let as the lessee cannot be trusted to look after the trees.

Annual standing crops, particularly cotton in Bulemeezi, are sold. The purchaser in such a case assumes responsibility for cultivating the crop until he harvests it. The tenant of the plot does not have to seek his landlord's permission to the sale and he remains responsible for paying *envujjo* in respect of the crop to his landlord and for burning the cotton plants after the harvest in accordance with the law.[1] After the harvest full use of the plot reverts to the tenant.

Trees must be separated into their various categories in order to understand the powers under customary law connected with them. Only the landowner has the right to sell trees of economic value, firewood for brickmaking or bush for the burning of charcoal.[2] Dry firewood is usually not sold but left for the tenants to collect for their own use. The tenant has no right to sell any trees, not even barkcloth trees, nor firewood. He has power to cut down the barkcloth trees, fruit trees and coffee trees on his plot without asking his landlord's permission but must not do so just prior to leaving the plot. The tenant may sell any of the produce of such trees, of course, such as barkcloths or fruit without his landlord's permission. If he was to cultivate a plantation of economic trees, such as *nsambya* or eucalyptus he must first come to an agreement with his landlord as to such a project and in particular as to the dues (empoza) which he will pay the landlord on selling the trees. A plantation becomes the property

---

[1] Agricultural Rules, Rule 6, Rev. Edn., pp. 224–226.
[2] See P.C.C.C. 218 of 1957, *Mukasa* v. *Lwanga*, 1957 C.L.R. 95.

of the landowner on the departure from the plot of the tenant who planted it, not of the incoming tenant—*superficies solo accedit.*[1] Such a landowner, however, may reach an agreement with the new tenant regarding payment of dues for the plantation, in which case he may give the new tenant authority to cut and sell the trees. Most of this customary law regarding trees has been embodied in section 9(a) of the Busuulu and Envujjo Law.

Even a landowner cannot remove trees connected with spirit worship (emiti egy'okusamiramu).

A contract of sale of hardwood trees (mivule) by a landowner binds his successor in title also.[2]

The former procedure for a tenant who wished to build a house in permanent materials on his plot was to ask his landlord for permission. This is still the procedure on many estates in Buganda but in other parts, notably in Bugerere and Kyaggwe, allegedly following the decision of the High Court in a *cause célèbre*,[3] a new practice has arisen on private mailo of the tenant building a permanent house without seeking his landlord's permission. On official estates there is a standing order that no tenant is to erect a permanent building without permission. Any tenant may build a mud hut thatched with grass or roofed with corrugated iron sheets without asking his landlord's permission.

On leaving a plot a tenant may remove his corrugated iron roofing providing he rethatches the house with grass or papyrus and he may, despite an early attempt by the Lukiko to rule otherwise,[4] remove his wooden doors and windows providing he fills the resultant gaps with doors and windows of reeds.

Trespass to land will be considered under the law of torts in Chapter 16.

COMMON RIGHTS IN LAND[5]

Since 1900 the practice has arisen, contrary to the ancient custom, whereby clan elders now have to ask the mailo owner's

---

[1] P.C.R.O. 38 of 1936, *Masajage* v. *Gweweyigira* (upholding Lukiko Court Case 594 of 1935) (unreported).

[2] P.C.C.C. 102 of 1955, *Botobewa* v. *Katumwa and Another* (amount of damages awarded alone varied in H.C.C.A. 31 of 1959) (unreported).

[3] *Isaka of Kigu* v. *Hamu Mukasa, Sekibobo*. I regret I have been unable to trace the year or the case number.

[4] *Ebigambo Ebyatesebwa Olukiko Olukulu olwe Buganda Awamu Nebiragiro ebirala*, 1918, p. 8.

[5] Some ancient public rights and easements are laid down in section 2(h) of the Possession of Land Law.

permission before bringing a corpse onto his land for burial in
what was the ancient *butaka* of the clan. But:

> " According to the customs of the Baganda a person is not
> denied access to land other than his own that he may tend his
> tombs; and there is the further point that a person can exhume the
> bodies of his deceased relatives and can take them to his own land
> if he wishes."[1]

As to rights of way, a landowner cannot prevent people using
ancient footpaths (amakubo) but he can stop them from making
new ones without his permission. The same legal principle applies
to cattle paths (kyikute), but is only enforced near areas of heavy
population. The permission of the landowner must, however,
be sought before a track is cut or increased in size for motor
transport whether it be an official track (bulungi bwansi) or a
village track (obweyagalire). Anybody may herd cattle on un-
occupied bush belonging to another but not on fallow land
(bisambu). Fallow land becomes classed as bush if left uncultivated for three consecutive years. (To herd cattle on someone else's cultivation is, of course, cattle trespass which will be
considered in Chapter 16 under the law of torts). There are no
private rights of grazing even on one's own bush or close to one's
house unless an area is enclosed with fencing (olukomera) or
barbed wire (ssengenge). But neither barbed wire nor fencing
can be erected by any tenant whether on private or on official
mailo without the permission of the landlord. Indeed on the
Kabaka's mailo no lesser authority than the Minister of Finance
may grant such permission. The bias against the erection of
barbed wire is because it prevents people moving freely in the
area to fetch water, firewood or grass.

Kalinda-luzzi of the Colobus Monkey Clan (Ngeye) is the
guardian of the Kabaka's well in the Lubiri (Palace). Each
village too has its keeper of wells. If a villager does not go to do
maintenance work on a well, when summoned by the village
chief, he is prevented from using the well and is also fined a goat
or a calabash of beer. If an individual digs a well for drinking
water, anybody may draw water there but if a person does so he
must thereafter assist in the maintenance of the well.

If a dog is allowed by its owner to drink in a well set apart
for human consumption, the dog's master commits an offence
and the penalty is to dig a new well. Similarly cattle must be

---

[1] P.C.C.C. 158 of 1949, *Mukasa* v. *Mukasa*, 1940–1955 C.L.R.

taken to separate water places other than wells used for human consumption.

There is no restriction on watering cattle at rivers or swamps. But those who dig dams for the watering of cattle (byesero) have a collective right to prevent others who do not assist in the digging from watering their cattle there. Likewise a private individual who digs a dam for watering his cattle can prevent others from watering their cattle at his dam.

There are the following rules which apply to wells set apart for human consumption:

(i) no-one may go to fetch water unless his hands and legs are free of soil;

(ii) no person may take his pipe there (for if he does so he is counted a wizard);

(iii) no-one may wash himself in the well;

(iv) no-one may wash clothes in the well;

(v) nobody may put a sooty pot or kettle in the well;

(vi) a woman is not allowed near a well during her menstruation.

Fruits of the land can usually be taken by anybody if permission is sought. For example, in the last century building poles and grass were taken freely without permission being sought but nowadays the landlord must be requested to allow the cutting of building poles, particularly of *nsambya* and *nkoma* trees, and the tenant must be asked for permission to cut his grass. Wild damsons (mpafu) or wild cherries (misaali) may be gathered in the bush but it is the practice to give a basketful to the chief of the village. If those trees stand on a tenant's plot, the fruit is his. The same rules apply to the collection of wild honey. As the Ganda proverb runs:

Nnanyini ffumu tasubwa nnyama—The owner of the spear is not passed over as regards meat.

The landowner receives a share of mushrooms and edible ants (enswa) gathered by his tenant; in default the tenant, at any rate in ancient times, was fined a goat.

The Kabaka's prerogative to produce of the land will be considered in Chapter 9.

Manure was used in ancient times to doctor knots on the bark-cloth tree (omutuba) so that the bark grew over them. In those days anyone could take as much cattle manure from a kraal as he wished without asking permission. Nowadays owing to the growing appreciation during the last ten years of the value of manure in agriculture the practice has arisen of first asking permission before removing the manure. This practice is becoming more general at any rate in peri-urban areas because of the trade in manure which is developing on a small scale.

URBAN DEVELOPMENTS

The most startling examples of urban development on mailo land are the suburbs of Katwe and Kisenyi within the Kibuga and on the perimeter of the Kampala municipal area. Southall's description of the land tenure in Kisenyi, the result of careful and detailed research, gives a clear picture and I accept it readily subject to two minor points:

> " In Kisenyi today the class of landowners remains, but the class of customary tenants has virtually disappeared. This process is clearly due to the fact that land in Kisenyi is now put to quite different uses from those originally envisaged. Its main value now is not for the subsistence cultivation of peasants, nor even for the planting of cash crops but for commercial and residential building sites. . . .
>
> Residential and commercial plots in Kisenyi resemble in status these temporary residential plots of immigrants rather than customary peasant holdings. The commonest fee charged for them is now ten shillings a month, but plot holders who have shops, or whose plots have good frontages, are paying from 300 shillings to 1,000 shillings a year. . . .[1]
>
> The outstanding feature of the mailo land system in its application to densely occupied areas, and perhaps elsewhere under modern conditions, is the contrast between the very low return on mere ownership and the high return accruing to the developer. . . .[2]
>
> The development of mailo land in urban areas probably yields a higher rate of profit together with a higher degree of security than any other form of investment in Uganda at the present time. In many instances such investments can be capitalised at 50%. Yet this is partly due to the fact that comparatively few Ganda landlords have developed their land, and property values are for this reason unnecessarily inflated."[3]

The two points on which I consider Southall's account should now be modified are:

(i) his statement that it has not yet been clearly established

---

[1] Southall and Gutkind, *op. cit.*, p. 31.
[2] *Ibid.*, p. 34.
[3] *Ibid.*, p. 35.

in the courts that the Busuulu and Envujjo Law does not allow a tenant to erect rooms on his plot in which to accommodate lodgers.[1] Reference to a recent decision of the Principal Court indicates that that Court has decided that section 8(2) of the Law prohibits such practices without the landlord's prior permission.[2]

(ii) his statement that a tenant who pays his dues cannot be rightfully evicted even with compensation.[3] This is certainly not true of tenancies under the Busuulu and Envujjo Law;[4] and in the case of tenancies of plots by agreement, outside the provisions of that Law, it is the simplest of procedures well-recognised by the courts of law for the landlord to give his tenant notice.[5]

Those two small points do not, however, detract from the great value of this independent sociological survey of conditions in the main centre of African activity near Kampala and in support of that account of the general trend of development of mailo in such areas comes part of a judgment of the Principal Court on an action to cancel unfulfilled agreements to purchase land:

> " Land in the Kibuga area varies in price almost every year; and therefore the Plaintiff in refusing to give his land for the prices that were current about four years past is not in the wrong, since it was the Defendant's laziness in that he did not fulfil what he contracted. The Defendant failed to purchase the land and loses the case."[6]

THE BUSUULU AND ENVUJJO LAW

Because of the great volume of litigation concerning land and the inter-connection of native law and customary law already described, I propose to stray in this particular instance from the main objective and briefly to review the decisions of the courts on the principal piece of legislation regulating the relationship of landlord and tenant on mailo land—the Busuulu and Envujjo Law:[7]

---

[1] Southall and Gutkind, *op. cit.*, p. 32.

[2] P.C.C.A. 74 of 1958, *Bangisibanno* v. *Lubogo*, 1958 C.L.R. 87.

[3] Southall and Gutkind, *op. cit.*, p. 33.

[4] Busuulu and Envujjo Law, sections 11, 12 and 16, and see cases quoted at p. 168, below.

[5] *E.g.*, H.C.C.A. 38 of 1949, *Kisalita* v. *Kabangala and Bros.*, Notes 37, and H.C.C.A. 27 of 1950, *Luboyera* v. *The Buganda Government*, Notes 43.

[6] P.C.C.C. 19 of 1955, *Musigire* v. *Sebabenga* (upheld in J.A.C.A. 92 of 1955 and H.C.C.A. 26 of 1956), 1940–1955 C.L.R.

[7] Rev. Edn., pp. 168 *et seq.*

Section 2—a plot (kibanja) comes within the Law when the rent (busuulu) paid is only Shs. 8/50 (*i.e.* Shs. 1/50 having been deducted for Land Tax[1]);[2]

Section 3—the landowner has power to ask the court for an eviction order if rent remains unpaid for 3 years;[3]

Section 4—the payment of *envujjo* (dues) for barkcloth;[4]

Section 6—the tenant must consult the landlord when he wishes to cultivate more than 3 acres of economic crops;[5]

Section 8—a person who nurses a sick man does not necessarily on his death succeed him as heir to a plot;[6]

Section 10—theft by the tenant of his master's goat is disrespect to the master;[7]

Section 11—eviction of tenant: order is to specify the value of all improvements made by him;[8]

Section 12—the landlord is responsible to the tenant for damage to his crops by new tenants whom he admits to plot before eviction order made;[9]

Section 15—does not apply to land which is in excess of the *kibanja* and the 3 acres permitted for the cultivation of economic crops;[10]

Section 16—the establishment of the landlord's *embuga*;[11]

Section 18A(b)—tenant leasing his plot for commercial purposes.[12]

---

[1] See the Land Tax Law, sections 3 and 4, Rev. Edn., pp. 210 *et seq.*

[2] P.C.C.A. 106 of 1956, *Sekweyama v. Kabangala*, 1956 C.L.R. 67.

[3] P.C.C.A. 146 of 1957, *Kamulegeya v. Bossa*, 1957 C.L.R. 105.

[4] P.C.C.A. 38 of 1956, *Mukasa v. Ziryawulamu*, 1956 C.L.R. 73.

[5] P.C.C.C. 53 of 1950, *Kewaza v. Byandala* (unreported), and P.C.C.C. 336 of 1956, *Kaliramujjira v. Banabakintu*, 1957 C.L.R. 111.

[6] P.C.C.A. 110 of 1956, *Kasirivu v. Kukulakwetta*, 1957 C.L.R. 117.

[7] P.C.Cr.A. 64 of 1958, *Kasoma v. Lukiiko*, 1958 C.L.R. 81.

[8] E.A.C.A. C.A. 9 of 1949, *Zedi Mulika v. Ismail Mohamed* (1949), 16 E.A.C.A. 51.

[9] H.C.C.A. 29 of 1957, *Mikando v. Mukezi*, Notes 83, see also P.C.C.A. 104 of 1957, *Wamala v. Ssessanga*, 1957 C.L.R. 107, P.C.C.C. 205 of 1956, *Mukezi v. Mikando*, 1957 C.L.R. 109 and P.C.Cr.A. 83 of 1957, *Lukiiko v. Twase*, 1957 C.L.R. 113.

[10] H.C.C.A. 12 of 1953, *Sawabiri v. Serumaga*, Notes 71.

[11] H.C.C.A. 12 of 1953, *Sawabiri v. Serumaga*, Notes 71, P.C.C.A. 104 of 1957, *Wamala v. Sessanga*, 1957 C.L.R. 107 and P.C.C.A. 41 of 1957, *Kawagga v. Lubega*, 1957 C.L.R. 115.

[12] P.C.C.A. 74 of 1958, *Bangisibanno v. Lubogo*, 1958 C.L.R. 87.

JURISDICTION IN LAND CASES

It is not only the law governing mailo land which is involved, being a conglomeration of native law, customary law and Protectorate legislation but the very jurisdiction of the courts is hedged about with problems. Twenty-six years ago GRAY, Ag. J., observed:

" With the best will in the world Native Courts are often unable to enforce their judgments—more especially those for specific performance of a contract to sell land. They lack the coercive powers of dealing with a dishonest vendor who contemns the Court's order.

As long as the jurisdiction in regard to cases concerning freehold land tenure in Buganda which is a modern creature of the Uganda Agreement, 1900, is exclusively confined to Native Courts, it is inevitable that hardships of this description will arise amongst Baganda."[1]

A more detailed aspect of this problem is to be found in an order of the Acting Judicial Adviser on the 9th February, 1942:

" As to the order for withdrawal of the caveat, the question arises whether the Principal Court has jurisdiction to make such an order. I do not think that section 11 (1) of the Buganda Courts Ordinance, which provides in effect (as I interpret its meaning) that cases arising under Part VII of the Registration of Titles Ordinance shall be tried only by the High Court, precludes the order being made. This was not a ' case arising under part VII ' but an action to compel the defendant to transfer land to the plaintiff in pursuance of an agreement. But I feel that it is doubtful whether such an order could be enforced if the plaintiff refused to withdraw the caveat. Disobedience to the Court's order would not amount to any of the forms of contempt of court specified in section 18 of the Buganda Courts Ordinance, and I know of no other machinery for the enforcement of such an order. It seems to me, therefore, that any order by the Principal Court directed to a party to a suit to take any such steps affecting the Mailo Register as the removal of a caveat is ineffectual. Section 11 (3) of the Buganda Courts Ordinance appears to contemplate the compulsory removal of a caveat being effected, not by an order of the Principal Court directed to a party to a suit, but, by an order of the High Court or Judicial Adviser directed to the Registrar of Titles."[2]

The duty of the High Court when considering the confirmation of a decision of the Principal Court in the matter of title to or interest in mailo land was defined by AINLEY, J., as follows:

---

[1] H.C.Misc.C. 10 of 1933, *Daudi Busulwa* v. *Texas Co. (South Africa) Ltd.*, 5 U.L.R. 55.

[2] Confirmation Cause, *Sematimba* v. *Lupyazitta*, P.C.C.C. 58 of 1940 (unreported).

" That Section in the Buganda Courts Ordinance which lays upon this Court the duty of confirming or varying the judgments of the Principal Court in Mailo land cases was not intended, I think, to give both parties the opportunity of criticising the judgement, or of asking for more than the judgement has given, or of asking that a judgement from which they have not appealed be set aside. Nor do I think that this Court was intended to substitute its own idea of what is right and fair for the opinion of the Principal Court. I think that the legislature which has already given a right of appeal to aggrieved parties, handed this confirmatory power to the High Court because the legislature had, for one reason or another, already handed the trial of Mailo land cases, cases which are governed by the Registration of Titles Ordinance, to a Native Court which was not empowered to administer that Ordinance, and which in any event would be unlikely to understand their untranslated, and untranslatable Ordinance. This Court's duty when considering a case under the Section is confined to ensuring that the decisions of the Principal Court are not contrary to the law laid down or taken for granted, by the Registration of Titles Ordinance, and to making the written and frequently vague directions of the Principal Court, workable and enforceable."[1]

---

[1] H.C.Conf.C. 13 of 1951, *Kaddu* v. *Kawesa* (unreported).

CHAPTER 9

MOVABLE PROPERTY

LIVESTOCK

Cases involving cattle in Buganda are fraught with peculiar difficulties. Often the claims are for many head of cattle each of which nowadays is valued at around seven hundred shillings. Despite the high value of the subject-matter generally in these cases the quantity and quality of the evidence produced by either party is almost without exception lacking in every way. The transactions generally occurred many years before between illiterate pastoral nomads.

As examples of these points and because of their intrinsic historical interest in view of the Royalty concerned we may take two cases:

The first was a claim for seventy head of cattle, valued in 1934 at seven thousand shillings, filed by a Prince of the royal blood of Ankole in the Principal Court of Buganda. The Prince was the son of another famous Prince of Ankole, Gumira. Gumira was deported from Ankole in 1902 and lived in Buganda for many years during which time his cattle were sent to Buganda from Ankole. He died in hospital in 1925 and his body was sent to Ankole for burial. According to the plaintiff Prince, his son, who succeeded to his father's property as a minor under the guardianship of the Omugabe (King) of Ankole, as soon as Gumira's death became generally known the herdsmen in charge of his cattle commenced to conceal them. In 1933 the plaintiff started prosecuting enquiries as to the whereabouts of his father's cattle left in Buganda in charge of various herdsmen of whom the defendant was one. The plaintiff Prince was successful in his suit.[1]

The second case was a claim filed by the Kabaka of Buganda, against the son of his own former Chief Herdsman (Omusumba Omukulu), responsible for the Kabaka's herds in Buddu and

---

[1] P.C.R.O. 3 of 1935, *Alifuledi Binyogambwa, Omulangira of Ankole* v. *Lweterima, Munyankole* (upholding Lukiko Court Case 704 of 1934) (unreported).

Mawogola, for 892 head of cattle allegedly misappropriated eleven years before in 1930 by herdsmen working under Mulisi Kigemuzi Yaye, the defendant's father by then deceased. The Kabaka was successful in his claim before the Principal Court but that Court's judgment was reversed on appeal to the High Court.[1]

In such cases one readily sympathizes with the sigh of a former Chief Justice of Uganda:

> " The question at issue was whether certain cattle which were in the possession of plaintiff's husband Kweita up to the time of his death and are now in the possession of the appellant belonged to him or were merely looked after by him as a shepherd as successor to his father Ibuza, who, the appellant says, was the shepherd of his father Kabututu. . . .
>
> The case is rendered the more difficult by the fact that the real question seems to be who owned the cattle or rather their ancestors some thirty years ago."[2]

Acquisition

Cattle may be acquired in several ways:

(1) by natural increase;
(2) by inheritance (a method which will be considered in Chapter 11);
(3) by gift to friends and relatives, particularly daughters;
(4) by barter (a method which will be considered in Chapter 13 under the law of contract);
(5) by purchase (see also under Chapter 13);
(6) by way of compensation in litigation—
    (a) in ancient times a fine of livestock having been levied;
    (b) at present time in clan cases;[3]
(7) by the practice of entrusting cattle to another for herding and keeping (okusibira ente) (a method which will be considered at length in the following section).

Okusibira ente

The entrusting of livestock usually occurs with cattle (ente y'obusibi or ente y'obusibirwa) but occasionally with goats

---

[1] H.C.C.A. 7 of 1942, *Joseph Kyera Yaye* v. *Stanule Kisitu for H. H. Kabaka of Buganda* (reversing P.C.C.C. 12 of 1941) (unreported).

[2] H.C.C.A. 9 of 1941, *Haroun L. Senkubuge for Zedekia Lwanchwende* v. *Funga* (*Shepherdess*) (upholding P.C.C.C. 8 of 1941) (unreported) (*per* WHITLEY, C. J.).

[3] I am informed that in a recent dispute in the Buffalo Clan, the Kabaka, as Ssabattaka, decided in favour of the Head of Clan who was given authority to fix the compensation to be paid to himself by his Head of Ssiga and he settled on one cow.

(mbuzi mugwa). The object of this practice may be to obtain better pasturage or water supplies for the herd, to subdivide large herds and so avoid the ravages of disease, to avoid responsibility for herding or to help a herdsman or a relative, say a sister, who will benefit from the milk produced. The owner entrusts his cattle to a friend or a relative for an indefinite period and it is the trustee's responsibility to employ a herdsman. The owner is liable to refund to the trustee part at any rate of the herdsman's pay, if he is so minded, any damages arising from trespass by his cattle, money spent on the purchase of cattle salt and veterinary fees. For all such payments the trustee is saddled with primary responsibility. To satisfy part of these financial liabilities the owner receives the proceeds from the sale of milk.

Nowadays an agreement in writing, being a memorial of the trust, is necessary. Witnesses to such a document are necessary and the owner's wife is always a witness of his cattle entrusted elsewhere and in like manner the trustee's wife of cattle entrusted to her husband. The calves of such cattle may be shared between the owner and the trustee in accordance with the agreement but if the matter is not covered in the agreement, the owner has a discretion to share the calves. The usual practice is for the trustee to be recompensed with one calf in every three and with one kid in every two reared.

Each head of cattle has a name usually according to its colour markings. In former times no agreement nor special witnesses were called for as the trust was founded on good faith but the trend of the times as has been noted above is now to record such a trust in an agreement. Further, a movement permit is necessary if the cattle are to move from one ggombolola to another, together with a letter of introduction from the ggombolola chief and the particulars of number, owner and trustee of the cattle are entered in the record book of the muluka chief in whose area they are going to be herded. In addition the veterinary staff inspect and inoculate from time to time. All this official activity may form evidence subsequently of the trust. Of recent years, because of the introduction of personal assessment for graduated tax, in some areas care is beginning to be taken by trustees of cattle and by the taxing authorities to ascertain and apportion the ownership of cattle but the system of tax assessment on cattle is by no means fully developed.

A trustee cannot use the cattle entrusted to him for his private purposes. Nor can he entrust to another cattle entrusted to him

without the owner's agreement. He may, however, lend out a
bull entrusted to him for stud. In such a case the stud fee is one
in every four of the calves born and that calf is given into the
charge of the trustee and is the property of the owner. As to
whether a trustee may castrate a bull entrusted to him without
the owner's permission there appears to be varying practice but
certainly the owner must be informed either before or afterwards.
A trustee may without the owner's permission pass a calf to
another kraal for a couple of months to rest the cow.

A trustee must exercise reasonable care in the keeping of the
cattle entrusted to him but as long as he follows the procedure
laid down he is not responsible to pay the owner compensation
for cattle which die or have to be killed on account of sickness.
If a cow disappears, the trustee must try and find it in order to
explain its fate to the owner. If a cow dies the trustee must
immediately report the circumstances to the owner.[1] If a cow
sickens or is injured, the trustee must make a neighbour a witness
to the fact that the cow entrusted to him is ailing before he kills
it. The trustee cannot kill a sound beast. In every case of death
of a beast the trustee must preserve the hide in order to account
later to the owner for the cattle which died or were killed. The
meat from the slaughtered cow must be sold, if possible, and the
proceeds of the sale then go to the owner. If it is not possible to
sell the meat, the trustee can consume what he likes, often after
giving the landowner his customary joint of one side of the chest,
and he has no liability to pay the owner for the meat consumed.

There is a duty placed on the owner to visit his cattle so entrusted from time to time and the Principal Court has held that
where an owner alleged he left fifty head of cattle with another
in 1936 and did not contact him until fourteen years later, in
1950, then the claim could not succeed.[2] If the trustee is seen to
be slack in keeping the cattle, the owner usually takes the cattle
away from his charge without prior notice, but the trustee must
be told of their removal. Nowadays the owner's representative
bearing written authority can go to collect the cattle from the
trustee; formerly only a well-known member of the owner's
household could do so but without written authority.

If the trustee dies when in possession of another's cattle, the
owner must immediately go to the deceased's home and call for

---

[1] P.C.R.O. 14 of 1921, *Twalabekyo* v. *Gawede* (unreported), and see proverb
in Appendix 6, p. 334, *post.*
[2] P.C.C.C. 73 of 1954, *Lukonzolwa* v. *Kakoba* (unreported).

the book kept by the trustee showing the history of his cattle in order that he may reclaim them. The deceased trustee's wife will also give her statement as to the whereabouts or fate of the cattle in trust.

Herdsmen are of three grades:

(1) the *basumba* who are a highly trusted class of herdsmen employed to herd cattle at a considerable distance from the owner's residence. They receive no pay but all the milk from the herd. Out of that milk they supply their master with lumps of butter (empomero y'omuzigo) every month. Their tax is not paid for them by the owner. These conditions of service approximate to those obtaining for herdsmen in ancient times.

(2) the *omulalo omusenze* (the tenant herdsman) who invariably lives nearby his master (owa waka). The customary arrangement is that the owner gets the morning milk and the herdsman the evening milk. Here again the herdsman gets no pay but his master does pay his herdsman's taxes. Where the owner's residence is near a town the owner often contracts out of this customary arrangement with the herdsman because of the ready sale of milk.

(3) the *omulalo omupakasi* (the porter herdsman) who, as his title implies, is paid a porter's wage and usually gets his rations including some milk. But the milk is his master's and he has no right to it.

Herdsmen may be made to pay the compensation for cattle trespass in which case the trustee or owner usually deducts it from his pay.

In ancient times when a beast was killed the herdsman had a right to a shoulder and foreleg but that right has long since become obsolete.

Herdsmen are not given notice to quit but are dismissed instantly for fear they may take cattle with them on departure.

The temporary entrusting of cattle to a relative, friend or steward during a short absence is not classed as a trust of cattle (okusibira ente) but as a mere stewardship (obusigere).

Before leaving this practice of *okusibira ente* mention may be made of an interesting application of the principle to modern conditions, which came before the courts:

In 1935 and 1936 a certain Kalibbala ran the Aggrey Memorial School and he devised a system whereby the parents of the pupils entrusted cows to him and the parents were then credited with school fees for their children to the extent that the school received revenue from the sale of the milk. Then Kalibbala left, the school eventually closed down and ten years afterwards, when the position regarding these cattle had become vague, one of the parents, who had slept on his rights until then, filed an action reclaiming cattle allegedly entrusted to the school and revenue from sale of milk. It was held by both courts that the suit must fail.[1]

Herding

In the reign of the late Kabaka the leading chiefs who were practically the only cattle owners used to employ a system of rotation whereby part of their milking herds was at any one time being herded near to Mmengo so that they might obtain milk while attending the Lukiko, often for long periods at a time. This practice is now only maintained by ministers and high officials continuously working at Mmengo.

Indeed owners of large herds usually divide their cattle into a milk herd which is kept at home and the rest which are owing to the shortage of pasture herded elsewhere.

An ancient custom still exists whereby as many as ten cattle-owners may place their cattle with their several herdsmen to be herded from one kraal—in a kind of collective herding.

It is the duty of a herdsman to build a proper kraal (olugo lw'ente) and to construct a proper door (mulyango) and bars (emiyingo). He must also keep the cattle inside during the night. Should the cattle stray from the kraal at night, the herdsman becomes liable for cattle trespass through his failure to construct a proper kraal.

A kraal may not be constructed without the agreement of the landowner.

If stray cattle are found, the peasant tells his landlord who passes the information to the parish chief (ow'omuluka) and he in turn reports to his ggombolola chief. The stray cattle are kept at the headquarters of the muluka or the ggombolola chief. The ggombolola chief advertises the finding of the cattle and if the owner does not appear within a reasonable time sells them in auction. The proceeds go into the treasury. The owner may claim back his cattle before the auction or after the sale may claim

---

[1] P.C.C.C. 63 of 1946, *Kabi* v. *Kiyimba and Others* (upheld by AINLEY, J. in H.C.C.A. 19 of 1947) (unreported).

compensation out of the treasury on proof of ownership. The owner is not charged a fee for the impounding of the cattle while they are at the chief's headquarters.

Rights of ownership

There is a custom of *ente enkobane* (collective purchase of a cow by two partners). The offspring of the cow belong to both partners. If the cow is killed, each partner takes half. If one of the partners dies, the heir of that partner inherits the half beast and the share of the calves that the cow may produce.

A husband keeps his wife's cattle for her but the produce is hers. The milk and butter are used in the home. She must, however, consult him before selling any cattle. A divorced wife takes all her cattle away with her, both those she brought and those given her by her husband.

If a father gives cattle to a child who is still living at home then those cattle are herded with the father's and the child cannot sell them without consulting his father. But if the child lives in a different homestead he may take there any cattle given him and then has complete authority to dispose of them.

It is not the practice for cattle herded by friendly arrangement within the family to be the subject of contracts to pay for that herding.[1]

Minor animals

Goats, sheep and chickens may be separately owned by wife or children but, according to the better opinion, they have to consult the husband or father as the case may be before disposing of such livestock.

The Ganda did not keep pigs in ancient times so that there are no special customs but the general rules for livestock apply.

Dogs were used by the Ganda from early times for hunting and as watchdogs. The responsibility for looking after them was on the wives of the household.

The usual stud fee for dogs and pigs is that the owner of the dog or boar takes one of the litter.

As has been already mentioned, the barter and sale of cattle are considered under the law of contracts in Chapter 13; the inheritance and guardianship of cattle are dealt with in Chapters 11 and 12; cattle trespass falls under the law of torts in Chapter 16 and cattle theft under the law of crimes in Chapter 17.

---

[1] P.C.C.C. 107 of 1954, *Kasiga* v. *Kasiga* (unreported).

Care has been taken to exclude from the above account customs pertaining to cattle such as " *mpano* " and " *eggwako* " which are not Ganda but Nkole customs sometimes practised by Nkole or Ruanda herdsmen in Buganda.

OTHER PROPERTY

While the marriage subsists the wife must consult her husband before disposing of her own property. Generally she is allowed also to dispose of produce she has cultivated or articles she has made but the husband usually takes his share (ndobolo). This is a concession to womankind of recent years for in ancient times whatever the wife produced by her toil belonged to her husband. As with livestock so with other movable property, a wife who separates from her husband takes all her property with her both that which she brought into the marital home and that which her husband has given her. The Ganda consider it an offence to strip a wife of her goods (okwambula·omukazi). Household property, except the baskets (ebibbo) brought by the wife, all belongs to the husband and on separation stays with him.

A case[1] filed twelve years ago in the Principal Court provides a good example of the respective rights of husband and wife in movable property in the home:

The suit was for desertion and removal of the husband's property to the value of Shs. 8,750/30 cents. The couple had been married for fifteen years but while her husband was away the wife removed everything in the house and refused to return any to the husband. The defence to the suit was that the husband had threatened to kill the wife and had married another woman. So the wife had deserted him taking her own acquired property and what her husband had given her. Judgment was given for the plaintiff husband as to the property which appeared to be his. The wife was to retain property which she needed in everyday life. The Court further opined that the wife should, on deserting or on being expelled by the husband, have obtained written confirmation as to what was her property and should have removed it in her husband's presence.

The property of minor children and succession to movable property will be considered in Chapters 12 and 11, respectively.

---

[1] P.C.C.C. 172 of 1947, *Kabalu* v. *Kabalu*, 1940–1955 C.L.R.

This appears to be a convenient point to consider the Kabaka's rights to movable property which formed the basis of the ancient system of taxation:

> " Taxes were imposed in Uganda before the advent of the white man. The fundamental principle of the State was that all things and persons were the property of the King, and were absolutely at his disposal. When he had need of anything that the country contained, he commandeered it. The articles taken were fish, kauri shells, edible grasshoppers, earthenware pots, bark-cloth, hoes, shields, fowls, eggs, cattle, bananas and beans. These imposts were not made annually, for it is only recently that time has been recognised as divided into years; but when the King wanted certain articles, the word was passed and the articles were forthcoming."[1]

Mair describes the method of levying the barkcloths:

> " Taxation consisted in barkcloths at the rate of one from each man, which were collected at such times as the King ordered, and were made fresh for the purpose. A barkcloth represented two days' work. They passed through the hands of two chiefs, the peasant's immediate superior and the head chief of the district, each of whom took out his own share. As far back as any informant remembered 250 cowries could be given as an alternative."[2]

This procedure whereby each chief took his share of the produce exacted on the way up to the Kabaka is the source of the Ganda proverb:

Musolo gwanswa osolowooza nga olyako—While you exact the tax of edible ants, you partake of them.

All these taxes of the produce of the land were paid to the Kabaka as a tax in his capacity of Ssabattaka (The Head of all the Clans). If there was default in the payment of tax, there was an offence punishable by a fine of goats.

---

[1] Cunningham, *op. cit.*, p. 232.
[2] *An African People in the Twentieth Century*, p. 133.

CHAPTER 10

METHODS OF ACQUISITION

FISHING

Sir Apolo Kagwa[1] and Roscoe[2] have described at length the ancient customs of Ganda fishermen and the nature of the occupation is such that the customs have changed little over the years even with the introduction of outboard motors as accessories to the traditional Ssesse canoe. I shall confine consideration to liabilities and shares of the fish caught.

The village chief, the ssaza chief and ultimately the Kabaka received a share of fish landed. In the last century the village chief was entitled to receive a share of all fish landed in his village. Then there was no fishing by net, only by hook (amaloba) and line (miganjo) or with baskets (emya). The fishing expedition was often a family one; otherwise the boat-owner used to get an equal share with those who fished.

Nowadays fish caught are divided in the following proportions:

the landowner onto whose landing the fish are brought gets one fish in ten, in accordance with the provisions of section 9(b) of the Busuulu and Envujjo Law;

the boat-owner also gets one fish in ten;

the owner of the nets, that is the real fisherman, gets the remaining eight fish in every ten he catches.

If the boat is lost, the boat-owner has no claim against the net-owner or those who fished. If the net-owner loses his nets, he likewise has no claim. The loss lies where it falls: as the Ganda proverb runs:

Kitta akimanyidde ennyanja etta muvubi—It kills the person who knows it, the lake kills the fisherman.

If the net-owner employs porters then they receive a monthly pay, not a share of the fish landed although they usually get the odd fish to eat.

---

[1] *Empisa*, Chap. 29, p. 278.
[2] *Op. cit.*, pp. 391 *et seq.*

If the net-owner takes his fish to market, then he pays the market fees laid down and which are described in Chapter 14.

The owner of the landing (nnannyini mwaalo) only has responsibility in keeping the landing clear of bush in accordance with the sleeping sickness legislation which was first introduced in 1908 after the disastrous outbreak of the disease which started in late 1900 and had grown into an epidemic in the islands in 1901.[1]

Finally under customary law, anyone may fish anywhere whether in lake or river. Nowadays there are restrictions of this customary right to fish under the sleeping sickness legislation.

HUNTING

Here again the two great authorities on ancient Ganda custom have each devoted a chapter[2] to hunting and I propose to consider just a few legal aspects of the pursuit.

The first principle of customary law, still vigorously maintained in discussion and sometimes in practice despite the game legislation, is that any person could hunt as he liked anywhere. Hunters (abayizi) are even permitted to enter a chief's courtyard (embuga) or the Kabaka's Palace (olubiri), where entry is normally forbidden, if the hunted animal has passed that way. Nowdays, however, this dispensation is not extended to hunters armed with guns (abatujju).

The most detailed piece of customary law concerns the division of the beast's carcase:

(i) the man who first spotted the animal (omuzizi) receives a back leg, the head, the guts and the skin;

(ii) the tracker (omugoberezi) receives a side of the chest;

(iii) the first to spear (omussi) receives a back and a front leg;

(iv) the second to spear (wabikya) receives the neck (ensikya);

(v) the third to spear (manyinganyi) receives the lower ribs;

(vi) the followers (abagoba) receive the remaining front leg, out of which

(vii) the man who cuts up the meat receives the lower part of the front leg (nnyama ya bulenge);

---

[1] Hattersley, *op. cit.*, p. 121.

[2] Sir Apolo Kagwa, *Empisa*, Chap. 24, p. 247 and Roscoe, *op. cit.*, Chap. XIV, p. 445.

(viii) the man who cleared the boundary of the hunting area (omutemi w'olwenda lw'ekizigo) receives the remaining side of the chest;
and the landlord (nnannyini ttaka) receives the back (kigongo).[1]

Guineafowl, whether caught by net in accordance with the ancient method or shot by gun, are not subject to the liability to give the landlord a share.

If a hunter intends to spear an animal but spears his fellow hunter instead, there is no case under Ganda customary law.[2]

WAR

Warfare, it has already been observed, was one of the principal ways in ancient Buganda to acquire wealth. It is not surprising, therefore, that once again Sir Apolo Kagwa and Roscoe each devote a chapter to the peculiar customs of that pursuit.[3] Here I shall attempt to explain the legal aspects against a background description mainly gained from informants.

First the background of politics and resultant treaties must be considered. It has already been observed that when the British began to take an interest in Buganda in the second half of the last century, the Kingdom of Buganda was at the zenith of its conquests of neighbouring tribes. In the first treaty of 1890 between King Mwanga and Captain Lugard on behalf of the Imperial British East Africa Company were the following Articles:

" 3. With a view to carrying out the obligations into which they now enter, the Company engage to send to the Court of Uganda a fully accredited agent. His powers shall be as follows: . . .
(f) His consent shall be obtained and his counsel taken by the King before any war is undertaken, and in all grave and serious affairs and matters connected with the State. . . .
6. The King, assisted by the Company, shall form a standing army, which the officers of the Company will endeavour to organise and drill like a native regiment in India."[4]

Those Articles were repeated in the 1892 Treaty and then in

---

[1] See Sir Apolo Kagwa's statement at p. 24 of *Akatabo ke Biragiro*, 1916–1919.
[2] *Ibid.*, p. 25.
[3] Sir Apolo Kagwa, *Empisa*, Chap. 14, p. 152 and Roscoe, *op. cit.*, Chap. X, p. 346.
[4] See Wild, *op. cit.*, pp. 41–45.

the Provisional Agreement between King Mwanga and Sir Gerald Portal in 1893 the following clause appears:

> " 10. No war or warlike operation of any kind shall be undertaken without the consent of Her Majesty's Representative. . . ."[1]

The wording of that clause was reproduced in Article 10 of the Buganda Agreement, 1894, between King Mwanga and Colonel Colville.

Finally Article 13 of the Buganda Agreement, 1900, which remains unaffected by the 1955 Agreement, states:

> " 13. Nothing in this Agreement shall be held to invalidate the pre-existing right of the Kabaka of Uganda to call upon every able-bodied male among his subjects for military service in defence of the country; but the Kabaka henceforth will only exercise this right of conscription, or of levying native troops, under the advice of Her Majesty's principal representative in the Protectorate. In times of peace, the armed forces, organised by the Uganda Administration will probably be sufficient for all purposes of defence; but if Her Majesty's representative is of the opinion that the force of Uganda should be strengthened at any time, he may call upon the Kabaka to exercise in a full or in a modified degree his claim on the Baganda people for military service. In such an event the arming and equipping of such force would be undertaken by the administration of the Uganda Protectorate."

On at least two occasions in the early days of British influence in Buganda, these treaty rights were employed:

(i) a force of 5,000 warriors were produced within a few days instead of the 3,000 requested to disperse marauding Nandi;

(ii) 400 fighting men were sent to Bunyoro to disperse Sudanese mutineers.[2]

Only the Kabaka under Ganda customary law can declare war. The royal drum Mujaguzo must first be beaten by the Kabaka himself. Then the chief drummer Kawuula beats the drum *Ggwanga mujje* (" My people come "). Its beat is " Gwangă ggwangă mŭjjĕ ". It is the great war-drum of Buganda. As soon as its beat was heard the rest of the Kingdom resounded to the beat taken up by other drums.

Thereupon the able-bodied Ganda men painted their faces and bodies with red ochre (basaba ggerenge), white ashes and pot-black. Each warrior wore his barkcloth as a loincloth and

---

[1] See Wild, *op. cit.*, p. 63.
[2] *Africa No.* 7 (1901), General Report by Sir H. Johnston on the Uganda Protectorate dated 10th July, 1901.

grasping two spears and his shield and bedecked with his charm (jjembe) and his horn (ngombe) he went off to report to the village chief (nnannyini kyalo).

Any man who was afraid and hid to avoid the muster was arrested after the campaign by the village chief. The punishment consisted of publicly dressing him up in a barkcloth like a woman with the points of plantain flowers (empumpumpu) stuck inside as breasts.

When the warrior reached the village chief, the latter asked him—" Onotabaala?" (Do you go to war?) whereupon the brave would reply—" Bwe ntabaala, ntabaala " (Yes, when I go to war, I go to fight). Others would hesitate and say—" Bwe nsigala waka nsigala; bwe ntabaala ntabaala ", (lit. = When I stay at home I stay at home; when I go to war I go to fight, but really meaning " No, I want to stay at home "). These latter waverers were sent in front of the army and sometimes were punished by being speared in the back during the fighting. In the light of that custom, one can understand the Ganda proverb:

Kabaka tajemerwa—No-one rebels against the Kabaka.

The village chief led his warriors to the great chief (omukungu ow'ekitongole) who in turn led his warriors gathered from all his villages to the ssaza chief. The ssaza chief led his contingent to the Katikkiro and the Katikkiro led the army to the Kabaka. When the levies were finally assembled the Kabaka appointed his general (omugabe) to command the army. The army then placed the royal head-dress (engule) on the general's head and the general took the oath of allegiance standing before the Kabaka seated on the Nnamulondo (throne). Behind the general stood two of his wives carrying gourds of beer on their heads. The general then retired backwards out of the audience chamber and led the army to war with some of the Kabaka's royal drums, including *Ggwanga mujje*, bagpipers (abakondeere) and flutists (abalere). Not only did the chiefs take their wives to cook and their concubines (abasebei) as camp-followers but often Princesses went along to keep high the morale of the army. It was the Kasujju's duty to build their camp and that for the Princes on campaign.

The general's camp was styled " the Palace of the King " (Olubiri lwa Kabaka) and was built for him by his warriors. For as Ggomotoka explains[1] people had to respect him as if the

---

[1] *Op. cit.*, p. 35.

general were the Kabaka himself. The general had the power to inflict the death penalty on offenders and to burn cowards in battle to death without right of appeal. An offence against the general equalled an offence against the Kabaka himself.

The general deployed his troops and allotted tasks to his lieutenants but himself remained with a headquarters guard in his Lubiri while his warriors skirmished, fought and plundered. The lieutenants would return with their divisions to the general bringing to him the plunder which they had won. On the way these lieutenants and their chiefs would have made their first sample choice of the booty they had plundered (okukuba embwagulo) and later the general would send his staff to review the booty and to make the selection of his personal share according to the amount each chief had obtained (okukuba omuwambiro). Finally before reaching the capital the general would again cause the booty of all the contingents to be inspected and his staff would select the Kabaka's share (okubala omwandu or okugereka). The Queen-Mother (Namasole) and the Queen-Sister (Lubuga) were alone exempt from the general's orders as to the disposition of the booty.[1]

The army was then led back to find the Kabaka seated on the Nnamulondo. Thereupon the general and the leading chiefs asked permission to drink with a ladle from a jar of beer (akawulula). As each chief asked, the warriors would shout " sena " (ladle out) or " tasena " (he is not to ladle out) according to whether they had been properly led by the chief concerned during the campaign or not. Those, refused permission to drink, were immediately bound by Senkole, the Chief Executioner, and taken away to be burnt.

Not only the men on the campaign but also the women left at home had to obey certain customary laws. A warrior's wife must not have sexual relations with another man while her husband was away at the war. If she did and her husband or one of his sons was killed on the campaign, her punishment was administered by her husband's clansmen who would purposely delay to complete the funeral rites (okwabya lumbe) for two or three years. During that period the wife had by custom to remain unwashed, her hair uncut and without a barkcloth being given her to wear.

While her husband was away on the campaign she had to

---

[1] Sir Apolo Kagwa, *Empisa*, pp. 157–158.

H

refrain from leaving home except to fetch water and had to light the fire early in the evening to give her absent husband strength. So the Ganda proverb runs:

Siyomba na munyoro nga bazze atabaadde—I do not quarrel with the Munyoro when my husband has gone to war.

When her husband returned, the wife had first to give him a glass of water to drink. That night they had sexual intercourse to put an end to the campaign. But if next day when the husband was due to go to a parade before the chief, he had a belly-ache and did not appear, then his wife was held to have been unfaithful to him while he had been away.

PART IV

THE LAW
OF SUCCESSION

SUMMARY

		PAGE
CHAP. 11. Succession	. . . .	189
CHAP. 12. Guardianship	. . . .	225

CHAPTER 11

SUCCESSION

Following Southwold[1] I shall refer to the person styled *omusika omukulu* in Luganda (sometimes translated as " the principal heir ") as " the successor ", and to the *abasika abalala* (sometimes called " the minor heirs ") as " the heirs " in order to avoid confusion. In fact only the successor (omusika) actually succeeds (okusikira) to the estate. The others (abasika balala) do not succeed at all but receive a share in the distribution (okugabana) of the deceased's property.

DEATH AND BURIAL

The ancient Ganda customs pertaining to death and burial have already been described by three eminent authorities.[2] I shall therefore concentrate this section on a review of the modern rites.

On a death a wail goes up (okukuba ebiwobe or okukuba emiranga). The body is then laid out (okumugolola) in the doorway of the house, with its chin tied up and covered with a barkcloth up to the neck. This barkcloth has been lightly wrapped round the body soon after death so that it can come to life quickly. The body stays there on view for one or two days (okulaga omulambo).[3] The object of exposing the body is so that the relatives of the deceased can see that their kinsman is dead, not that they may ascertain whether he died of witchcraft.[4] Each relative or friend brings a barkcloth or a roll of unbleached calico (ejjoola lya japon or lya merikaani = a roll of cloth of

---

[1] Martin Southwold, *The Inheritance of Land in Buganda*, U.J., Vol. 20, No. 1, March 1956, p. 88.

[2] Sir Apolo Kagwa, *Empisa*, Chap. XXI, p. 196, Roscoe, *op. cit.*, Chap. IV, p. 98, and Mair, *An African People in the Twentieth Century*, Chap. VIII, p. 206.

[3] *Pace* Mair, *op. cit.*, p. 208. The exposure is still practised as described and no such Government orders, as alleged, exist or existed (even in the 1930's) except in respect of those who died of a contagious disease. Indeed if the body is buried quickly, the relatives are prosecuted in the clan.

[4] *Pace* Mair, *op. cit.*, p. 206.

about 30 yards).[1] They may bring a money contribution ranging from ten shillings to fifty cents towards the purchase of barkcloths. After two or three days the body is completely wrapped in many barkcloths—the equivalent of a grand funereal cortège by western standards. In the case of the deceased having been a parent, the body is clothed with a loin-cloth (kikooyi) before being wrapped in the barkcloths. Then the death is formally announced to the senior clansman in the area and the chief (okubikka) and both still send their representative to the burial even though it be of a peasant. It is held to be an indication that a person is a witch, if he fails to follow the custom of announcing the death (okubikka), by telling anyone he meets " So-and-so has died (gundi afudde)."

It may be noted at this point that the ancient customs of *empambo* (the heir eating seed of a squash (ensujju) out of the hand of his dead father) and *omuzigo* (smearing the corpse with butter) are obsolete.

To continue with the narrative of modern rites, the clansmen of the deceased decide where and when to bury his body. There is a growing custom of burying on the deceased's own private mailo which he acquired in his lifetime or on his plot (kibanja). But if the deceased so willed or if he was sufficiently distinguished then his clansmen will usually still decide to bury him on the clan *butaka* land. The decision on burial site lies within the absolute authority of the clan heads and they may over-rule the provisions of the will in this matter. As has been observed already,[2] they cannot do so unless they obtain the permission of the owner of that *butaka* land and he can easily refuse. But if he agrees to the burial on his land, then his tenant cannot object to the burial taking place within his plot (ekibanja) if the tombs (ebiggya) of the clan's ancestors are situated there.

Relatives and friends " keep the funeral " (okukuuma olumbe) by staying at the deceased's home during the period prior to the burial and for a few days afterwards. They keep a fire (gwoto) alight in the deceased's courtyard and everybody helps to dig the grave (ntaana). It is a criminal offence under Ganda customary law punishable with a fine to stay away and not to assist in the digging of the grave and the burial.[3]

---

[1] *Pace* Mair, *ibid.*—not white butter muslin.
[2] See p. 163, above.
[3] P.C.Cr.C. 537 of 1958, *Lukiiko* v. *Kigozi*, 1958 C.L.R. 41; and see Sir Apolo Kagwa's statement at p. 20 of *Akatabo ke Biragiro*, 1916–1919.

Beer is purchased and provided after the burial for those who have taken part. Then beer bananas are cut for brewing the beer for the wake (omwenge ogw'esumwa) which is drunk about seven days later when the period of *okukuuma lumbe* (keeping the funeral) is over.

After the burial in ancient times the best bull in the herd (engundu), a prime billy-goat (sseddume) and a cock (sseggwanga) were killed for the feast if the deceased was a rich master of the household (ssemaka). Nowadays no cattle are killed even if the deceased was rich unless he so instructed in his will.[1] If cattle are killed without authority in the will of the deceased, the head of the sub-consanguinity (omukulu w'olunyiriri) will bring a case in the clan against the head of the courtyard (ow'oluggya) and if the clan case is successful the matter is then pursued in the courts of law as a civil case. The Principal Court has shown itself unsympathetic towards those who illicitly satisfy their ancient craving for meat.[2] The only exception to this modern rule is that if the house-holder (nnannyini maka) dies then a cock is killed, if it exists; indeed it cannot be permitted to sleep in its deceased master's house.

When a father of twins (ssalongo) or a mother of twins (nnalongo) is buried, the wild vine (ebbombo) is spread on top of the grave and a strip of barkcloth (olufuvu) is left to run from the corpse below, to which it is tied, up to the ground above. Twins themselves are buried in the same way as other people but a curious custom relates to the afterbirth (ebitanyi) when twins are born. It is placed in a hole in an anthill in the bush underneath a cooking-pot (entamu). Gorju observed:

> " Ce role est devolu à un ancien du village. Il porte son dépôt dans la brouse, ou mieux sur la lisière de la forêt, placé dans une écuelle (kibya) ou dans une de ces petites termitières noires à forme de crâne, qui servent de pierres de foyer."[3]

It is said that if one attempts to uncover the afterbirth by taking off the cooking-pot, one is burnt white as a European by the twins (abalongo okwokya).

When a twin or a parent of twins dies, the death is announced

---

[1] This was the general view but the Head of the Nsenene Clan disputed it alleging that the clan authorities always set aside one or two cattle out of the estate of the deceased even if not allowed in will, for the feast at *okwabya lumbe* (see below). If there are few cattle then money is set aside to purchase meat.

[2] P.C.C.C. 85 of 1958, *Nakuzabasajja* v. *Kakembo*, 1958 C.L.R. 109.

[3] Gorju, *op. cit.*, p. 350.

in a special way—" omulongo (or ssalongo or nnalongo) abuuse "
(the twin has passed over). No-one cries at their death but drums
are beaten as the body is buried at 6 p.m.

Whenever a death occurs in either of the families of the parents
of twins, the twins' umbilical cords are untied (okubikkira
balongo). When the funeral rites are completed the cords are
smeared with butter and beer and put in the sun. Money is
showered on the cords by well-wishers before the cords are tied
up again. This money the parents of the twins have a right to
take.

MOURNING

The period of mourning lasts until the successor is appointed.
There has been some modification of the customs of mourning
described by Mair[1] in the quarter of a century that has passed
since she wrote:

The mourners still do not shave their heads but they do wash
their bodies, the standards of personal hygeine having been
raised considerably since the nineteenth century.

The grass strewn in the house is still not changed but after
seven days or so cultivation by relatives starts again. Cultivation
by fellow-villagers, not of the deceased's family, usually starts
about three days after the burial. Anyone who breaks this
traditional embargo on cultivation is prosecuted.

It is still the custom not to have sexual intercourse with the
widows of the deceased during the mourning period but that
custom is not always followed. Certainly the grown-up children
of the deceased do not observe sexual abstinence after drinking
the *mwenge ogw'esumwa*. The ancient custom of not allowing the
bull of the deceased's herds (engundu) to have access to the cows
until the funeral rites are completed is no longer generally
observed.

The little presents, which are still brought by relatives paying
visits of condolence, are called *mataba* and the beer brought by
the relatives-in-law is called *omwenge gw'okubagizza*.

The reason why the sanctions on cultivation and sexual intercourse are ceasing to be observed by the relatives of deceased
for the whole period of mourning, as previously, is that, whereas
in olden days the installation of the successor took place two or
three weeks after the burial, nowadays, particularly if there is

---

[1] *Op. cit.*, p. 209.

any dispute about land in succession, the installation may often be delayed for months or years.[1]

INTERIM ADMINISTRATION OF ESTATE

As soon as the burial is completed, the clan council and the relatives of the deceased choose the " president of the funeral " (omukulu w'olumbe). He is usually the father or grandfather of the deceased, that is, the head of the household (ow'oluggya), for the Ganda proverb runs:

Ekika kisookera mu luggya—The clan begins in the courtyard.

The *mukulu w'olumbe* assumes responsibility for the administration of the deceased's estate and becomes guardian meanwhile of his widows and children.

At that council meeting also the deceased's will is read, if one exists.

OKWABYA LUMBE

The ceremony of completing the funeral rites (okwabya lumbe) used only to be celebrated in respect of some deceased married person whose decease called for a successor to that position in society,[2] but deceased batchelors now have their own funeral rites if they died possessed of property, in particular land. Children have no separate funeral rites unless a child has inherited land, in which case that child too must have an heir. The practice is to mention the deceased child at the funeral rites next following of a near adult clansman or relative. A wife on her decease is the subject of two ceremonies for the completion of her funeral rites, one at her husband's home and then the other at her family home.

The period elapsing between the burial and the completion of the funeral rites, as has been already observed, varies considerably. In general a peasant's funeral rites, there being little property and usually no mailo land involved, are completed after a comparatively short interval of weeks whereas a rich man's or chief's, there being usually land and cattle in the estate, after months or years.

When the clan authorities have approved the heir under the

---

[1] *Pace* Mair, *loc. cit.*, who gives quite the reverse of the modern situation on this matter.

[2] See Mair, *op. cit.*, p. 210.

will in the testate succession or have selected the heir in an intestate succession, the ceremony of *okwabya lumbe* can be held. If there is land in the estate the heir must first be introduced and confirmed by the Kabaka,[1] before the ceremony can be held. The village chief is informed that the ceremony of the completion of the funeral rites is to take place. The head of the next grade in the clan hierarchy personally attends the ceremony in respect of his deceased subordinate, that is, at the ceremony of a deceased head of consanguinity (ow'omutuba) the head of the sub-clan (ow'essiga) attends; but unless specifically invited the representative of the head of clan (ow'akasolya) only goes to the funeral rites when land is involved in the succession.

On the eve of the ceremony the heir leads the party to cut beer bananas and to brew. Then in the evening the heir is taken by the clan head to the village chief's headquarters. A calabash of beer is given to the chief and he is asked to approve the heir and invited to the ceremony next day. Then the party retrace their steps; the *engalabi* drum is beaten and dancing begins. The relatives keep the fire going in the courtyard and build temporary shelters (ensisira) in the plantain garden. The members of the deceased's family (ab'oluganda) occupy one set of shelters and the relatives-in-law (abako) another set. The largest shelter is occupied by the president of the funeral rites (omukulu w'olumbe).

On the day of the ceremony the heir's " sister " (olubuga) is selected, usually at the last minute, to go through the ceremony of installation with the heir or heiress so that he or she may not be lonely. The Lubuga is chosen from the clan of the heir or heiress but from outside the sub-consanguinity (olunyiriri). This arrangement is copied by the people from the custom of appointing the Queen-Sister (Lubuga) to accompany the new Kabaka at his installation.

The actual ceremony and its aftermath have social rather than legal interest and those who wish to refer to the details can consult the works of Sir Apolo Kagwa,[2] of Roscoe[3] or of Mair.[4]

CATEGORIES OF HERITABLE PROPERTY
There are three main categories of heritable property:

---

[1] See below p. 210 for procedure.
[2] *Empisa*, p. 203.
[3] *Op. cit.*, p. 122.
[4] *Op. cit.*, p. 212.

immovable, movable and, what for want of a better name I propose to style, titular.

Immovable property comprises ownership of land, tenancy to land and buildings, trees and such things as go with land. Ownership of land calls for a particular procedure in distribution of the estate which will be considered below.[1]

Movable property comprises, first in importance, cattle and then all other property whatsoever. Cattle are handled in a particular manner during the distribution of the estate which we will consider below.[2]

Finally under titular property are included the headship of a clan or of one of its branches, certain hereditary chieftainships and the headship of the household.[3] It will be convenient to consider this type of property now.

Succession to the headship of a clan always has been hereditary. The headship of the clan in the last century also carried with it the clan's *butaka* estates but nowadays that type of land, as has been already noted, is mainly in private ownership. The procedure is for the elders of the clan to chose the successor to the headship and to submit their recommendation to the Kabaka through the Ddiiro for approval (*vide* the Uganda Agreement (Clan Cases), 1924). Succession to the headship of the subordinate branches of a clan, that is to say, of the sub-clan, consanguinity, and sub-consanguinity, proceeds in like manner with the proviso that in such cases the head of clan obviously has a powerful voice as to who the successor shall be. The traditional procedure has been described by Mr. Justice Carter[4] and the occasions when such succession operates are so limited that I do not propose to go into the details here. Suffice it be to mention two modern developments: there was an attempt recently made at the funeral rites of the late Namwama, Head of the Kkobe (Yam) Clan, to prevent his personal successor from succeeding also to the headship of the clan but the attempt was unsuccessful. Secondly the ancient rule that a *mutaka* who accepted office as a *mukungu* or *mutongole* automatically vacated his headship of the clan no longer is observed under modern conditions: there are two ssaza chiefs who are also heads of clans, at least two other ssaza chiefs

---

[1] See section on Machinery of Succession at p. 209.
[2] See p. 221 below.
[3] See P.C.R.O. 40 of 1917, *Lukiko* v. *Kauwa and Others* (unreported) (claim for share in inheritance of Kabakaship).
[4] *Loc. cit.*

who are heads of sub-clans (amasiga) and a ggombolola chief who is a head of clan.[1]

Succession to hereditary chieftainships nowadays is a mere rump of the ancient widespread practice which at any rate appears to have obtained up to the reign of Junju in the late eighteenth century.[2] Then six ssaza chieftainships at least were hereditary now only that of Kamuswaga of Kkooki, by virtue of a treaty in 1896 between the former Kingdom of Kkooki and the Kingdom of Buganda, remains. The office of Mugema does, however, still exist and though it has ceased long since to carry with it a ssaza chieftainship, the office is normally hereditary and the incumbent has important duties to perform at the accession of a Kabaka.[3]

Finally when the head of a family dies his successor not only succeeds to a large part at least of the estate but also to the rights and responsibilities of the pater familias. As already observed, that may well involve marrying the deceased's wives or some of them; it will certainly involve caring for his minor children, and becoming responsible for the various relationships of the family's members.

Before leaving this subject of categories of heritable property, it must be appreciated that there is no distinction under Ganda customary law between succession to inherited and to self-acquired property.

LAW AND JURISDICTION

There is very little real legislation which governs succession, including guardianship, among the Ganda. By order of the 22nd January, 1906, made under section 337 of the Uganda Succession Ordinance, 1906,[4] all natives of the Protectorate were exempted from the operation of that Ordinance and the rules for distribution of intestate estates were not to apply to Muhammadans.

---

[1] The hereditary ssaza chief Kamuswaga of Kkooki is also Ssababiito, Head of the Ababiito Clan of Kkooki; the head of the Nsuma (Fish) Clan, which originated in the ancient Kingdom of Buvuma, later absorbed in Buganda, is Kibondwe and he is at present Kayima also, ssaza chief of Mawokota; the ssaza chiefs Ssebwana of Busiro and Kasujju of Busujju are respectively heads of sub-clans in the Edible Rat (Musu) and Scaly Ant-eater (Lugave) Clans; and finally Mugalula, the head of the Edible Grass-hopper (Nsenene) Clan is a ggombolola chief in Ssingo Ssaza.

[2] Hailey, *op. cit.*, Part I, p. 14.

[3] See Nsimbi, *op. cit.*, pp. 38 *et seq.*

[4] Now section 333 of Cap. 34.

Guardianship was the subject of one of the first native laws of Buganda enacted in 1904—the Guardianship Law. Testamentary disposal of mailo and intestate succession to mailo were permitted by the Land Law, 1908.[1] In 1912 the procedure of succession was further explained by the Land Succession Law and in 1916 by the Wills Law. The Coming of Age Law, 1920, fixed the age of entitlement to be put in possession of property by guardians at twenty years.

The development of jurisdiction in clan cases has already been generally described up to the making of the Uganda Agreement (Clan Cases), 1924.[2] It is now desirable to proceed further and to consider the jurisdiction in succession matters in detail. Fortunately on this difficult question we have over the last eighteen years acquired a wealth of authority both in the decisions of the High Court and strangely enough, there being no right of appeal from the Principal Court of Buganda, in the decisions of the Court of Appeal for Eastern Africa. The most practicable way is to review these decisions in chronological order.

The first proceedings of note are the case of Kulanima S. Kabali versus Marko Kajubi. These proceedings originated in the Principal Court[3] and went on appeal to the High Court;[4] against that appellate judgment of the High Court, for reasons which are by no means clear,[5] the Court of Appeal for Eastern Africa entertained a further appeal.[6] The short facts were that Kabali's father,

> " Yokana Kamya Bafirawala Masembe, a Muganda owning considerable landed property in Buganda, a member of the Nsenene Clan, died in 1940 intestate. He left no less than fifty children surviving him. He was lawfully married under the Marriage Ordinance and left surviving him seven children of that marriage. The remaining children are the issue of irregular unions with other women. There is no dispute as to their paternity."[7]

Kajubi, the clan head after consultation with the clan council selected Kabali, the eldest son of the deceased and a child of the lawful marriage, to be Masembe's successor. Kabali, under

---

[1] Now the Possession of Land Law, Rev. Edn., p. 154.
[2] See p. 75, above.
[3] P.C.C.C. 25 of 1942.
[4] H.C.C.A. 21 of 1942 (unreported).
[5] *Per* AINLEY, J. in H.C.Misc.A. 13 of 1949 (unreported).
[6] E.A.C.A. C.A. 2 of 1944, (1944) 11 E.A.C.A. 34.
[7] *Per* GRAY, C. J., *ibid.*

Kajubi's scheme for the distribution of the deceased's estate, got the lion's share and the balance was distributed in unequal shares amongst the other children, both legitimate and illegitimate. The Kabaka confirmed Kabali's appointment as successor and Kajubi's scheme of distribution. The children, other than Kabali, of the statutory marriage complained that they should receive greater shares under the distribution than the children of the irregular unions. Kabali, as successor, then in accordance with practice filed this suit against the clan head on their behalf praying for a redistribution of the estate and claiming thereby preferential treatment for the children of the Christian marriage. In the course of its judgment the Principal Court made a statement of the customary law of succession on an intestacy in Buganda and as this statement was held to be " unimpeachable at law and also one which no court ought to try to go behind "[1] it is worth quoting the translation which appears in the judgment of GRAY, C. J., on the Court of Appeal:

> " All the illegitimate children in Buganda are regarded as children of the deceased, unless somebody claims that they are not the children of the deceased. In this case nobody claims that these illegitimate children are not the children of the deceased. . . . According to Buganda customs all these illegitimate children must have a share from their father's property. . . .
> In Buganda when a person dies intestate, the head of clan and the relatives of the deceased are the people who distribute the property of the deceased and choose the heir. According to our customs, when His Highness the Kabaka confirms the heir or heirs and all their respective shares, there is no alteration in what he has confirmed."

The Principal Court accordingly dismissed the suit.

On appeal to the High Court, PEARSON, J. partly allowed the appeal, holding that the children of the married wife should be considered " senior " to the natural children and as such entitled to larger portions, but left the matter " for reconsideration by the clan head and native authority in that light ". The reasons for that decision need no special consideration here as they were subsequently over-ruled by the Court of Appeal. But there are two passages in his judgment which refer to the " Buganda Succession Ordinance 1926 " which are germane to our present purpose. The learned Judge was, of course, really referring to the Buganda Succession Order, 1926.[2]

---

[1] *Per* GRAY, C. J., E.A.C.A. C.A. 2 of 1944, (1944) 11 E.A.C.A. 34.

[2] See Appendix 4, p. 320, below.

" Appellant cites also a document entitled ' Buganda Succession Ordinance 1926 '. This is interesting and relevant to the issues herein, but it goes no further than to state that the eldest son of a registered marriage shall succeed as heir, and this is already granted to this appellant at all stages of these proceedings. This Court however has no cognizance of the said document, and it does not appear to have been duly published in the *Gazette* as required by the Buganda Agreement, 1910. . . .

He again cites the ' Buganda Succession Ordinance 1926 ', s.19, which purports to provide that ' all debts due to land agreements shall be dealt with by the Head of the Clan, who may pay all debts due '. This puts the clan head in the position of personal representative in English law. That ' Order ' however has not the force of law—it may be thought that clan heads are not yet ripe for such responsibility."

"Later a stop order was put by the learned Judge on the registration of the shares in the land as set out in the schedule of distribution approved by H.H. the Kabaka. The learned Attorney General then applied on behalf of the clan head for a review of the judgment the result of which was that the learned Judge finding that nothing had been done by the clan head in pursuance of his judgment set aside the distribution of the clan head and directed a distribution of the estate by the Court in its equitable jurisdiction."[1]

As has been already mentioned, the Court of Appeal allowed the appeal, restored the judgment of the Principal Court and set aside the stop order of the High Court. In the course of his judgment SHERIDAN, C. J., opined:

". . . in my opinion neither the High Court nor this Court, has any authority to interfere with the distribution effected by the clan head."

GRAY, C. J. further opined after referring to section 2(f) of the Land Law, 1908, and section 3 of the Land Succession Law, 1912:

" Therefore on an intestacy in Buganda the native customary law of succession applies in a case in which the deceased is a Muganda."

In 1945 MANNING, J., held, as already noted,[2] that jurisdiction granted under subsection 11(1) of the Buganda Courts Ordinance, 1940, must be read not only in conjunction with the Buganda Agreement (Clan Cases), 1924, but also in conjunction with section 9(e) of the same Ordinance, which expressly deprives all native courts of jurisdiction in any proceedings to which the Agreement relates.[3]

---

[1] *Per* SHERIDAN, C. J., E.A.C.A., C.A.2 of 1944.
[2] See p. 43, above.
[3] H.C.C.A. 8 of 1945, *Saku and Another* v. *Mugema and Others*, Notes 15.

In 1949 PEARSON, J., as has also already been mentioned,[1] found it well established that all succession matters are regarded as clan matters and held that the Principal Court has no jurisdiction in matters of succession which are disposed by the Kabaka himself.[2]

In the same month of October 1949, the same learned Judge could find no authority for regarding the Ddiiro as a court of justice and so the defence of *res judicata* could not lie in respect of one of its previous decisions. PEARSON, J., continued:

> " By the Uganda Agreement (Clan Cases), 1924, no native court shall take cognizance of any case or matter affecting clans. It is well established that this embraces—or excludes—matters of succession and inheritance."

By implication a little later in his judgment the learned Judge mentioned not only succession and inheritance as matters affecting " the interests or authority of the clan " but also so classed the appointments of executors or guardians.[3]

In 1950 AINLEY, J., examined the law of succession among the Baganda[4] and as that judgment has been cited with approval subsequently[5] it is worth quoting at some length here:

> " Here it is necessary to examine the law of succession among the Baganda. It is well known that the law is mainly customary. Why in fifty years of administration and legislation a written law has not been promulgated reducing the custom to essentials and certainty, and providing prompt and certain representation of estates of deceased persons I do not know.
>
> It is however well known that among the Baganda there is no rigid, preordained scheme of succession on intestacy as there is in English law. When a clansman dies it is the concern of the clan, acting by the Clan Head to choose a successor or principal heir. Custom may give some guidance in the choice, but there seems to be no hard and fast rule as to who the successor should be. The Clan Head makes his choice in council certainly with family members, and in cases of importance in council with clan elders. The matter is a clan and family affair. The successor usually takes the lion's share of land and often no doubt of personal goods. As to what is left, this is distributed according to what seems right and

---

[1] See p. 75, above.

[2] H.C.Misc.A. 9 of 1949, *Nabyonga and Others* v. *Sewava* (unreported).

[3] H.C.C.A. 4 of 1949, *Male* v. *Kayongo and Another*, Notes 29.

[4] H.C.Misc.A. 13 of 1949, *Musoke and Others* v. *Head of the Nsenene Clan and Another*, Notes 35 (part).

[5] H.C.C.A. 61 of 1951, *Waswa* v. *Sebuliba* (unreported) H.C.Misc.C. 42 of 1952, *Re Kagwa* (unreported) and E.A.C.A., C.A. 30 of 1954, *Sewava* v. *Kamalya Kagwa and Others* (unreported).

proper in the circumstances, though again custom may give general guidance.

It strikes one immediately that the particular problems which the Clan Head is called on to decide could not adequately be dealt with by a Court of Law sitting either at the first instance or in an appellate capacity, and it is certainly well established that disgruntled family members cannot run straight from the Clan Head to any Court of law. The Clan Head's task being completed, the Kabaka is next turned to.

There seems to me to be some distinction between the Kabaka's function in respect to succession to land and his function in respect to succession to personalty. Fairly clearly in the old days the only land which was regarded as hereditable was land held under Butaka tenure. With land held under the Butaka tenure went the power to rule, and land so held had either been granted by the Kabaka or had been held immemorially by local hereditary rulers. It is not then surprising to find that the rule was that the successor to a deceased Mutaka having been chosen by the Clan (I rely very largely here on Mr. Justice Carter's exposition of Native Customs Law printed at the end of Vol. 1, U.L.R.), had to be presented to the Kabaka for his approval. The Kabaka in registering his approval or disapproval was not as it appears to me performing a judicial act. The propriety of his decision could certainly not be enquired into by a Court of Law if any had existed. His decision was the decision of a ruler, an overlord, and would be based to some extent at any rate on questions of policy and loyalty.

Where the estate was merely personalty the position seems to have been different (see Mr. Justice Carter's exposition printed at the end of Vol. 1, U.L.R.). The Kabaka was probably not interested in the successor to a Mukopi's chickens. But still in such cases an appeal by a dissatisfied member of the family did lie to the Kabaka. In such an appeal of course the Kabaka performed judicial functions.

Now in 1900, when the brand new Mailo tenure was created, the requirement that the successor to Butaka land should be presented to the Kabaka seems to have been attached to the successor to Mailo land, not perhaps with such good reason. Whether with the advent of Mailo land some other scheme should have been devised I will not discuss. No scheme was promulgated to take the place of such presentation, and the custom relative to Butaka land became so I think the custom relative to Mailo land, and that custom has been acted on for 50 years or so and cannot now be disregarded. Indeed the Succession Law of 1912 I think endorses the custom for it will be noted that Certificates of Succession to Mailo Land are issued not by a Court of Law but by the executive Lukiko, a striking and significant fact. As to the modern state of customary law regarding estates of pure personalty, little need be said for I apprehend that very little turns on that question in the present case, I merely note that in such cases the Kabaka has apparently continued to exercise his appellate function. Nobody has ever supposed that the Principal Court in spite of its very wide jurisdiction has absorbed this function of H.H. the Kabaka and at this stage in history it would be absurd to say that family squabbles should go straight from the clan head to the Principal Court.

It seems to me then that generally in regard to all matters of intestate succession and particularly in regard to succession to estate of land H.H. the Kabaka occupies a very special and peculiar position. We see that it is the Kabaka's executive council that issues Certificates of Succession, not the Principal Court. We see that historically the function of the Kabaka in ' approving ' successors to land cannot have been any concern of any judicial body. Even today the problems to be decided by the Kabaka and the Clan in these matters are not really problems with which a court of justice could adequately deal. I do not myself consider that H.H. the Kabaka can then be regarded as some kind of Court intermediate between the Clan and the Principal Court or between the Clan and this Court. It was known that H.H. the Kabaka performed these special functions when the Buganda Courts Ordinance was passed, but no one I think would argue that because that Ordinance does not in explicit terms refer to these functions they have been taken from H.H. the Kabaka and handed to the Principal Court. Clearly they are still in his hands, and there is no indication in any Ordinance, law or agreement that the Principal Court may act as a Court of Appeal from H.H. the Kabaka's decisions or that they may exercise any supervisory power over his functions."

Later in the same judgment the learned Judge considered the problem of what a clan case consists:

" Now it is said that the choice by the clan head of a successor to a deceased intestate particularly where land is involved is plainly a matter ' affecting clans ' and/or is a ' clan case '. It is of course a difficult matter for this Court to interpret an agreement between His Majesty and His Highness the Kabaka. What did the contracting parties intend? There is no doubt I think what the executive Government of Buganda thinks was intended. They have refused permission for this case to proceed. Nor is there any doubt as to what the executive Government of Uganda thinks was intended, for the legal adviser to the Executive Government, the learned Attorney General, intervened in the case of Kajubi *v.* Kabali and urged upon this Court that succession matters *were* matters affecting the clan. It would be somewhat strange if I were to tell both sides to the Agreement that they had misinterpreted their own agreement. I do not however find it necessary to do so. It is really I think quite impossible to say that a matter which from time immemorial has been the peculiar concern of the clan, which native public opinion has always regarded as being a matter to be decided by the clan is not a matter which ' affects ' the clan. If the matter did not in the mind of the Baganda affect the clan how comes it that the clan makes the matter its concern? It is therefore my opinion that the choice of a successor or principal heir is a matter ' affecting clans ' and is a matter which does fall within the said Agreement, and accordingly that it is a matter excluded from the jurisdiction of the Principal Court by Section 9 (e) of the Buganda Courts Ordinance. I would here most emphatically state that nothing which I have said is intended to give the impression that the Kabaka or his Council have something in the nature of Chancery jurisdiction, or have jurisdiction as a Court in each and every matter which may in some way link up with succession. I have seen references in one case to something called a Diro Court which Court may be assuming very wide jurisdiction in succession matters; I leave the question as to whether or not there has been an irregular assumption of jurisdiction there entirely open. Disputes as to whether the deceased transferred or sold property to individuals prior to death cannot, obviously be regarded as ' clan cases ' because H.H. the Kabaka has confirmed a successor as owner of the land in dispute, and plaintiffs cannot I think be barred in any way from raising their claims in such circumstances before a Court of law simply because of such confirmation. But the choice of a successor to a deceased intestate is to my mind a matter which is not within the jurisdiction either of the Principal Court or of this Court and is the sole concern of the clans and H.H. the Kabaka."

The learned Judge then opined *obiter* that the High Court had no power to issue an order of *certiorari* or similar process against the Kabaka should the Kabaka fail to abide by the ancient custom of his people in deciding matters affecting clans.

The same year the same learned Judge gave judgment in another appeal[1] arising out of the same deceased's estate as the case just cited, namely that of Seperia Rosiko Kadumakasa, which was to provide a fertile source of litigation for the next four years. The facts of the case and the legal manoeuvres resorted to are so involved that we would be detracted from our present purpose in studying them. Those proceedings, however, have given posterity a wealth of judicial decision and opinion on the Ganda law of succession. In the instant case AINLEY, J., examined succession to mailo land:

" By virtue of the Land Succession Law of 1912 neither a devisee of land of a deceased Muganda nor one chosen as successor to such land upon an intestacy may meddle with the land until he has obtained a Certificate of Succession to the land issued by the Lukiko. Having obtained this Certificate the next step for the devisee or successor is to obtain transfer of the land to his name upon the Mailo Register which is maintained under the Registration of Titles Ordinance. The sole section which deals with the transmission of land upon death in that Ordinance is Section 141 which provides for the registration as proprietor of the grantee of letters of administration or probate. No provision is made for the direct

---

[1] H.C.Misc.A. 8 of 1950, *Re Kadumakasa* (unreported).

transmission to an heir or devisee. As however the Baganda are not subject to the Succession Ordinance neither probate nor letters of administration can be granted to them.

But since in the Interpretation section of the Registration of Titles Ordinance it is provided that the phrase ' Letters of Administration ' includes certificates of succession the difficulty is in some sort overcome, and it would appear that by treating the person named in the Certificate as the grantee of letters of administration, whether he be devisee, successor on intestacy, guardian or executor, a transfer is accomplished. It appears to be the practice though it involves I think some divergence from what is laid down in Section 141 to register the Certificate as an instrument effecting a transfer from the deceased to the person named in the Certificate and then to make the appropriate change in the Register."

And the creation of mailo tenure:

" Further, though I may be profoundly mistaken, it seems to me wrong to regard the tenure of Mailo land as something emanating from Native Custom, as being linked in some way with the ancient customary tenures. I do not think that the Land Law of 1908 was intended to be based upon custom, it was an attempt to deal with something new and strange, *viz.* private land ownership; further I do not think that that law attempted to create some special tenure to be called Mailo tenure, having its own peculiar incidents, and its own peculiar limitations. Simply it seems to me the more important features of what an English lawyer would regard as ownership of land have been set forth and that nothing exhaustive was intended.

When the Buganda Agreement was made in 1900 it seems to have been assumed by the signatories that there existed in Buganda private land owners who held their land as a private possession and at their complete disposal. This from all I have been able to gather was an incorrect assumption. I will not go into the various forms of tenure existing prior to 1900. It is sufficient to say that from all I can gather the idea of land ownership as an Englishman understands it, the idea of land as a freely alienable possession seems to have been alien to the mind of the Baganda. Yet under that Agreement allotments of land were made to some 1000 individuals to hold not under the ancient forms of tenure but as possessors with complete rights of disposal. This position is reflected in the Land Law of 1908 though certain wise restrictions were imposed from political motives, not with the intention of reflecting custom. There seems then to have been a clean break with custom. There is nothing customary about the free rights of alienation by sale, gift and will spoken of in the Land Law, and it seems to me that so far as the Land Law or any other law goes the owner of Mailo land is as fully an owner of his land as any lawyer, English or otherwise could imagine. Then if a man has full rights of ownership whether you call his tenure freehold, Mailo, or what you will, may he not do what he chooses with his own? "

Finally the learned Judge held:

" If a man is capable of full ownership then I see no reason in law nor common sense reason why he should not be capable of joint ownership, not why he should not by will or otherwise create joint ownership which is certainly not greater than individual ownership. I do not see any reason why the mere fact that this Certificate declares that three persons are the joint successors to this land should prevent its registration, nor why the persons named therein should not be registered as joint proprietors."

This decision was followed by PEARSON, J., when the involved question of two separate certificates of succession in respect of the same land, which was the core of these proceedings, next came before the High Court in the following year.[1] But the learned Judge decided that he must leave to the Kabaka and his Lukiko the decision on which certificate of the two should be cancelled.[2] The Kabaka indicated through the Katikkiro to the Office of Titles that he had rescinded the first Certificate issued by the issue of the second Certificate of Succession. Issue was then joined before Low, J.,[3] as to whether a Certificate of Succession once issued could be altered or rescinded by the Kabaka or the Lukiko. Referring to the Uganda Agreement (Clan Cases), 1924, the learned Judge opined:

" There can be no question that up to the time of issue of a certificate of Succession the clan and the Kabaka or the Kabaka acting on his own can vary the choice of successor and the distribution of an estate. It is a clan matter and no court can interfere. The point for my determination is whether the issue of a certificate carries things beyond the sphere of a ' matter affecting clans '. I have come to the conclusion that it does."

The learned Judge referred to the Land Succession Law and then gave these reasons for his conclusion:

" The position is therefore this: when a mailo landowner dies intestate the clan chooses a successor and H.H. the Kabaka signifies his approval. Thereafter the Land Succession Law steps in and decrees that the successor shall be given a certificate of succession stating that he is entitled to the land and entitled to deal with it as he pleases; until he obtains that certificate he shall do nothing with the land.

From the purely practical aspect I cannot imagine the Registrar of Titles ever registering a change of ownership without seeing such certificate as authority for so doing. He would be the first person to insist that the Land Succession Law be complied with. It is true

---

[1] H.C.Misc.C. 17 of 1951, *Re Sewava* (unreported).

[2] The basis for this decision was queried by BRIGGS, J. A., in E.A.C.A., C.A. 30 of 1954.

[3] H.C.Misc.C., 42 of 1952, *Re Kagwa* (unreported).

that the certificate is issued by the Lukiko in a non-judicial capacity but I cannot see that it affects the matter: by law they are not only authorised but compelled to issue it. Suppose for example they refused to issue a certificate to a successor elected by the clan and approved by the Kabaka: that would be a breach of Section 3 of the Land Succession Law. They could be compelled to do so by Writ of Mandamus and it would be a tenuous answer to plead that the writ could not issue as the matter was one affecting clans.

It seems to me, therefore, that in performing their duty in accordance with the provisions of the Land Succession Law they are doing something which can no longer be said to be a matter affecting clans and consequently their act or acts can be examined by the High Court. I consider, further, that in the absence of any express permission given by the Land Succession Law they cannot cancel a certificate once they have issued it."

When that decision came before the Court of Appeal,[1] BRIGGS, J. A., opined that up to the time of confirmation questions of intestate succession are within the Clan Cases Agreement and further:

" On the death intestate of an owner of mailo land, the Land Succession Law, 1912, provides that a certificate of succession ' shall be given according to the customs of succession in Buganda '. . . . When it has been done, the equitable title to the land vests forthwith, as it seems to me, in accordance with the tenor of the certificate. Registration is no doubt required to vest the legal estate."

However, the learned Justice of Appeal expressly reserved the question as to whether the power might exist for the Kabaka to remedy a situation created by a certificate of succession having been issued through mistake or fraud, by alteration or revocation.[2]

Referring to section 2(f) of the Land Law, 1908, JENKINS, Ag. V-P., was of the following opinion:

" The ascertainment is, as has already been stated, made according to the old customary butaka procedure and the clan recommendations are put before the Kabaka for confirmation. The ' rules of the law of succession ' are not contained in any legislative enactment, but an attempt seems to have been made in 1926 by the Kabaka to deal with the matter by Order. A printed copy of the draft Succession Order, 1926, is in evidence, . . . but it did not receive the necessary approval of the Governor and so never came into force as a legislative enactment. It seems that in cases of dispute the rules of the law of succession would have to be proved in the usual way for proving Buganda customary rules."

---

[1] E.A.C.A. 30 of 1954, *Sewava* v. *Kagwa and Others* (unreported).
[2] See p. 224, below.

Worley, Ag. P., agreed

> " that His Highness's confirmation of the recommendations of the clan council was a quasi-judicial act which could not be revoked after having been given formal expression in the issue of the Certificate of Succession."

The learned Acting President deemed it unnecessary to express any final opinion on whether, if fraud or mistake is discovered before a certificate of succession has been registered, His Highness or the Lukiko could revoke it, but held that once the distribution of the estate has been settled and expressed in formal Certificates, the Kabaka and Lukiko are *functus officio.*

The appeal was dismissed.

There is one other case the mention of which perforce has now been pushed out of its chronological order but it is convenient to note it here. In 1952 Pearson, J., held that the clan, after it has determined the succession and distribution of the estate of a deceased person, is *functus officio*; any claim therefore in respect of a sum of money coming subsequently into the successor's hands in the management of the estate can properly be entertained by the Courts.[1]

Let us revert in time to the making of the Uganda Agreement (Clan Cases), 1924, which was the point we reached before reviewing the case law.[2] It is clear from an inspection of the printed publication *Ekiragiro ekyo Busika ekyo Mwaka, 1926* (" The Succession Order, 1926 ") that the late Kabaka with the advice of the Lukiko made that Order at Mengo on the 15th September, 1926. The approval of the Governor was not given to the Order. It appears from the printed publication that originally such consent was considered necessary but the copies issued had the printed words to that effect deleted in ink. From 1926 until the present day that Order has been strictly observed by every clan authority and by the Kabaka's courts. By Resolution No. 90 of 1956 the Lukiko passed the Law of the Succession and Wills of the Natives of Buganda, 1956. This draft native law was submitted to the Governor for his approval, as is required under Article 26 of the Constitution of Buganda, but his approval was withheld on the grounds that the draft law would be in conflict with the Uganda Agreement (Clan Cases), 1924.

---

[1] H.C.C.A. 42 of 1951, *Bugembe* v. *Kiwanuka and Others*, Notes 47.
[2] See p. 197, above.

It is desirable, if possible, to ascertain the legal affect, if any, of the 1926 Order. The High Court has no cognizance of this Order which did not appear to PEARSON, J., to have been duly published in the *Gazette* as required by the Buganda Agreement (Native Laws), 1910.[1] It may be freely conceded that not only was this Order never published in the *Gazette* but it never received the Governor's approval. The Order plainly is not a native law within the definition accepted. Further it was not embodied either in a subsequent agreement nor in any ordinance. It may be freely conceded also, therefore, that the Order was never contained in any legislative enactment.[2]

It is submitted that the Kabaka having been given exclusive and absolute jurisdiction in " any case relating to the headship, membership or other matter affecting clans " by the 1924 Agreement, there cannot be any reasonable bar on the Kabaka making an administrative order as to how such jurisdiction shall be exercised. As the superior courts have themselves referred to these powers of the Kabaka at times to be " quasi-judicial ", a statement as to what procedure will be followed in their employment, it is suggested, is the more welcome. The approval of the Governor was not given to the Order, if indeed it was in fact ever sought, for, it is suggested, the same reason which led the present Governor to withhold his approval to the recent draft native law. For the Governor to give such approval would be in conflict with the 1924 Agreement which bestowed on the Kabaka exclusive and absolute power in clan cases. Since the order, which embodies Ganda custom, has been scrupulously followed for the last twenty-three years by the Kabaka, Chiefs and people of Buganda and has been recognised by the Kabaka's Courts which have from time to time taken cognizance of it,[3] it is submitted that the Order is by the standards set by the Privy Council,[4] a statement of Ganda customary law on testate and intestate succession and inheritance, administration, execution and distribution of estates and guardianship.[5] The English text of the Order together with a commentary has accordingly been provided as Appendix 4 to this book.

---

[1] H.C.C.A. 21 of 1942 (unreported), see p. 199 above.
[2] See judgment of JENKINS, Ag. V-P., in E.A.C.A. 30 of 1954 (unreported) at p. 206, above.
[3] *E.g.* P.C.C.C. 59 of 1949, *Balikolamanyi* v. *Tonondola*, 1940–1955 C.L.R.
[4] *Eshugbayo Eleko* v. *Nigeria Government*, [1931] A.C. 662 at p. 673.
[5] See H.C.C.A. 4 of 1949, cited at p. 200, above.

MACHINERY OF SUCCESSION

It may well assist the administration of justice in courts of law if those courts may ascertain what machinery is set in motion on testate and intestate successions, in regard to the distribution of immovables and movables. Certainly it will enable us the better to consider the substance of the law of succession later described.

If there is a will, it is passed by deceased's family to the *ow'olunyiriri* (head of sub-consanguinity), by *ow'olunyiriri* to the head of the consanguinity (omutuba), by him to the head of the sub-clan (essiga) and by the latter to the head of clan (ow'akasolya). If the estate consists merely of movable property the head of clan, subject to certain special procedure regarding cash,[1] has power to confirm the will or reject it.

If, on the other hand, the estate contains land, the head of clan first writes a " search letter " to the Protectorate Office of Titles, requesting as the title implies a search of the register, and sends a copy to the Lukiiko Land Officer who supervises the head of clan's actions in regard to land matters. If there are any outstanding transfers of land remaining unsigned by the deceased at his death, an assistant in the Titles Office sends them to the Lukiko Land Officer for submission to the three senior Ministers to sign in accordance with Section 5 of the Possession of Land Law. Thereafter the head of clan makes his report and his recommendations for the distribution of the estate to the Katikkiro's Office.

Until March 1954, such recommendations were entered in handwriting in the Succession Register and were then copied by a clerk onto separate papers, the Kabaka alone signing the Register. Because of human error in copying the system has been changed and now consists of the head of clan putting his recommendations in the form of a typewritten memorandum which he takes first to the Lukiiko Land Officer. This officer examines the recommendations as to immovables and if satisfied that the land proposed for distribution is available in the estate stamps the memorandum with a certificate to the effect that it is in order. The head of clan then takes his memorandum so stamped to the Ddiiro Office where the Assistant Katikkiro stamps it if he considers the recommendations are all in order. The Assistant Katikkiro submits the recommendations so stamped to the Katikkiro who if personally satisfied submits to the

---

[1] See below at p. 213.

Kabaka. The Kabaka's signature confirms the succession from the date of that signature.

At this point it should be observed that if there is an intestacy, the head of clan has power to approve the distribution recommended to him by his subordinates if the estate consists of movables only. But if the estate includes land, then the above procedure as in the case of testate succession is followed with the additional provision that the recommendations may be amended by the Ddiiro prior to submission to the Katikkiro.

After the Kabaka has confirmed by his signature a succession whether testate or intestate, the successor and the heirs to land bring a stamped letter of introduction from the head of clan to the Lukiiko Land Officer in order that the land may be transferred to them in accordance with the succession confirmed. The Lukiiko Land Officer puts the letter of introduction on a file and sends it to the Ddiiro where the Succession Registers are kept. Lukiiko Mailo Form No. M.8 is then completed. This form reads as follows in translation:

*Lukiiko Mailo Form No. M.*8

KINGDOM OF BUGANDA

No. . . . .

SUCCESSION CONFIRMED BY HIS HIGHNESS THE KABAKA ON . . . .

INSTRUMENT PERMITTING THE TRANSFER OF THE SUCCESSION

Name of deceased   Date of death

Village   County

Number of Certificate of Title   Folio   Volume

Area of land which he held   Acres

Present Whereabouts of Certificate of Title

Name of Successor

Acres which he succeeds to

Signature of Successor

Amount of Lukiiko fees Shs.

Amount of Lukiiko fees Shs.   and of obeisance
                          (okulanya)

      Date   19   Signature of Clerk of Succession Affairs in the
                     ·   Ddiiro

                           Signature of Clerk in Lukiiko Land Office

      Date   19   Signature of Lukiiko Land Officer

            The Lukiiko gives consent   19

      Date   19

                                          Katikkiro

Other heirs who have not yet transferred their inheritance
have the following acres of land.

1	Acres
2	Acres
3	Acres
4	Acres
5	Acres
6	Acres
7	Acres

The fees, for the introduction to the Kabaka before the Lukiko, consisting of Shs. 8/– to be paid by the successor and Shs. 6/– by the other heirs are then paid into the Lukiiko Treasury. The successor and heirs are then so presented to the Kabaka.

Thereupon, the Katikkiro's signature having been obtained to that form, the Lukiiko Land Officer makes out Lukiiko Mailo Form 12 which is a Certificate of Succession to be signed by the Katikkiro and six members of the Standing Committee of the Lukiiko. That form reads:

Lukiko Mailo Form No. 12

THE LAND SUCCESSION LAW, 1912

Reg. No. . . . .

CERTIFICATE OF SUCCESSION

We certify that

of   his/her Chief

died on   day of

having land in Buganda and that

of   his/her Chief
is entitled according to law to have possession and to sell the land which is written below thus.

This Certificate of Succession is given to
spoken of above, because he/she is entitled according to law to it:—
As having been willed it by the above-mentioned " deceased "
                          will come of age on the   day of
his/her guardian

1
2
3   Katikiro
4   •   and
5   Members of
6   the Lukiko
7

Mengo

.... 19 ....

When the Certificate of Succession has been so signed the successor or heir, as the case may be, is given a copy or is sent a copy through the post under cover of form " M ", the appropriate assistant to the Registrar of Titles being sent a copy which has previously been signed at the bottom by the successor or heir concerned on his visit to Mmengo so that the Office of Titles may check that witnessed signature against the claimant's. Form " M " in translation reads:

Ref: No. " M "   /   /
Lukiiko Land Office,
H.H. The Kabaka's Government,
Mmengo Buganda
P.O. Box 91, Kampala

19

Mr./Mrs.

MAILO REGISTER

Volume   Folio

Certificate of Title

Acres   at   Ggombolola   Ssaza

I send you Certificate of Succession No.

of the   19   , by which you may cause to be transferred   acres from the succession of the late   .

You should take it to the Titles Office at together with the fees for the registration of your land.

Encl. 1.   *Lukiiko Land Officer*

Copy to: The Assistant Registrar of Titles,
              Mailo Office
              P.O. Box

        Signature of the Successor

        In the presence of

        Date   19

The successor or heir then takes his Certificate of Succession to the appropriate assistant Registrar of Titles who stamps it with the date of production and on payment of the required fees issues a Certificate of Title to the claimant. It will be an indication of the volume of this work to observe that in the year 1957 about 1,750 successions were registered which comprised 136 successions to whole estates and 4,716 successions to portions.[1]

There is a special procedure which is followed when the deceased's estate includes funds deposited with banks. This special procedure is of recent growth and owes its origin to the suggestion of the former Katikkiro, Oweekitiibwa M.E. Kawalya Kagwa, that an officer be appointed to supervise the distribution of movable property and in particular money. Such an officer, the Succession Secretary, was appointed on the 27th October, 1950. What happens is that the head of clan applies to the Katikkiro to obtain the deceased's money from a bank and submits his passbook. The Succession Secretary on behalf of the Katikkiro takes the matter up with the bank concerned. When the money has been received from the bank all the approved recipients, that is successor or heirs or both, come to the Succession Secretary and receive each their shares of the money for which they sign.

Revision of the distribution approved takes place if a debt against the estate is subsequently proved or if extra land or moneys of the deceased are discovered to which there must be an additional succession. The procedure is for the head of clan to put up his recommendations in writing and to send them, in the case of fresh land, to the Lukiiko Land Officer who on being satisfied as to the existence of the land sends the recommendations to the Ddiiro to be stamped. If there is no land for additional distribution then the recommendations go to the Katikkiro's office and so to the Ddiiro. The Ddiiro stamps the recommendations if it approves and sends them through the Katikkiro to the Kabaka. If the Kabaka approves the additional distribution he issues a letter of approval to that effect. On receiving that letter the Katikkiro writes to the head of clan, with a copy to the Lukiiko Land Officer if land is involved, conveying the Kabaka's approval. All the correspondence regarding such an additional succession is then entered in the Succession Register at the page of the original distribution.

---

[1] Figures given by Registrar of Titles on 12th April, 1958.

The above system of dealing with succession to land started in 1904 when the records were kept in the Lukiko Diary, which also contained records of cases decided by the Lukiko Court from 1904 onwards. The first separate register of Succession was opened in 1915. As has already been mentioned,[1] up to the middle 1940's the work of the Lukiko Land Officer included transactions in respect of the exchange, sale and gift of mailo land, the Lukiiko Endagaano being handled by him. On the cessation of those activities the Lukiiko Land Officer's work was restricted to succession to land.

CHOICE OF SUCCESSOR AND DISTRIBUTION OF ESTATE

Prior to the reign of Kabaka Muteesa I the pattern of succession was for a man to succeed to the estate of his paternal uncle, a woman to succeed to the estate of her paternal aunt. Succession was then always patrilineal, with the special exception of the royal family, and succession followed sex.

As a result of frequent disputes over successions by nephews and on the advice of his Katikkiro Kaira, Muteesa I ordered that a child of the blood should inherit, that is that the successor must be the son or grandson of the deceased and only on failure of such sons or grandsons could the succession go to the brother's line. Muteesa at the same time ordered that the successor was to be chosen by the daughters of the deceased from among the deceased's male descendants. Thereafter the practice grew up during the last century whereby a man succeeded to his grandfather's estate and when his father died another, that is a grandson, became his father's successor. This practice indeed is still followed in the case of a testate succession where the will is not disputed by the testator's son and is subsequently confirmed by the Kabaka. Should the testator's son dispute such a will he would usually succeed in upsetting it.[2] Intestate succession now never goes to a grandson if there is a surviving son.

The reason for this former practice of a grandson succeeding to deceased's estate may be found in the custom of the grandfather treating his grandson with especial favour. At his grand-

---

[1] See p. 154, above.

[2] Famous recent examples are: by the Kabaka's decision Serwano Kulubya succeeded to his father Ezeki Mugambe in preference to a grandson; Servano Sekazza likewise succeeded to Amoni Bazira, Kaggo; Matiko succeeded to Sensali in like manner; and Leonard Bassudde succeeded to Daudi Bassudde. But the grandson of the late Speaker Rafaeri Kasule succeeded to the estate in accordance with the will as the deceased's son did not dispute the will.

father's home, the grandson was called " nnannyinimu " (owner of the house) and his grandfather's wives were said to be his wives. The grandson was counted the grandfather's brother and could perform the *kukuza*[1] rite with his grandfather's wives. Even when he has grown up, the grandson can sleep and stay in his grandfather's house contrary to the usual Ganda custom of grown-up children having to sleep in other houses than their parents. This relationship was not all one-sided: the grandfather could carry out his grandson's prerogative of fixing the marriage consideration on the marriage of the grandson's sister. The grandfather and his grandson were in truth of the same rank—*ab'olubu lumu*.

It was and is thus possible for the same person to succeed several deceased providing the grandfather involved in each succession is different. But in respect of each succession he must have a different Lubuga (" sister ", co-heiress). Such a Lubuga is chosen, as is the custom, from outside the successor's sub-consanguinity (olunyiriri). The Lubuga does not in fact succeed to any part of the property but may be given part by the successor.

In the nineteenth century there were no heirs other than the successor (omusika) and his Lubuga. The successor even in polygamous households took the whole estate. It is true that all deceased's clansmen who attended the ceremony of completing the funeral rites (okwabya lumbe) took some small keepsake and indeed if he did not get such a memento he was supposed to have been disowned by the clan: as the Ganda proverb goes:

Sikayanira mu lumbe: alinda kuboolwa—" I do not dispute at the funeral " says the man who waits to be expelled.

That was called *okugabana ebintu by'omufu* (distribution of deceased's property). But it was not until after the mailo system was introduced in 1900 that the practice arose of distributing valuable portions of the estate, in particular land (okugabana ttaka), to the other heirs (abasika abalala).

While the practice after Muteesa I's edict was for succession by a son, it should be noted that the son who succeeded was not the eldest son. There was no rule of primogeniture in succession. In a *cause célèbre* in 1925 it was held:

" In regard to the particular contention raised by Bamutta firstly that there are several *basika*, secondly that he has a claim as the

---

[1] See p. 219, below.

eldest son, I think he has no case. Judge Carter's monograph, pp. 116 and 118, show that there can be only one *musika* and also that the succession of the eldest son was clear contrary to primitive custom and has only recently come in."[1]

It was soon after that there was a public outcry led by Christian feminists demanding that

" in a case of intestacy only the eldest son of the first wife should inherit and that no-one might leave property to the children of any but this wife."[2]

The late Kabaka acceded to the first demand for the most part which is embodied in his Succession Order of the following year[3] but not to the second. The qualification on the acceptance of the first demand was that neither did the Kabaka's Succession Order specify nor have the clans paid the slightest attention to the religion of the marriage. The eldest child, providing he is a child of the blood, succeeds no matter from what union he sprang.[4]

The eldest natural son can only be debarred from succeeding to his father if he commits an act of abomination (omusango gwa kivve), if he steals or if he suffers from mental disorder.

The testator may however still circumvent this rule of primogeniture of the male issue by making a token nomination of the eldest son while at the same time bequeathing his substance to another. The Ganda term that *okusikira omusai* (succession to blood) as contrasted with *okusikira ttaka* (succession to land). The successor must inherit the homestead and some land if the estate contains land but not necessarily the larger portion under a will. If under the will all the property has been distributed to others than the successor, the clan head persuades the donees to give some portion to the heir. The sanction is that until the will is confirmed by the Kabaka the heirs cannot get their land out of their inheritance and if the successor does not get some land he cannot be introduced to the Kabaka and confirmed when an estate contains land; the heirs (abasika abalala) are not so introduced.

---

[1] P.C.R.O. 28 of 1925 (upholding Lukiko Court Case 91 of 1924), *I. G. Mwaziza v. I. Kato* (unreported).

[2] Mair, *An African People in the Twentieth Century*, p. 102.

[3] See Appendix 4, clause 12(a), p. 324, below.

[4] The outstanding exception to the rule is that the Kiwewa, the Kabaka's first-born son, never succeeds to the Kabakaship; but that exception springs from ancient custom.

If the succession is intestate, the successor gets the larger share.[1]

If the successor is absent when due to succeed the deceased's relatives (ab'oluganda b'omufu) keep the property in collaboration with the village chief (nnannyini kyalo) until the successor returns to take his inheritance. If the successor goes missing nowadays it is usual for the clan authority to advertise in the press for him and if there is no reply within a period of about three months, then another successor to the deceased is selected by the clan council.

To turn to the women of the deceased's family, it should first be noted that they are not without influence nor without portion nowadays in the estate. In 1922 the Lukiko resolved that when a man begat daughters only and died without making a will, his successor should be selected in the sub-consanguinity (olunyiriri) to which the deceased belonged but his daughters should receive each a share in their father's land.[2]

It is now a general rule that daughters as well as sons receive land in the distribution of the estate, whether the succession be testate or intestate, providing the land suffices.

Further in an intestate succession the recommendation of the daughters as to which of their brothers should succeed as being best suited to look after them has since the time of Muteesa I been given great weight by the clan authorities. Should there be a single surviving daughter, she, in the absence of any male kin eligible as heir, may choose a short list of male candidates in the clan from whom the clan heads select the successor.

The position of widows has changed considerably. Before Muteesa I's reign a widow who had been married to the deceased by customary marriage (muwase) had to marry the successor and had no power to leave his courtyard (oluggya). After Muteesa I a widow who had borne the deceased a child did not marry the successor; she could leave the successor's courtyard and there was no question of compensation being paid to the successor by her family. At no time could a slave-wife (omuzaana) of the deceased leave the courtyard; whether she had borne children or not she was allotted to another clansman to take to wife. Later a practice arose of putting widows under the care of the village chief if the successor was not going to live on

---

[1] See Southwold, *op. cit.*, p. 94, who places the amount at 40% on the average.

[2] *Amateka ne Biragiro ebyatesebwa Olukiko Olukulu okuva* 1922–1923, p. 6.

I

the deceased's plot, but that is now obsolete because of the scramble for *bibanja*.[1]

A widow never has inherited anything from her deceased husband as she is of a different totem. But he may have willed her something or in an intestate succession if the clan head considers she has been a good, faithful wife who has borne the deceased children, he may give her something from the estate. And if he does not, the Ddiiro usually allots her something under those circumstances.

If a widow marries again and takes a child of her first marriage to the stepfather's home, that child can only succeed or inherit within the sub-consanguinity (olunyiriri) of its natural father not within that of its stepfather.

In the nineteenth century there was a practice of a man who was without a son, even if he had wives, adopting a male child of one of his brother's in the same sub-consanguinity. It was then understood that the child was to be treated as his favourite son and that he would become his successor. This practice still operates but nowadays a written will is a usual necessary preliminary condition.

Female succession, as has been already mentioned, runs from paternal aunt to niece not from mother to daughter and this custom ancient though it is still holds good today. A daughter is usually given something from her deceased mother's property but the widower gets nothing. When there are children of the marriage the widower usually acts as agent cum trustee of his deceased wife's land for the good of their children but he cannot transfer the land to himself and, of course, he must not abuse his agency. He has no authority in respect of his former wife's succession because she is of another clan.

When a woman dies, the heiress has another girl to be her Lubuga (co-heiress), just like a male successor.

When an heiress succeeds to the estate of a deceased wife she is usually the deceased's brother's daughter or the deceased's younger sister. In ancient times a girl who succeeded to the estate of her paternal aunt used to marry the widower and bring up the children. This practice fell somewhat into abeyance under mission influence but even today such heiresses still marry the widower particularly when the widower has come to an understanding with his relatives-in-law on the matter. On the night

---

[1] Compare Mair, *op. cit.*, p. 219.

of the *okwabya lumbe* the widower performs the *kukuza* rite with the heiress. This rite which occurs frequently in Ganda social customs consists of the formal ceremony whereby the woman sits on the ground with her legs stretched out in front of her and the man jumps over them. If, however, the man is attracted to the woman he has sexual intercourse with her instead of the merely formal ceremony. Such intercourse cannot subsequently be the basis of legal proceedings even if a pregnancy should result. So it sometimes happens that the widower thereby takes to wife his former wife's heiress. Should that not happen, the heiress nowadays only stays a few days at the widower's home if she is unmarried. It is then up to the widower to make his own arrangements.

An exception to the general rule of female succession is found among families displaced from their homelands by capture during the Bukedi, Bunyoro or other wars of the last century. If the deceased woman's clan cannot be traced outside Buganda in order that a successor to her estate may be obtained, then her family, which will have settled here for many years, usually select one of the deceased's grand-daughters, that is a daughter of one of her sons to succeed her.

If a wife fell sick of the disease called *makiro*, said to be caused by sexual excess, then her parents would say on her death that her husband had not looked after her properly and would refuse to provide a successor to her estate.

As to minors a father succeeds to his minor son's property and her sister to that of an unmarried girl. As has been stated above, there are no separate funeral rites for children and so no formal successor or heirs to their estates.

Succession by someone outside the deceased's clan has never been common.[1] The only true example as regards male succession was where a dispute arose in a blood-brotherhood and a series of successors of one side kept dying; thereupon to avoid further misfortune the son of the deceased's daughter (mujjwa) would be chosen to succeed to the estate, since not being of the deceased's clan he would be immune from the blood-brother's curse.[2]

The only other true example is that described above in respect of female succession by the deceased woman's grand-daughter—a practice arising from the wars of the last century. Such a

---

[1] *Pace* Mair, *op. cit.*, p. 211.
[2] The example was restricted to blood-brotherhood disputes and not a general possibility, as Mair stated (*op. cit.*, p. 211).

grand-daughter would, of course, be of her father's totem and his totem would be her grandfather's not her grandmother's.

There were two pseudo-cases where succession outside the clan was apparent rather than real, to wit between blood-brothers and masters and slaves. In both cases the stranger had in fact been adopted into that clan. A slave, as has already been mentioned,[1] did not normally succeed to property but his property could be inherited by the clan which had adopted him.

By ancient custom the Kabaka used to receive a portion of the estate of every chief who died, in the shape of women and cattle, but this custom was relinquished by Mwanga on his return from flight.[2] About that same time village chiefs for their part relinquished their claim to a portion of a deceased peasant's estate.[3] Nowadays neither the Kabaka nor the landowner (omutongole) receive portions out of the estate of a deceased person unless there is specific provision to that effect in the will.[4]

The heads of sub-clan (ow'essiga), of sub-consanguinity (ow'olunyiriri) and of household (ow'oluggya) still receive a share (omugabo) in the distribution of the estate. Relatives now receive merely a small keepsake.

Certain property can only pass to a male on succession: shield, shoes, spears, sticks, axe, barkcloth hammer, hunting and fishing nets. Similarly certain property can only pass to females in succession: knife, barkcloth, hoe, gardening and cooking utensils.

Land in succession calls for the observance of some particular provisions of customary law. There is no limit to the subdivision of an area of land or a plot, which is reckoned to be 35 yards square or four to an acre. Often two or three heirs inherit one plot jointly particularly in the densely populated and rich agricultural ssazas of Kyaddondo, Busiro, Mawokota, Bulemeezi, Kyaggwe and Buddu " where ", informants told me, " they even count out the coffee trees ".[5] The head of sub-clan (ow'essiga) must not rely on mere hearsay in arranging the distribution of

---

[1] See p. 66, above.

[2] Carter, *op. cit.*, p. 118 and Roscoe, *op. cit.*, p. 270.

[3] Carter, *ibid.*

[4] A recent example was the bequest of cattle to the Kabaka by the late ex-Regent Kyemwa.

[5] And see P.C.C.C. 8 of 1955, *Namutebi* v. *Nansubuga* 1956 C.L.R. 63.

land.[1] The heirs (abasika abalala) must survey their portions of land before the successor (omusika).[2]

Cattle are part of the estate for distribution although they may be separately bequeathed under the will. If the cattle are nearby the deceased's home they are brought to the funeral rites. Otherwise the president of the funeral rites (omukulu w'olumbe) sends emissaries to inspect them.[3] If some cattle are distributed under a will, the balance go to the heir.

The Kabaka's courts have recognised two Hima customs in respect of Hima herdsmen and their cattle in Buganda: the succession of a daughter to her father[4] and the custom, which rather smacks of Theocritus, whereby the deceased's cattle are brought to the burial that they might low for the person who used to herd them.[5]

RIGHTS AND DUTIES OF SUCCESSOR

The successor follows " in the footsteps of the deceased " (ajja mu bigere by'omufu) from the moment he dons (okusumuka) the barkcloth of succession, taking over the duties and responsibilities of the deceased as well as his rights. This responsibility does not now, even if it did previously,[6] extend to the debts outstanding owed by the deceased, for the simple reason that such as are admitted and can be paid are paid off by the clan authorities before the successor is put in possession of his inheritance.[7]

The duties and responsibilities of the successor in regard to the widows and the minor children of the deceased are considered in the chapter on the law of guardianship.[8]

DEBTS FOR OR AGAINST THE ESTATE

Debts may be admitted against the estate in various ways: the deceased on his death-bed may have requested that a certain debt be paid and payment of that debt will then invariably be made either out of the estate or, if it does not suffice or there is

---

[1] P.C.C.C. 257 of 1955, *Mwanula* v. *Serruga and Another*, 1956 C.L.R., 63.

[2] P.C.C.C. 5 of 1953, *Nanfuka and Others* v. *Mpiso and Another* (unreported) P.C.C.C. 225 of 1955, *Kasule* v. *Namunyaka and Another*, 1956 C.L.R. 65 and P.C.C.C. 329 of 1957, *Kasajja* v. *Nyanjabulye*, 1958 C.L.R. 111.

[3] See p. 174, above.

[4] H.C.C.A. 11 of 1943, *Kaika* v. *Buyingira* (unreported), P.C.C.C. 376 of 1956, *Byandazo* v. *Nsubuga*, 1957 C.L.R. 159.

[5] P.C.C.A. 153 of 1956, *Lutanzira* v. *Kichweka*, 1957 C.L.R. 157.

[6] Carter, *op. cit.*, p. 119.

[7] Succession Order, 1926, Clause 21.

[8] See p. 225, below.

none, out of the pockets of the relatives of the deceased; alternatively if the deceased had property, the president of the funeral rites (omukulu w'olumbe) collects claims against the estate, sometimes by advertising in the newspapers, and then places such claims before the head of clan who decides which are to be paid,[1] usually relying on the evidence of the widow. But if a deceased had no property and has not given instructions either on his death-bed or in his will as to payment of certain debts, then those debts die. It is, of course, the duty of the head of clan to ensure payment into the estate of any outstanding credits.[2] Reference is invited to clauses 18 to 21 inclusive of the Succession Order, 1926, regarding debts due to or by deceased persons generally.[3]

Dispositive Succession

The nomination of one's successor or an oral will is of ancient origin as a Ganda usage.[4] The occasion, at any rate prior to Muteesa I's reign, used to be when a man's brother came to visit him. The householder made a feast providing a goat and a calabash of beer in his brother's honour. The feast was attended by the householder's friends, neighbours, relatives and wives who were witnesses essential to the validity of such a testamentary disposition.[5] The householder would then verbally will his property to his brother or his brother's son. All the witnesses were then supposed to keep that nomination secret until the householder's death. At that time the nominated successor might be far away but the witnesses would support his succession before the clan authorities. Those clan authorities, of course, had the final decision as to the approval of the successor nominated but it was rare for such an oral will to be upset.[6] Prior to his death the testator could always disinherit the successor he had previously nominated and providing he did so before witnesses, the principal of whom would be his wives, the previous nomination would be cancelled.

Oral wills are still permissible providing the nomination is made before two witnesses and providing there is no land in the

---

[1] P.C.C.C. 38 of 1957, *Kabusu* v. *Semugoma and Others*, 1958 C.L.R. 107.

[2] P.C.C.C. 176 of 1946, *Sebuliba* v. *Kamya and Others* (unreported).

[3] Appendix 4, p. 328, below.

[4] H.C.C.A. (1915), *Mikaya Nkangoli* v. *Stanislaus Mugwanya*, 2 U.L.R. 140 and Gorju, *op. cit.*, p. 358.

[5] H.C.C.A. (1915), *Nkangoli* v. *Mugwanya*, 2 U.L.R. 140.

[6] Carter, *op. cit.*, p. 120.

deceased's estate. If there is land, a written will is required or the estate will be treated as an intestate succession.

Gifts of property *inter vivos* are common. The property can either be transferred to the donee immediately or left in donor's care until his death.[1] In the latter case such gifts must be confirmed by the evidence of at least two witnesses or by a document duly witnessed. A court will, however, take into account the fact that a donee has built his house on a certain area and sold to others from that area when considering which part of the deceased's estate shall be allotted to satisfy a gift made *inter vivos*.[2] A gift *inter vivos* may be reduced by the donor subsequently[3] or cancelled by him. The High Court has held that if between the incomplete gift and the death of the donor was interposed the will which showed no intention of giving in accordance with the previous gift, the gift must fail.[4]

It is also possible in emergency for a dying man to call forward a favourite child, hold him by the hand and pass him to a friend standing beside him. This act was counted as an indication of the dying man's selection of his heir and providing witnesses were present, notably a wife, would usually be approved by the clan authorities.

It was, and is, also a well-recognised usage for gifts to be made on the death-bed (*donatio mortis causa*).

Written wills were not known among the Ganda until the closing years of the last century but that is understandable when one takes into account that writing itself was unknown to them until the reign of Muteesa I (1852–1884). By 1916 the written will had become so common that it was necessary to enact the Wills Law. That Law, it has already been observed, was omitted from the Revised Edition of the Buganda Laws, 1957, but its provisions were in fact duplicated for the most part by Clause 3 of the Succession Order, 1926, which still stands.[5] A testator's powers are unrestricted subject to the Succession Order, 1926, and the clan authorities culminating in the Kabaka. As has already been mentioned, a testator may will away all his property from his successor. But the Kabaka has power to alter the succession under a will.[6] A testator can disinherit or cancel the

---

[1] P.C.C.C. 59 of 1948, *Zamwanguya* v. *Kabali and Another* (unreported).
[2] P.C.C.C. 39 of 1949, *Kiggundu* v. *Mubiri*, 1940–1955 C.L.R.
[3] P.C.C.C. 135 of 1948, *Mbazira* v. *Senkubuge*, 1940–1955 C.L.R.
[4] H.C.C.A. 10A of 1947, *Nakabugo* v. *Nkoyoyo*, Notes 19.
[5] See Appendix 4, p. 320, below.
[6] P.C.C.C. 43 of 1950, *Kiviri* v. *Damba and Another*, 1940–1955 C.L.R.

provisions of the will providing he does so in writing formally before witnesses. A later will is superior to an earlier will by the same testator.[1] But a will written out and signed by the beneficiary is invalid![2] As regards alterations in a will the judgment of GRAY, Ag. J., enunciates the well-known principles:

> " The presumption to be made in such circumstances is that, in the absence of any satisfactory evidence proving the contrary, such addition was made after the execution in proper form of the will by the testator. If this presumption is not disproved, the addition forms no part of the will and must be disregarded in carrying out the testator's wishes. Common sense points this out as the only possible course to take. If one held otherwise, it would be fatal to the whole object of the Wills Law. . . . These and many others are very obvious dangers, which the Wills Law was designed to prevent by requiring that all wills should be only executed with certain formalities."[3]

A rather curious case in 1934 gives a precedent for upsetting a certificate of succession on the grounds of fraud,[4] and also an example of criminal proceedings in respect of succession under a will. The Provisional Commissioner's revisional order reads:

> " Accused's son, who was a minor, inherited some land from his uncle. His father, the Accused, went to the head of the clan with the will and said that his son had died, and as a result the Clan Council decided that as the heir was dead, Accused should succeed to the land.
>
> This was confirmed by the Kabaka, and a certificate of succession was issued and the land registered in Accused's name.
>
> When the boy who was the rightful heir, came of age he reported himself to the Head of the Clan. The matter was taken to the Lukiko Arbitration Court and eventually the Kabaka ordered the inheritance to be transferred from Accused to his son.
>
> The Lukiko Court have now convicted the Accused of having obtained his son's inheritance by giving false information, and have sentenced him to 1 year's imprisonment."[5]

---

[1] P.C.C.C. 43 of 1952, *Kafero* v. *Kalulengwa*, 1940–1955 C.L.R.
[2] P.C.C.C. 83 of 1954, *Lutaya* v. *Kikasima and Another*, 1940—1955 C.L.R.
[3] H.C.C.A. 21 of 1932, *Susani B. Muyinda* v. *Stanley Kitaka*, 5 U.L.R. 19.
[4] See above p. 206.
[5] P.C.R.O. 108 of 1934, *Lukiko* v. *Kibirango* (upholding Lukiko Court Case 230 of 1934) (unreported).

CHAPTER 12

GUARDIANSHIP

The fate of the widows on the death of their husband has already been considered:

    (i) they remained in the courtyard, sometimes as the successor's wives; or

    (ii) they were married off to the brothers of the deceased with the successor's agreement; or

    (iii) they were taken back by their family with the successor's agreement.

It was not, therefore, surprising that in ancient times the successors, with the prospect of nothing but wives to look after, attempted frequently to escape succession. The mailo distribution put an end to any such faintheartedness.

If the widow was not taken to wife by the successor and she was young enough to remarry, she inclined to leave her children by the deceased with his clan. It was to prevent such an eventuality that the Guardianship Law, 1904, was enacted so that such a widow should be prevented from deserting and should be compelled to stay to nurture her child.

When the father dies, his successor assumes responsibility for the well-being of the deceased's children. If the successor has not grown up, the clan council selects clansmen of the *lunyiriri* (sub-consanguinity) to look after the children unless the deceased has willed others outside the clan to be guardians of his children. Usually, however, two to four such guardians are selected from the family of the deceased. The successor too, if he is a minor, has guardians appointed to look after him if he is young until he comes of age.

Guardians are entrusted with their ward's property but work under the orders of the clan head. In the last century the clan head was empowered to remove a guardian but now that power is vested in the Principal Court.[1] If a guardian dies the clan council selects another in his stead.

Not only does the successor have a general responsibility along

---

[1] Guardianship Law, section 6, and see P.C.Cr.A. 31 of 1957, *Nakityo* v. *Lukiiko*, 1957 C.L.R. 153 and P.C.Cr.A. 150 of 1958, *Senfuma* v. *Lukiiko*, 1958 C.L.R. 105.

with the guardians appointed in respect of minor children, but the widow does also in respect of her young children's property. She has no power herself to deal with the minor child's property but if she considers that the guardians, to whom that property is invariably entrusted, are neglecting the children's interests she can complain to the clan of her deceased husband. If need be, she may pursue her accusation of maladministration or misappropriation against the guardians in the courts of law.[1] On the other hand the guardians can expel the widow if she is idle in regard to the children and can assume the care of the children in their own homes, as they have been chosen to represent the deceased father. They can also sue the widow for misappropriation of the minor's property.[2]

The successor, although he is not entrusted with the property of the deceased's minor children is " their father " (kitaabwe) and it is he, not the guardians, who is concerned in the social ceremonies such as the betrothal of one of the deceased's daughters. If the successor neglects the minor children of the deceased he can be sued before the clan council and fined a calabash of beer, a goat and a cow, which are consumed by that council. If he remains stubborn in his neglect the clan may refer the case to the courts of law. The custody of the minor children can then be removed from him and placed in another. A successor cannot be removed from his inheritance for neglect of deceased's minor children,[3] since only an act of abomination (kivve) which expels him from the clan can remove him from his inheritance.

The head of the household (ow'oluggya), usually the deceased's elder brother who had presided at his funeral rites, has a residual authority to arbitrate between the successor, the guardians and the widow in the interests of the minor children.

The guardians hold land, cattle and other property for the heirs but cannot dispose of the ownership of that property which is in trust for those heirs. The property must be distributed by the guardians to each child when that child comes of age[4] or marries. The ward can complain to the clan council concerning any shortfall in the property so received from the guardians and may sue them in courts of law.[5]

---

[1] *E.g.* P.C.C.C. 84 of 1955, *Kulikiri* v. *Lutalungibwa* (guardian being stepfather) (unreported).

[2] P.C.C.C. 59 of 1949, *Balikolamanyi* v. *Tonondola*, 1940–1955 C.L.R.

[3] *Pace* Mair, *op. cit.*, p. 217.

[4] P.C.C.C. 405 of 1956, *Bawakanya* v. *Masembe*, 1958 C.L.R. 103.

[5] *E.g.* P.C.C.C. 108 of 1949, *Nunga* v. *Kibirango*, 1940–1955 C.L.R.

So far we have been considering the guardianship of minor children when their father dies. Quite a different procedure is followed when their mother dies. In the last century the paternal grandmother and the paternal aunt assumed responsibility for the minor children in such circumstances. If the paternal aunt was married then the children might go to her home; but if she was unmarried then she might go to her brother's home to care for them. That method is still sometimes followed; indeed nowadays if the father is poor the children may be distributed to the paternal grandmother, paternal aunt or to any adult friend.

There is an ancient practice, which has already been mentioned,[1] and which is still occasionally seen, and that is for the deceased woman's family to take counsel and to choose another woman of their family to go and cook for and look after the widower's children. If the woman and the widower suit each other she eventually becomes his wife.

If the mother of a child dies at childbirth, the child is sent to the paternal grandmother to rear. Formerly it is said that such a child was suckled by the grandmother who resorted to Kiganda medicine for the purpose. But nowadays the baby is reared on cow's milk and it is its father's responsibility to send all requirements for its nurture. If the husband has a second wife who is suckling a child then the babe is handed to her rather than to the grandmother.

If both parents die the paternal grandfather, uncle and aunt assume major responsibility for the upbringing and supervision of the orphans. This responsibility exists even though the clan council may appoint other guardians. If the paternal relations are unable to bear this responsibility then the maternal relatives, in particular the brothers of the deceased mother, assist.

A review of cases decided over the last fifteen years shows that the courts have been vigilant in preserving minor children's property. The restrictions on guardian's powers in relation to land were considered in 1954 by AINLEY, J.:

> " There is not the slightest indication in this case of the existence of any custom whereby it is permissible for the head of a clan (even with the consent of the Katikiro) to sell or give away the lands of infant members of the clan in the name of those infants. In any event the Land Succession Law, 1912, makes things perfectly clear. Clause 2 of that Law reads ' when a Muganda dies having land in Buganda there is no man who shall be able to do to that land any-

---

[1] See p. 218, above.

thing at all except after he has obtained from the Lukiko a certificate of succession which says that he is entitled according to law to have control of it.' Provision is later made for the issue to guardians of certificates of succession, but care has been taken to tell guardians that they are not permitted to do anything with the land contrary to their duties as guardians.

These old land laws of the Baganda were drafted with great simplicity and wisdom, but the pity of it is that they have been repeatedly ignored both by the Courts and even occasionally, I speak with all respect, by the Office of Titles."[1]

The Principal Court similarly has held that guardians erred in selling a minor heir's land allegedly in order to obtain funds for his education.[2] The High Court has further held that a guardian may only sell a ward's land if he had obtained a certificate of succession and such land can only be conveyed to a purchaser under an instrument of transfer signed by the Ministers under section 5 of the Possession of Land Law.[3]

The courts have also held a guardian who assumed responsibility for funds exceeding Shs. 77,000/– to have been negligent in failing to open a ledger account at the beginning of his assumption of power.[4] The High Court instructed the Principal Court in a suit by wards against guardians for failure to account properly for their dealings with the estate that a full account of the guardian's dealings with the estate should be taken by an accountant and that he should report to the Court.[5] At the suit of the widow guardians have been ordered to hand over the minor heir's immovable property and to pay moneys being the proceeds of sale of vehicles he inherited into a bank.[6] Cattle are frequently a bone of contention between the widow or ward and guardians and in general the Principal Court has inclined to order that the mother and child be given access to the cattle so that the child may benefit from the milk.[7]

---

[1] H.C.C.A. 10 of 1952, *Hamu Mukasa and Another* v. *Muguluma* (P.C.C.C. 54 of 1950) (unreported).

[2] P.C.C.C. 31 of 1953, *Seruwagi* v. *Gitta and Others*, 1940–1955 C.L.R.

[3] H.C.C.A. 49 of 1952, *Wamala* v. *Muguluma*, Notes 53.

[4] P.C.C.C. 30 of 1950, *Buza* v. *Lubega and Others* (H.C.C.A. 71 of 1951) (unreported).

[5] H.C.C.A. 17 of 1948, *Nnamulondo and Others* v. *Musigire and Others* (P.C.C.C. 54 of 1946), Notes 23.

[6] P.C.C.C. 263A of 1950, *Nantumbwe* v. *Kasozi and Another*, 1940–1955 C.L.R.

[7] P.C.C.C. 54 of 1944, *Kiteteyirwano* v. *Byalugaba*, 1940–1955 C.L.R.; P.C.C.C. 38 of 1946, *Namirembe* v. *Kalembe and Others*, 1940–1955 C.L.R.; P.C.C.C. 177 of 1949, *Kalekye* v. *Lulyambalyamba*, 1940–1955 C.L.R.; P.C.C.C. 128 of 1952, *Lutemesa* v. *Muwairoha*, 1940–1955 C.L.R.

PART V

MERCANTILE LAW

SUMMARY

		PAGE
CHAP. 13. Contracts	. . . .	231
CHAP. 14. Markets	. . . .	241
CHAP. 15. Corporations and Associations	. . . .	244

CHAPTER 13

CONTRACTS[1]

The ancient relationship of peasant (omukopi) to village chief (nnanyini kyalo) was considered in Chapter 4 under the law of persons and the modern development of this contractual relationship in Chapter 8 under the law of land.

The contractual relation of a slave to his master was also considered in Chapter 4 under the law of the status and capacity of individuals.

The marriage contract was examined under Chapter 6.

Contracts Creating or Transferring Interests in Property

Barter

Prior to the introduction of cowry shells by the Arabs in the reign of the Kabaka Suna (1810–1852),[2] barter was the only type of contract for acquiring interest in property. My information is that it was customary to barter cattle without there being witnesses; but Sir Apolo Kagwa goes so far as to state that a sale of anything not brand-new between two persons was impossible unless they had arranged for a third party to be a witness of their transaction in consideration of a fee (engobolo).[3] Frequently cattle and goats were bartered between a peasant and his chief, for the chief was in the habit of giving feasts whereas the peasant could not afford to butcher his stock. Or peasants would barter among themselves the legs of a goat (amagulu g'embuzi) for beer bananas (mbidde). Indeed barter is still practised in respect of cattle, goats, chicken and what is nowadays of far greater intrinsic importance, land. Land started to be bartered about 1907, at first at the ridiculous rate of a calabash of beer and a goat for an acre.

---

[1] I have followed Dr. A. N. Allott's classification of African customary contracts.

[2] Gorju, *op. cit.*, p. 306, footnote.

[3] *Empisa*, pp. 241–242.

Sale

Contracts of sale began to be made in the nineteenth century as the use of cowry shells as money began to spread.

There is a custom of buying on credit which though of ancient origin still exists. It is usually styled *nte ngiguze* (I have bought the cow) or *nkuguziza mbuzi* (I have sold you the goat). The practice consists of an agreement to purchase and to sell without any consideration passing. Such a contract is binding: the vendor could not sell to another but the purchaser can sell again before he has paid the purchase price and then pay his debt out of the proceeds, thereby usually reaping a profit.

This custom is still in practice particularly among cattle-dealers and butchers. The mere handshake (okusika mukono) completes the sale agreement and is binding at law. It is then the responsibility of the vendor to take the cattle to the agreed market, often distant, and the purchaser pays for the cattle which arrive there. This custom is also observed in the fish trade but in the *matooke* (plantain) trade part payment is usual.

Purchase by part payment (okusigaza ebbanja) was well known in the nineteenth century. It is the usual method of purchase, nowadays the part payment being a security (omusingo) for the sale. A development of this method is sale by instalments. In such case it is usual to have a time limit. Should the purchaser fail to complete the contract, the money paid is returned or the vendor resorts to court action to claim the balance of the debt.

The verbal agreements of the nineteenth century gave way to the written agreements of the twentieth particularly in respect of cattle and then land. Sharp practice was a primary cause for this change but there was also the need to evidence a purchase—in respect of cattle to the Kabaka's Chief Herdsman (Ssebalijja) who would demand evidence that the cattle in question were not the Kabaka's, and in respect of land to the Registrar of Titles in order to effect the transfer. Nevertheless, verbal contracts on proof are still valid today in respect of all property.

Cowry shells were not the only currency in the nineteenth century. Ivory also was among the nobility a medium of exchange. It is said that Kabaka Mwanga first sold villages to chiefs for ivory.[1]

---

[1] Kabaka Mwanga so sold Manyangwa estate to Sir Apolo Kagwa, Makerere to Semei Kakunguru and Samwiri Mukasa, Seta to Abudulazizi Bulwadda and part of Rubaga to Semei Kakunguru.

Plots (bibanja), trees and crops were not sold until recent times and their sale has been described in Chapter 8.

On the 8th July, 1901 a notice issued prohibiting the importation of cowry shells. The resulting confusion has been described by Cunningham:[1]

" The money question has always been a vexed one and a most difficult one to tackle. Great efforts have been made to get rid of the cumbersome cowrie shells, but that is more easily attempted than accomplished. Large quantities have been burned, and importation prohibited, but still they come, no-one seems to know from where. The natives still prefer these troublesome representatives of coins (?) as they are so easy to hang in strings round their necks—a great convenience to men who have no pockets.

Pice, sixty-four (?) to the rupee, have been tried for several years, but numbers of natives still refuse to sell their produce for anything but cowrie shells. . . . Shells, though so many are still used in the country, are not obtainable in sufficient quantities for our daily needs owing to Government's determined efforts to rid the country of them. Pice have proved unsatisfactory in many ways, as they vary so in value to the rupee, and are not small enough for a country where most things in daily use have so very low a value. The Government are trying to cope with the difficulty by introducing the decimal coinage, the rupee still being the standard and 100 cents being of the value of one rupee. The smallest coin will therefore be the hundredth part of 1s. 4d., roughly six cents, which is the value assessed for a penny postage stamp. The cents are of aluminium. In the middle of the coin a hole is punched, and the natives greatly appreciate this, for they dearly like anything they can put on strings and hang round their necks. The quarter and half-rupee silver coins are still to be circulated, and there will be also 10, 25 and 50 cent pieces of silver, but other and smaller values of the old coinage are to be withdrawn."

Loan

The loan is of ancient usage in Buganda as the proverb bears witness:

Sempola nnume azza omugongo—The man who borrows a bull returns a cow.

Cowries were borrowed and interest used to be charged.[2] The loan was evidenced by a large cowry-shell (ensimbi ennyami) or wild banana seed (ensigo y'olutembe) being given to the creditor in the presence of sureties (abayima) from both sides. The debtor might borrow from his clansmen, neighbours, friends,

---

[1] *Op. cit.*, p. 41.
[2] *Pace* Mair, *op. cit.*, p. 143.

relatives-in-law or chief to repay the debt. But if he could not otherwise repay the debtor would give his daughter or female slave (envuma) in satisfaction of the debt.[1] If the debt were denied resort was had to trial by ordeal (amaduudu).

After the 1900 distribution the loan came into prominence in regard to mailo land.

Gift

In the nineteenth century a verbal gift passed ownership but it was usually made by the fireplace (ku kyoto) at a feast before neighbours and wives. Gifts which were thereupon taken away could not be revoked. If the gift was to a child who was still staying at home then the gift could be revoked if the child committed an act of abomination (omusango gw'ekivve). The child would then be sued in the clan, the gift forfeited and the child expelled. But property given to a child who stayed at home could not be used without consulting the child, although the child could give it to another without consulting the father.

After 1900 a gift of land could be revoked, providing it had not been transferred by instrument, for unfilial treatment by a son.

Gifts to wives (abawase) were not recoverable by the husband. Valuable gifts were in fact given only to properly married wives (abawase) not to slave wives (abazaana).

CONTRACTS OF SERVICE

In the nineteenth century a household consisted of wives and slaves male and female, possibly totalling forty or so. It was they who did the work and no contract labour was required. The peasants performed further the customary services for the village chief without pay.

There was the custom, however, of peasants working for food (" abasasi " from *okusaka mmere*); they cultivated a strip allocated (lubimbi) for a bunch of plantains (ettooke). This practice is still widespread in Buganda today.

Barkcloth-makers used in the last century to buy bark by contracting to hand back seven out of ten finished barkcloths, themselves keeping the balance of three.

Porterage was first engaged in by Ganda in 1896 when porters carried a safari of Swahili traders to Nandi in Kenya. But it was

---

[1] See also Roscoe, *op. cit.*, p. 14.

not till the 1920's that Ganda themselves started to employ porters in order to cultivate larger areas of cotton. There are, besides the *abasasi* mentioned above, two other types of porter:

(i) the casual labourer (omupakasi owe lejjalejja) who is given a fixed task which he completes in his own time and is then paid in money;

(ii) and the labourer employed at a monthly wage (omukozi wa mpeera y'omwezi).

There was a special custom in regard to contracts with medicine men (abasamizi). The sick man or his relative or friend on engaging the medicine-man gave him an initial payment called *kikuba nsiko* (it beats the bush), the meaning being that it was a sum to cause the medicine-man to go and fetch a herbal remedy (eddagala) from the bush. On recovery the patient was expected to give the medicine-man a calabash of beer, a goat and a cock. If the patient defaulted, the medicine-man hit the tree from which he had obtained the medicine and shouted " So-and-so has not paid us, so let him fall sick again." If the patient did not recover, there was no liability to pay the medicine-man the second sum. Hence the Ganda proverb runs:

Ow'endoga mbi akoma ku kikubansiko—The man who has had bad medicine stops at the payment for " beating the bush ".[1]

Contracts of agistment of cattle (okusibira ente) have already been considered under Chapter 9.

Some co-operative herding arrangements also were there considered and co-operative associations will be further reviewed in Chapter 15.

CONTRACTS OF GUARANTEE

Such contracts are not common but a good example is afforded in a case which occurred in 1943 and can be summarized as follows:

Kabi borrowed Shs. 500/– from an Indian with a promise to repay within 221 days the capital sum together with Shs. 300/– interest. Musoke guaranteed the debt. Both Kabi and Musoke signed a promissory note for Shs. 800/– making themselves liable jointly and severally thereon. Kabi failed to repay any part of the loan or of the interest by the due date. The Indian lender endorsed the promissory note to another Indian who sued Kabi

---

[1] Ggomotoka, *op. cit.*, p. 21.

and Musoke in a Protectorate Court and obtained judgment for
Shs. 800/– and costs. Thereupon the Indian judgment creditor
obtained an order of attachment on Musoke's salary for the
judgment debt, costs and interest. Musoke claimed before the
Principal Court that Kabi was liable to indemnify him. Kabi
replied that he was only liable as to half as he alleged he had
only received Shs. 250/– on loan. The Principal Court found
for the plaintiff to the effect that Kabi had received the whole
sum of Shs. 500/– and that he was liable to indemnify Musoke
as to the whole capital loan, interest and costs.[1]

Contracts of guarantee are in fact of recent growth and are a
product of the increasing participation of Ganda in commerce.

CONTRACTS OF AGENCY

The agent or deputy (omusigere) is a well-established figure in
Ganda custom but the proverb goes:

Omusigere asala bitono—The deputy decides small matters.

Without specific authority the usual type of *omusigere* left in
charge of an estate can only introduce tenants to his master,
show them their plots' boundaries and collect rents and dues.
The remuneration of such an agent is a plot on the estate.

But other types of agent are now coming to be known in the
commercial sphere—*e.g.* an agent selling milk for another.[2]

MODERN DEVELOPMENTS

There is no doubt that the Ganda customary law of contracts
has developed rapidly during the last twenty years and continues
to develop apace. That development is the outcome of a great
increase of commercial activity and contact with non-African
business men and their methods. Building contracts account for
quite a lot of the litigation: contractors have failed to complete
the work[3] and have failed to use proper materials.[4] Damages of
over twenty thousand shillings have been awarded for leaving
without permission the work of constructing a beer-hall.[5] The

---

[1] P.C.C.C. 21 of 1943, *Musoke* v. *Kabi* (upheld by Ag. J. A. in J.A.C.A. 25
of 1943), 1940–1955 C.L.R.

[2] P.C.C.C. 174 of 1954, *Damulira* v. *Sekubunga* (unreported).

[3] P.C.C.C. 19 of 1950, *Mukuye* v. *Sejongo* (upheld in H.C.C.A. 4 of 1951)
(unreported) and P.C.C.C. 71 of 1948, *Kimbowa* v. *Mayanja* (upheld in
H.C.C.A. 34 of 1949) (unreported).

[4] P.C.C.C. 31 of 1941, *Mufubyagenda* v. *Kabangala*, 1940–1955 C.L.R.

[5] P.C.C.C. 29 of 1952, *Sebuliba* v. *Gonzabato and Others*, 1940–1955 C.L.R.

repair of motor vehicles has also been a fertile source of litigation: damages have been awarded in the alternative if the written agreement to repair was not fulfilled within two months[1] and after obtaining a garage report from an expert expenses incurred at another garage to set right work badly done by defendant were set off against repair bill and an order was made for the payment of Shs. 30/- *per diem* after the date of judgment if the lorry were not returned immediately.[2]

Purchases by instalments of goats[3] or of motor vehicles[4] have come before the courts. So have a lease of a printing press,[5] the hire of a typewriter at a monthly rate,[6] an alleged contract of agency for the sale of a printed book at a commission,[7] the mortgage of a motor-car[8] and a contract to run a school.[9]

The above examples show the diversity of contracts which are now coming before the Kabaka's courts to be decided under customary law.

CASE-LAW

Mair's allegation[10] that natives do not charge one another interest is refuted by a decision of the Lukiko Court, in the very year that her book was published, ordering a debtor in respect of a debt which had been outstanding for $2\frac{1}{2}$ years to pay interest at 3%.[11] The High Court in 1951 held that interest at the rate of 120% per annum over a period of two years and nine months on a loan of five hundred shillings was, in view of the very ample security of land given, utterly extortionate.[12] And interest has from time to time been awarded since:

> " The appellant further claimed interest at the rate of 6%. The Principal Court rejected this claim. I have no doubt that under native customary law as it has developed since the enactment of

---

[1] P.C.C.C. 223 of 1950, *Kato* v. *Kasule*, 1940–1955 C.L.R.

[2] P.C.C.C. 199 of 1947, *Nansibo* v. *Nsubuga*, 1940–1955 C.L.R.

[3] P.C.C.C. 159 of 1952, *Zirabamuzale* v. *Kiggundu* (upheld in H.C.C.A. 25 of 1954) (unreported).

[4] *E.g.* P.C.C.C. 113 of 1955, *Gulemye* v. *Mukasa* (unreported).

[5] P.C.C.C. 216 of 1955, *Lutaya* v. *Mugambe* (unreported).

[6] P.C.C.C. 269 of 1950, *Lwanga* v. *Makumbi*, 1940–1955 C.L.R.

[7] P.C.C.C. 84 of 1952, *Kyazze* v. *Mukubira for The Baganda Co-operative Society* (upheld in H.C.C.A. 20 of 1954), 1940–1955 C.L.R.

[8] P.C.C.C. 129 of 1940, *Kakungulu* v. *Maweje*, 1940–1955 C.L.R.

[9] P.C.C.C. 158 of 1957, *Musoke* v. *Educational Secretary General*, 1958 C.L.R. 65.

[10] *Op. cit.*, p. 153.

[11] P.C.R.O. 132 of 1934, *Kasule* v. *Kiwanuka* (upholding Lukiko Court Case 255 of 1934) (unreported).

[12] H.C.C.A. 25 of 1950, *Nkeretanyi* v. *Kabanda*, Notes 43.

the Buganda Courts Ordinance it is competent for the courts in
Buganda to award interest and I have seen cases where they have
done so but it is not an established practice or right as in the
Protectorate Courts and I cannot say that the Court erred in
rejecting this part of the claim.''[1]

At the same time as the rapid development of the law of contracts under Ganda customary law, there has been a conscious
adoption and adaptation of English legal principles. Decisions
of the Principal Court over the last three years which have been
reported in the Customary Law Reports illustrate the point: the
Principal Court has considered:

the capacity of an infant to enter into an agreement for the
sale of land;[2]

an unwritten wagering contract;[3]

an unsigned agreement in writing;[4]

the exclusion of oral by documentary evidence;[5]

a tacit agreement to the user of land;[6]

the principle of caveat emptor;[7]

the express terms of a contract of sale of land[8] and of
marriage;[9]

a separation agreement;[10]

a conditional contract;[11]

a condition precedent to the sale of land;[12]

the implied terms of a contract of tenancy;[13]

the breach of the implied terms of a contract of service;[14]

the breach of a contract of education;[15]

delay in repaying a loan;[16]

and the taking of accounts of a shop under a contract of
service.[17]

---

[1] *Per* SHERIDAN, J., H.C.C.A. 40 of 1955, *Sewalu* v. *Musajakawa*, Notes 71.
[2] P.C.C.C. 207 of 1954, *Kibuka* v. *Lukwago and Another*, 1956 C.L.R. 47.
[3] P.C.C.A. 190 of 1956, *Mukasa* v. *Luboyera*, 1956 C.L.R. 51.
[4] P.C.C.A. 17 of 1956, *Musema* v. *Katabazi*, 1956 C.L.R. 49.
[5] P.C.C.C. 105 of 1955, *Musoke* v. *Kabazzi*, 1956 C.L.R. 49.
[6] P.C.C.C. 171 of 1958, *Kasali* v. *Kaggwa*, 1958 C.L.R. 95.
[7] P.C.C.C. 162 of 1953, *Kayongo* v. *Kiwanuka and Another*, 1956 C.L.R. 53.
[8] P.C.C.C. 140 of 1957, *Mutulakungo* v. *Kalibuggyawa*, 1958 C.L.R. 63.
[9] P.C.C.C. 264 of 1956, *Magezi* v. *Mutegombwa and Another*, 1957 C.L.R. 143.
[10] P.C.Cr.A. 91 of 1957, *Lukiko* v. *Gavamukulya and Another*, 1958 C.L.R. 99.
[11] P.C.C.C. 267 of 1957, *Mambule* v. *Kavuma*, 1958 C.L.R. 61.
[12] P.C.C.C. 274 of 1955, *Kyeyune* v. *Sekayiba*, 1957 C.L.R. 125.
[13] P.C.C.A. 142 of 1953, *Mutumba* v. *Ssonko*, 1956 C.L.R. 53.
[14] P.C.C.A. 130 of 1955, *Luganda* v. *Kateregga*, 1956 C.L.R. 53.
[15] P.C.C.A. 167 of 1956, *Wasswa* v. *Lubega*, 1956 C.L.R. 51.
[16] P.C.C.A. 16 of 1957, *Mwanje* v. *Mulindwa*, 1957 C.L.R. 93.
[17] P.C.C.C. 88 of 1954, *Gavamukulya* v. *Kawesa*, 1958 C.L.R. 69.

The High Court has held:

(i) that without doubt there exists in native law a principle corresponding to the doctrine of undue influence;[1]

(ii) that, while the English rules as to limitation of actions do not apply in native courts and where an ancient liability is clearly established it can be enforced, nevertheless there may be cases where failure to sue for a debt for many years may create a strong doubt as to the very existence of the debt;[2]

(iii) that, in a contract for the sale of mailo land, time of payment of the purchase price is of the essence of the contract, if the express terms of the contract itself require payment by a specific date;[3]

(iv) that under the Buganda Coming of Age Law a person under the age of 20 years has no contractual capacity and is incapable of making an agreement which will bind himself or anyone else.[4]

There are two more recent decisions of the High Court which call for more detailed consideration: when the question arose as to whether a mortgage agreement on land had subsequently changed to one of sale SHERIDAN, J., opined:

> " I am by no means satisfied that under native law or native customary law prevailing in Buganda it is necessary for such an agreement (*i.e.* of sale) to be supported by consideration. The law does not provide for contracts under seal. . . . As far as I am aware the Indian Contract Act is not an applied Act under s. 10(e) of the Buganda Courts Ordinance which the Principal Court has been authorised to administer and enforce under s. 12 of the Ordinance."[5]

The second decision was made by LEWIS, J., in June 1959,[6] when a claim for the return of a part payment for a motor-car which the defendants failed to deliver was before the Court. One of the defences went to the jurisdiction of the High Court, all parties being African. The plaintiff replied that his was a claim under the Sale of Goods Ordinance and therefore the Buganda Courts had no jurisdiction. The learned Judge held:

---

[1] H.C.C.A. 11 of 1944, *Musoke* v. *Luyombya and Another*, Notes 13.

[2] H.C.C.A. 35 of 1948, *Zake* v. *Bazongere*, Notes 25.

[3] H.C.C.A. 41 of 1951, *Mulindwa* v. *Musoke*, Notes 49.

[4] H.C.C.A. 44 of 1951, *Buko* v. *Kiddu*, Notes 51.

[5] H.C.C.A. 6 of 1956, *Lumu* v. *Nsubuga*, Notes 73.

[6] H.C.C.C. 826 of 1958, *Bukenya* v. *Mutebi and Another*, Bulletin 51/59.

". . . the answer is to be found in the form in which the claim is framed. The plaintiff sued the defendants for the return of Shs. 4,200/– and pleaded a written agreement embodying the contract. The Sale of Goods Ordinance is not mentioned and so far as I can see need never be invoked. . . . It is extremely difficult to say with certainty what suits are and what suits are not triable by African courts. The pleadings are a guide but not conclusive. . . . It depends, I think, whether a plaintiff has to plead and invoke a particular section of an Ordinance to succeed. No general rule can be laid down."

In the instant case the learned Judge held that the proceedings were not taken under any Ordinance and as the Principal Court had jurisdiction the case must be transferred.

CHAPTER 14

MARKETS

The customary law of markets may most conveniently be considered now. There is no question that markets are an ancient institution in Buganda[1] but the law governing them is somewhat abstruse.

The control and supervision of native markets in Buganda has been vested by the Kabaka in his Chief Market Master (Sentala).

> " Since the Market Ordinance does not apply to Buganda there is no written law governing these cases. It is a well established and recognised fact however that the Kabaka may appoint market masters to superintend and supervise the proper running of markets."[2]

In 1916 the Chief Sentala's motion that no-one should be permitted to sell goats, sheep or cattle in a place other than a market was passed by the Lukiko and approved by the Provincial Commissioner.[3] This resolution was clarified by another of the following January (1917) wherein the slaughtering for sale of cattle, goats or sheep outside markets was forbidden but the sale of live cattle or the slaughtering of cattle for one's own domestic consumption were permitted elsewhere.[4] The objects of this resolution were to prevent the sale of bad or diseased meat and to increase the revenue to the Lukiko. In the latter connection a resolution of the Lukiko in January 1920 is of interest: it was decided that every rupee of revenue from markets should be allocated as follows:[5]

to the Lukiko	40 cents;
to the ssaza chief	4 cents;
to the Ggombolola Chief	5 cents;
to the Muluka Chief	4 cents;

---

[1] See Roscoe, *op. cit.*, Chap. XV, at p. 452.
[2] P.C.R.O. 75 of 1934 upholding Lukiko Court Case 163 of 1934.
[3] *Akatabo ke Biragiro na Mateka ebyatesebwa Olukiko Olukulu olwe Buganda okuva 1916 okutusa*, 1919, p. 4.
[4] *Ibid.*, p. 6.
[5] *Ibid.*, p. 64.

to the landowner	25 cents;
to the Chief Sentala	10 cents;
to the Chief Sentala's representative	3 cents;
to the Chief Sentala's representative	3 cents;
to the Ssaza Chief's Sentala	3 cents;
to the Ggombolola Chief's Sentala	3 cents.

At the same session the Lukiko decided that the responsibility for building the markets was on the butchers and traders who traded permanently therein and on those who collected the fees.[1]

The same month the Kabaka's Ministers issued orders laying down prices for fat and lean beef and goat's meat and for the prevention of overcharging.[2] A like order of the Katikkiro in December 1922 declared that the collection of fees in markets was the Chief Sentala's responsibility.[3]

In 1928 the Busuulu and Envujjo Law provided:

> " The mailo owner shall be allowed to take a 10 per centum due of fish so long as he shall carry out all sleeping sickness instructions with regard to the upkeep of landings and other fishing places:
>
> Provided that when the mailo owner is unable to provide any men for such work he shall receive only 5 per centum and the Kabaka's Government shall receive the other 5 per centum."[4]

The question of market dues payable to the Kabaka's Government in respect of markets on Crown Land came before the courts in 1935. The suit for Shs. 2/– being market dues in respect of a cow slaughtered at Lutoboka landing place came before the Lukiko Court and went ultimately on a petition for revision to the Provincial Commissioner. In his order the following passage occurs:

> " They (*i.e.* the Lukiko Court) then, very rightly, called the Chief market master in Buganda to give evidence on customary practice in Buganda. His evidence was to the effect that the Native Government collected market dues on all local produce sold anywhere in Buganda except in markets established by the British Government. They then accepted as evidence some administrative instructions given by the Provincial Commissioner in 1927 which supported the evidence of the Chief market master.
>
> *Held:* It is an old established custom for the Native Government to collect market dues everywhere in Buganda except in gazetted markets on Crown Land. . . . If traders were exempted from

---

[1] *Akatabo ke Biragiro na Mateka ebyatesebwa Olukiko Olukulu olwe Buganda okuva 1916 okutusa 1919*, p. 65.

[2] *Amateka ne Biragiro ebyatesebwa Olukiko Olukulu okuva 1922–1923*, p. 25.

[3] *Ibid.*, p. 27.

[4] Section 9(b).

market dues when sales took place on Crown Land there would be constant attempts to evade dues by traders moving onto Crown Land."[1]

Consequent upon a resolution of the Lukiko in December 1953, the Chief Sentala of Buganda issued new rates of market dues on a wide variety of foodstuffs and handicrafts on the 5th May, 1955.[2] Of those fees 10% is refunded to the market master, 30% is refunded to the landowner and 60% is taken by the Kabaka's Government. A claim for fees collected is enforceable by civil suit in the Courts.[3]

About the same year the Chief Sentala made orders for the control of markets[4] prohibiting *inter alia*:

smoking of pipes or cigarettes;

spitting or clearing the throat;

sale of bad meat, fish or vegetables;

sale by a person suffering with an infectious disease;

.the introduction of motor vehicles or the riding of bicycles;

the carrying of sticks;

the entry of dogs;

the subletting of shops or stalls without permission;

the butchering and sale of meat except when butcher is clad in a white coat;

the lighting of fires;

stay in the market except between 6 a.m. and 5.30 p.m.

---

[1] P.C.R.O. 190 of 1935, *Musuza, Sentala of Ssesse* v. *Katanda* (upholding Lukiko Court Case 525 of 1935) (unreported).

[2] Repeated by the Sentala's Circular No. 47/99 of 12th March, 1958.

[3] P.C.C.C. 62 of 1945, *Muzito* v. *Ngalombi* (unreported).

[4] *Ebiragiro ebifuga Akatale* (undated).

CHAPTER 15

CORPORATIONS AND ASSOCIATIONS

Ganda tradition asserts that the first corporate commercial enterprise undertaken by a Ganda was the renting of a printing press by Sepiriya Kadumukasa about the years 1925–1927 for the printing of the *Uganda News*. In the same year, 1925, another famous Ganda businessman, Kulanima Musoke, became president of K. M. Nakalyakoni & Co. Ltd., a company of blacksmiths at Wandegeya, an African suburb of Kampala. The next remembered commercial corporate venture was Yusufu Bamutta's Baganda Cotton Company in 1930, which produced considerable litigation the following year. About 1934 D. S. K. M. Mukubira founded the Baganda Co-operative Society and in 1942 similar co-operative societies were started in Kyaggwe (Kikuba Growers) and Bugerere (Bugerere Growers).

Since the jurisdiction of the Kabaka's Courts in regard to African companies and partnerships has from time to time been queried, it will be most useful to our present purpose first to trace the customary case-law as it appears to have developed in regard to such bodies during the last thirty years and then to turn to consider the opinions expressed and decisions made on such cases by Her Majesty's Judges.

The first case that I can trace came before the Lukiko Court in 1930. The two parties entered a partnership for the hire of a motor-car for six months but the car broke down after one trip and spent the next seven months in a garage. The partners made a compromise agreement with the owner of the car but one of the partners subsequently refused to honour it. The owner then sued him for the whole amount for the full period the car had been out of his control and obtained judgment against him. That partner then sued his fellow for a contribution as to half of that judgment sum.[1]

Two years later a plaintiff successfully sued to recover rent from the acting secretary of the Baganda Printing and Publishing

---

[1] P.C.R.O. 50 of 1930, *Galiwango* v. *Gavamukulya* (unreported).

Co. Ltd. in respect of premises rented to that company.[1] The same year a plaintiff sued for the balance of a sum given to the defendant on behalf of the Baganda Produce Agency for the purchase of cotton and other produce.[2] In 1934 the Lukiko Court considered the case of a partnership formed in 1930 for the purpose of selling meat in Kampala but without a written agreement to show how business was to be carried on or how profits were to be divided.[3] Again in 1935 the Lukiko Court was faced with another such case of a partnership business to run an eating house in Kampala. The capital of the partnership was Shs. 300/–, each of the two partners contributing Shs. 150/–. That capital was spent on rent of premises, furniture and foodstuffs. A vague bank account existed but no books were kept.[4] In 1936 there was a similar action to recover a like sum of Shs. 300/–, comprising a contribution of Shs. 150/– and interest thereon of a like amount, in respect of a partnership business started in 1933 wherein no books were kept.[5] The same year the Lukiko Court heard a claim for Shs. 300/–, being Shs. 100/– for capital invested in a company of defendant's to buy cotton and Shs. 200/– being the amount assessed by him as his share of the profits gained on the capital.[6]

There appears to have been a lull in such cases for about five years but in 1942 there is a claim for a share of revenue from land bought jointly and again the venture was not evidenced in books of account.[7]

In 1943 a claim for repair of a bus was filed in the Principal Court which in view of a judgment of the High Court[8] and because the present plaintiff company was limited advised the plaintiff to sue in a British Court.[9] But in making that ruling the Principal Court *obiter* opined that the matter should be considered by Government in view of the jurisdiction of the Buganda

---

[1] P.C.R.O. 85 of 1932, *Lutalo* v. *Kiddu* (upholding Lukiko Court Case 316 of 1932) (unreported).

[2] P.C.R.O. 102 of 1932, *Sajjabi* v. *Kyadze* (unreported).

[3] P.C.R.O. 55 of 1934, *Nyanzi* v. *Bikanduse* (unreported).

[4] P.C.R.O. 160 of 1935, *Kubo* v. *Kiwanuka* (unreported).

[5] P.C.R.O. 26 of 1936 upholding Lukiko Court Case 358 of 1935 (unreported).

[6] P.C.R.O. 97 of 1937, *Mugalasi* v. *Lubwama* (unreported).

[7] P.C.C.C. 42 of 1942, *Musoke* v. *Kintu*, 1940–1955 C.L.R.

[8] H.C.C.A. 34 of 1942, *K. M. Nakalyakani & Co. Ltd.* v. *Kulanima M. N. Musoke* (unreported), see p. 254, below.

[9] P.C.C.C. 25 of 1943, *Baganda Bus Coy. Ltd.* v. *Sewanaku*, 1940–1955 C.L.R.

Courts to entertain suits between Africans and in view of the likely increase of African limited companies.

In 1944 the Baganda Co-operative Society unsuccessfully claimed in detinue for a printing press allegedly sold them but retained by the vendor.[1] And in the same year an Islamic religious society successfully claimed damages against a former *muwalimu* (mullah) who on his retirement removed the corrugated iron roofing of the mosque.[2]

1945 proved a fruitful year for litigation involving corporations:

(i) the Buganda Growers and Agricultural Co-operative Society, Kasenene, unsuccessfully claimed damages for wrongful removal of maize;[3]

(ii) the General Cattle Traders Co. claimed for some plants;[4]

(iii) a society entitled Kabasanda Baganda Kwebera unsuccessfully sued alleging wrongful distress of goods in a shop;[5]

(iv) the General Cattle Traders Co. again sued one of its partners in respect of a sum given him to buy cattle;[6]

(v) finally the Gayaza Growers Society successfully sued the Kasenene Agricultural Growers Society for the repayment under an agreement of a loan to buy maize and interest thereon.[7]

In the year 1945 and during the subsequent year there were at least nine successful claims by individuals and an association (*i.e.* the Uganda Farmers Association, Masaka) against the Baganda Credit Bank for moneys deposited in the Bank and interest thereon.[8] The trustees of the Bank were a certain Joachim Matovu and four other Africans. The evidence of the Registrar of Business Names was called and relied upon by the Principal Court in its judgments.

Two cases in 1946 were prosecuted successfully in the Principal

---

[1] P.C.C.C. 22 of 1944, *Baganda Co-operative Society* v. *Mugwanya* (unreported).

[2] P.C.C.C. 34 of 1944, *Ekibina kya Isiramu* v. *Nswemu*, 1940–1955 C.L.R.

[3] P.C.C.C. 1 of 1945, *Buganda Growers and Agricultural Co-operative Society* v. *Mutanda* (upheld in H.C.C.A. 14 of 1946) (unreported).

[4] P.C.C.C. 74 of 1945, *General Cattle Traders Co.* v. *Lule* (unreported).

[5] P.C.C.C. 88 of 1945, *Kabasanda Baganda Kwebera* v. *Sekanyo* (unreported).

[6] P.C.C.C. 93 of 1945, *General Cattle Traders Co.* v. *Matovu* (upset by Ag. J. A. in J.A.C.A. 49 of 1947 on facts although Principal Court's jurisdiction was considered and confirmed. See below at p. 251. The Ag. J. A.'s decision was subsequently upheld by AINLEY, J., in H.C.C.A. 25 of 1947) (unreported).

[7] P.C.C.C. 52 of 1945, *Gayaza Growers Society* v. *Kasenene Agricultural Growers Society* (unreported).

[8] P.C.C.C.'s 104, 105, 106, 107, 108 of 1945 and 8, 10, 22 and 28 of 1946 (unreported).

Court against managers of African companies representing those companies.[1] In the same year there was an important commercial case tried by the Principal Court which not only involved an African company but also questions of an agreement allegedly made under stress at an extortionate rate of interest.[2] The claim was for Shs. 4,375/– being the balance of Shs. 15,000/– borrowed on agreement for 15 months at 50% interest. The defence was that the interest was extortionate, the agreement having been made under financial stress. It was held that the defendants made the agreement voluntarily and even though the interest was high they must pay up. Interest on the claim at 6% per annum from the date of payment under the agreement until payment was ordered.

In the same year a partnership agreement to buy and run a lorry for trading purposes was examined by the Principal Court, which thereafter in view of the actual wording of the agreement refused to allow one of the partners to avoid his responsibilities just because the lorry on the way home from collection broke down.[3]

In 1947 an unregistered business sued one of its partners for misappropriation of the firm's funds.[4] It was alleged by the plaintiff firm and found by the court after an inspection of the books that the defendant had sold the firm's shop on the instructions of the other partners but had then retained the proceeds and had avoided rendering an account.

In the same year there was a successful claim for Shs. 4,000/– being the balance not refunded of Shs. 5,000/– put into a company floated for the manufacture of tiles and bricks in 1944. A temporary receipt only had been given pending the registration of the company. Judgment was for the Shs. 4,000/– and interest thereon at $1\frac{1}{2}$% from the date of investment to the date of repayment.[5]

In 1948 the former manager of a registered company, the Mawokota Gomba Farmers, which carried on the trade of selling

[1] P.C.C.C. 18 of 1946, *Matovu* v. *Manager of General Cattle Traders Co.* (unreported), and P.C.C.C. 180 of 1946, *Seninde* v. *Manager of Nakatema Store Co., Kampala* (unreported).
[2] P.C.C.C. 42 of 1946, *Katwe Cattle Dealers and Butchers Co.* v. *Mukasa and Others* (unreported).
[3] P.C.C.C. 184 of 1946, *Sempa* v. *Sempagama* (unreported).
[4] P.C.C.C. 97 of 1947, *Serunkabidde & Co.* v. *Serunkabidde* (unreported) (H.C.C.A. 31 of 1950 but the jurisdiction not argued nor decided).
[5] P.C.C.C. 202 of 1947, *Nanfuma* v. *Mugwanya* (unreported).

milk in the Kibuga, sued the new manager for a refund of a judgment debt made against him in respect of the rent of a building in Katwe used by the company. The defence was that it was a private debt never brought to the company's notice. The court took notice of the fact that the agreement for lease of the building was not changed into the company's name when the plaintiff gave up the management. The Principal Court, however, held that it had no jurisdiction to entertain a suit between members of a registered company.[1]

A cattle-trading partnership to operate in Bukedi was to have been financed by the two partners in equal shares. The defendant did not contribute his full share and withheld information as to cattle-trading and also the proceeds therefrom.[2]

The year 1950 saw several partnership cases before the Principal Court:

An agreement was made for the setting up of a partnership to buy fish. Later the plaintiff was told when he wished to withdraw his share of the profits that all the shares had been dissipated. He examined the books and found the funds including the profit had not disappeared.[3]

A partnership agreement was made for the building and renting of a house. Before the house was completed one partner was arrested and imprisoned. The other partner borrowed money to finish the house and then started to collect rent. When the imprisoned partner was released after a year he started to collect rent from the tenant placed in the house by his partner without enquiring into the method by which the house had been completed. The Principal Court decided it was for the partners to settle their own affairs.[4]

A loan to a partnership was ordered to be repaid with interest at 6% from the date repayment was due.[5]

A case wherein one partner entrusted with contributions by 35 others with which to trade and then he decided to expel 32 of them from the partnership was brought before the court by those partners claiming the return of their shares. The domineering partner was given three months to pay.[6]

---

[1] P.C.C.C. 31 of 1948, *Mubito v. Senyanga*, 1940–1955 C.L.R.

[2] P.C.C.C. 119 of 1949, *Mukasa v. Mulindwa* (unreported) (upheld by J.A.C.A. 16 of 1951).

[3] P.C.C.C. 169 of 1950, *Wayononye v. Mwebe and Another*, 1940–1955 C.L.R.

[4] P.C.C.C. 234 of 1950, *Sekubwa v. Kazibwe* (unreported).

[5] P.C.C.C. 279 of 1950, *Nakkaka v. Kibuka and Brothers* (unreported).

[6] P.C.C.C. 277 of 1950 *Loto v. Alata* (unreported).

In 1951 the Principal Court ordered specific performance in respect of a transfer of land sold by a registered company.[1] In another unregistered company members sued their fellow member for losing their capital in running a shop.[2]

The only case of note in regard to these matters filed in 1952 was an action for the taking of the accounts of a partnership formed for the buying of foodstuffs and their re-sale at a profit. Proper books of account had not been kept and there was a dispute as to respective liabilities after the partnership had been dissolved. The Principal Court referred the partnership books to an accountant.[3]

A contract for the building of a beerhall combined with a partnership agreement for the running of the beerhall was the subject of a suit for the contract sum plus the anticipated profits from the partnership.[4]

The Principal Court held that a partnership agreement to buy and run a lorry envisaged the sharing of debts between the partners and therefore refused a claim by one of the partners to withdraw his share on leaving the partnership after it had fallen into debt.[5] A like claim in another case was defeated for lack of proof.[6]

Finally in 1957 the Principal Court held there was a joint liability of shareholders for a company's debts;[7] and considered what proof was required of a partnership.[8]

Let us now turn to the decisions of the High Court on proceedings wherein African corporations were parties. The first which it is important to consider is that of MANNING, Ag. C. J., on a claim by two African partners against their seven fellow African partners for the taking of accounts, the dissolution of the partnership and the appointment of a receiver. The proceedings were instituted in the High Court and an application was then made by the defendants to transfer it to an African Court. The learned Acting Chief Justice held that these were proceedings

---

[1] P.C.C.C. 132 of 1951, *Sekinnemye* v. *Mmengo African Traders Ltd.* (confirmed by H.C.Conf.C. 4 of 1952), 1940–1955 C.L.R.

[2] P.C.C.C. 24 of 1951, *Musajjakawa* v. *Ddungu and Another* (unreported).

[3] P.C.C.C. 82 of 1952, *Wasswa and Others* v. *Sempa and Another* (upheld in part in H.C.C.A. 53 of 1955, see p. 252 below) (unreported).

[4] P.C.C.C. 157 of 1953, *Mukasa* v. *Abdalla* (unreported).

[5] P.C.C.C. 187 of 1955, *Zake* v. *Kasajja and Others* (unreported).

[6] P.C.C.C. 217 of 1955, *Kiberu* v. *Ba Bulemezi Bus Co.* (unreported).

[7] P.C.C.C. 310 of 1956, *Rusoke* v. *Ntambi and Others*, 1957 C.L.R. 161.

[8] P.C.C.C. 230 of 1955, *Bosa* v. *Seba*, 1957 C.L.R. 163.

K

taken under the English Partnership Act (which was a statute of general application before the enactment of the Partnership Ordinance in 1950) and therefore by section 9 of the Buganda Courts Ordinance no Buganda Court had jurisdiction to try the case. In the course of his judgment appears the following passage:

> " I have no doubt that the Partnership Act, 1890, is a Statute of general application and that it is in force in the Protectorate, and I am satisfied that there is no native customary law capable of dealing with the problems which arise when accounts have to be taken, a dissolution decreed, or a receiver appointed. If this case came before a Native Court it would have (to use the peculiar wording of the Ordinance) to ' administer ' the Partnership Act and the English law of Partnership as laid down in a large number of decided cases. Natives who are members of a firm have, in my opinion, a right to invoke the provisions of English law to protect themselves and to ascertain their rights, and it was precisely this kind of case that section 9 of the Buganda Courts Ordinance contemplated when it excluded from the jurisdiction of Native Courts proceedings ' taken under ' any English law unless such jurisdiction was expressly conferred by an Ordinance."[1]

The next leading case was decided by AINLEY, J., on the 27th May, 1946:[2]

> ". . . the Plaintiff's case is that the parties verbally agreed to refer a dispute as to partnership accounts to arbitration. That in pursuance of the agreement an arbitration was held and an award made which he is entitled to enforce against the Defendant.
>
> A preliminary objection has been taken that this Court has no jurisdiction to hear the suit since both parties are natives within the meaning of the Buganda Courts Ordinance and that by virtue of section 6(1) and section 7 of the Ordinance this Court should transfer the proceedings to a Buganda Court.
>
> Both parties are admittedly ' natives ' and the proceedings are of course civil proceedings.
>
> The short point is whether the case is excluded from the ordinary jurisdiction of the Buganda Courts by section 9(c) of the Buganda Courts Ordinance. . . .
>
> The Plaintiff's Advocate urges that these provisions apply to exclude the jurisdiction of the Buganda Courts and to base the jurisdiction of this Court for two reasons. Firstly because the English Partnership Act of 1890 applies to the case by reason of the action arising from a dispute between partners and secondly because the Arbitration Ordinance applies.
>
> As to the first point. I am prepared to agree that if a native asks for relief against another native which this Court and this Court

---

[1] H.C.C.C. 6 of 1944, *Kibalama and Another* v. *Basazemagya and Others*, 6 U.L.R. 137.
[2] H.C.C.C. 58 of 1945, *Yusufu Kayolo* v. *Yokana Kayondo* (unreported).

alone is entitled and equipped to give by virtue of the English Partnership Act, 1890, then the provisions of section 9(c) apply to give this Court jurisdiction to grant the relief. But I cannot agree that the mere fact that a relationship exists between two natives which an English lawyer would term a partnership ousts the jurisdiction of the Buganda Courts in all disputes arising out of the relationship, and as in this case the Court is not even asked to decide any problems arising out of the contract of partnership I can see no reason whatever for holding that the proceedings are ' brought under ' the English Partnership Act.

As to the application of the Arbitration Ordinance. Here again I agree that a submission to Arbitration falling within the scope of that Ordinance would clearly found the jurisdiction of this Court. But the Ordinance quite clearly applies only to written submission to arbitration. The submission in this case was admittedly oral and though I have carefully considered the cases quoted by the Plaintiff's advocate I cannot find, nor did I expect to find, any authority for saying that an oral submission can in any circumstances be considered as a written submission. I hold then that these proceedings are not ' brought under ' the Arbitration Ordinance.

It has occurred to me that under certain circumstances the expression ' English law ' used in the subsection might be interpreted as covering English Common Law and the rules of equity. But I consider that even if such an interpretation is admissible in any circumstances I would not be entitled in this case to hold that the proceedings were ' brought under ' English Common Law. There is here nothing more than an action to enforce a simple contract to abide by the decision of a third party. That problems will arise in the case which this Court administering a highly developed system of law is better equipped to deal with than a Buganda Court may be true. But I assume that the Buganda Courts will enforce a contracted obligation if such is proved to exist and that is all that in this case any Court is required to do, and I see no reason why the Buganda Courts' jurisdiction should be ousted. To hold otherwise in this case would be to say that all difficult disputes to which the Common Law would be applied if heard in this Court may be brought to this Court at the election of the parties, and I am satisfied that this was not the intention of the Buganda Courts Ordinance.

These proceedings are therefore transferred to the Principal Court of Mengo.''

These two leading cases were considered and thus distinguished by the Acting Judicial Adviser (now Mr. Justice SHERIDAN) in an appeal already mentioned which came before him in 1947:[1]

" On the face of it this appeal raises questions of Company or Partnership law which would be excluded from the jurisdiction of the Buganda Courts by section 9(c) of the Buganda Courts

---

[1] J.A.C.A. 49 of 1947, *Matovu* v. *Kalasi* (unreported), see p. 246 above.

Ordinance 1940 (*vide Kibalama* v. *Basazemagya High Court Civil Case No. 6 of 1944*). On the other hand it is very difficult to determine the status of ' the General Cattle Traders Company '. It is not registered anywhere. The Respondent describes himself as the managing partner and the Appellant as a partner. The ledger of the company has been exhibited in the case but the accounts have been kept in a half-hearted and unprofessional manner. I can only denominate the company as a group of Africans who have banded together for the purposes of trade. Even if a partnership does exist I am not prepared to hold that the jurisdiction of the Buganda Courts is ousted in view of the judgment of AINLEY, J., in *Kayolo* v. *Kayondo* (High Court Civil Case No. 58 of 1945). It is not easy to reconcile this case with the case quoted above but the learned judge found that he could decide it without any reference to the Partnership Act whereas the former case involved the taking of accounts. He held that the mere fact that a relationship existed between two natives which an English lawyer would term a partnership did not oust the jurisdiction of the Buganda Courts in all disputes arising out of the relationship. The only issue before me in the instant case is whether or not the Appellant repaid Shs. 500/– to the ' Company '. In my view this case was rightly brought in the Principal Court."

The decision of MANNING, Ag. C. J., in the case quoted was followed but qualified by PEARSON, J., who then observed that:

" Some kinds of partnership may be well established in native custom, e.g. a common venture in a fishing boat—in which disputes between partners can very well and perhaps best be settled in accordance with custom in native Courts."

But, said the learned Judge

" I respectfully agree with a learned brother that native customary law is not capable of dealing with problems which arise when accounts have to be taken and dissolutions decreed—in commercial partnerships."[1]

The next time that a matter concerning an African partnership was properly before the High Court was as an appeal[2] from original proceedings in the Principal Court already mentioned.[3] SHERIDAN, J. held:

" No proper books of accounts were kept and, owing to the dispute between the partners as to their respective liabilities, the Principal Court took the sensible course of referring it to an accountant. They had an opportunity of making representations to him and of producing any relevant records in their possession. . . .

---

[1] H.C.C.A. 11 of 1949, *Nsubuga* v. *Kasozi* (unreported).
[2] H.C.C.A. 53 of 1955, *Sempa and Another* v. *Wasswa and Others* (unreported).
[3] P.C.C.C. 82 of 1952, see p. 249 above.

For myself I must confess that from a perusal of the copy record of the proceedings I had great difficulty in following the calculation of the sums involved, and on this point I have received no assistance from the appellants, but I am satisfied that on the material available the Principal Court and the accountant did the best they could, and I am unable to say that they reached a wrong conclusion subject to this qualification. The claim was framed as being for the embezzlement of partnership monies. In fact it was an action for the taking of accounts."

On the 31st October, 1958, Sir Audley McKisack, C.J., delivered an important judgment in the case of *Mengo Builders and Contractors Limited* v. *K. M. L. Kasibante*.[1] This judgment is so germane to our present consideration of the jurisdiction in respect of limited companies consisting of Africans that I propose quoting extensively from it:

" In the Principal Court of Buganda Mr. Kasibante, respondent in the present appeal, brought a suit against a limited company called Mengo Builders & Contractors Ltd., the present appellants, concerning the ownership of land. At the hearing of the suit the Company took the preliminary objection that the Principal Court had no jurisdiction over companies. The Principal Court held, however, that it did have such jurisdiction, by virtue of subsection 8 of section 3 of the Interpretation and General Clauses Ordinance (Cap. 1). It is against that ruling that the company has appealed.

The Buganda Courts Ordinance (Cap. 77) gives the Principal Court ' full jurisdiction, civil and criminal, throughout Buganda over all " Africans " ' (section 3(1)). Section 2 of that Ordinance defines the term ' African ' as follows:—

' " African " means any person whose tribe is a tribe of the Protectorate or of the Colony and Protectorate of Kenya, the Trust Territory of Tanganyika, Nyasaland, the Sudan, the Belgian Congo or the Mandated Territory of Ruanda-Urundi, and includes a Swahili.'

There is no mention in this Ordinance of jurisdiction in relation to companies or other corporations (save for a reference in section 6(4) to jurisdiction in respect of proceedings by or against the Crown or the Buganda Government).

Subsection 1 of section 3 of the Interpretation and General Clauses Ordinance, which was enacted in 1951, provides that:—

' In this Ordinance and in every other Ordinance, unless there is something in the subject or context inconsistent with such construction or unless it is therein otherwise expressly provided, each of the terms " African " and " native " means any person who is a member of or one of whose parents is or was a member of an indigenous African tribe or community.'

The subsection goes on to exclude from the definition of ' African ' certain persons whom it is not necessary to particularise for the

---

[1] H.C.C.A. 77 of 1958 (arising out of P.C.C.C. 189 of 1958) (unreported).

purposes of this appeal. Subsection 8 of the same section—and it is upon this that the Principal Court relied in the ruling which is the subject of this appeal—is as follows:—

> ' Save and except in regard to the provisions of the Income Tax Ordinance and any Ordinance amending or replacing the same, any company, association, partnership or body of persons corporate or unincorporate all of whose members are Africans within the meaning of subsection (1) of this section shall be deemed to be an African so long as all the members thereof are Africans as aforesaid. . . .'

The definition of ' African ' in the Interpretation and General Clauses Ordinance does not apply to that term as used in the Buganda Courts Ordinance, because the latter Ordinance has its own definition of that term. It will be seen that the definition in the former Ordinance is much wider than the one in the Buganda Courts Ordinance and would include, for example, members of West African or South African tribes or communities, who are not included in the term as defined in the Buganda Courts Ordinance. When the Interpretation and General Clauses Ordinance says that a company of which all the members are Africans within the meaning of that term as defined in that Ordinance is to ' be deemed to be an African ', it means that the company is to be deemed to be African as defined in that Ordinance. It does not mean that it is to be deemed an African as differently defined in any other Ordinance. Consequently it cannot mean that the company is to be deemed an African as defined in the Buganda Courts Ordinance. And the Buganda Courts Ordinance gives jurisdiction only over those Africans who are defined in that Ordinance. If the ruling of the Principal Court were correct, it would mean that that court would have jurisdiction over a company all of whose members were West Africans, whereas it has no jurisdiction over an individual West African. Such a result would be quite illogical.

In support of the appeal Mr. Pinto referred me to two cases. The first was *K. M. Nakalyakani & Co. Ltd.* v. *Kulanima M. N. Musoke*, Uganda High Court Civil Appeal 34 of 1942 (unreported), in which MANNING, J., held that the Principal Court had no jurisdiction over a limited company because the definition of the term ' native ' (since replaced by the term ' African ') in the Buganda Courts Ordinance ' was never meant to include an incorporated company, even if at any given moment all its shareholders happened to be natives.' That decision was, however, given in 1943 when there was in force nothing equivalent to section 3 of the Interpretation and General Clauses Ordinance now in force. The last-mentioned provision was first introduced in 1945 by the Interpretation (Definition of ' Native ') Ordinance, 1945, and this is in substantially the same terms as section 3 of the Interpretation and General Clauses Ordinance.

The other case cited by Mr. Pinto was a decision of PEARSON, J., given in 1952; see High Court Civil Case 194 of 1951 (unreported), *E. D. N. Kubo* v. *Buganda Butchers Ltd.* The question there arose whether the High Court had jurisdiction in a case in which a limited company was a party, or whether, under the provisions of section 7 of the Buganda Courts Ordinance, the case had to be transferred to the Principal Court on the ground that the latter court had jurisdiction in the matter. PEARSON, J., in the course of his ruling said:—

> ' In fact all the members of this company are, and must by the Articles of Association be, natives within the definition of section 2, and I hesitate to hold that such natives lose the privilege of suing in their native courts by registering under our Companies Ordinance. On the other hand the company is a distinct legal entity, and I cannot hold that, where a registered company is a party, the Court is concerned with the question of the nationality or race of the members. The company is within the jurisdiction of this Court (*i.e.* the High Court of Uganda). This Court will proceed to hear.'

Although this decision was given after the provisions relating to the interpretation of the word ' African ' (now to be found in section 3 of the Interpretation and General Clauses Ordinance) had been in force for some time, no reference is made to it in the decision. Nevertheless, for the reasons I have given, I do not doubt that PEARSON, J. would have come to no different conclusion had he thought it necessary to consider those provisions.

The appeal succeeds, and I reverse the ruling of the Principal Court that that Court has jurisdiction in the suit in question. It follows that the Principal Court should dismiss the suit for want of jurisdiction. . . ."

It is hardly necessary to record that that decision which is binding on the Principal Court has in fact been followed by that court in at least two cases which came before it in 1959.[1]

That decision does, however, at first sight appear to be to some extent contradicted by a more recent order of LYON, J., delivered on the 21st September, 1959.[2] The three plaintiffs before the Principal Court, who were partners in a concern named Sapoba Bookshop Press, claimed damages for a libel contained in an edition of a vernacular newspaper, *Obugaga*, alleged to be published by the Mengo Blue Gardens Limited, a limited liability company incorporated in Uganda. The alleged libel was in respect of an item of " News " which stated that the plaintiffs and their partnership had become bankrupt. The defendants submitted that the Principal Court had no jurisdiction because the case involved a partnership and a limited liability company. That submission was over-ruled by the Principal

---

[1] P.C.C.C. 66 of 1954, *Nakifuma Galyawamu Co.* v. *Lwanga and Another* (unreported) and P.C.C.C. 224 of 1958, *Gingo Radio Ltd.* v. *Uganda Electricity* (unreported).

[2] H.C.C.A. 51 of 1958, *Samueli Kasule* v. *Lameka Ntambi for Mengo Blue Gardens* (P.C.C.C. 36 of 1958) (unreported).

Court which ordered that the hearing continue. Against that order, an appeal was filed. The learned Judge's attention was drawn to the judgment in the Mengo Builders Case but he held that no question of company nor of partnership law could arise and the suit was merely a claim for damages, a suit within the jurisdiction of the Principal Court.

It is difficult if not impossible to reconcile all those decisions of the High Court. It is clear that the Kabaka's Courts have no jurisdiction to entertain proceedings brought under the Companies Ordinance or under the Partnerships Ordinance in respect of registered companies and partnerships. By inference it is also clear that Protectorate legislation and therefore the High Court and subordinate Protectorate courts do not recognise unregistered companies and partnerships. If such unregistered companies and partnerships are composed entirely of Africans any proceedings arising in respect of them are justiciable by the Kabaka's courts. The conflict of decisions comes in that class of case which is normally within the jurisdiction of the native courts, such as a contract or a claim for damages, but in which a registered company or a registered partnership, albeit composed entirely of Africans, is one of the parties.

In fact nowadays most African companies, partnerships and societies are registered for the public otherwise suspect the enterprise of being a swindle. For that reason and because advocates are usually engaged by such corporate bodies the trend is for the majority of such proceedings to go to the Protectorate courts.

PART VI

THE LAW OF WRONGS

SUMMARY

			PAGE
CHAP. 16	Torts	. . . .	259
CHAP. 17	Crimes	. . . .	268

CHAPTER 16

TORTS

The Ganda like other African peoples have always had a conception of compensation for wrong suffered indeed in ancient times there were few wrongs classed by the state as crimes. The principal object in the ancient courts when trying cases of alleged wrong done was to restore the equilibrium.[1]

Generally responsibility for the wrong or tort was and is laid on the individual who did the act which caused the damage. The only clear exception to this rule is an accidental spearing of a fellow hunter when hunting.[2] There is also a quasi-exception in the case of cattle fighting and one killing the other; the owner of the animal killed takes the killer and the owner of the killer the carcase.[3]

As has already been observed,[4] not only was there an individual responsibility in tort but also the family and ultimately the clan were liable for wrongs done by a member of their group. The final sanction against an habitual wrongdoer was, of course, to expel him from the clan. Nowadays only individual responsibility, at any rate in the courts of law, is enforceable except in certain specified cases which tend to follow the English law of vicarious liability.

A man is not liable for the acts of his associates[5] but he is liable as a master for the tort committed by his servant in the course of his employment[6] but not for an independent act by his servant which is not so connected with the authorised act as to be a mode of doing it.[7] Nor is a man liable for a wrongful act of an independent contractor.[8]

---

[1] See J. H. Driberg, " The African Conception of Law ", *Journal of Comparative Legislation and International Law*, 1934.
[2] See p. 182, above.
[3] Sir Apolo Kagwa, *Empisa*, p. 246.
[4] See pp. 115 and 73, above.
[5] P.C.C.C. 12 of 1956, *Kezimbira v. Nakalogo*, 1956 C.L.R. 55.
[6] P.C.C.C. 120 of 1956, *Kaggwe v. Kalibala*, 1956 C.L.R. 55.
[7] H.C.C.A. 62 of 1953, *Walusimbi v. The Buganda Government*, Notes 63.
[8] P.C.C.C. 218 of 1957, *Mukasa v. Lwanga*, 1957 C.L.R. 95.

There is a line of cases concerning the liability of chiefs in tort. This line can be split into two branches: the first branch consists of an allegation of despoliation against the chief, a type of accusation that was current after the 1949 riots, which is treated as a case of damage to goods.[1] The second branch is a series of cases where persons arrested by chiefs have sought to fasten on them responsibility for alleged thefts of their property which were said to have occurred while the plaintiffs were in custody. The courts have held repeatedly that such damage even if the theft were proved and on the assumption that the arrest was wrongful and the imprisonment false was too remote to fall upon the shoulders of the chief and *a fortiori* of the Government.[2] It has further been held that there is no responsibility on a *mutongole* chief to look after the property of a person whom he arrests; it is for the prisoner to request facility to make his own arrangements for its safe-keeping.[3] An interesting case in this class was a suit for the loss of forty bunches of plantains (matooke) valued at Shs. 110/– which resulted from their ripening when the plaintiff, a vendor, was charged by the market authority for overcharging in selling the plantains. The Principal Court held that he could have nevertheless sold the *matooke* pending the criminal proceedings and the responsibility for the loss was not the authority's.[4]

INJURIES TO PROPERTY

Trespass to land by itself without causing damage or diminution of rights is not actionable under Ganda customary law with one important exception. The exception is to pass through a compound at the back of a house (okweyitiriza emanju). Because of the suspicion that a person who so trespassed was attempting to have an illicit affair with one of the women of the house, such a trespass in ancient times was counted a crime.[5] A man who so

---

[1] *E.g.* P.C.C.C. 164 of 1950, *Nyonyintono* v. *Sewanyaga and Another*, 1940–1955 C.L.R. and P.C.C.C. 187 of 1950, *Sempa* v. *Sewanyaga and Another*, 1940–1955 C.L.R.

[2] H.C.C.A. 5 of 1950, *Gyotogendanga* v. *Sekabira*, Notes 41; H.C.C.A. 90 of 1956, *Iga* v. *O. C. Mengo Police*, Notes 81, arising from P.C.C.C. 157 of 1956, 1956 C.L.R. 59.

[3] P.C.C.C. 49 of 1949, *Sentongo* v. *Kulazikulabe*, 1940–1955 C.L.R.

[4] P.C.C.C. 185 of 1948, *Mukasa* v. *Buganda Government and Another*, 1940–1955 C.L.R.

[5] But is no longer, see Sir Apolo Kagwa's statement at p. 24 of *Akatabo ke Biragiro*, 1916–1919.

trespassed in a chief's compound was likely to lose his eyes or his ears and even one who trespassed in a peasant's was liable to be speared.

It is, however, a tort wrongfully to occupy another's land[1] and more particularly so if one leaves buildings on it and uses them after the land has become another's property.[2] To demolish or destroy by fire a tenant's house while he is still in lawful possession is an actionable trespass creating a liability in damages.[3] Nor can a man evict his ex-mistress from a house she built on a plot of which he was tenant and deprive her of her property therein.[4] The Kabaka's Government has, however, been held not to be liable for demolishing official buildings on vacating a plaintiff's land[5] nor for removing a building under a demolition order issued by the health authority.[6] It is understandably an actionable wrong to build a mosque on a person's land without his permission.[7]

Damages are payable for excavating another's sand,[8] for digging another's clay to make bricks,[9] for removing another's stone[10] or for felling his trees.[11] Indeed in the latter event exemplary damages have been awarded.[12]

Accidental burning of another's house and property by allowing a grass-burning fire (oluira) to spread there has always been a wrong under Ganda customary law calling for compensation. In ancient times the offender had to rebuild the house and compensate for the other property destroyed.[13] Even crops destroyed by fire spreading over the boundaries of a plot may be the subject of compensation if the owner of the crops has taken all reasonable precautions to prevent such an eventuality

---

[1] H.C.C.A. 45 of 1949, *Kasozi* v. *Mukasa*, Notes 41.

[2] P.C.C.C. 251 of 1955, *Musoke* v. *Mivule and Another*, 1957 C.L.R. 131.

[3] H.C.C.C. 37 of 1957, *Lukwayo* v. *Singh and Another*, Bulletin 7/59 (an action against a non-African lessee and the African lessor but the native law was considered), and P.C.C.C. 197 of 1951, *Mbowa* v. *Dr. Kaggwa*, 1940–1955 C.L.R.

[4] P.C.C.C. 118 of 1940, *Nakalema* v. *Kapalaga* (unreported).

[5] P.C.C.C. 31 of 1946, *Luima* v. *Buganda Government* (unreported).

[6] P.C.C.C. 183 of 1955, *Kiwanuka* v. *Buganda Government* (upheld in H.C.C.A. 86 of 1957) (unreported).

[7] P.C.C.C. 10 of 1952, *Lule* v. *Nakikulu* (unreported).

[8] P.C.C.C. 5 of 1953, *Nanfuka and Others* v. *Mpiso and Another* (unreported).

[9] P.C.C.C. 9 of 1950, *Kisitu* v. *Kitaka* (unreported).

[10] P.C.C.C. 118 of 1954, *Kitakule* v. *Nsimbe* (upheld in H.C.C.A. 46 of 1955) (unreported).

[11] P.C.R.O. 17 of 1923, *Bavunanyeki* v. *Samwiri Mukasa*, *Kangawo* (unreported).

[12] H.C.C.A. 1 of 1950, *Nduga* v. *Masitula Nkinzi Nnaalinnya*, Notes 37.

[13] Sir Apolo Kagwa, *op. cit.*, p. 243.

and if the offender has not done what is required of a reasonable man.[1]

To damage another's plantains by driving a tractor through his plaintain garden is not unnaturally an actionable wrong.[2]

Sir Apolo Kagwa recounts[3] that the ancient remedy for cattle trespass was to seize the animals and to force the herdsman to redeem them by giving the owner of the crops damaged a hoe; otherwise the offending beast was consumed. Cunningham records a sterner penalty exacted on a herdsman who inadvisedly let his animal trespass on royal land:

> " The writer has seen a poor wretch who had his ears cut off because his goat, in passing along a path, nibbled a blade of corn on the King's land."[4]

It is probable that in ancient times there were few cases of cattle trespass taken to the courts, not because there was no liability[5] but because in the majority of cases the owner of the cattle was the chief of the peasant whose crops had been damaged. Certainly cattle trespass is now an actionable wrong[6] and damages may be recovered both from the owner of the cattle and the herdsman.[7]

As long ago as 1923 the owner of a cow was cast in damages by the Ggombolola, Ssaza and Lukiko Courts on the ground that he took insufficient care when leading along the highway an animal he knew to be dangerous and it then injured the plaintiff's cycle.[8]

But often it is the cattle which are damaged in such encounters. In ancient times if an animal fell down an excavation on someone else's land and was injured, far from receiving any compensation the owner of the animal would find that one haunch of the slaughtered beast would be taken by the hands of the man who dug the hole to the village chief as his share of an animal caught in a trap and he was then permitted to take away the rest.[9] But if a shepherd struck another's goat and broke its

---

[1] P.C.R.O. 14 of 1925, *Mikulumya* v. *Waswa* (upholding Lukiko Court Case 297 of 1924) (unreported).

[2] P.C.C.C. 119 of 1954, *Binagwa* v. *Muwonge* (unreported).

[3] *Op. cit.*, p. 246.

[4] *Op. cit.*, p. 147.

[5] *Pace* Mair, *op. cit.*, p. 157.

[6] P.C.C.C. 160 of 1950, *Sajjabi* v. *Musoke* (unreported).

[7] P.C.C.A. 20 of 1958, *Katende* v. *Luyulu*, 1958 C.L.R. 73.

[8] P.C.R.O. 16 of 1923, *Kasule* v. *Seputemba* (unreported).

[9] Sir Apolo Kagwa, *Empisa*, p. 245.

leg the owner had a right enforceable in the courts of taking in its place one of the other's uninjured goats.[1] Of course, the modern customary law of tort in running-down actions is a development of the ancient but the Principal Court has held that there is no *prima facie* liability in the vehicle driver if his vehicle strikes a cow.[2] Indeed that court has held that if a cattle-owner allows his cattle to wander on the road at night without a herdsman and without a warning lamp then he has no right to damages if his cattle are struck by a vehicle.[3] But damages have been awarded for cattle killed by vehicles.[4]

Damages have been awarded against the driver found to have caused a collision between two vehicles by his negligence.[5] An owner-driver who rammed a shop with his motor-car has, as one would expect, been found liable for the damage caused.[6]

What appears to be similar to a suit for detinue is also well-known to the Kabaka's courts. There have been suits for refusing to hand over to the successor the testator's will[7] and for refusing either to return a printing press or to pay its value.[8] A widow has successfully sued in detinue for her deceased husband's property wrongfully taken.[9] The High Court has held that a mechanic is responsible for taking reasonable care of a car as bailee and must return in substantially the same condition or pay appropriate damages.[10]

PHYSICAL INJURIES TO THE PERSON

Plaintiffs who had been awarded compensation in prior criminal proceedings for assault resulting in loss of work were unsuccessful in attempting to obtain more damages in subsequent civil suits.[11] But another similarly claiming was successful.[12]

---

[1] Sir Apolo Kagwa, *Empisa*, p. 245.
[2] P.C.C.A. 72 of 1952, *Katabazi v. Mukasa*, 1956 C.L.R. 57.
[3] P.C.C.A. 23 of 1958, *Ddamulira v. Mabirizi*, 1958 C.L.R. 71.
[4] P.C.C.C. 33 of 1948, *Sebuliba v. Kyebatenda and Another* (unreported).
[5] P.C.C.A. 58 of 1945, *Mutasa v. Mukibi* (upheld in J.A.C.A. 56 of 1946) (unreported).
[6] P.C.C.C. 429 of 1956, *Muwanga v. Mukuta*, 1957 C.L.R. 97.
[7] P.C.C.C. 26 of 1941, *Musoke v. Kasaliko* (unreported).
[8] P.C.C.C. 56A of 1945, *Nkalubo v. Mukibi and Another* (unreported).
[9] P.C.C.C. 112 of 1953, *Nakabugo v. Naddibanga* (unreported).
[10] H.C.C.A. 13 of 1951, *Kasule v. Kato*, Notes 47.
[11] P.C.C.C. 274 of 1950, *Namungona v. Mutyaba*, 1940–1955 C.L.R. and P.C.C.C. 165 of 1956, *Tibyasa v. Sempala*, 1957 C.L.R. 99.
[12] P.C.C.C. 45 of 1946, *Senfuma v. Mbago* (upheld in J.A.C.A. 61 of 1946 and H.C.C.A. 45 of 1946) (unreported).

A plaintiff, whose collar bone was broken and cycle damaged, failed to prove his claim against another cyclist with whom he collided.[1]

The Kabaka's courts recognise a claim for damages for false imprisonment.[2] And indeed such damages have been awarded.[3]

SEDUCTION

The ancient ritual which took place when an unmarried girl was found to be pregnant (amawemukirano) is still occasionally followed in the way described by the authorities.[4] But nowadays the usual procedure in such an eventuality is for the girl's father to summon the youth to appear before him and to enquire whether he is going to marry the girl. If the youth refuses, the father demands compensation and has if need be a claim for damages enforceable at law. If the fathers of both the youth and the girl live in the same village then sometimes an alternative procedure is followed—the two fathers meet at the summons of the girl's father and reach agreement.[5] Such pregnancies do not in practice usually lead to marriage. The natural father is expected to make some presents to the girl's parents (by'okulongoosa oluggya = lit. for the cleaning of the courtyard) and takes the child after weaning. The girl is then married off to another man.

The responsibility in the youth for the pregnancy and the upbringing of the child would cease if after their love-making the girl went with other men.

In ancient times if an unmarried girl had a miscarriage, the seducer used to take a barkcloth and a gourd of beer to her father who made a small feast. The matter ended there (gafuka mawemukirano). Nowadays the father of the girl can proceed to sue the seducer for spoiling his daughter's chances of marriage.

If the girl seduced dies in childbirth the seducer is never sued nor does he pay compensation. But if the child survives, he takes custody of it.

---

[1] P.C.R.O. 56 of 1924, *Kyewalabye* v. *Simwogerere* (unreported).

[2] P.C.Cr.A. 54 of 1956, *Mukasa and Another* v. *Lukiiko*, 1956 C.L.R. 59.

[3] P.C.C.C. 97 of 1952, *Kabangala* v. *Wakulira* (upheld in H.C.C.A. 60 of 1952) (unreported).

[4] Sir Apolo Kagwa, *Empisa*, p. 179, Roscoe, *op. cit.*, p. 263 and Mair, *op. cit.*, p. 75.

[5] P.C.C.A. 70 of 1956, *Kiwesi* v. *Balinya*, 1957 C.L.R. 103.

If the seducer makes an unmarried woman pregnant for a second time then on the second occasion he does not pay compensation and is not sued. If he wants to marry her, he is allowed to do so. Otherwise her parents give her in marriage to another and the children are handed over to the seducer.

If after betrothal the betrothed pair have pre-marital sexual intercourse and the girl becomes pregnant, the man is not sued unless he seeks to discontinue with the marriage. A girl's father has no power to stop the marriage because of the girl becoming pregnant during the period of betrothal if the man completes the payment of the marriage consideration fixed.

The Principal Court has been in the practice of carefully scrutinizing the claim of the girl's father for damages.[1] That court's decisions on the bases for damages have, however, been various. In a case decided in 1954,[2] the court held that the girl's father could not claim for moneys expended on the education of the girl but only damages for the loss of expectation of marrying her off satisfactorily. But two years later the same court took into account not only her spoiled future chances of respectable marriage but also her present difficulty of continuing her education.[3] But in a case decided in 1957, the three heads of damage were:

(a) seduction and removal of the girl from school;

(b) making her a wanton;

(c) making her pregnant.

The facts of that case indicate that the girl was made pregnant at the earliest possible age and that the seducer ignored the warning given him by the girl's father. He had also refused to marry the girl. The court therefore ordered him to pay damages calculated on the bases of school fees for the five years the girl had been at school, of the lying-in expenses of the girl and of Shs. 50/– a month for the rearing of the child for the period from birth until the child should go to school[4] (when presumably it would be handed over to the seducer).

A case of this nature came before AINLEY, J., in 1951[5] and the learned Judge then held that it was proper that such an action should lie at the suit of the parents as they would have the burden

---

[1] P.C.C.A. 74 of 1957, *Katongole* v. *Ddaki*, 1957 C.L.R. 99.
[2] P.C.C.C. 130 of 1953, *Nsobeddwa* v. *Kivumbi*, 1940–1955 C.L.R.
[3] P.C.C.A. 104 of 1955, *Musoke* v. *Zavuga*, 1956 C.L.R. 57.
[4] P.C.C.C. 468 of 1956, *Nzalambi* v. *Ssonko*, 1957 C.L.R. 103.
[5] H.C.C.A. 39 of 1950, *Nabanja* v. *Kayinja*, Notes 45.

of maintaining the child born if the seducer made no provision and that there were two heads of damage:

  (i) the diminution of marriage consideration that the parent might have received for the daughter; and

  (ii) the sum which the parent could reasonably be expected to expend in feeding and clothing the child until the daughter could fend for herself.

It is convenient here to consider three other classes of case in which the Principal Court has found the defendant liable in tort and has awarded damages:

A husband sued civilly his wife and her adulterer for expenses incurred in her pre-natal treatment and in the nursing of the mother and child after birth. It was held that the husband had no claim against his wife as he was bound to sustain her in any case but that he could recover against the adulterer.[1]

A man, whom the woman had named as the natural father when she became pregnant before marriage and who had expended considerable money on maternity fees, compensation, the feeding and maintenance of the mother after childbirth and who had been given the child five years before the action to place at school, recovered damages for his outlay when the woman after ten years changed her story, alleged that another man was the true father and took the child away from the plaintiff.[2]

Finally an unmarried mother successfully sued the natural father for neglect of their children and recovered as damages moneys she had expended on their upbringing.[3]

PSYCHIC INJURIES TO PERSON

Torts of this kind are rare in Ganda customary law as most cases of defamation have in the past been prosecuted criminally on a charge of " speaking unfounded words " (okwogera bya kalebule).[4]

Sir Apolo Kagwa, however, records that a herdsman who herded his livestock on graves was liable to forfeit the offending beast which the relatives of those therein buried ate unless it was ransomed by giving them a goat as compensation.[5]

---

[1] P.C.C.C. 288 of 1955, *Mugadya* v. *Namusoke and Another* (unreported).
[2] P.C.C.C. 63 of 1958, *Batulabudde* v. *Nalubowa and Another*, 1958 C.L.R. 77.
[3] P.C.C.C. 347 of 1957, *Kalule* v. *Mulira*, 1958 C.L.R. 73.
[4] See below in Chapter 17.
[5] *Empisa*, p. 246.

A curious modern case might also be put in this class: a building contractor sued the person for whom he was building a house for trespass in that he removed the doors and windows that he had supplied for his own house because of a dispute as to payment. Thereby the contract had been terminated and the plaintiff's professional reputation as a builder damaged.[1]

---

[1] P.C.C.C. 12 of 1952, *Makerere Builders and Concrete Pipe Manufacturers* v. *Lule* (unreported).

CHAPTER 17

CRIMES

Criminal law is a subject of supreme importance for by far the larger number of cases brought to the courts are of a criminal nature. It is also an indisputable fact that the bulk of native criminals in Buganda are dealt with by the Kabaka's courts rather than the Protectorate Courts.[1] Paradoxically the law of crimes is, apart from one or two exceptional offences, a dull field of customary law which is of comparatively recent growth.

There is fair authority, and in such an hierarchic cephalous society as the Ganda it is indeed probable, that in ancient times certain crimes such as treason against the Kabaka, witchcraft, incest, sexual perversions, adultery with the royal wives or chief's wives, theft and cowardice in war were classed as crimes against the State and were punished with death or at the least mutilation.[2] Other offences were dealt with as torts and were settled by the payment of compensation to the injured party.[3]

Through contact with British administrators, police, lawyers and judges over the last seventy years the Ganda have come to recognise as crimes those offences which are set out in the Protectorate Penal Code. Indeed from the early years of the century until about 1940 there were frequent convictions in the Buganda courts allegedly made under sections of the Penal Code or the Gambling Regulations although in a strict law those courts had no jurisdiction to administer that legislation.

This process of adoption of English law particularly in the field of criminal law was apparent twenty years ago and was thus described by the then Attorney-General:

"... the fundamental conception of native law is surely and rapidly changing; the difference between civil and criminal law, as we know it, is becoming appreciated so that it is recognised that the enforcement of the latter is the affair of the State rather than the individual, while the system and principles of the administration

---

[1] See Hone, *op. cit.*
[2] *Ibid.* and see Driberg, *op. cit.*
[3] See Chapter 16, above.

of justice in the native courts is rapidly becoming indistinguishable in form and substance from that prevailing in the British courts. This has not been brought about by legislation nor by the forcing of any alien system upon the native courts. It is the inevitable result of the change from primitive to civilised conditions and the consequential adaptation and readjustment of the native mental processes to the demands of a more highly organised mode of life and outlook.

A most important conclusion, on the facts, is thus that, however widely the system of native justice may have differed originally in form and appearance from our own civilised system, it has in the last fifty years developed along similar lines to our system and has indeed arrived at a stage of development that, in regard to criminal law in particular, its main principles and concepts are now in close approximation to our system."[1]

Such a development has continued since and is continuing at a more rapid pace every year as more and more of those administering justice in the Kabaka's Courts obtain a deeper grasp of the English legal principles. It would appear to be a process acknowledged throughout the length and breadth of Africa to be highly desirable.[2]

The more important criminal proceedings tried in the Principal Court during the last few years have been reported in the published Customary Law Reports. It will be convenient in the following pages to follow the arrangement of the various offences to be found therein; and to reduce the volume of cases cited I shall refer to the authority of cases by the pages of those reports.

General Rules to Criminal Responsibility

Following a decision of the Privy Council on a famous Nigerian case,[3] MANNING, J., held in 1942 that it should always be a legitimate ground of appeal that the act complained of was not a criminal offence and that it must be apparent that the custom would be assented to by the law-abiding members of the community if they had an opportunity of doing so.[4]

The Principal Court has found a boy of thirteen years of age to have been of an age capable of a sexual offence.[5]

---

[1] Hone, *op. cit.*
[2] See Lewin, *op. cit.*, Chapter III.
[3] *Esugbayi Eleko* v. *Government of Nigeria*, A.I.R. 1931 P.C. 253.
[4] H.C.Cr.A. 125 of 1942, *Kivu* v. *Lukiiko*, Notes 3 and see also H.C.Cr.A. 98 of 1953, *Musoke* v. *Lukiiko*, Notes 53, and H.C.Cr.A. 300–304 of 1957, *Sebanakirya and Others* v. *Lukiko*, Notes 87.
[5] 1957 C.L.R. 1.

That Court has also held that the act of a chief's deputy in his absence cannot cause the chief himself to be charged with an offence.[1]

Provocation is recognised as a possible defence or at any rate as a mitigating factor.[2] So is intoxication.[3]

Self-defence has been accepted repeatedly as a defence to a charge.[4]

The Principal Court has also followed the Protectorate Code in deciding the degree of force permitted in effecting an arrest.[5]

OFFENCES AGAINST THE KABAKA'S AUTHORITY

These offences may be divided into those held to be against the Kabaka's person and those committed against the Kabaka's representatives.

In a criminal revision which came before the High Court in 1922, GRIFFIN, C. J., accepted a statement of native law contained in the judgment of the Lukiko Court to the following effect:

> " It is well known in the Kingdom of Buganda that this is an absolute taboo, and the Kabaka is never abused; further in the old days no-one would even attempt to speak or even to make any sign which would be calculated to be abusive to the Kabaka and if found out, he would be instantly killed."

The learned Chief Justice held that there could be no doubt that sedition is an offence against and is punishable by every Government that has ever existed.[6] Indeed any disrespect to the Kabaka is still an offence under customary law.[7]

Other offences against the Kabaka's person were to squat on one's haunches in his presence (okusitama), to whistle (okufuuwa oluwa) in the Lubiri, to cough, sneeze or blow one's nose in Lukiko,[8] to urinate in the Lubiri or to carry weapons in the Lubiri.[9] It is forbidden to have sexual intercourse with a woman in the Lubiri because as the saying goes:

---

[1] 1956 C.L.R. 1.
[2] 1957 C.L.R. 3 and 1958 C.L.R. 3.
[3] 1956 C.L.R. 3 and 1958 C.L.R. 5.
[4] 1957 C.L.R. 3 and 1958 C.L.R. 7.
[5] 1957 C.L.R. 5.
[6] H.C.C.R. 43 of 1922, *Rex* v. *Paulo and Others*, 3 U.L.R. 98.
[7] 1956 C.L.R. 5 and 1958 C.L.R. 13.
[8] Roscoe, *op. cit.*, p. 258.
[9] Speke, *op. cit.*, p. 374.

Empologoma eri emu yekka mu Lubiri—There is only one lion in the Palace.

Mention has already been made of the prohibition on the Queen-Sister (Lubuga) marrying.[1] Neither she nor a princess could in ancient times bear children on pain of death.[2] To commit adultery with one of the Kabaka's wives or concubines entailed instant death. Even to look at them resulted in the loss of ears or eyes or both. Similarly anyone who gave a prince a girl to wife was liable to be put to death immediately as having treasonable designs.[3] It almost goes without saying that anyone convicted of treason or rebellion against the Kabaka was put to death.[4]

Trespass in the Lubiri (okweyitiriza manju) in ancient times was punished with instant death.[5] Nowadays it is an offence punishable under customary law with imprisonment.[6]

Any act which smacks of witchcraft committed against the Kabaka is not unnaturally still an offence punishable with imprisonment.[7]

To turn to the second division of offences being those committed against the Kabaka's representatives, it is clear that a messenger sent by the Kabaka was sacrosanct as to his person and his actions.[8] On the other hand such messengers had to be swift in their journeys and exact in their missions on pain of having a leg broken or even of death.[9] To impersonate one of the Kabaka's emissaries is still a punishable offence.[10]

Sir Apolo Kagwa, in his résumé of certain Ganda customs for implementation published in 1919 for the guidance of the chiefs and the public, declared that from ancient times it was a punishable offence to show disrespect to a chief in any way.[11] There is rather a quaint example of such a case which one may be excused for digressing for a moment to cite:

---

[1] See p. 55, above.
[2] Roscoe, *op. cit.*, pp. 84–85.
[3] *Ibid.*
[4] Roscoe, *op. cit.*, p. 266 and see p. 184, above.
[5] Roscoe, *op. cit.*, p. 50.
[6] 1956 C.L.R. 5 and 1957 C.L.R. 7.
[7] 1958 C.L.R. 9.
[8] Roscoe, *op. cit.*, p. 266.
[9] Roscoe, *op. cit.*, p. 12.
[10] 1956 C.L.R. 7.
[11] *Empisa za Baganda ezalondebwamu ezimu okukolerako* in *Akatabo ke Biragiro na Mateka ebyatesebwa Olukiko Olukulu olwe Buganda okuva* 1916 *okutusa* 1919, pp. 18–27 is in general a condensed repetition of passages occurring in his book *Empisa za Baganda.*

"... it appears that the accused has been sentenced to 7 days R.I. for not having dismounted from his bicycle in accordance with native custom on meeting Owesaza Mukwenda on the Entebbe road on 6.4.16. The sentence has been imposed as stated in the judgment with a view to effectively impressing the younger Baganda with the necessity of giving due respect of their Chiefs."[1]

It is an offence punishable with imprisonment to personate a public servant, the usual guise being that of a detective.[2]

There are also a whole body of offences in this division which amount to breaches of public duty which every Ganda owes to the Kabaka and his Government. Such offences comprise failing to answer a drum, failing to answer an alarm, neglecting to keep a path clear of weeds, refusing to help build a bridge, refusing to hunt pigs, delay in delivering a despatch and omitting to inform the chief of the area of happenings therein.[3] These offences are commonly classed as refusal to do a public duty (bulungi bwansi).

OFFENCES RELATING TO THE ADMINISTRATION OF JUSTICE

Roscoe's explanation of the reason why the ancient Ganda sometimes told the truth is akin to the Spartan idea of morality:

" Though there was no veneration for the truth as an abstract idea, the violation of it, if it caused inconvenience to a superior, was sure to meet with punishment. In other cases lying would be laughed at. Sometimes it would even be thought clever and amusing.

The oath of blood-brotherhood was binding; it was considered a solemn compact, and the violation of it was dreaded. Other oaths, such as the common oath ' By my Mother ', were lightly made, and lightly set aside. It was worth while telling the truth to those in authority, unless a man had time to escape before his lie could be discovered, since the penalty for lying was mutilation."[4]

However, there is now no question but that to lie to a court in evidence is an offence under customary law frequently punished by the courts with a fine or even imprisonment.

There is no doubt[5] that in ancient times litigants would discreetly offer the court bribes during the hearing of a case by sign

---

[1] P.C.R.O. 5 of 1916, *Owesaza Mukwenda* v. *Zavuga* (unreported).
[2] P.C.R.O. 10 of 1912, *Lukiko* v. *Lwanga* (unreported).
[3] Sir Apolo Kagwa, *ibid.*
[4] *Op. cit.*, p. 268.
[5] Hamu Mukasa, *op. cit.*, p. 21.

language: a hand held towards the ground indicated the bribe would take the form of a goat, fists clenched on the chest that of a girl.[1] In the evening out of court the bribe would be handed over. The fact that allegations of bribery or even of improper behaviour are now rarely made against the members of the Buganda judiciary would seem to indicate that there is in fact today little, if any, corruption in these courts. An allegation of bribery made against the judges of the Principal Court in 1956 was held to be an offence against customary law.[2]

An attempt to corrupt a court orderly was punished with a sentence of six months imprisonment and a fine of two thousand shillings.[3]

In 1926 the High Court held that it is a serious contempt of court to attempt to influence the decision of a native court in a pending case.[4]

Compounding a criminal offence is itself an offence;[5] as also is aiding a prisoner to escape.[6]

OFFENCES RELATING TO RELIGION

Disturbing the practice of religion[7] and hindering a wife from burying her dead husband[8] have been held offences under customary law.

NUISANCES

The Ganda proverb ran:

Aliziba n'aligula bonna benkanye obusungu—He who blocks a path and he who opens it are both equal in their rage.

The meaning was that they would fight each other. Under ancient customary law anyone who blocked a path without an announcement from the chief was fined a goat or even a cow. Nowadays also such an act is held to be a criminal offence.[9]

To block up a well similarly is an offence.[10]

---

[1] See Roscoe, *op. cit.*, p. 260, followed by Jules Le Clerq, *op. cit.*, p. 205.
[2] 1956 C.L.R. 7.
[3] 1957 C.L.R. 13.
[4] H.C.C.C. 8 of 1926, *Rex v. X.Y.*, 3 U.L.R. 202.
[5] 1956 C.L.R. 9.
[6] 1957 C.L.R. 15.
[7] 1956 C.L.R. 9.
[8] 1956 C.L.R. 11.
[9] 1957 C.L.R. 17 and see p. 164, above.
[10] 1958 C.L.R. 17 and see p. 164, above.

DEFAMATION

Defamation, that is criminal libel as understood by English lawyers, was really unknown in ancient times in Buganda. Its place was filled by the customary offence of " Kalebule " (speaking unfounded words). To quote a definition of the Principal Court:

> " Cases of unfounded words contain important statements which have the purpose of disturbing the peaceful existence of the person of whom they are spoken. . . ."[1]

If a man speaks unfounded words of another to his face, the person maligned has to raise an alarm immediately and there must be the evidence of a third person to satisfy a court. *Kalebule* has always been considered a serious offence in Buganda and in proceedings brought in ancient times before the village chief an offender was usually fined a calabash of beer, a goat or a chicken but if serious enough to be taken before the clan, a cow.

It is, however, well-established that a customary law exists and can be enforced forbidding the public use of words having a seditious intent although no native custom can debar an inhabitant of the Protectorate from honestly, decently, unmaliciously pointing out the mistakes of their rulers whether they do so in public or in private.[2] The Principal Court has for more than thirty-five years been gradually assimilating the elements of the offence of defamation for in 1923 its conviction of the publishers of a vernacular newspaper of defamation for publishing an article in which it was said that the Native Treasurer was suffering from an infectious disease and ought to be removed from his office was upheld by the High Court on the grounds that it was a statement of fact and was not fair comment on a matter of public interest.[3] Recently the Principal Court distinguished the crime from the tort basing its decision on the dictum of COLERIDGE, C. J., in 1889.[4]

OFFENCES AGAINST MORALITY

In ancient Buganda there was no distinction at customary law between having sexual intercourse with a married woman by

---

[1] 1957 C.L.R. 18.
[2] *Per* AINLEY, J., in H.C.Cr.A. 505 of 1945, *Sekkuma* v. *Lukiko*, Notes 15.
[3] H.C.Cr.A. 4 of 1923, *The Publishers of " Munyonyozi "* v. *Lukiko*, 3 U.L.R. 124.
[4] 1958 C.L.R. 19.

force and having it with her consent. The offence was ranked as a murderous act against the husband for the strange man would go armed, as discovery meant death, and in any case he was bound to offend the husband's fetiches and so lay the husband exposed to an enemy's attack.[1] The ancient customary law governing such offences is said to have been a severe enactment entitled the " Law of Kasagira " and is variously reputed to have been enacted by Kabaka Kamanya[2] and Kabaka Suna II.[3] The law, which was not written, of course, but handed down by report, appears to have embraced various aspects of adultery:[4] an adulterer was to be punished with death, mutilation or confiscation of property and even a wife's parents were to be prosecuted and punished for not looking after her if she had been staying with them when the intercourse took place. If the exact identity of the adulterer could not be determined the law allowed the confiscation of the property of the inhabitants of the village from which it was suspected he came. The law also provided the right of direct access to the royal court without first bringing a charge in the lower court. Speke gives a stirring eye-witness account of such a trial:

"... and, finally, a large body of officers came in with an old man, with his two ears shorn off for having been too handsome in his youth, and a young woman who, after four days' search, had been discovered in his house. They were brought for judgment before the King.

Nothing was listened to but the plaintiff's statement, who said he had lost the woman four days, and, after considerable search, had found her concealed by the old man, who was indeed old enough to be her grandfather. From all appearances one would have said the wretched girl had run away from the plaintiff's house in consequence of ill treatment, and had harboured herself on this decrepid old man without asking his leave; but their voices in defence were never heard, for the King instantly sentenced both to death, to prevent the occurrence of such impropriety again; and, to make the example more severe, decreed that their lives should not be taken at once, but, being fed to preserve life as long as possible, they were to be dismembered bit by bit, as rations for the vultures, every day, until life was extinct. The dismayed criminals,

---

[1] Roscoe, *op. cit.*, p. 261.
[2] Ggomotoka, *op. cit.*, p. 32.
[3] I am indebted to Mr. C. N. Mukuye, a Magistrate, for the information supplied on this law. One of his father's servants, a certain Bowazi, who died in 1947, was one of the last persons to be mutilated under this law—he lost his ears—by order of Mukasa, Katikkiro to Muteesa I.
[4] Sir Apolo Kagwa's version (*op. cit.*, p. 26) does not appear to be corroborated elsewhere.

struggling to be heard, in utter despair, were dragged away
boisterously in the most barbarous manner, to the drowning music
of the milélé and drums."[1]

There appears to have been apportionment of the penalty
according to the status of the husband; a man who had intercourse with a peasant's wife might be fined a cow, a goat and a
gourd of beer and if it was a case of rape a barkcloth too for the
woman; but one who dared to have intercourse with a chief's
wife at least lost his ears or the sight of his eyes and *a fortiori* with
a royal wife there was only one penalty—death.

Ashe, though writing in 1890, is clearly describing the pre-
valence and treatment of adultery in this period in the middle
of the nineteenth century when he writes:

> " These women (*i.e.* ladies of chief's harem), in the absence of
> their lord, are left pretty much to themselves, and are generally on
> the look-out to be unfaithful. If discovered, then the most frightful
> punishments are inflicted upon the guilty persons, such as burning
> to death, or frightful semi-roasting and various mutilations; and
> yet, in spite of these drastic measures, offences of this kind appear
> to be utterly unchecked."[2]

Only a man who stood in the relation of blood-brother to a
chief could escape the death penalty, according to Sir Apolo
Kagwa, but even he was mutilated by losing eyes and ears.[3]

Torture was usually inflicted on the wife if she was unwilling
to disclose the identity of her paramour or on the suspected
adulterer if he denied the charge.[4]

Kabaka Muteesa I did away with the death penalty for
adultery. But even thereafter an adulterer appears to have been
ostracized in a village and when opportunity arose on campaign
he would be speared in the back.

Nowadays both rape and adultery, and indeed other sexual
offences, are triable under a native law.[5] There is, however,
certain customary law dealing with practice and evidence in
such cases which is not to be found in the written law.

Only the outraged husband or in his absence his brother on
his behalf can prosecute a case of adultery. A private person
other than the brother cannot do so without the husband's
express authority. If the husband can prosecute his wife and

---

[1] *Op. cit.*, p. 374.
[2] *Life in Uganda*, p. 293.
[3] *Empisa*, p. 240.
[4] Roscoe, *op. cit.*, pp. 261 and 263.
[5] The Adultery and Fornication Law, Rev. Edn., pp. 2 *et seq.*

her lover for adultery but delays to do so, despite the Luganda proverb[1] the case falls and cannot afterwards be revived. To stay with the wife afterwards is counted to be evidence of having forgiven her and the adulterer. Nowadays a wife can be prosecuted for adultery even though the adulterer is unknown.

A successor cannot prosecute adultery if the woman is a widow who has not married again but has remained in deceased's courtyard. If the widow has been taken to wife by the successor or a brother of the deceased then the charge may be brought in the usual way.

The husband cannot accept a blatantly adulterous child as his own even though he may have forgiven the adulterous pair. If a husband suspects that a child is adulterous he may force his wife to tell the truth even by tying her up with plantain fibre (ebyai) and the adulterer so disclosed is then summoned and attends with his parents. Compensation of goats or money is then demanded and the child is then taken by the adulterer. If a suspicion arises after the husband's death and the widow confesses her fault, then the adulterer can go to the funeral rites of the deceased husband and on admitting his offence can pay compensation to the deceased's clansmen for the offence and for the expense of rearing the child (ebikunta) whom he may then take away. If a woman refuses to disclose the identity of a child's natural father then the child takes her husband's totem but is debarred from succession by the clan.[2]

There is no fixed amount of compensation for adultery. Nowadays a wife can be made to pay compensation to her husband.

Customary law lays the responsibility on the man to go to the woman's brother to ascertain what her marital status is. Even if she pretended to him that she was unmarried, that would be no defence to a charge of adultery. There was in ancient times a custom called *emomboze* whereby providing a man reported finding another's stray wife to his chief she might after a period of six months become his wife; if her original husband later appeared to reclaim her he could do so but any children she had borne meanwhile remained with the man who had found her; and the latter could not be charged with adultery. This custom is now obsolete.[3]

---

[1] *Omusango teguvunda*—see Appendix 6, p. 334, below.
[2] Mair, *op. cit.*, p. 57.
[3] Sir Apolo Kagwa, *Empisa za Baganda ezalondebwamu* (1917), p. 21.

The evidence required to prove adultery can consist firstly of evidence that the pair were caught *in flagrante delicto*. But whoever so catches them must then and there raise an alarm in order to preserve the evidence. The adulterer cannot be allowed to slip silently away if such evidence is to be accepted later. Only a member of the family or the husband's steward (omusigere) can raise such an alarm. If an alarm is raised and the adulterer is injured when attempting to escape the injury becomes evidence as to his identity at the trial. The only other evidence that can prove adultery is the birth of a child which could not possibly be the husband's. It should be noted that a wife's confession does not now suffice as evidence in the courts. Nor does the fact that the suspected man submitted to a beating at the hands of a suspicious husband without complaint. Nor is the contraction of venereal disease by the wife taken as evidence of adultery—she is merely treated.

Gutkind's allegations[1] that

> " any native court would rule in favour of a man who brought a case against his wife on the grounds of adultery "

and that

> " few men take such a case to court knowing that the court is not empowered to order the repayment of bride-wealth "

are completely untrue. The number of cases of adultery taken each year in the Kabaka's courts is very high and there is no noticeably higher rate of convictions in such prosecutions than in any other type of case.

To return to the subject of rape, the Principal Court tries many cases of such crime every year and has classed some as aggravated.[2] The High Court has on appeal insisted on the lodging of a complaint by the prosecutrix at the earliest reasonable opportunity and her earliest possible medical examination after the alleged offence.[3] That Court has also drawn attention to the need for corroboration of her story.[4]

Unnatural offences are regarded as crimes of abomination (kivve) by the Ganda and from ancient times have been tried in

---

[1] *Op. cit.*, p. 155 and *pace* Southall, *ibid.*, p. 68.
[2] See 1956 C.L.R. 11–17.
[3] H.C.Cr.A. 194 of 1952, *Nyonyintono* v. *Lukiko*, Notes 51 and H.C.Cr.A. 361 of 1956, *Kayongo* v. *Lukiko*, Notes 79.
[4] H.C.Cr.R. 50 of 1935, *Rex* v. *Asitasio Kiyimba*, 5 U.L.R. 124 and H.C.C.R. 100 of 1935, *Rex* v. *Sebbowa*, 5 U.L.R. 128.

the regular courts. Those convicted were taken to the ggombolola of Bukomero in Ssingo and were either thrown in Lake
Mutukula after passing over a stream from which there was no
return (" Katadde ") or were done to death on Mujokero Hill.
Cases of bestiality still occur from time to time and are heavily
punished.[1]

Incest is also a crime of abomination (kivve) and used to be
punished in the same manner as unnatural offences.[2] Incest was
formerly tried in the clans being a most flagrant breach of the
prohibition on endogamy. Nowadays such cases come before the
ordinary courts. Sexual relations between parent and child or
brother and sister are not the only incestuous ones under Ganda
customary law: it is incestuous to have sexual intercourse with
a maternal or paternal aunt[3] or a first cousin.[4]

Offences Against the Person

The jurisdiction in the homicide cases previously held by the
Lukiko Court[5] was relinquished under the 1917 Proclamation[6]
and any consideration of the ancient customary law governing
such cases is, therefore, purely academic.[7] The salient points are
that simple murder resulted in a clan feud (okuwolera eggwanga)
if blood-money in the shape of livestock, barkcloths and women,
was not paid but murder by witchcraft carried the penalty of
being burnt alive; to murder one's wife or slave was no crime as
they were one's property; and killing by accident (okutanwa)
was no offence.[8] Attempted murder has always been and is an
offence under Ganda customary law.[9] A person who made
people drunk and then at his drinking party a murder was
committed was guilty of a crime under customary law apparently.[10]

---

[1] 1956 C.L.R. 17.
[2] 1956 C.L.R. 19 and Gorju, *op. cit.*, p. 285.
[3] Gorju, *ibid.*
[4] 1958 C.L.R. 21 and see p. 120, above.
[5] H.C.Cr.A. (1909), *Nakaka and Another* v. *Rex*, 1 U.L.R. 60 and H.C.Cr.A.
(1911), *Basajabalaba* v. *Rex*, 2 U.L.R. 29.
[6] The Lukiko Court's inability by European standards to deal with the trial
of murder cases (see P.C.R.O.'s 8 of 1912, 38, 46, 51, 52 and 54 of 1914 and
1 of 1915) led to the removal of this jurisdiction and as a *quid pro quo* that Court
was given jurisdiction over natives other than Ganda.
[7] See Roscoe, *op. cit.*, pp. 20 and 266.
[8] *Pace* Roscoe, *loc. cit.*
[9] 1957 C.L.R. 19.
[10] Sir Apolo Kagwa, *op. cit.*, p. 25.

Suicide has always been treated by the Ganda with abhor-rence.[1] It has usually been committed by hanging. The son of the suicide's sister (omujjwa) is brought to cut the cord with a knife on a pole and so drops the body onto a barkcloth spread beneath. He then has to run away without looking back. On his way he collects a goat, which is his reward. The male villagers then, without looking at the body, take it on the bark-cloth to a sandy depression where they bury it without any women being present and without lamentation. Each villager then goes his way home. If the suicide hung himself from a tree the tree is felled, uprooted and burned. If the act was committed in a house then the house is burnt down. The significance of getting a man from another clan (omujjwa) to cut the body down and in not looking at it is so that the abomination (kivve) may not recur. Formerly there were no funeral rites for a suicide nor did he have a successor. But of recent years the custom has changed to the extent that they are now succeeded but they have no separate funeral rites of their own. Their succession is merely mentioned at the funeral rites of others like deceased minors.[2]

Attempting suicide has always been and is an offence under Ganda customary law.[3]

The basic principle of customary law in regard to assaults is that the person who strikes the first blow is in the wrong.[4] Wounding is only culpable if intentional.[5] If a child blinded another in one eye when at play, then the injured child was compensated with livestock in either case but if a boy with a girl also.[6] The Principal Court has viewed an assault on a mistress[7] or on a chief[8] as an aggravated assault. Dangerous wounding is severely punished.[9] It is an offence under customary law to bully people on the road.[10] Riot (kasasamalo) under customary

---

[1] Roscoe, *op. cit.*, p. 20.

[2] See p. 193, above. A notable exception to this rule was Yosia Serwali, who shot himself about 1950, but who was so rich that he had his own funeral rites (olumbe) in breach of custom.

[3] 1956 C.L.R. 19 and 1958 C.L.R. 25.

[4] Sir Apolo Kagwa, *Empisa*, p. 241.

[5] Sir Apolo Kagwa, *Empisa za Baganda ezalondebwamu ezimu okukolerako* (1917), p. 25.

[6] Sir Apolo Kagwa, *Empisa*, p. 245.

[7] 1956 C.L.R. 21.

[8] 1956 C.L.R. 21.

[9] 1958 C.L.R. 23.

[10] Sir Apolo Kagwa, *Empisa za Baganda ezalondebwamu ezimu okukolerako* (1917), p. 26.

law seems to mean much the same as the English legal term " riot ".[1]

Forcible deportation has been held to be an offence against customary law.[2]

Kidnapping of children is an offence committed in ancient times and of recent years by women who desired to pretend to their husbands that they had given birth—particularly in the metropolitan area of the Kibuga.[3] Quite often there are religious reasons for the kidnapping of a child, namely the desire to circumcise if the natural father is a Muslim.[4] But an adult may be kidnapped.[5]

Selling a person as a slave, whatever the position may have been eighty years ago, is now well recognised as an offence against customary law.[6]

OFFENCES RELATING TO PROPERTY

Theft was severely punished in Buganda in the last century: a thief of plantains caught in a garden by night might be killed and his body thrown on the path with a bunch of plantains tied round his neck.[7] A woman caught so stealing food was enslaved.[8] Generally theft, even by children,[9] was punished by the cutting off of hands.[10] Only the chief's food might be stolen by his peasant with impunity for as the Ganda proverbs go:

Omwami takayanira emmere—The chief does not quarrel about food.

Embuga ye bibwa—The chief's headquarters means things to eat.

Alya ekya mukamawe ng'atasenguse taba mubbi—He who eats his master's while he stays with him is no thief.

Anybody coming across cooked food or sweet bananas (amenvu) in a village might eat with impunity.[11]

---

[1] H.C.Cr.A. 123 of 1950, *Semijja* v. *Lukiko*, Notes 35.
[2] 1957 C.L.R. 21 and H.C.Cr.A. 300–304 of 1957, *Sebanakirya and Others* v. *Lukiko*, Notes 87.
[3] 1956 C.L.R. 21.
[4] 1956 C.L.R. 23.
[5] 1958 C.L.R. 21.
[6] 1956 C.L.R. 23 and 1957 C.L.R. 23.
[7] Roscoe, *op. cit.*, pp. 15 and 264 and Sir Apolo Kagwa, *op. cit.*, p. 22.
[8] Sir Apolo Kagwa, *Empisa*, p. 244.
[9] Roscoe, *op. cit.*, p. 267.
[10] Roscoe, *op. cit.*, p. 10.
[11] Sir Apolo Kagwa, *Empisa*, p. 241.

L

Cattle thieves were killed when convicted unless ransomed.[1]

Burglary is said to have entered Buganda from Busoga. Burglars were speared under customary law.[2]

Nowadays theft, burglary, storebreaking, robbery and dacoity are all crimes under customary law.[3]

It need hardly be stated that the High Court in this century has not held the killing of thieves to be justifiable homicide.[4]

The Principal Court has defined burglary under customary law on the lines indicated in the Protectorate Penal Code.[5]

It may be of interest to philologists that the word " kkondo ", which is commonly used nowadays by the Ganda to describe a gang-robber, was coined by an Indian, one Soleya of Kalennamu, from *okumenya kakondo* (breaking the bolt) when prosecuting the notorious robber Mulalira for shopbreaking and theft before the Resident Magistrate, Mr. D. JEFFRYS JONES, in 1953.

To wander about at night without a light is an offence against customary law.[6] The existence of this custom in ancient times is proved by Ashe:

> " Indeed, it is against the law for anyone to be found even on the high-roads after dark, as it is supposed that he can be out for no good purpose, and the King's executioners go out periodically at night and kill all and sundry whom they find on the roads."[7]

MALICIOUS INJURIES TO PROPERTY

An incendiary, who had no good grounds for burning down his fellow's house such as known witchcraft or adultery, and who was caught red-handed was punished by being thrown into the fire of the burning house. If he was not caught in the act but suspected of arson he was in ancient times expelled from the village, led to the next village and announced as an incendiary.

Not only is arson a crime under customary law[8] but also a verbal threat to harm just prior to a house being burnt is an offence.[9]

---

[1] Sir Apolo Kagwa, *Empisa*, p. 244.
[2] Roscoe, *op. cit.*, p. 10.
[3] 1956 C.L.R. 25–27.
[4] H.C.Cr.C. (1918), *Rex* v. *Yokhana Mukasa and Another*, 2 U.L.R. 276.
[5] 1958 C.L.R. 27.
[6] *Amateeka ne Biragiro ebyatesebwa Olukiko Olukulu okuva* 1922–1923, p. 22.
[7] *Life in Uganda*, p. 294.
[8] 1956 C.L.R. 27 and 1957 C.L.R. 27.
[9] 1957 C.L.R. 25.

Wilful destruction of another's document has been held to be an offence.[1] So has malicious damage to a vehicle.[2]

WITCHCRAFT

There were two classes of wizard in Buganda:
  (i) *abalogo*, who were the normal type operating by night or by day;
  (ii) *abasezi*, who were cannibals who killed to satisfy their hunger for human flesh but also ate corpses[3] and prowled (okusera) by night only, uprooting (okuzinda) plantains and crops.[4]

The penalty they suffered on capture differed for each class: *abalogo*, ordinary wizards, were burnt alive[5] but *abasezi*, the prowlers, were killed by the stems of plantain leaves (mizingoonya) being stuffed (okusokkota) up their anus.

All witchcraft is now justiciable by the Kabaka's courts under the Witchcraft Ordinance, 1957, but those courts have very naturally interpreted the provisions of that Ordinance in the light of Ganda customary law and beliefs in regard to witchcraft.[6] The various practices of witchcraft[7] and the nature of witchcraft instruments[8] have been so described.

---

[1] 1958 C.L.R. 29.
[2] 1956 C.L.R. 29.
[3] P.C.R.O. 29 of 1926, *Aliziwangula* v. *Takantwa* (unreported).
[4] See also Mair, *op. cit.*, p. 248 and 1956 C.L.R. 29, P.C.C.A. 64 of 1956.
[5] 1958 C.L.R. 39.
[6] 1956 C.L.R. 31.
[7] 1957 C.L.R. 31 and 1958 C.L.R. 41.
[8] 1957 C.L.R. 37 and 1958 C.L.R. 43.

PART VII

PROCEDURAL

SUMMARY

CHAP. 18 Procedure 287

PAGE

CHAPTER 18

PROCEDURE

ANCIENT RULES OF PRACTICE

There appears to have been little, if any, difference between the procedure followed in the trial of criminal and civil cases in the last century. Indeed, as has already been mentioned,[1] it was not until well into this century that the Lukiko Court distinguished between the two categories of case in its registers.

The most complete description of the ancient method of opening proceedings is to be found in the works of Sir Apolo Kagwa.[2] The injured party took to the chief a fee of twenty-two cowries or, earlier still before money was current, an untanned goat skin (nkanamu). The chief then sent his messenger to fetch the defendant and when he arrived the hearing took place.

The complainant first stated his case and then the defendant replied. Afterwards the witnesses, if any, the plaintiff's first and then the defendant's, were heard.[3] The chief then decided on the fees to be paid by each party. When they brought those fees the chief heard the pleadings again and then gave his judgment and, if against the defendant, ordered him to compensate the plaintiff and refund to him the fees paid.

Before proceeding further it is important to appreciate that the payment of fees, in courts other than the Kabaka's,[4] was without doubt[5] well-established in ancient Buganda. These fees appear to have been paid by both parties or at any rate by the plaintiff just before judgment and are variously referred to as *mpozensinge*[6] or *obuzza*.[7]

If the evidence did not suffice, the parties would resort to trial by the ordeal. As Hone observed:

---

[1] See p. 37, above.
[2] *Empisa*, p. 238.
[3] Ggomotoka, *op. cit.*, p. 27.
[4] Sir Apolo Kagwa, *Empisa za Baganda ezalondebwamu* (1917), p. 22.
[5] Roscoe, *op. cit.*, p. 260, and Hone, *loc. cit.*
[6] Sir Apolo Kagwa, *ibid.*, and *Empisa*, p. 246.
[7] Ggomotoka, *op. cit.*, p. 26.

" Usually the guilt of the accused was common knowledge and
the business of the court was not to find the facts but to declare
the quantum of punishment. Where, however, there was a denial
of guilt, recourse was had to trial by ordeal. . . ."[1]

Such a test was often resorted to also after the litigants had
exhausted their rights of appeal by appealing to the superior
chiefs, to the Katikkiro and then to the Kabaka.[2]

The ordeal customary in ancient Buganda was by intoxication
and consisted of the two litigants drinking a liquid containing
the crushed fruit of *amaduudu* (a tree of the moonflower (datura)
species). The procedure has been described by all of the main
authorities[3] and I therefore propose to consider this ordeal only
cursorily here with a few additional points. The intoxicating
potion was prepared on appeal from the Kabaka's court by
Magunda of the Civet Cat (Ffumbe) Clan living at Lwanga. In
courts other than the Kabaka's it was permissible for a party to
get a stand-in to submit to the test on his behalf, but it need
hardly be said that no such substitutes were employed when the
charge was of witchcraft or the appeal was from the Kabaka's
court, as failure in the ordeal often meant death. After drinking
the potion, and waiting for the stupefaction to have effect, the
litigants had to get up and step over a plantain stem and thank
the chief in the customary manner (okweyanza). He who failed
to do so or who died from the ill-effects of the potion was held to
have lost the ordeal.

A lesser used alternative method of trial by ordeal was by
passing a hot iron down the litigant's legs, the party who was
burnt losing the test.[4]

If a witness refused to appear at the hearing the court would
arrange for him to be brought by force.[5]

If a man's goods were stolen and he suspected another of
having his property, he could apply to the chief of that area for
a messenger to go and search the suspect's home.[6] If a man met
subsequently a defendant whom he wished to sue but who had
previously disappeared from their area, he could ask a passer-
by to take them to the chief having jurisdiction and he would

---

[1] *Loc. cit.*

[2] Sir Apolo Kagwa, *Empisa*, p. 239.

[3] Sir Apolo Kagwa, *Empisa*, p. 239, Roscoe, *op. cit.*, pp. 266 and 341,
Ggomotoka, *op. cit.*, p. 28 and Mair, *op. cit.*, p. 190.

[4] Roscoe, *op. cit.*, p. 341 and Fraser, *The Native Races of Africa and Madagascar*,
p. 331.

[5] Ggomotoka, *op. cit.*, p. 27.

[6] Sir Apolo Kagwa, *Empisa*, p. 240.

summon their own chiefs to take the parties back to decide the case.[1]

Execution of a judgment debt was made by the successful party having obtained a messenger from the chief.[2] Execution usually consisted of obtaining payment of goods from the losing party or his relatives and, if necessary, plundering his home to obtain all property of value. The property so obtained was taken by the successful party and the official messenger to the chief who took his share and the balance was handed to the successful party.[3]

MODERN RULES OF PRACTICE

The first published collection of rules of court was a booklet of Omulamuzi's *Instructions*, 1916–1918.[4] It contains an undigested mass of instructions issued to ssaza chiefs by the Omulamuzi and translations of communications from the Provincial Commissioner to the Omulamuzi on judicial and prison matters together with specimen forms for court proceedings and returns. The booklet also contained a translation of the 1917 Proclamation. Blasio Kagwa reported in 1927 that the chiefs considered these instructions possessed the force of law and even took precedence over the laws themselves. He accordingly recommended in place of these instructions the drawing up of proper Rules of Court approved by the Chief Justice of Uganda. Such Rules of Procedure were in fact signed by the late Kabaka on the 15th August, 1929, and consisted of twenty-four rules governing the institution of suits, the manner of hearing cases, cases of serious crime, rules of evidence and fees. Unfortunately these rules were never printed but in 1937 another undigested mass of Omulamuzi's circular instructions issued over the preceding six years were published.[5]

The lacuna was not remedied until after the enactment of the Buganda Courts Ordinance, 1940. In 1941 the then Omulamuzi published Directions printed in Luganda and in English made

---

[1] Sir Apolo Kagwa, *Empisa*, p. 240.
[2] Ashe, *Life in Uganda*, p. 294.
[3] Mair, *op. cit.*, p. 133.
[4] This publication was the only one produced to Blasio Kagwa for his examination in 1927.
[5] *Ekitabo ky'Ebiragiro by'Emisango mu Gombolola z'Obwakabaka bwe Buganda*, 1931–1936.

by himself on the advice of the Resident, in fact of the first Judicial Adviser on the Residency staff, under section 20 of the Ordinance for the trial of criminal and civil cases.[1] These Directions were slightly amended as to the several jurisdictions of ggombolola courts, ssaza courts and the Principal Court by a subsequent Omulamuzi on the 20th March, 1951, but otherwise are still in force today. The Directions were probably at that time the most comprehensive set of rules of procedure made for any native courts in Africa and covered in Part I complaints and arrests, the trial of criminal cases, the jurisdiction of various grades of court, evidence, appeals, court forms, juveniles and fees, and in Part II an explanation of the difference between civil and criminal cases, claims, summonses, order of proceedings, plaintiff's duty to prove his case, claim by defendant, procedure when defendant admits the claim, judgments, costs, *ex parte* decisions, adjournments, exemption from court fees, enforcement of judgments, appeals and notes on certain Buganda laws and Protectorate ordinances in relation to civil cases. The Omulamuzi also on the 27th February, 1941, made additional Directions for the trial of criminal cases in the Ggombolola Court of Omukulu we Kibuga, the metropolitan ggombolola, where the existence of the Chief of Police and the Kabaka's Government Police called for modifications of the principal Directions for the trial of criminal cases. These additional Directions were never printed but presumably also still remain in force.

No further booklets of Omulamuzi's instructions were published after 1937 but two such circulars need special mention here:

(i) On the 20th June, 1941, Criminal Direction 55 which awarded the court 5% of the compensation ordered in a criminal case was cancelled and thereby the ancient practice of the court taking *Obuzza* was abolished, a step which had been recommended by Blasio Kagwa in 1927.

(ii) On the 29th May, 1946, the then Omulamuzi ordered that in criminal proceedings if the case could not be brought to trial within a period of six months owing to the disappearance of some party then the case should be closed and that in civil proceedings a similar procedure but with the period at one year should obtain. In either category the case could subsequently be reopened.

---

[4] Directions, Part I, Criminal Cases and Part II, Civil Cases.

It will be convenient at this point to review the decisions of the courts over the last thirty years on procedural points. The first recorded comment is by a Magistrate in 1928 who wrote of a proceeding in the Lukiko Court:

> " The trial was presided over by the Omuwanika in the absence of the Mulamuzi and was conducted in a most unsatisfactory and perfunctory manner."[1]

The procedure of the Lukiko Court was hardly better when the Omulamuzi presided for in the same year we find:

> " The Court of Mengo Lukiko consisting of the Mulamuzi and nine members heard the appeal from the lower Court. The Mulamuzi and one member found the accused guilty. The other eight members found him not guilty. In spite of this heavy majority in favour of the accused he has been convicted and sentenced to one year's R.I."[2]

In a case in 1931 only the Omulamuzi signed a judgment and one of the judges of the Lukiko Court was a close relation of the accused. An order for re-trial was made.[3] In 1954 the High Court held that an appellant had not had a fair trial when he was convicted for forgery by the same judges who had tried a related civil case.[4] But it was not until 1958 that the High Court clamped down on an abuse which was becoming rampant through frequent changes of the judges of the Principal Court, and held that the judges constituting a Principal Court must hear all the evidence themselves before giving judgment otherwise the trial is a nullity.[5]

The former practice of the Buganda courts as to the hearing of witnesses is recorded in a judgment of the first Judicial Adviser exercising the revisional power of the Provincial Commissioner in 1939:

> " The procedure which was adopted by the Lukiko Court follows the customary practice of that Court. On appeals from subordinate native courts it is the practice of the appellate court to call the appellant, the respondent and all or any of the witnesses who gave evidence in the lower court. Their former statements are read over to them and they are questioned by the appellate court and the parties to the suit. If it appears that witnesses have not been called who might have been called, the appellate court calls them and

---

[1] A. H. Cox in P.C.R.O. 125 of 1928, *Kagwa* v. *Kasaja* (unreported).
[2] P.C.R.O. 161 of 1928, *Luboyera* v. *Serunkuma* (unreported).
[3] P.C.R.O. 51 of 1931, *Namayanja* v. *Bamutta* (unreported).
[4] H.C.Cr.A. 75 of 1954, *Kajwala* v. *Lukiko*, Notes 63.
[5] H.C.C.A. 84 of 1956, *Ndiwalana* v. *Katera*, Notes 87.

records their evidence. As regards the swearing of witnesses, it has been the practice of the Lukiko Court to swear witnesses, but if a witness is unwilling to take the oath he is not compelled to do so, and the court merely records that the witness has not been sworn."[1]

This practice of regularly calling witnesses to give additional evidence on appeal was condemned by BENNETT, J., who held that the power must be judicially exercised in accordance with the principles well-recognised under English law.[2] Grounds worthy of consideration in hearing applications to appeal out of time[3] or as a pauper[4] have been indicated by the High Court which has also ruled that there is no right of appeal to it from an interlocutory order of the Principal Court.[5]

In criminal causes and matters the Principal Court has made decisions regarding authority to prosecute,[6] the duty of chiefs,[7] the institution of proceedings,[8] the choice of tribunal,[9] joinder of charges,[10] trial of two counts,[11] the constitution of the court,[12] the summary trial of offences,[13] pleas of guilty,[14] changes of defence,[15] compounding criminal offences,[16] failure to call witnesses,[17] admission of previous convictions[18] and grounds of appeal.[19]

On appeal from the criminal cases originally tried in the Principal Court, the High Court has ruled on prosecution,[20] trials unduly protracted by adjournments,[21] the presence of the accused through the trial,[22] the innocence of the accused,[23] acquittal as

---

[1] P.C.R.O. 23 of 1939, *Serwada* v. *Mukasa* (unreported).
[2] H.C.C.A. 67 of 1953, *Nyanzi* v. *Kayima*, Notes 65.
[3] H.C.C.A. 12 of 1946, *Katende* v. *Musigere and Another*, Notes 19.
[4] H.C.C.A. 14 of 1948, *Kagwa* v. *Parma*, Notes 23.
[5] H.C.C.A. 107 of 1956, *Zzimula* v. *Buganda Government*, Notes 75.
[6] 1956 C.L.R. 33 and 1957 C.L.R. 39.
[7] 1957 C.L.R. 43.
[8] 1957 C.L.R. 41.
[9] 1958 C.L.R. 55.
[10] 1956 C.L.R. 35.
[11] 1958 C.L.R. 55.
[12] 1957 C.L.R. 47.
[13] 1956 C.L.R. 37.
[14] 1957 C.L.R. 81.
[15] 1957 C.L.R. 81.
[16] 1958 C.L.R. 57.
[17] 1957 C.L.R. 79.
[18] 1957 C.L.R. 83.
[19] 1957 C.L.R. 83.
[20] H.C.Cr.R. 43 of 1922, *Rex* v. *Paulo and Others*, 3 U.L.R. 98 and H.C.Cr.A. 178 of 1946, *Musoke* v. *Lukiko*, Notes 17.
[21] H.C.Cr.A. 50 of 1954, *Ediyamu* v. *Lukiko*, Notes 61.
[22] H.C.Cr.A. 63 of 1943, *Lubega and Others* v. *Lukiko*, Notes 9.
[23] H.C.Cr.A. 401 of 1949, *Lwasa* v. *Lukiko*, Notes 27.

a bar to further proceedings,[1] a previous criminal record,[2] assessment of sentences,[3] the imposition of corporal punishment,[4] bail pending appeal[5] and references to the Omulamuzi.[6]

In civil proceedings the Principal Court has considered *inter alia* authority to sue,[7] improper joinder,[8] the power to call witnesses,[9] the service of summonses,[10] payment into court,[11] *ex parte* procedure,[12] *res judicata*[13] and a bailiff's responsibility.[14]

On appeal from civil proceedings originally heard by the Principal Court, the High Court has ruled that the Civil Procedure Ordinance and Rules do not apply,[15] and upon *res judicata*,[16] the value of the subject-matter,[17] a claim for damages subsequent to the date of judgment,[18] *ex parte* procedure[19] and advocates costs in appeals.[20]

Before leaving this subject, the arbitral proceedings which come before the *batongole* and *miruka* chiefs must be considered. No fees are paid for such proceedings;[21] indeed exaction of such fees by a chief is a criminal offence.[22] The procedure of these arbitral authorities has been well described by Gutkind:

---

[1] H.C.Cr.A. 401 of 1949, *Lwasa* v. *Lukiko*, Notes 27.

[2] H.C.Cr.A. 135 of 1940, *Kiyaga* v. *Lukiko*, Notes 1.

[3] H.C.Cr.A. 72 of 1942, *Mukasa* v. *Lukiko*, Notes 1 and H.C.Cr.A. 15 of 1943, *Kafero* v. *Lukiko*, Notes 7.

[4] H.C.Cr.A. 198 of 1940, *Masumbuko* v. *Lukiko*, Notes 1 and H.C.Cr.A. 580 of 1949, *Buteraba* v. *Lukiko*, Notes 31.

[5] H.C.Cr.A. 300–304 of 1957, *Sebanakirya and Others* v. *Lukiko*, Notes 79.

[6] H.C.Misc.A. 10 of 1956, *Mulira and Another* v. *Lukiko* (1957), E.A. 584.

[7] 1957 C.L.R. 165.

[8] P.C.C.C. 173 of 1955, *Mayanja* v. *Mukasa and Another*, 1940–1955 C.L.R.

[9] 1956 C.L.R. 77.

[10] 1957 C.L.R. 169.

[11] 1957 C.L.R. 171.

[12] 1958 C.L.R. 113, 1956 C.L.R. 77 and 1957 C.L.R. 173.

[13] P.C.C.C. 56 of 1954, *Kajugujwe* v. *Mugwanya* (unreported), 1957 C.L.R. 171 and 1958 C.L.R. 113.

[14] P.C.R.O. 25 of 1933, *Balinevumagana* v. *Weraga* (upholding Lukiko Court Case 364 of 1932) (unreported).

[15] H.C.C.A. 35 of 1958, *Ntambi* v. *Jumba*, Bulletin 35/58, and H.C.C.A. 69 of 1956, *Serunkuma* v. *Nandyose*, Bulletin 12/59.

[16] H.C.C.A. 5 of 1953, *Musoke* v. *Mpanga*, Notes 59 and H.C.C.A. 74 of 1957, *Kasolo* v. *Sekubwa* (unreported).

[17] H.C.C.A. 16 of 1945, *Kasozi* v. *Mukasa*, Notes 17.

[18] H.C.C.A. 10 of 1955, *Nantumbwe* v. *Kalibwani*, Notes 69.

[19] H.C.C.A. 27 of 1948, *Sentongo* v. *Katende*, Notes 23, and H.C.C.A. 98 of 1957, *Nakuzabasajja* v. *Mukasa*, Notes 81.

[20] H.C.C.A. 10 of 1941, *Ndagire* v. *Kasozi*, Notes 5.

[21] 1956 C.L.R. 37.

[22] P.C.R.O. 27 of 1928, *Balikupu* v. *Mukasa* (unreported).

"At times, when a case was being tried and the disputants stood in front of the chief and his court, some people collected and listened. They might tender advice but usually the chief would tell them to pass along. The chief, or his assistant, kept a record book. At the conclusion of every meeting, entries were made either by the chief or his assistant or one of the headmen who was selected for this task because of his unusually good handwriting. Sometimes no entries were made even though business had been transacted. There was no special reason for this; it resulted simply from the casual nature of the council and the fact that the book is not a legal record which has to be presented to a higher authority. In some parishes no book whatever is kept, which makes research very difficult, if not impossible. The book records the matters which have been dealt with, and when a case has been tried the disputants sometimes signify their agreement with the court's recommendations by writing their names in the book or by leaving their marks. . . .

As the parish chief and the council have no legal power to enforce their decisions, the disputes brought to the court are often of an unimportant nature. Only occasionally are really serious cases brought forward and the attitude seems to be that presentation to the parish council is just the necessary first step in the hearing of the case. When disputants were asked why they had taken their case to the parish council, they almost always answered that it was the traditional thing to do, adding however that their faith in the court was almost nil. Although both the plaintiffs and defendants often accept the advice of the court, they do so only out of their own goodwill. A number of people come to the court not to have their cases heard, but only to tell the court that there has been a case which they have already solved among themselves. Having told the court this, they then thank it for its deliberations and advice."[1]

The writer then gives a number of specimen cases which illustrate his view.[2]

The language of the Kabaka's courts is Luganda but if any party or witness is unable to use that language an interpreter into and from Luganda into a language known to the person in question is employed.

EVIDENCE

Particularly in the field of evidence can the assimilation of English legal principles by the Kabaka's courts be most clearly observed. Those courts are not bound to follow the English law of evidence[3] nor does the Evidence Ordinance apply to trials before them.[4] They in fact are only bound to follow rules of

---

[1] *Op. cit.*, pp. 200–201.
[2] *Ibid.*, pp. 201–209.
[3] H.C.C.A. 90 of 1955, *Nkeretanyi* v. *Gazanyawo* (unreported).
[4] H.C.Cr.A. 1 of 1944, *Baziwane* v. *Lukiko*, Notes 11.

commonsense and justice in their handling of evidence[1] and such Directions as have been made by the Omulamuzi.[2] The clearest illustration of this assimilation is the subject of hearsay evidence. The High Court has repeatedly held that the rule against the admissibility of hearsay does not apply to native courts,[3] but in 1957 the Principal Court on two occasions at least rejected such evidence in criminal proceedings.[4]

An earlier decision of the High Court that proof of customary law required two witnesses[5] was not followed in the leading " Namasole Case ",[6] wherein WHITLEY, C. J., held that it was wrong to require that custom should be proved in Native Courts in the same way in which it must be proved in British Courts.

The High Court has also ruled on the onus of proof in criminal trials,[7] on the value to be attached to unsworn statements by the accused,[8] on unsworn statements of witnesses taken in rebuttal of a defence,[9] on a witness called by the court at the close of the defence,[10] on a co-accused's evidence,[11] on the inadmissibility for the prosecution of her husband of the evidence of a wife married monogamously[12] and the doctrine of recent possession.[13]

The widescale acceptance by the Principal Court of the English rules regarding burden of proof, quantum of proof, no case to answer, complaint in sexual cases, confessions, benefit of doubt, a *prima facie* case and expert evidence may be readily observed on reference to the Customary Law Reports for the last three years.[14]

There is, however, one indigenous rule of evidence which must also be mentioned and that is evidence of alarm. Alarms must be raised when violence occurs and alarms when raised must be answered by all men who hear them.[15]

---

[1] H.C.C.A. 5 of 1953, *Musoke* v. *Mpanga*, Notes 59.
[2] See p. 289, above.
[3] See H.C.Cr.A. 1 of 1944, H.C.C.A. 90 of 1955 (both cited above) and H.C.Cr.A. 131 and 132 of 1949, *Mubiru and Another* v. *Lukiko*, Notes 25.
[4] 1957 C.L.R. 55–59.
[5] H.C.C.R. 41 of 1921, *R.* v. *Mberebezi*, 3 U.L.R. 79.
[6] H.C.Cr.A. 149 of 1942, *Kigozi* v. *Lukiko*, Notes 7.
[7] H.C.Cr.A. 223 and 224 of 1955, *Kalenzi and Another* v. *Lukiko*, Notes 69.
[8] *Ibid.*
[9] H.C.Cr.A. 101 of 1952, *Nakabale* v. *Lukiko*, Notes 49.
[10] H.C.Cr.A. 263 of 1957, *Ssango* v. *Lukiko* (1958), E.A. 265.
[11] H.C.Cr.A. 31 of 1953, *Kakembo* v. *Lukiko*, Notes 57.
[12] H.C.Cr.A. 64 of 1932, *Petero Sebaggala* v. *R.*, 5 U.L.R. 4.
[13] H.C.Cr.A. 69 of 1956, *Kigundu* v. *Lukiko*, Notes 73.
[14] 1956 C.L.R. 39 *et seq.*, 1957 C.L.R. 51 *et seq.* and 1958 C.L.R. 47 *et seq.*
[15] 1956 C.L.R. 45 and 1957 C.L.R. 61.

Treatment of Offenders

The penal sanctions imposed in Buganda in the last century are described by Ashe:

> " The ordinary punishments in Buganda are death by fire, being hacked to pieces by reed splinters, fine, imprisonment in the stocks (' mvuba '), or in the slave fork (' kaligo '), also mutilation. It is most common to see people deprived of an eye, or in some cases of both eyes; persons lacking their ears are also frequently met with. . . . Other hideous mutilations, but less often practised, are cutting off the lips and nose. Sometimes a hand or both hands or arms are cut off, but this very often proves fatal."[1]

Ggomotoka mentions also imprisonment particularly in the close and strict prison called Nnawanga kept by a person entitled Ssebatta at Mutundwe.[2] The better view, however, appears to be that there were no real prisons until after the advent of the British administration and that previously persons held in custody pending trial or under investigation were confined in the stocks or in a pillory.[3] There does appear to have been a system of bail obtainable from the guards for a fee.[4] At any rate in the closing years of the nineteenth century two main prisons had been established one by the Katikkiro Apolo Kagwa under the custody of a certain Njabule[5] and the other on Rubaga Hill by the Catholic Katikkiro Stanislaus Mugwanya under the custody of a certain Mugatira. On the abolition of the second post of Katikkiro and the creation of the new post of Omulamuzi under the 1900 Agreement, these two prisons were amalgamated.

The collective responsibility of clansmen for their clansman's offence has already been described.[6]

The treatment of offenders which obtained in Uganda in 1918 was considered by Carter, C. J., in the following terms:

> " In this country I consider that the Courts must be governed by the same principle in passing sentence, but the application of the principle requires in my opinion very great modification owing to the circumstances of Uganda.
>
> In the first place the native is accustomed to exceedingly severe punishment at the hands of his chiefs and too sudden a change is inadvisable. Secondly, imprisonment to a native is undoubtedly

---

[1] *Life in Uganda*, p. 293.
[2] *Op. cit.*, p. 26.
[3] Roscoe, *op. cit.*, pp. 22, 23 and 264, Mair, *op. cit.*, p. 188 and Hone, *loc. cit.*
[4] See Roscoe, *ibid.*, and Mair, *ibid.*
[5] The Mmengo prison is still popularly called " wa Njabule ".
[6] See above, p. 73 and Mair, *op. cit.*, p. 189 and Roscoe, *op. cit.*, p. 22.

a very much less severe punishment than it is to a European in England. Thirdly, a lenient sentence is regarded, as a rule, as a sign of weakness. Fourthly, we have no Borstal system, no reformatories and no provision for preventive detention after the expiration of imprisonment."[1]

Figures are available for the prison population of certain years in the 1930's:

in 1932 there was a total of 759 imprisoned of whom 411 were tax defaulters;

in 1933 the total was 481 of whom 242 were tax defaulters;

in 1934 the total was 616 of whom 262 were tax defaulters;

and in 1936 the total had risen to 857 of whom 411 were tax defaulters and 50 were females.

Of recent years the Principal Court has given increasing attention to the appropriate treatment of juvenile offenders[2] and female offenders[3] and to the preventive detention of recidivists.[4]

CONFLICT OF LAWS

There is for practical purposes no conflict of laws in the Kabaka's Courts. Those courts administer and enforce customary law, native law and certain specified Protectorate legislation, but not English law.[5] Where any conflict might have occurred between the customary law and enacted native law or Protectorate legislation, the unwritten customary law is automatically revoked.[6] There is no provision for resolving conflict between native laws and Protectorate legislation but since the former under Article 26 of the Constitution of Buganda require the Governor's prior approval no such conflict should arise. The only conflict which might arise is between Ganda and foreign customary law. The attitude of the Kabaka's courts to such a possible conflict has already been described[7] and the rule appears to have been evolved that if both parties are foreigners and their contract was under foreign customary law the Kabaka's courts

---

[1] H.C.C.R. (1918), *R. v. Astaliko Ngobi*, 2 U.L.R. 287.

[2] 1956 C.L.R. 39, 1957 C.L.R. 85 and *Report of the McKisack Committee of Enquiry into the Problem and Treatment of Juvenile Delinquency in Uganda*, 1958, paras. 120–125.

[3] 1957 C.L.R. 87.

[4] 1957 C.L.R. 91.

[5] See p. 29, above.

[6] And see section 8 of the Adultery and Fornication Law.

[7] See p. 70, above.

will apply that law.[1] The Principal Court also has accepted a defence of foreign custom to a criminal charge based on Ganda customary law although made under the Witchcraft Ordinance, 1957.[2] That court has permitted proof of foreign customary law.[3] But has refused to allow a male Ganda plaintiff to plead foreign customary law as the law governing his marriage to a woman of another tribe.[4]

English law, as has been stated, is not administered by the Kabaka's courts but those courts particularly in the spheres of the laws of contracts, corporations, torts and crimes and of procedure including evidence have, as has been described, shown a desire to adopt and assimilate that law. To the extent that that assimilated English law conflicts with the ancient customary law, the customary law is ousted. But this conflict rarely arises although the assimilation of English law is now wholesale because that law is generally adopted to fill lacunae in the customary law or native law.

There is and has been, however, some conflict between the jurisdiction of the Buganda courts and the jurisdiction of the Protectorate courts.[5] This conflict usually arises in regard to serious crime committed outside townships or municipalities which is within the jurisdiction of the Buganda courts but which the Protectorate Police not unnaturally prefer to prosecute under the Protectorate Penal Code. There is a decision of the High Court that once the charge has been laid under the Penal Code the accused cannot be tried for a similar offence under customary law and so the case cannot be transferred from a Protectorate to a Buganda court which has no jurisdiction in respect of the particular section of the Penal Code.[6] In civil matters there is a recent decision of the High Court already noted[7] that if a plaint is framed under Protectorate legislation not administered by the Buganda courts the latter's normal jurisdiction in suits of that nature would be ousted.

---

[1] 1956 C.L.R. 1.
[2] 1957 C.L.R. 1.
[3] 1958 C.L.R. 1.
[4] 1957 C.L.R. 143.
[5] See E.A.C.A., C.A. 7 of 1939, *Nadiope* v. *Mwebe* (1939), 6 E.A.C.A. 44 and H.C.C.C. 20 of 1957, *Kaluba* v. *Kajaya* (1957), E.A. 312.
[6] H.C.Cr.R. 42 of 1942, *R.* v. *Yoanna Muigira*, 6 U.L.R. 118.
[7] See p. 239, above.

APPENDICES

SUMMARY

PAGE

APPENDIX 1   Diagrams of Judicial Systems
     (a) Pre-1940   301
     (b) 1940–1954   301
     (c) Modern   301

APPENDIX 2   List of Clans   302

APPENDIX 3   Chronological Tables
     (a) Orders in Council   304
     (b) Agreements   306
     (c) Native Laws   307
     (d) Protectorate Legislation not specified   .   .   313
     (e) Protectorate Legislation specified   .   .   314
     (f) Protectorate Legislation affecting Buganda
        Courts   317

APPENDIX 4   The Succession Order, 1926   .   .   .   320

APPENDIX 5   List of Ministers of Justice   .   .   .   332

APPENDIX 6   Luganda Proverbs connected with the Administra-
     tion of Justice   333

APPENDIX 7   Glossary of Luganda Terms   .   .   .   335

APPENDIX 8   Bibliography   336

APPENDIX 1

DIAGRAMS OF JUDICIAL SYSTEMS

(Full lines indicate appeal, dotted lines revision).

(a) <u>Pre-1940</u>

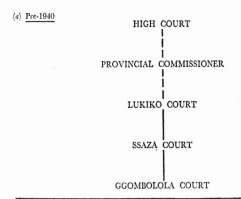

HIGH COURT

PROVINCIAL COMMISSIONER

LUKIKO COURT

SSAZA COURT

GGOMBOLOLA COURT

(b) <u>1940-1954</u>

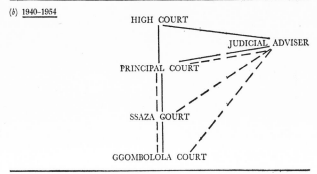

HIGH COURT

JUDICIAL ADVISER

PRINCIPAL COURT

SSAZA COURT

GGOMBOLOLA COURT

(c) <u>Modern</u>

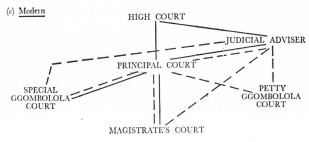

HIGH COURT

JUDICIAL ADVISER

PRINCIPAL COURT

SPECIAL GGOMBOLOLA COURT

PETTY GGOMBOLOLA COURT

MAGISTRATE'S COURT

APPENDIX 2

LIST OF CLANS

Clan	Clan (English translation)	Title of Head of Clan	Ssaza where Headquarters are	Remarks
Ekirangira	Princely	Ssabalangira	Busiro	
Ababiito (Bunyoro)	Favourites (Bunyoro)	Kitahimbwa	Bugangazzi	
Ababiito (Kkooki)	Favourites (Kkooki)	Ssababiito Kamuswaga	Kkooki	Kamuswaga is the descendant of the ancient Kings of Kkooki and the only hereditary ssaza chief now in Buganda
Ababiito (Kiziba)	Favourites (Kiziba)	Lutayinzibwa	Buddu	
Mmamba	Lungfish	Gabunga	Busiro	The largest clan
Nkima	Monkey	Mugema	Busiro	
Ffumbe	Civet cat	Walusimbi	Busiro	
Mpeewo	Oribi	Kibaale	Kyaddondo	
Lugave	Scaly ant-eater	Ndugwa	Mawokota	
Ngo	Leopard	Mutesasira	Butambala	
Butiko	Mushroom	Gunju	Busiro	
Katinvuma	Small shrub	Kyaddondo	Kyaddondo	
Ngeye	Colobus monkey	Kasujja	Busiro	
Kasimba	Genet	Kabazzi	Mawokota	
Mpologoma	Lion	Namuguzi Ssebuganda	Bulemeezi	
Ngabi	Bush-buck	Nsamba	Mawokota	
Kkobe	Yam	Namwama	Mawokota	
Nsenene	Edible grasshopper	Mugalula	Ggomba	
Mbogo	Buffalo	Kaira	Ssingo	
Nngonge	Otter	Kisolo	Busujju	
Mutima	Heart	Kakeeto	Buddu	
Kibe	Jackal	Muyige	Kyaggwe	
Njaza	Reed-buck	Kitanda	Kyaggwe	
Mbwa	Dog	Mutasingwa	Busujju	
Ntalaganya	Blue duiker	Bbambaga	Ggomba	
Mpindi	Bean	Mazige	Busiro	
Nvubu	Hippopotamus	Kaita	Kyaggwe	
Njovu	Elephant	Mukalo	Busiro	
Nte	Cow	Katongole	Buddu	
Nnonyi Ennyange	White egret	Mbaziira	Kyaggwe	

Clan	Clan (English translation)	Title of Head of Clan	Ssaza where Headquarters are	Remarks
nonyi nakinsige	Brown grass finch	Kyeyune	Kyaggwe	This clan came into separate existence out of the main Nnonyi Clan in September 1958
namungoona	White shouldered crow	Kajabuwongwa	Ggomba	
gaali	Crested crane	Mawesano	Buddu	
kaliisa	Tick-eater	Kaliika	Buddu	
kerebwe	Squirrel	Kiddimbo	Ssingo	
ayozi	Jumping-rat	Magambo	Mawokota	
1usu	Edible rat	Muyingo	Mawokota	
1azzi-ge-kisasi	Rainwater	Woyo	Buddu	
1suma	Fish	Kibondwe	Buvuma	
kejje	Sprat	Kikwata	Kyaggwe	
inyomo	Red ant	Nakigoye	Buddu	
ukato	Bodkin	Lutagi	Bugangazzi	
1swaswa	Monitor lizard	Mayengo	Buvuma	
1sogasoga	Castor oil berry	Makweyenge	Ssingo	A very small clan
kula	Rhinoceros	Senkula	Bugerere	
1jobe	Marsh antelope	Kiyise	Ssingo	
iwere	Rumex plant	Luwombo	Ssingo	
1kebuka	Dung	?	?	This clan from understandable embarrassment first pretended its clan name was Nswera (Fly) and then dispersed into large clans like the Mmamba (Lungfish) and Ngabi (Bush-buck)
1diga	Sheep	Lwomwa	Mawokota	

APPENDIX 3

CHRONOLOGICAL TABLES

(a) ORDERS IN COUNCIL

Title	Remarks
The Africa Order in Council, 1889 The Africa Order in Council, 1892 The Africa Order in Council, 1893 The Africa (Acquisition of Lands) Order in Council, 1898 The African Protectorates (Capital Sentences) Order in Council, 1898	Repealed with certain provisoes by the Uganda Order in Council, 1902
The Uganda Order in Council, 1902	
The Eastern African Protectorates (Court of Appeal) Order in Council, 1902	Repealed by the Eastern African Protectorates (Court of Appeal) Order in Council, 1909
The East Africa and Uganda (Currency) Order in Council, 1905	
The Eastern African Protectorates (Court of Appeal) Order in Council, 1906	Repealed by the Eastern African (Court of Appeal) Order in Council, 1909
The East Africa and Uganda (Currency) Order in Council, 1906	
The Colonial Prisoners Removal Order in Council, 1907	
Order in Council of 4th July, 1908	Providing for depositions for the purposes of the Workmen's Compensation Act, 1906
The Eastern African Protectorates (Court of Appeal) Order in Council, 1909	Repealed by the East Africa (Court of Appeal) Order in Council, 1921
The Eastern African Protectorates (Appeal to Privy Council) Order in Council, 1909	Repealed by the East Africa (Appeal to Privy Council) Order in Council, 1921
Order in Council of 18th October, 1909	Applying the Evidence (Colonial Statutes) Act, 1907, to certain countries including Uganda
The Uganda Order in Council, 1911	
The Uganda Order in Council, 1913	Repealed by the Uganda Order in Council, 1920
The Uganda Order in Council, 1920	
The Uganda (Amendment) Order in Council, 1953	
The Buganda (Powers of Regents) Order in Council, 1954	Revoked by the Buganda Agreement, 1955, Order in Council, 1955

Title	Remarks
The Uganda (Amendment) Order in Council, 1954	
The Buganda (Transitional Provisions) Order in Council, 1955	Revoked by the Buganda Agreement, 1955, Order in Council, 1955
The Buganda Agreement, 1955, Order in Council, 1955	
The Uganda (Amendment) Order in Council, 1955	
The Buganda Constitution (Appeal to Privy Council) Order in Council, 1958	Regulating procedure in appeals from High Court on reference by Governor for interpretation of the Constitution of Buganda
The Uganda (Amendment) Order in Council, 1958	

(b) AGREEMENTS

Title	Remarks
The Uganda Agreement, 1894	
The Uganda Agreement, 1900	Amended by the Buganda (Transitional) Agreement, 1955 and the Buganda Agreement, 1955
The Uganda Agreement (Poll Tax), 1904	Cancelled by the Uganda Agreement (Poll Tax), 1909
The Uganda Agreement (Judicial), 1905	Divorce Cases were transferred to the High Court by order thereunder dated 23rd January, 1905
The Uganda Memorandum of Agreement (Forest), 1907	
The Uganda (Payment to Chiefs) Agreement, 1908	
The Uganda Agreement (Poll Tax), 1909	Cancelled by the Uganda Agreement (Poll Tax), 1920
The Buganda Agreement (Native Laws), 1910	Revoked by the Buganda (Transitional) Agreement, 1955 and the Buganda Agreement, 1955
The Buganda Agreement (Allotment and Survey), 1913	
The Uganda Agreement (Payments by the Government), 1913	Amended by the Uganda Agreement (Payments by the Government), 1920
The Uganda Agreement (Poll Tax), 1920	
The Uganda Agreement (Payments by the Government, 1920	
The Uganda Agreement (Taxation of Natives), 1922	Expired 31st December, 1925
The Uganda Agreement (Clan Cases), 1924	
The Uganda Agreement (Taxation of Natives), 1926	Expired 31st December, 1926
The Buganda (Declaratory) Agreement (Native Laws), 1937	Revoked by the Buganda (Transitional) Agreement, 1955 and the Buganda Agreement, 1955
The Buganda (Transitional) Agreement, 1955	
The Buganda Agreement, 1955	
The References to the High Court (Procedure) Directions, 1958	
The References to the High Court (Procedure) (Amendment) Directions, 1958	

(c) NATIVE LAWS

Date of Enactment	Non-Disallowance	Title	Remarks
8th April, 1904	—	The Vaccination Law, 1904	Superseded by the Prevention of Small-pox Law, 1915
3th May, 1904	—	The Law for the Registration of Births and Deaths, 1904	Repealed as to the registration of births by the 1923 law and consolidated with the 1923 law in the Revised Edition, 1941
8th May, 1904	—	The Guardianship Law	
6th June, 1904	—	The Rape Law, 1904	Repealed by section 6 of the Adultery and Fornication Law, 1917
6th June, 1904	—	The Prevention of Abortion Law, 1904	Repealed by the Law to Prevent Abortion, 1947
6th June, 1904	—	The Tax Collection Law, 1904	Repealed by the Busulu and Envujo Law, 1927
6th June, 1904	—	The Prevention of Cheating Law, 1904	
6th June, 1904	—	The Carrying of Knives Law, 1904 .	
6th June, 1904	—	The Hut Tax Evasion Law, 1904	
6th June, 1904	—	The Njayi Law, 1904	Repealed by Notice of 14th January, 1918
7th April, 1906	—	The Law of Using Indecent Language	Repealed by the 1947 Law
1th April, 1908	—	The Law for Prevention of Spreading Sleeping Sickness, 1908	
5th June, 1908	—	The Land Law, 1908	
4th June, 1909	—	The Land Law, 1909	Repealed by the Land Law, 1909 (Repeal) Law, 1938
2nd July, 1909	—	The Land Law (Survey), 1909	
3th Jan., 1910	—	The Law for the people who do not pay their taxes before the end of the year for which it is due, 1910	Repealed by Repeal Law, 1941
3th June, 1911	—	The Boundary Marks Law, 1911	
1th July, 1912	27th July, 1912	The Land Law, 1912	
5th Oct., 1912	23rd Oct., 1912	The Land Succession Law, 1912	

Date of Enactment	Non-Disallowance	Title	Remarks
6th June, 1913	—	The Law for preventing Venereal Disease, 1913	
22nd Sept., 1913	—	The Land Law (Survey), 1913	
4th Sept., 1915	—	The Prevention of Smallpox Law, 1915	
6th Sept., 1916	—	The Wills Law, 1916	Omitted from the Revised Edition of the Buganda Native Laws, 1957, as about to be superseded by more comprehensive legislation
12th Oct., 1916	—	The Law for preventing the Native Tabulu Dance and certain other Native Dances, 1916	
14th June, 1917	—	The Native Liquor Law, 1917	Repealed by the Native Liquor Law 1938
24th May, 1918	4th June, 1918	The Adultery and Fornication Law, 1917	
12th May, 1919	28th Aug., 1919	The Prevention of Smallpox (Amendment) Law, 1919	
15th July, 1919	30th June, 1919	The Cotton Cultivation Law, 1919	Repealed by the Buganda Cotton Cultivation Law, 1938
18th Aug., 1920	31st Aug., 1920	The Coming of Age Law, 1920	
1st Oct., 1920	8th Sept., 1920	The Luwalo Law, 1920	Repealed by the Luwalo Law, 1927
1st March, 1921	12th March, 1921	The Luwalo (Amendment) Law, 1921	Repealed by the Luwalo Law, 1927
2nd June, 1921	—	The Luwalo (Amendment No. 2) Law, 1921	Repealed by the Luwalo Law, 1927
27th Oct., 1921	21st Dec., 1921	The Law to provide for the payment for food supplied to the labourers employed in cutting and clearing Mailo Boundaries, 1921	Repealed by the Mailo Survey (Fees) Law, 1933
8th May, 1922	15th June, 1922	The Law relating to the payment of Fees for preparation of Final Certificates, 1922	Repealed by the Mailo Survey (Fees) Law, 1933
24th May, 1923	25th May, 1923	The Buganda Births Registration Law, 1923	
4th April, 1924	31st Jan., 1925	The Native Liquor (Amendment) Law, 1924	
10th March, 1927	23rd March, 1927	The Incendiarism (Prevention) Law, 1927	Repealed by the 1932 Law
25th April, 1927	4th May, 1927	The Native Liquor (Amendment) Law, 1927	

Date of Enactment	Non-Disallowance	Title	Remarks
4th July, 1927	12th Aug., 1927	The Busulu and Envujo Law, 1927	
18th Aug., 1927	19th Dec., 1927	The Luwalo Law, 1927	Repealed by the Luwalo Law, 1930
14th March, 1928	25th May, 1928	The Land Tax Law, 1928	Repealed by the Land Tax Law, 1932
15th Oct., 1928	7th Nov., 1928	The Land Tax Law, 1929	Repealed by the Land Tax Law, 1932
25th March, 1929	27th March, 1929	The Land Law, 1929	
13th Nov., 1929	3rd Dec., 1929	The Land Tax (No. 2) Law, 1929	
17th May, 1930	21st May, 1930	The Luwalo Law, 1930	Repealed by the Luwalo Law, 1939
1st Nov., 1930	17th Dec., 1930	The Luwalo (Amendment) (No. 1) Law, 1930	
17th Nov., 1930	9th Dec., 1930	The Cultivation of Food-stuffs Law, 1930	Repealed by the Agricultural Law, 1946
27th Nov., 1931	10th Dec., 1931	The Luwalo (Amendment) Law, 1931	
7th Dec., 1931	12th Dec., 1931	The Baganda Township Sanitary Law, 1931	Repealed by the Repeal Law, 1941
4th May, 1932	8th June, 1932	The Incendiarism Prevention Law, 1932	
9th May, 1932	12th July, 1932	The Land Tax (Amendment) Law, 1932	
26th May, 1932	17th June, 1932	The Law to provide for the payment of food supplied to the labourers employed in cutting and clearing Mailo Boundaries Law, 1932	Repealed by the Mailo Survey (Fees) Law, 1933
29th July, 1932	—	Order under section 2 of the Land Tax (Amendment) Law, 1932	
16th Aug., 1932	24th Aug., 1932	The Baganda Township Sanitary (Amendment) Law, 1931	Repealed by the Repeal Law, 1941
16th Dec., 1932	28th Dec., 1932	The Land Tax Law, 1932	Repealed by the Land Tax Law, 1939
4th March, 1933	23rd March, 1933	The Mailo Survey (Fees) Law, 1933	
15th March, 1933	6th April, 1933	The Land Tax (Amendment) Law, 1933	
9th Oct., 1933	27th Oct., 1933	The Luwalo (Amendment) Law, 1933	
27th April, 1934	12th May, 1934	The Busulu and Envujo (Amendment) Law, 1934	
10th Jan., 1938	29th Jan., 1938	The Buganda Cotton Cultivation Law, 1938	Repealed by the Agricultural Law, 1946

Date of Enactment	Non-Disallowance	Title	Remarks
31st May, 1938	—	The Land Law, 1909 (Repeal) Law, 1938	
31st May, 1938	—	The Carrying of Knives (Amendment) Law, 1938	
31st May, 1938	—	The Adultery and Fornication (Amendment) Law, 1938	
31st May, 1938	—	The Native Liquor Law, 1938	Repealed by the Native Liquor Law, 1941
21st April, 1939	—	The Land Tax Law, 1939	
29th April, 1939	L.N.19/40	The Luwalo Law, 1939	Repealed by the Graduated Tax Law, 1954
16th Aug., 1939	L.N.19/40	The Land (Agreements) Law, 1939	
28th Dec., 1940	L.N.161/41	The Vagrancy Law, 1940	Repealed (erroneously) by the Vagrancy Law, 1945
15th Feb., 1941	L.N.190/41	The Prevention of Prostitution Law, 1941	
15th March, 1941	L.N.190/41	The Native Liquor Law, 1941	Notices of commencement of certain sections in L.N.'s 190 and 210 of 1941
24th April, 1941	L.N.206/41	The Preservation of the Amenities of the Lubiri Law, 1941	
13th May, 1941	L.N.229/41	The Revised Edition of the Buganda Laws Law, 1941	Repealed by the Revised Edition of the Buganda Laws Law, 1957
17th May, 1941	L.N.274/41	The Repeal Law, 1941	
27th March, 1942	L.N.193/42	The Busulu and Envujo (Amendment) Law, 1942	
17th April, 1942	L.N.204/42	The Land (Amendment) Law, 1942	
23rd Dec., 1943	L.N.102/44	The Vagrancy (Amendment) Law, 1943	Repealed by the Vagrancy Law, 1945
9th Feb., 1944	L.N.102/44	The Planting of Trees Law, 1944	
11th Feb., 1944	L.N.102/44	The Busulu and Envujo (Amendment) Law, 1944	
30th Oct., 1945	L.N.6/46	The Law to empower the Kabaka to acquire land for purposes beneficial to the Nation	

Date of Enactment	Non-Disallowance	Title	Remarks
4th Nov., 1945	L.N.241/45	The Law for Selecting Un-official Representatives to the Councils, 1945	Ceased to apply to election of repre-sentatives to the Great Lukiko under the 1953 Law
3th April, 1946	L.N.9/47	The Vagrancy Law, 1945	
0th Sept., 1946	L.N.70/47	The Busulu and Nvujo (Amendment) Law, 1946	
0th Sept., 1946	L.N.70/47	The Luwalo (Amendment) Law, 1946	
5th Nov., 1946	L.N.70/47	The Agricultural Law, 1946	Corrigendum in L.N.76/47
5th Nov., 1946	L.N.48/57	The Mailo Survey Fees (Amendment) Law, 1946	
3th Dec., 1946	L.N.70/47	The Luwalo (Amendment) (No. 2) Law, 1946	
0th June, 1947	—	The Law to Prevent Abor-tion, 1947	
0th June, 1947	—	The Law to Prevent the Use of Indecent Language, 1947	
0th June, 1947	—	The Native Liquor (Amend-mend) Law, 1947	
0th June, 1947	—	The Luwalo (Amendment) Law, 1947	
0th June, 1947	—	The Town Planning Law, 1947	Repealed by the Buganda Town Planning and Build-ing Law, 1958
0th Nov., 1950	L.N.201/51	The Law for the Establish-ment of Lower Councils in Buganda	Corrigenda in L.N.'s 30/51 and 60/57
0th Nov., 1950	L.N.201/51	The Law to amend the Law for Selecting Non-official Representatives to the Coun-cils, 1950	Corrigendum in L.N.234/52
1st March, 1951	—	The Law to amend the Law to empower the Kabaka to acquire land for purposes beneficial to the Nation	
1st March, 1951	—	The Busulu and Nvujo (Amendment) Law, 1951	
2nd March, 1951	—	Notices under the Native Liquor Law, 1941	Amending First and Second Schedules
7th Sept., 1951	L.N.202/52	The Buganda Government Shop Law, 1950	
7th Sept., 1951	L.N.202/52	The Buganda Government Shop Building Law, 1950	
0th Oct., 1952	—	Notices under the Native Liquor Law, 1941	
2nd May, 1953	—	The Education Tax Law	
5th Oct., 1953	—	The Law for the Establish-ment of Lower Councils in Buganda (Amendment) Law, 1953	Order altering date L.N.282/53

Date of Enactment	Non-Disallowance	Title	Remarks
6th Oct., 1953	—	The Great Lukiko (Election of Representatives) Law, 1953	
21st July, 1954	—	The Adultery and Fornication (Amendment) Law, 1954	
7th Oct., 1954	—	The Busulu and Envujo (Amendment) Law, 1953	Alteration of Fir Schedule L.N.29 54
28th Dec., 1954	—	The Graduated Tax Law.	Corrigendum L.N.8/55
28th Dec., 1954	—	The Law for the Establishment of Lower Councils in Buganda (Amendment) Law, 1954	
15th July, 1955	—	The Repatriation of Undesirable Foreigners Law of 1954	
20th Jan., 1956	—	The Salary of the Speaker Law	
24th Jan., 1956	—	The Law for the Establishment of Lower Councils in Buganda (Amendment) Law, 1955	
24th Dec., 1956	—	The Land Tax (Variation of Areas) Order, 1956	
24th Dec., 1956	—	Order under the Graduated Tax Law	Adding Grade VI
8th May, 1957	—	The Revised Edition of the Buganda Laws Law, 1957	Notice of bringi into force L.N.13 58
6th Jan., 1958	—	The Adultery and Fornication (Amendment) Law, 1957	
6th Jan., 1958	—	The Buganda Government Shop Law, 1950—Variation of Schedule	
28th March, 1958	—	The Buganda Town Planning and Building Law, 1958	

(d) Protectorate Legislation Not Specified

Year	Ordinance No.	Title	Remarks
1897	4	The Uganda Land Regulations, 1897	Secs. 6 and 8 repealed
1900	29	The Hut Tax Regulations, 1900	
	30	The Native Gun Tax Regulations, 1900	Repealed
	35	The Native Liquor Regulations, 1900	Repealed
1901	2	The Gambling Regulations, 1901	
	5	The Uganda Marriage Ordinance, 1902	Repealed
	7	The Native Liquor Ordinance, 1902	
	8	The Uganda Land Regulations, 1902	See cap. 113
	11	The Uganda Marriage (Amendment) Ordinance, 1902	
1903	2	The Crown Lands Ordinance, 1903	See cap. 117
	14	The Native Marriage Ordinance, 1903	See cap. 111
1904	2	The Uganda Marriage (Repeal) Ordinance, 1904	
	3	The Uganda Registration of Documents Ordinance, 1904	
	8	The Uganda Registration of Documents (Amendment) Ordinance, 1904	
	15	The Divorce Ordinance, 1904	See cap. 112
1905	4	The Registration of Documents Ordinance, 1905	
1906	3	The Uganda Land Transfer Ordinance, 1906	
	6	The Native Marriage Fees Ordinance, 1906	
	7	The Uganda Muhammadan Marriage and Divorce Ordinance, 1906	See cap. 110
	10	The Native Liquors Ordinance, 1906	
1908	11	The Registration of Land Ordinance, 1908	
1909	16	The Land (Perpetual Succession) Ordinance, 1909	
1910	4	The Poll Tax (Baganda and Basoga) Ordinance, 1910	
1918	9	The Illiterates Protection Ordinance, 1918	
1919	15	The Native (Official Estates) Ordinance, 1919	Cap. 122, amended. O.3/20 and L.N.213/56
	17	The Native Authority Ordinance, 1919	Cap. 72 amended. O.14/23, 2/55 and 22/58
1920	3	The Native Official Estates Ordinance, 1920	
1920	27	The Poll Tax Ordinance, 1920	
1921	27	The Buganda Taxation Ordinance, 1921	
1922	14	The Native Land in Buganda (Provisional Certificates) Ordinance, 1922	Cap. 121
	22	The Registration of Titles Ordinance, 1922	Cap. 123
1923	14	The Native Authority (Amendment) Ordinance, 1923	
1938	8	The Native Administration (Incorporation) Ordinance, 1938	Cap. 73 as amended O.46/58
1939	12	The Survey Ordinance, 1939	Cap. 125 amended O.18/55
1944	6	The Land Transfer Ordinance, 1944	Cap. 114 amended O.18/56
1955	2	The African Authority (Amendment) Ordinance, 1955	

M

(e) PROTECTORATE LEGISLATION SPECIFIED

Date Specified	By Legal Notice or by Warrant	Legislation	Courts Empowered	Cancellation
1st Sept., 1940	Warrant	Poll Tax Ordinance, 1939 Witchcraft Ordinance, Cap. 140 Diseases of Animals Ordinance, Cap. 55 Public Health Ordinance, Cap. 145 Sleeping Sickness Ordinance, Cap. 158 Masters and Servants Ordinance, Cap. 106; Section 58(1)	All Ssaza and Ggombolola Courts	Replaced by new warrants—27-9-54
1st Sept., 1940	Warrant	Townships Ordinance, 1938	Ggombolola of Omukulu we Kibuga Ssaza and Ggombolola Courts	Replaced by new warrant—27-9-54
13th May, 1943	L.N.139/43	Defence (Amendment of Laws) (No. 12) Regulations, 1942 (relating to offence of engaging in green hide trade without a licence)		
5th July, 1944	L.N.158/44	Defence (Control of Prices and Distribution) Regulations, 1943, regulation 11(1).	Ssaza and Ggombolola Courts	Replaced by L.N.103/47
22nd Dec., 1945	L.N.271/45	Penal Code, sections 173 and 174	All Buganda Courts	Replaced by warrant—27-9-54
26th July, 1946	L.N.141/46	Defence (Control of Prices and Distribution) Regulations, 1943, regulations 15, 16 and 17(2)	Ssaza and Ggombolola Courts	Replaced by L.N.103/47
19th Dec., 1946	L.N.78/47	Prevention of Cruelty to Animals Ordinance, Cap. 139	All Buganda Courts	Replaced by warrant—27-9-54
6th Mar., 1947	L.N.57/47	Defence (Control of Prices and Distribution) Regulations, 1943, regulations 15, 16 and 17(2)	All Buganda Courts	Replaced by L.N.103/47
20th May, 1947	L.N.103/47	Defence (Control of Prices and Distribution) Regulations, 1943, regulations 11(1), 11(2), 15, 16, 17(2) and 25	All Buganda Courts	Replaced by L.N.116/53

Date	L.N. No.	Legislation	Courts	Repealed
7th July, 1948	L.N.120/48	Census Ordinance, Cap. 25	All Ssaza and Ggombolola Courts	Repealed
2nd May, 1949	L.N.127/49	Cotton Ordinance, 1927, Section 50	All Buganda Courts	Replaced by warrant—27–9–54
27th June, 1950	L.N.146/50	Police Ordinance, 1939, sections 67, 68 and 69	All Buganda Courts	Replaced by warrant—27–9–54
3rd July, 1950	L.N.161/50	Uganda Employment Ordinance, 1946, sub-section 67(1)	All Buganda Courts	Replaced by warrant—27–9–54
24th Sept., 1952	L.N.256/52	Hide and Skin Trade Ordinance, 1951, sections 4, 13 and 15(2) and rule 11 of Hide and Skin Trade Rules, 1951	All Buganda Courts	Replaced by warrant—27–9–54
20th May, 1953	L.N.116/53	Distribution and Price of Goods Ordinance, 1952, sections 6, 7, 8, 9, 10, 11, 12 and 13	All Buganda Courts	Replaced by warrant—27–9–54
27th Sept., 1954 onwards	Warrant	Penal Code, Cap. 22, sections 162 and 163 Police Ordinance, Cap. 56, sections 63, 64 and 65 Uganda Employment Ordinance, Cap. 83, section 68(1)(a) Public Health Ordinance, Cap. 98 Sleeping Sickness Ordinance, Cap. 100 Townships Ordinance, Cap. 102 Diseases of Animals Ordinance, Cap. 158 African Poll Tax Ordinance, Cap. 187 Hide and Skin Trade Ordinance, 1951, sections 4 and 13 and rule 11 thereunder Cotton Ordinance, 1952, section 31 Distribution and Price of Goods Ordinance, 1952, sections 6, 7, 8, 9, 10, 11, 12 and 13 Witchcraft Ordinance, Cap. 23 Prevention of Cruelty to Animals Ordinance, Cap. 157	Buganda Magistrate's Courts (as and when established)	Repealed 1–1–59

Date Specified	By Legal Notice or by Warrant	Legislation	Courts Empowered	Cancellation
1st Oct., 1954	Warrant	Ditto (with exception of Townships Ordinance, Cap. 102	Special Ggombolola Courts (as and when established)	
4th Oct., 1954	L.N.279/54	Townships Ordinance, Cap. 102	Ggombolola Court of Mutuba III, Bulemeezi	Repealed 1–1–59
4th Oct., 1954	L.N.280/54	Townships Ordinance, Cap. 102	Ggombolola Court of Mumyuka, Buweekula	Repealed 1–1–59
4th Oct., 1954	L.N.281/54	Townships Ordinance, Cap. 102	Ggombolola Court of Mutuba VI, Buddu	Repealed 1–1–59
28th May, 1955	L.N.174/55	Townships Ordinance, Cap. 102	Ggombolola Court of Ssabaddu, Buddu	Repealed 1–1–59
27th June, 1955	L.N.173/55	Townships Ordinance, Cap. 102	Principal Court	Repealed 1–1–59
3rd Nov., 1955	L.N.218/55	Townships Ordinance, Cap. 102	Ggombolola Court of Mutuba I, Mawokota	Repealed 1–1–59
18th Nov., 1955	L.N.2/56	Fish and Crocodiles Ordinance, Cap. 161, sections 5, 7(1), 7(3), 9, 18, 19, 20, 23, 24, 35, 36, 37, 39 and 41	Magistrate's Court Buweekula, Bugangazi and Buyaga and Ggombolola Court of Ssabaddu, Buyaga Petty	
1st Jan., 1959	Warrant	African Poll Tax Ordinance, Cap. 187.		

(f) PROTECTORATE LEGISLATION AFFECTING BUGANDA COURTS

Year	Ordinance No.	Title	Remarks
1902	10	The Subordinate Courts Ordinance, 1902	
1904	16	The Uganda Appeal Ordinance, 1904	
1905	10	The Native Courts Ordinance, 1905	Repealed by O.12/11
		Native Courts in Buganda Proclamation of 29th January, 1909	The first major definition of the powers and jurisdiction of the Buganda Courts
1909	15	The Native Courts Ordinance, 1909	Repealed by O.12/11
		Amending Proclamation of 4th November, 1909	Mubendi substituted for Kakumiro
1910	12	The Uganda Appeal Ordinance, 1910	Repealed by O.12/11
1911	12	The Courts Ordinance, 1911	
		Amending Proclamation of 3rd March, 1911	re Ssabaddu, Buyaga
		Amending Proclamation of 10th November, 1911	re Sesse and Buvuma
1912	1	The Courts (Amendment) Ordinance, 1912	Substituting definition for " Native of the District "
		The Appeal Rules, 1912	Made under Article 22 of the Ug.OIC 1902
1913		Amending Proclamation of 6th January, 1913	Adding Mutuba IV, Buyaga
		Amending Proclamation of 24th March, 1913	Adding Kibuga, Kyaddondo
	4	The Courts (Amendment) Ordinance, 1913	Repealing O.1/12
1914		Amending Proclamation of 22nd May, 1914	re Kabula and Mawogola
		Amending Proclamation of 24th June, 1914	re Mutuba IV, Busiro
1916		Proclamation of 18th May, 1916	Recital of Native Courts existing in Buganda
		Amending Proclamation of 6th July, 1916	Adding Court of the Lukiko
1917	12	The Courts (Amendment) Ordinance, 1917	Amending definition of " Native of the Protectorate "
		Native Courts in Buganda Proclamation of 27th October, 1917	The second major definition of the powers and jurisdiction of the Buganda Courts
1918		Amending Proclamation of 29th April, 1918	
		The Court Fees (No. 2) Rules, 1918	Fees prescribed on appeal or revision from Native Court
1919		The Courts Ordinance, 1919	
		The Criminal Procedure Ordinance, 1919	
		The Native Law Ordinance, 1919	
1924		The Legal Practitioners Rules, 1924	
1925		Proclamation and Notice of 30th April, 1925	re Bombo Special Native Court

Year	Ordinance No.	Title	Remarks
1927		Bombo Special Native Court Rules, 1925 Notice—Native Courts in Buganda—of 14th September, 1927	Conferring jurisdicti in 8 minor townshi
1929		Native Courts in Buganda Proclamation of 23rd January, 1929	Revoked by proc. mation of 22nd Se tember, 1932
1930		The Native Courts Record (Fees) Rules, 1929 Amending Proclamation of 24th January, 1930 Amending Proclamation of 20th April, 1930	Adding Mutuba Ssingo, Musale, B vuma and Sabagal Mawokota
1931	8	Native Courts Record (Fees) Rules, 1930 The Criminal Procedure Code, 1930 Amending Proclamation of 10th April, 1931	Adding Mutuba VI Kyaggwe and d leting Mutuba Sesse
		Amending Proclamation of 19th September, 1931	Deleting Mutuba VI Buddu and addi Sabagabo, Mawogo
1932		Native Courts in Buganda Proclamation of 22nd September, 1932	
1933		Amending Proclamation of 23rd June, 1933	
1934		Native Courts in Buganda Proclamation of 12th June, 1934	Revoked by L.N.15 34
		Amending Proclamation of 24th September, 1934	Adding Mutuba I Kyaggwe
		Native Courts in Buganda Proclamation of 26th September, 1934	L.N.150/34 — retr spective
1936		Amending Proclamation of 1936	Deleting Mutuba Sesse
1937	5	The Courts (Amendment) Ordinance, 1937	
1938	6	The Buganda Native Laws (Declaratory) Ordinance, 1938	Cap. 71, Schedule co taining 1937 Agre ment
		Proclamation of 11th January, 1939 Amending Proclamation of 12th June, 1939	re Judicial Adviser Adding Mutuba VI and IX Buddu
		Direction of 14th June, 1939	Mutuba IX Buddu have jurisdiction Masaka Township
		Proclamation of 28th December, 1939	Abolition of Nativ Court at Bombo
1940	3	The Native Courts Ordinance, 1940	Re process rules
	4	The Buganda Courts Ordinance, 1940 The Buganda Courts Rules, 1940	
		Revocation of Bombo Special Native Court Rules	L.N.13/40 of 13 January, 1940
		Amending Proclamation of 3rd June, 1940	Revoked by L.N.13 40
		Amending Proclamation of 28th June, 1940	L.N.130/40

Year	Ordinance No.	Title	Remarks
1941		Notice of commencement of Buganda Courts Ordinance of 23rd August, 1940	w.e.f. 1st September, 1940
		Notice of 16th June, 1941	Style of Principal Court
		The Native Courts (Process and Appeal) Rules, 1941	Rules 3–6 only apply to Buganda Courts
		The Buganda Courts (Amendment) Rules, 1941	
1945	10	The Buganda Courts (Amendment) Ordinance, 1945	
1946	28	The Buganda Courts (Amendment) Ordinance, 1946	
1949		The Buganda Courts (Amendment) Rules, 1949	New Schedule of fees
		Delegation of Governor's Powers to approve appointments	L.N.327/49 of 23rd December, 1949

APPENDIX 4

THE SUCCESSION ORDER, 1926

	English text	*Commentary*
Short Title	1. The Order shall be called " The Succession Order 1926 " and shall read with the " Wills Law 1916 ".	The Wills Law 1916 was omitte from the Revised Edition of th Buganda Laws, 1957.
Object of this Order	2. It is found that to safeguard the interests of deceased natives of Buganda that an Order be made empowering the disposing of in legal way immoveable property between the interested parties.	The Luganda text of which th English is an attempted translatio is the dominant text and indeed the text to which the late Kabaka name is appended. The Englis version of this clause is not a tru translation of the Luganda whic reads " that there be an Order whic shall be employed in succession Mailo and personal property Natives of the Country ". In oth words all property immovabl movable and titular comes withi the purview of the Order and n just immovable property as th English version states. The la words appear, quite properly, limit the application of the Ord to natives of Buganda.
Making of Wills	3. A person may make a Will disposing of all his or her property and such a Will shall be attested by two witnesses in conformity with the terms of " The Wills Law 1916 ". Such Will may be constituted in the following manner: (a) The Testator shall sign or affix his or her mark to the Will in the presence of two witnesses. (b) The two witnesses shall attest their signature marks in such way as to leave no room for any one to fraudulently sign or making unauthorised additions to it. (c) If a Will is written by the Testator in his or her own writing, such Will will be	Again the English text is not a tru translation of the Luganda versio It should read: " When any person dies, leaving Will he has written, by which he ha disposed of his property which possessed during the period of h life, that Will shall be followed, ju as the Kabaka's Order of the yea 1916 ordains. Such Will shall constituted in the following ma ner ": The reference to the Kabaka Order of 1916 appears to be to th Wills Law 1916.

	English text	Commentary
	deemed valid though it is not attested by any other person. No Will of any person who is of unsound mind will be deemed valid unless it is attested by two witnesses at the time of its being made. A Will that shall be deemed valid within the terms of this Law shall bear the latest date, and that such a Will may be passed in ordinary way by the Lukiko for His Highness's confirmation.	
Wills must be legibly written in Luganda language. Relatives of the deceased person to demand testators Will	4. Wills must be legibly written in the Native Language Luganda.	Clan authorities declare void lawyer-made wills written in English, (as occurred in the leading case of Bingo Sepiriya Kadumukasa).
	5. A Father or Brother of a deceased person may demand a Will of their deceased relative if the testator has left one disposing of his or her property, and that the terms of such a Will shall be followed in disposing of the property.	
To take Heir before the Head of the Clan	6. When there is a proper Will and there is no dispute, the Sub-Head shall submit (cases of succession) to the Head of the clan at Mengo or to his representative there, the Successor named in the Will of the deceased along with all children of the testator. After the usual performance of such occasions: The Head, Sub-Head, and the Consanguinity shall then take the heir before the Katikiro in the Upper Lukiko. The Katikiro shall enquire into all details concerning the Testator's property and if correct will fix the date when the heirs are to come back again for His Highness the Kabaka's confirmation of the Will, and Succession, and the disposal of the property. If, however, there is any doubt as to the validity of the Will Vide Clause 3 of this Law,	The head of the mutuba (consanguinity) who ranks between the head of the lunyiriri (sub-consanguinity) and the head of the sub-clan (essiga) is not mentioned. The head of the lunyiriri (sub-consanguinity) does in practice introduce the succession and the parties to him and he can, but rarely does as they are his own descendants, refuse to take the succession forward to the head of the sub-clan (essiga). Usually he introduces the matter to the ssiga and then returns home leaving the head of the sub-consanguinity (ow'olunyiriri) to take the interested parties forward to the head of clan (Kasolya) and the Lukiiko (Ddiiro). The third paragraph of the English version is an inaccurate translation of the Luganda. It should read:

English text	Commentary
such Will shall be pronounced void and null. The Katikiro will then order the Head, Sub-Head of the clan and the Consanguinity to inquire of their clan as to why the Will was not properly constituted. Again the Head, Sub-Head, of the clan and the Consanguinity shall bring all their findings or failures before the Lukiko who will go into the matter administratively and will then come to a decision. The matter will then go before His Highness the Kabaka, whose decision will be final and binding in all matters.	" But if he shall see that the Will not properly executed either i incorrect form or because it does n observe the laws—that is, the Orde explained above, a Will whic appears like that shall not be vali nor shall it be acted upon. Th Kabaka shall not confirm tha succession immediately." The English version of the la paragraph is not a true translatio but conveys the general sense of th Luganda.
7. It shall be an offence for anyone to cancel, destroy or make any unauthorised alterations in a Will, unless such alterations are done under Clause 6 of this Law. Such person if found shall be guilty of an offence and shall be liable on conviction to a fine not exceeding Shs. 300/- or to imprisonment of either description for a period not exceeding two months or to both.	The word " cancel " should reall read " conceal " (*okukweka* is th word in the Luganda). The word " on failure to pay " should b substituted for the words " of eithe description " and the period of " si months " for " two months " in th English text. The usual procedure in cases of thi kind is for the clan to make a pre liminary enquiry and then for th case to be transferred on th Katikkiro's order to the ordinar criminal courts. The sequence i that a succession submitted is no approved but sent back to clan fo further enquiry (under Clause 6) The clan after enquiry resubmit new proposals revealing a crimina offence to have been committed The Katikkiro then sends th criminal case for trial in the cour of law which alone have jurisdictio and powers to fine and imprison.
All property of a deceased person which is not mentioned in the will shall be disposed of by the Head of the clan	
8. Property left by a deceased person which is not mentioned in his Will, shall be deemed as though deceased had died intestate in respect of the property of which he has not made testamentary disposition. Such will remain the property of the children entitled to the	The Luganda version is not trul translated for the English expand generally and adds the words: " and shall be brought before th Kabaka for his confirmation." In fact the English text truly reflect the practice of listing the deceased property, which is not mentioned i the will, and of allotting it to hi

English text	Commentary

[marginal: n the usual vay.]

same and will be divided between the children of the deceased person, and shall be brought before the Kabaka for his confirmation.

children subject to the Kabaka's approval. Persons other than the deceased's children cannot be allotted such property.

[marginal: No Successor hall be willed who is not one of the dead person's amily, grandchildren or ineal descendant]

9. No person shall be allowed to make a Will of Succession in favour of a person who is not his or her descendants, but any person is free to will any of his or her property to any-one he or she wishes.

The English text is not a true translation of the Luganda. It should read:
" No person is allowed to make a will for a person who is not of his clan (Mugandawe) to succeed him, but this does not prevent a man from willing his friend some land or some of his property as a bequest."
The last words mean a friend outside the testator's clan. The marginal note should be adjusted accordingly. Although not mentioned in this clause, Kabaka Muteesa I issued an edict that a son shall succeed the deceased father. When that edict was issued in the last century written wills were unknown and so the edict primarily applies to intestate succession but it is also a guiding influence in considering testate succession. For if the will nominates a clansman to succeed to the estate when a son of the deceased is alive, the Kabaka does not usually confirm the will unless an important reason is adduced explaining why the child should not succeed. An example is of a child who has committed an abomination (omusango gwa kivve) and has been expelled from the clan.

[marginal: Council of the clan empowering to dispose of any property of intestate person]

Power of the Council of the Clan
10. The Council of the clan shall, before bringing any heirship before the Lukiko see that the intestate's property has been properly disposed of between his or her relatives. The Council will provisionally choose an heir or heiress to succeed the deceased person:
(a) The Council of the clan has power to either decide disputes between the interested parties or see that a fair distribution of deceased property is done.

Again the English text is not an accurate translation and in particular the words " between his or her relatives " in the fifth line do not appear in the Luganda. This clause refers to intestate distribution of estates.
Under clause 10(b), appeal lies first to the Katikkiro in Ddiiro and thence on second and final appeal to the Kabaka in his capacity of Ssabattaka. The word " Ddiiro " is derived from " the meeting of those who eat together " (enkunganya ya balya emmere bonna). The Ddiiro is in

	English text	Commenraty
Consanguinity	(b) Any person so interested may appeal to the Lukiko and if still dissatisfied will again appeal to His Highness the Kabaka, whose decision will be final and binding in all matters. *Re Property of the Intestates* 11. In the annexed Table of Kindred it is shewn what persons, and from whom, may be chosen to succeed the intestate or to receive a portion of the property. Such property shall be inherited by the children entitled to the same alone, but if deceased left no issue, his or her heir shall be selected among the persons mentioned hereunder who shall have power to distribute such property.	fact the advisory council of the Kabaka in clan matters, consisting of the heads of clans, and presided over by the Katikkiro, or nowadays usually by his Assistant. Under Clause 12(a) of this Order the eldest son shall succeed on his father's intestacy. This was a step further than the edict of Muteesa I. This order is now followed except when the eldest son has been expelled from the clan. Further if such expulsion has not been completed by the time that the father of the offender dies then the eldest son cannot be expelled subsequently nor can he be debarred from succession to his father. The ancient custom was that all of the sub-consanguinity (olunyiriri) had a share in the deceased's property. But nowadays in view of clause 12 of this Order, if the successor to the deceased is his only son then that son succeeds to all the deceased's property and there is no distribution. If there is no son of the deceased then his grandson succeeds; and if no grandson, his great grandson; and if no great grandson then succession goes to deceased's brother's descendants; and if there are none, to deceased's uncle's descendants under Clause 12(b). But whoever among those priorities succeeds, there is always a distribution of some of deceased's property to the sub-consanguinity (olunyiriri).
If a person dies intestate his or her relatives may recommend some one to succeed to the property	12. If any person dies intestate his or her father or elder brother or consanguinity or other of either may recommend a Successor to the deceased person's property or estate, and it may be done in the following manner: (a) If the deceased had male issues the elder son will succeed him (or her). The	The usual person who is selected to be " omukulu w'olumbe " (president of the funeral rites) is the deceased's elder brother living at home and so accepted by the household. The English text is a condensation of the Luganda and introduces one gross inaccuracy—the words " (or

	English text	Commentary
	Successor will have the largest share out his or her father's estate, and other male issued shall share the property proportionally.	her) "—because a male never succeeds a female under Ganda customary law.

English text:

Successor will have the largest share out his or her father's estate, and other male issued shall share the property proportionally.

If, however, the deceased person had a Butaka land such land will be entailed and on no account shall any portion of it be sold.

(b) If the deceased person had only female issues and if his brother had male children one of the sons of the brother shall be chosen to succeed to the estate of their Uncle. Daughters of the deceased person shall be consulted whilst a Successor is being chosen amongst their Uncle's sons, to succeed to their dead father's estate, and that their choice shall be given special consideration. Daughters shall be given a share each out of their father's estate according to their age.

(c) If the deceased person survives his children, his male children's issues will succeed to the property of their grandfather. All grandchildren shall each have a share out of their grandfather's property.

(d) If daughters survive their father, their issues will never succeed to the property of their grandfather, for, according to national custom they will be members of a different clan from that of their grandfather. However, such issues will be entitled to receive a share out of the estate of their grandfather and also mailo land which is not a Butaka land of the family.

(e) If a man dies and leaves his wife conceived then all heirship ceremonies shall be postponed till the wife delivers the child to succeed its father.

Commentary:

her) "—because a male never succeeds a female under Ganda customary law.

This Order was made when " the Butaka controversy " was at its height. Although modified butaka still exists, this clause has been seldom observed for what was butaka since 1900 has become private mailo and is transferable.

The English text misses the following passage in the Luganda which should be inserted before the last sentence of this sub-clause:

" If there are no uncle's sons, they shall choose from one of their sub-consanguinity from which the deceased sprang for the succession and he shall succeed their father."

The English text omits the point, which appears in the Luganda, that the head of the sub-clan (omukulu w'essiga) is the selecting authority in this event.

There is a slip in the translation at the beginning. It should read:
" If the father survives his daughters."

The Luganda text states that mailo land will stay with the clan, i.e. deceased's clan. In other words land, whether butaka or not, will not be distributed, as the English version alleges, to daughter's issue. But as already observed, such provisions about butaka are nowadays seldom observed.

The English text gives the sense in précis. The Luganda expression " lubuto olutategerekeka " means it cannot be ascertained at that time whether the child will be male or female. Only a posthumous male child would, of course, succeed the father.

	English text	Commentary
	(f) If the deceased had no issues the Sub-Head of the clan and the consanguinity shall choose amongst brothers of deceased or their male issues; failing these, then the deceased's other relatives may succeed to the property. Deceased's other relatives may receive a share out of the estate, as shewn in Section 11 of this Law. (g) If a man on his death had only sisters, such sisters are entitled to share in their brother's real estate, but they can never succeed their brother. Sub-Head and sisters of deceased, will, however, choose somebody from the nearest relatives, *i.e.* Nephew to succeed the deceased person. *Illustrations* (a) If a man had only sisters and that if such a man survives his sisters and dies without male issues and that if sisters had issues, then such grand-nephews shall be entitled to share in the estate of their Uncle, but they shall never succeed him. (b) The heir to succeed such deceased person shall be chosen amongst his nearest relatives Vide Clause 12(g).	The English text omits reference to the cousins german who rank after the deceased's brother's descendants for the succession.
Widow to receive share of her husband's estate Mother to receive share on her son's estate	13. If the Widow is the mother of above children or not, she will always be entitled to have a share out of her husband's estate. 14. The Mother of deceased person if she survives deceased shall be given as a share something from her deceased son's estate. *Guardians, Executors or Trustees* (a) Deceased person may appoint guardians to look after his son and heir during his minority and to generally look after other heirs of deceased along with his home. (b) Deceased is free to appoint any-one he wishes as	Guardians are usually appointed even though the successor has grown up. The guardian can be a friend from another clan.

English text	Commentary
a guardian, trustee, or executor. He may either appoint (a) Friend, (b) Brother or (c) Head of the clan to the guardianship. (c) It will be an offence for any one of the guardians if found fraudulently using for their own personal use properties left to children who are under their charge. Guardians shall be solemnly expected to be honest people carrying out duties in such a way so as to show that they are fulfilling their trust to the deceased person.	The first part of the English text is a palliative rendering of part of the Luganda and the second part of the English is a condensation of the next sub-clause (4) in the Luganda. The translation should read: " When a guardian appears to have fraudulently misappropriated the property of his wards, he shall be sued in court and tried; if he loses the case he shall return the property he took and shall be relieved of his guardianship; and if he cannot refund what he took he shall be imprisoned under civil law. The Lukiko shall then order the Head of the clan to select other Guardians." If there is no land in the succession then the head of clan (ow'akasolya) approves the succession whether testate or intestate and such a succession is not forwarded for the Kabaka's confirmation.

When a Will is rejected by the Lukiko of Buganda

15. If a Will is rejected by the Lukiko of the Kingdom of Buganda as given out in Clause 22(b), such heirship shall be treated as though the man died intestate. His Highness the Kabaka's sanction shall be first obtained before such heirship is confirmed.

Non-Allowance of clan after 6 months have passed from the date of confirmation of heirship

16. After a period of six months have passed from the date the Kabaka confirmed the heirship before the Lukiko nobody shall be allowed to bring any claim in disputation against the heirship. The heir will then bring a fee of Shs. 2/– and will do " Okulanya " before the Lukiko, when these formalities are completed, the Katikiro will hand over to the heir a letter to the Saza Chief concerned introducing him finally as the heir.

Power of the Head of the Clan

17. Head of the clan has power to advertise the death of a member of his clan, if it is necessary that children of deceased who were abroad be acquainted with their father's death:

	English text	Commentary
	(a) Advertisement is continually to go on for a period of at least three months. If, however, the wanted children come in before the above time expires no further advertisement shall be necessary. (b) Fee for such advertisements are to be deducted from the deceased's estate. An account of which shall be made out showing for what services the money was expended. (c) When a man dies, a period of at least six months from date of his death must pass before an heir is chosen and the distribution of estate takes place, but when the party advertised for arrives it shall not be necessary to wait for the prescribed period of three months. (d) During the time of advertising for the children of deceased person, deceased property shall be properly written and detailed on papers and left in the safe keeping of the Head of the clan, Sub-Head and the Consanguinity.	Advertisement is still made in the press as required, an example being the recent succession to the Gabunga, Headship of the Lung-fish Clan (Mmamba). The Luganda test stipulates three months not six as appears erroneously in the English translation. The estate meanwhile is in the hands of the head of the household (ow'oluggya) under the surveillance of the head of sub-consanguinity (ow'olunyiriri).
Debts due to and by deceased	*Debts due to or by Deceased and all Land Documents and etc.* 18. If a man dies and leaves a will showing all debts due to him or by deceased and also land agreements showing land bought him or sold by deceased, the terms of the will shall be strictly complied with. But if the deceased did not direct in a will as to how debts due to or by deceased shall be collected or paid then the Head of the clan, Sub-Head and the consanguinity shall collect such debts or pay same.	Debts introduced to the clan heads and proved may be added to the debts listed in the will. The practice is for the clan heads not to pay the debts out of the property themselves but to state them to the successor who pays out of the estate after the ceremony of completion of the funeral rites (okwabya olumbe). A debt which was not introduced at that ceremony for good cause, say, for example, the absence of the creditor abroad when the debtor died, or if the creditor was a minor can be admitted later by the head of clan on proof and an adjustment of the estate made.
Debts due to and by	19. If a man dies intestate, all debts due to land agreements	

	English text	*Commentary*
intestate deceased	shall be dealt with by the Head of the clan, Sub-Head of the clan and the consanguinity along with the guardians, who may pay all debts due by deceased or collect all monies from parties concerned. In fact to do all that which should have been done by deceased regarding the estate had he lived.	
If deceased's property and estates do not cover liabilities	20. If a person dies and leaves debts owed, the property and estates shall be sold and if deceased did not leave enough money to pay off liabilities so that creditors may be satisfied by paying them proportionally, according to the extent of the claim of each creditor, the heirs or heiresses will only take what is left out of the deceased's estate and property.	The words " the heirs or heiresses will only take what is left out of the deceased's estate and property " do not appear in the Luganda and are plainly nonsensical for there will be nothing left in such circumstances. The Luganda text correctly reads: " omusika tatwalenga kintu " that is: " the successor shall take nothing "; damnosa heriditas. Neither a successor rich in his own right nor the clan can be sued for the unpaid debts of the deceased, if no inheritance is left to satisfy those outstanding debts.
	The procedure to be followed in paying off Deceased's Debts (a) Before such sale takes place, members of the clan to which deceased belonged shall be consulted, and will be free to buy it or hold it and pay off the claims against their deceased relative.	
	(b) Again the Heir or the Head of the clan or the sub-Head or the consanguinity may stop such sale if they undertake to pay off and satisfy the creditors.	If they possibly can, there is a recognised obligation on the successor and the clan to redeem the property.
	(c) In such a case, there must be agreement between the parties which must be drawn up before the Lukiko.	
If a person dies destitute a debt will be regarded as forfeited	21. If a person dies and leaves behind debts and if that person is without any property or any thing to enable relatives to settle them, the Head of the clan and heir shall become legally free from any obligations of meeting such debts. If, however, the property of deceased	For the creditor to obtain satisfaction out of such hidden property unearthed afterwards, his debt must have been approved at the funeral rites.

	English text	*Commentary*
	person is found to have been purposely hidden to avoid paying debts deceased owed, such person who hid the property shall be summoned before a Gombolola Court, who are empowered to deal with such debts.	
	The Power of the Lukiko and Buganda Kingdom	
	22. The Lukiko of the Buganda Kingdom with His Highness the Kabaka shall settle all clan cases and disputes brought before them from clan councils.	
	(a) The Lukiko of the Kingdom of Buganda may reject any recommendations for heirship brought before them by the Clan Council if in their (the Lukiko) opinion the deceased died intestate, and more especially if rules of the distribution of intestate's estate were not properly followed, whilst the clan council were making their recommendations, the clan council may be directed to go back and re-submit fresh recommendations.	There is an important omission from the English translation. The words " or the Lukiko may distribute as it sees fit " should be added to the end of this sub-clause.
	(b) The Lukiko of the Buganda Kingdom are empowered to reject and send back any will which in their opinion was not properly executed.	Children not mentioned in the will may be admitted by the Lukiko on proof—even to the extent of upsetting the successor nominated in the will and of appointing the child so admitted in his stead.
Operation of this Order	23. This order will come into operation from the date His Highness the Kabaka approves it, along with that of the Governor's consent.	The words " along with that of the Governor's consent " have no basis in the Luganda version, are untrue and for reasons explained in the appropriate chapter above should be ignored. The English text does not indicate that the late Kabaka signed the order or that he did so on the date given but the Luganda text covers both points and for convenience the appropriate insertions have been made in italics.

Signed under my Seal at Mengo, on the *15th* day of *September, 1926.*

   Daudi Chwa
  KABAKA OF BUGANDA

SCHEDULE VIDE CLAUSE 11

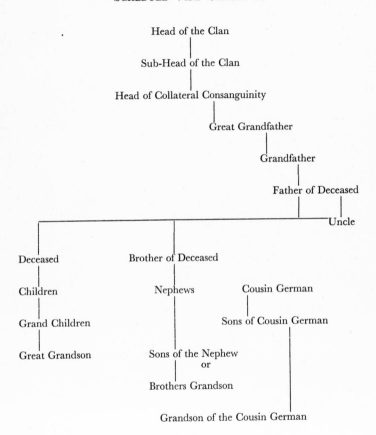

Head of the Clan

Sub-Head of the Clan

Head of Collateral Consanguinity

Great Grandfather

Grandfather

Father of Deceased

Uncle

Deceased

Brother of Deceased

Children

Nephews

Cousin German

Grand Children

Sons of Cousin German

Great Grandson

Sons of the Nephew
or
Brothers Grandson

Grandson of the Cousin German

APPENDIX 5

LIST OF MINISTERS OF JUSTICE

Years	*Name*	*Clan*
1900–1921	Stanislaus Mugwanya	Butiko (Mushroom)
1921–1935	Anderea Kiwanuka	Mbogo (Buffalo)
1935–1945	Rauli Kiwanuka	Lugave (Scaly Ant-eater)
1945–1950	Matiansi Kigonya	Mmamba (Lung-fish)
1950–1955	Matayo Mugwanya	Butiko (Mushroom)
1955–1959	Antonio Gitta	Katinvuma (Small Shrub)
1959–	Yozefu Musoke	Ngabi (Bush-buck)

LUGANDA PROVERBS CONNECTED WITH THE ADMINISTRATION OF JUSTICE

Principles of Justice

Enkima tesala gwa kibira	No man shall be judge in his own cause (lit. The monkey does not decide an affair of the forest).
Tosala gwa kawala nga tonnawulira gwa kalenzi	*Audi alteram partem* (lit. Do not decide the girl's case until you have heard the boy's).
Omusango omukadde gwe gusala omuggya	*Res judicata* (lit. The old case it is which decides the new).
" *Nkuwawaabidde* " *takuviirako awo*	Whoever sues you causes you loss (even if you win).
Ne gw'oyagala omusalira omusango ne gumusinga n'omuliyirira	Even the man you like you must convict and then help to pay.

Pleadings

Okuwoza tekubongola mannyo	Pleading does not crumble the teeth.
Omusango bijanjalo, ogukkuta kiro	A case is like beans, it reacts at night (*i.e.* on second thoughts).
Ogusula (omusango), gwe gukuwa empoza	Adjournment offers chance of preparing further pleadings.
Wodizza omulalu mu kyama, ng'ayogera obulungi tomulabye	When you seek advice from a madman, it means you have no-one better than him.
" *Agudde ddalu* " *kuwona mabanja*	So says plaintiff when defendant feigns madness to escape debt.
Omutamiivu tabaaga mbwa	The drunken man does not skin his dog.
Akamwa akabi katta " *siroganga* "	Evil speech cancels the plea of not bewitching.
" *Gunsinze* " *aliwa bitono*	" I plead guilty " he says and then pays a little.
Gw'otoyise naye si muzibu kulimba	It is not difficult to lie to the man with whom you did not go (*i.e.* the judge).
Atava ku mulungi afa awoza	Importunate pleading results in death.

Procedure

Ntyi lubale w'omulamu tasamirirwa	The injured party must file the suit.
Ebya basumba bigwera ku ttale	Young boys have their cases decided among their fellows in the bush.
" *Bya mpuna* " *ng'akubbye wa mu nju*	Domestic offences should not be publicised.
Bakuyita embuga, si buganzi	Care should be exercised in going to the chief.

Ogw'embuga gutta ogw'obuko — If you are summoned, attend and leave other duties.

Omusango tegumanya nnyumba mbi — All people try and compound offences (lit. The case does not know the lowly house).

Ka ntanyi, kaggweerawo — If you are asked to pay a fine, pay it then and there.

Omusango teguvunda — A case does not rot.

Tigumazibwa mbiro — Flight does not end the case.

Clan responsibility

Ogutaggwa guboolanga abataka — A continuing case brings hatred to the clan.

Omulya mmamba aba omu n'avumanganya ekika — The whole clan is shamed by the clansman's offence.

Omusango oguzzanga ku busenze n'otogussa ku butaka — There is no help from the clan in a clan case.

Cattle

(Ente) ensibirwa lw'efa: lw'emanyibwa nyiniyo — When an entrusted cow dies, its death is known by its owner.

Debt

Ekiri mu bbanja tekinunula mwaana — A debt does not ransom anybody.

Ky'owola otudde okibanja oyimiridde — What you loan sitting down you have to stand up to recover.

Akunoonya ameewola takunoonya masasula — The man who seeks you for a loan does not look for you to pay.

Contract

Akalagaane tekaggya buliika — The terms of a contract are binding.

Tort

Kyeyendere, bbwa lya njola — *Volenti non fit injuria.*

Theft

Bakubanja n'otobba — Better get into debt than steal.

Akatali kabbe, eggumba osuula mu mulyango — What is not stolen, you are not afraid to show (lit. You throw the bone in the doorway).

Fraud

Omulyazamanyi alya gw'asinze, ensega terya mulamu — The cheat devours the person he has overcome, the vulture does not eat a live man.

Corruption

" *Toba agwe* ", *we wawonerwa* — If you had not been in the chair, I should have been convicted.

Akuweerera ekigambo, akira akuweerera envuma (ng'ogenda mu masengere) — Advice on going to court is better than the gift of a slave.

APPENDIX 7

GLOSSARY OF LUGANDA TERMS

(Titles are arranged alphabetically, nouns alphabetically according to prefix with the initial vowel placed before in brackets and verbs alphabetically according to stem with the infinitive prefix and initial vowel placed before in brackets.)

(o)busuulu	rent.
(o)butaka	clan land.
(o)butongole	official land.
(o)bwesengeze	land belonging to an individual.
(E)Ddiiro	Council of the Lukiko in clan matters.
(e)ggombolola	sub-county.
(e)kkanzu	long white robe.
(a)Kasolya	headship (of clan).
kasuze katya	beer given to bride's parents on evening before wedding.
Katikkiro	Prime Minister.
Katikkiro we Byalo bya Ssaabasajja Kabaka	Chief Steward of His Highness the Kabaka's estates.
(e)kibanja	tenancy plot.
kigula luggi	beer given to lover's brother.
(e)kika	clan
(e)kita ky'omwenge	calabash of beer.
(o)Lubiri	Palace.
Lubuga	Queen-sister, also called Nnaalinnya.
(o)luggya	courtyard.
Lukiko	Council.
(o)lunyiriri	sub-consanguinity
(o)mukungu	a great chief.
(o)muluka	parish.
(o)musango gw'ekivve	case of abomination.
(o)mutaka	clan elder.
(o)mutongole	village chief.
(o)mutuba	consanguinity.
Nnaalinnya	Queen-sister, also called Lubuga.
Nnamasole	Queen-mother
(e)nvujjo	tithe.
Omukulu ow'Olubiri	Major domo in Kabaka's Palace.
Omulamuzi	Minister of Justice.
Omwanika	Minister of Finance.
Omwanika ow'Enkuluze	Private Treasurer of the Kabaka.
Ssabaganzi	maternal uncle of Kabaka.
Ssabalangira	Head of the Princely Clan.
Ssabataka	Head of all the clans—title of the Kabaka.
(e)ssaza	county.
(oku)sibira ente	to entrust cattle to another.
(e)ssiga	sub-clan.
(e)ttooke	bunch of plantains.

335

APPENDIX 8

BIBLIOGRAPHY

ANDERSON, J. N. D.—*Islamic Law in Africa*, London, 1954.

ASHE, R. P.—*Two Kings of Uganda*, Sampson Low, London, 1889.
Life in Uganda, Sampson Low, 1890.

BRUSHFIELD, T. N. N. and RELTON, A. J.—*Land Registration in Buganda*, Entebbe, 1955.

BUSTIN, E.—*La Décentralisation Administrative et L'Évolution des Structures Politiques en Afrique Oriental Britannique*, Liège, 1958.

CARTER, W. M.—" The Clan System, Land Tenure and Succession among the Baganda," *Law Quarterly Review*, Volume 25, 1909.

CUNNINGHAM, J. F.—*Uganda and its peoples*, Hutchinson, London, 1905.

EDEL, M. M.—*The Customs of the Baganda*, by Sir Apolo Kagwa, Columbia University Press, New York, 1934.

FRAZER, Sir J. G.—*Anthologia Antropologica, The Native Races of Africa and Madagascar*, Percy Lund Humphries, London, 1938.

GGOMOTOKA, J. T. K.—*Magezi Ntakke*, White Father's Printing Press, Bukalasa, 1934.

GOLDTHORPE, J. E.—*Outlines of East African Society*, photolithographed, Makerere College, 1958.

GORJU, P. J.—*Entre le Victoria l'Albert et l'Edouard*, Oberthür, Rennes, 1920.

HAILEY, LORD—*Native Administration in the British African Territories*, H.M.S.O., London, 1951.

HALL, M. J.—*Through my Spectacles in Uganda*, C.M.S., London, 1898.

HATTERSLEY, C. W.—*The Baganda at Home*, The Religious Tract Society, London, 1908.

HONE, H. R.—" The Native of Uganda and the Criminal Law ", *U.J.* 1938–39, Volume 6.

INGHAM, K.—*The Making of Modern Uganda*, Allen and Unwin, London, 1958.

KAGWA, Sir A.—*Ekitabo kye Mpisa za Baganda*, Kampala, 1905.
Ekitabo kya Basekabaka be Buganda, Luzac, London, 1912.
Ekitabo kye Bika bya Baganda, Mengo, 1949.

KINGDOM OF BUGANDA—*Akatabo ke Biragiro na Mateka*, 1916–1919, Mengo, 1919.
Ekitabo ky'Ebiragiro by 'Emisango, 1916–1919, Mengo, 1919.
Ebigambo Ebyatesebwa Olukiko Olukulu olwe Buganda, 1918, Mengo, 1919.
Amateka ne Biragiro 1922–1923, Mengo, 1925.
Ekitabo ky'Ebiragiro by 'Emisango, 1931–1936, Mengo, 1937.
Revised Edition of the Native Laws of Buganda, 1941.
Customary Law Reports, 1956.
Customary Law Reports, 1957.
Customary Law Reports, 1958.
Customary Law Reports, 1940–1955 (not yet published).
Notes of Selected Decisions of Her Majesty's High Court of Uganda on cases originating from the Buganda Courts, 1940–1958.
The Revised Edition of the Native Laws of Buganda, 1957.
The Native Laws of Buganda, 1957–1958, Supplement.

KIRWAN, J. D.—" Customary Land Tenure and the Legal System in Buganda ", African Studies Branch, Colonial Office, *Digest of African Local Administration No. 4*, September, 1948.

KULUBYA, S. W.—" Presidential Address to Uganda Society ", 1942, *U.J.*, Volume 9.
LECLERCQ, J.—*Aux sources du Nil*, Librairie Plon, Paris, 1913.
LEWIN, J.—*Studies in African Native Law*, Capetown, 1947.
LUGARD, Capt. F. D. (later Lord)—*The Rise of our East African Empire*, Blackwood, London, 1893.
MACQUEEN, P.—*In Wildest Africa*, Bell, London, 1910.
MAIR, L. P.—*An African People in the Twentieth Century*, Routledge, London, 1934.
Baganda Land Tenure, Africa, Volume VI.
Native Marriage in Buganda, O.U.P., London, 1940.
MEEK, C. K.—*Land, Law and Custom in the Colonies*, O.U.P., London, 1946.
MUKASA, H.—" The Rule of the Kings of Buganda ", *U.J.*, Volume 10, No 2, September 1946.
MUKWAYA, A. B.—*Land Tenure in Buganda—Present Day Tendencies*, E.A.I.S.R., Eagle Press, Kampala, 1953.
MULLINS, J. D.—*The Wonderful Story of Uganda*, London, 1904.
MUSOKE, S. B. K.—*The Baganda Clans*, typescript, E.A.I.S.R., 1958.
NSIMBI, M. B.—*Amannya amaganda n'ennono zaago*, Kampala, 1956.
PETERS, Dr. C.—*New Light on Dark Africa*, Ward, Lock, London, 1891.
PLACE, G.—*The Torrens System of Registration of Title as applied to the Uganda Protectorate*, Entebbe, 1923.
RICHARDS, A. I.—*Economic Development and Tribal Change*, Heffer, Cambridge, 1954.
ROLIN, H.—*Le Droit de l'Uganda*, Bruylant, Bruxelles, 1910.
ROSCOE, J.—*The Baganda*, MacMillan, London, 1911.
SOUTHALL, A. W. and GUTKIND, P. C. W.—*Townsmen in the Making—Kampala and its Suburbs*, E.A.I.S.R., Kampala, 1957.
SOUTHWOLD, M.—" The Inheritance of Land in Buganda ", *U.J.*, Volume 20, No. 1, March 1956.
SPEKE, J. H.—*Journal of the Discovery of the Source of the Nile*, Blackwood, London, 1863.
STRICKLAND, J. G.—" The Uganda Mailo System ", *Empire Survey Review*, 1936, Volume 3.
THOMAS, H. B.—" An Experiment in African Native Land Settlement ", *Journal of Royal African Society*, Volume 27.
THOMAS, H. B. and SCOTT, R.—*Uganda*, O.U.P., London, 1935.
THOMAS, H. B. and SPENCER, A. E.—*A History of Uganda Land and Surveys and of the Uganda Land and Survey Department*, Government Press, Entebbe, 1938.
UGANDA PROTECTORATE—*Bibliography of Land Tenure*, Ministry of Land Tenure, 1957.
VANDERLINDEN, J.—*Essai sur les jurisdictions de droit coutumier dans les territoires d'Afrique Centrale*, Academie royale des Sciences Coloniales, Bruxelles, 1959.
WILD, J. V.—*The Story of the Uganda Agreement*, Eagle Press, Nairobi, 1950.

INDEX

A

ABORTION, 122
ADMINISTRATION
estate, 193
justice, offences against, 272
ADULTERY, 274
AGENCY
contracts, 236
AGREEMENTS. *See* TREATIES.
ASSOCIATIONS, 244

B

BARBED WIRE, 164
BARTER, 231
BETROTHAL, 86
BLOOD-BROTHERHOOD, 70
BUGANDA
description, xxxviii
early history, 3, 6, 18
BUILDINGS, 163
BURIAL, 189

C

CATTLE
acquisition, 172
agistment, 172
herding, 176
ownership, 177
CHIEFS
ancient system, 5
hierarchy, 56
liability, 260
marriage, 83
modern system, 23
titles, 24
CHIEFTAINSHIP
succession, 195
CHILDREN
duties, 116
endobolo, 122
status, 68
twin, ceremony of, 117

CLANS

CLANS
matter affecting, 75
system, 72
COMPANIES, 244
CONCUBINAGE, 82
CONFLICT
jurisdiction, 298
laws, 297
CONTRACTS
agency, 236
barter, 231
gift, 234
guarantee, 235
loan, 233
sale, 232
service, 234
CORPORATIONS, 244
CORRUPTION, 47
COUNCILS
modern, representation in, 24
COURTS
chiefs', 12
Kabaka's, 15
Katikkiro's, 13
Lubuga's, 16
Namasole's, 16
reorganisation, 40
royal, modern, 47
CRIMES, 268
CROPS
lease, 162
sale, 162

D

DEFAMATION, 274
DIVORCE
effects, 111
grounds, 107
procedure, 109

E

ESTATE
debts, 221
distribution, 220
EVIDENCE, 294

F

FAMILY, 104
FATHER
  duties, 112
FISHING, 180
FUNERAL
  rites, completion of, 193

G

GIFT
  contracts, 234
  inter vivos, 222
GRAZING, 164
GUARANTEE
  contracts, 235
GUARDIANSHIP, 225

H

HERDSMEN, 175
HUNTING, 181
HUSBAND, 104

I

INCEST, 179
INDIVIDUAL
  capacity, 53
  status, 53
INJURIES
  physical, 263
  psychic, 266

J

JUDICIAL ADVISER
  creation of post, 38

K

KABAKAS
  land, 150
  marriage, 83
  offences against, 270
  tyranny, 4
KABAKASHIP
  succession, 55

KASAGIRA
  law of, 275
KINSHIP
  avoidances, 119
  responsibilities, 119

L

LAND
  Bataka problem, 136
  burial on, 163
  Busuulu and Envujjo Law, 167
  butaka tenure, 128
  butongole tenure, 129
  bwesengeze tenure, 130
  common rights, 163
  gifts, 161
  interest-holders, 148
  interests, 153
  judicial decisions, 156
  jurisdiction, 169
  Kabaka's mailo, 132
  landlord and tenant, 141
  " mailo " system, 132
  mortgages, 158
  peasant tenancy, 131
  registration of titles, 140
  rights of way, 164
  rights to fruits, 165
  right to manure, 165
  sale, 153
  tenure, pre-1900, 127
  urban development, 166
LANGUAGE
  courts, of, 294
  dominant, Agreements, of, 28
    native laws, of, 28
LAWS
  Busuulu and Envujjo, 167
  conflict of, 297
  English, 29
  foreign customary, 70
  Muteesa I's, 10
  native, 27
  Protectorate, 28
  recording, 11
  specified, 28
LEASE
  crops, 162
  land, 160
LEGISLATION. *See* LAWS.
LIABILITY
  tortious, 259
LIBEL, 274

LIMITATION
statutes, 161
LIVESTOCK
cases, 171
minor animals, 177
LOAN
contracts, 233
LUKIKO
ancient, 5, 9

M

MARKETS, 241
MARRIAGE
capacity, 84
ceremonies, 96
consideration—
ancient, 90
modern, 93
return of, 96, 108
formalities, 96
dissolution, 107
by death, 111
law, 77, 91, 100
negotiations, 86
payments, 90
preliminaries, 86
prohibited degrees, 84
registration, 103
subsequent ceremony, 102
types, 78
MORALITY
offences, 274
MOTHER
duties, 115
MOURNING, 192

N

NUISANCES, 273

O

OFFENCES
person, against, 279
unnatural, 278
OFFENDERS
treatment of, 296
ORDERS IN COUNCIL
Africa, 1889, 8
Uganda, 1902, 25

ORDINANCES
Buganda Courts, 1940, 38, 42
Native Courts, 1905, 31

P

PARENTS
control by, 111
PEASANTS
position, 61
tenancy, 131
PERSONS
injuries to—
physical, 263
psychic, 266
law of, 53
PROCEDURE
rules, ancient, 287
modern, 289
PROCEEDINGS
arbitral, 12, 45, 293
PROCLAMATIONS
Native Courts in Buganda,
1909, 32
1917, 34
PROPERTY
heritable, 194
injuries to, 260
Kabaka's rights to, 179
malicious injuries to, 282
offences relating to, 281
PUBLICATIONS
legal, 48

R

RAPE, 276, 278
RELIGION
offences relating to, 273
RESPONSIBILITY
criminal, 269
ROYAL FAMILY, 54

S

SALE
contracts, 232
crops, 162
trees, 162
SEDITION, 270

SEDUCTION, 264

SERVICE
    contracts, 234

SLAVERY, 281
    abolition, 64

SLAVES, 65

STRANGERS, 69

SUCCESSION
    dispositive, 222
    jurisdiction, 196
    machinery, 209
    Order, 1926, 207

SUCCESSOR
    choice of, 214
    duties, 221
    rights, 221

SUICIDE, 280

T

TERMINOLOGY, xxxvii

THEFT, 281

TORT
    liability in, 259

TRAINING
    legal, 42

TREATIES
    between Mwanga and Lugard,
        1890, 7
        1892, 8
    between Mwanga and Portal,
        1893, 8
    between Mwanga and Colville,
        1894, 9
    Buganda Agreement, 1900, 18
    Buganda (Judicial) Agreement,
        1905, 26
    Buganda (Clan Cases) Agreement,
        1924, 26, 75, 207
    Buganda (Declaratory) Agreement
        (Native Laws) 1937, 27
    Buganda Agreement, 1955, 25, 27

TREES
    sale, 162

TWINS
    ceremony, 117

W

WAR, 182

WELLS, 164

WIFE
    property, 178
    relationship, 104

WILLS
    oral, 222
    written, 223

WITCHCRAFT, 283

WOMEN, 66